Roman Presences

Receptions of
in European C

edited by
Catharine Edward

CAMBRIDGE
UNIVERSITY PRESS

CAMBRIDGE UNIVERSITY PRESS
Cambridge, New York, Melbourne, Madrid, Cape Town, Singapore, São Paulo

Cambridge University Press
The Edinburgh Building, Cambridge CB2 8RU, UK

Published in the United States of America by Cambridge University Press, New York

www.cambridge.org
Information on this title: www.cambridge.org/9780521591973

First published 1999
This digitally printed version 2007

A catalogue record for this publication is available from the British Library

ISBN 978-0-521-59197-3 hardback
ISBN 978-0-521-03617-7 paperback

Roman Presences

Receptions of Rome in European Culture, 1789–1945

This collection of essays explores aspects of the reception of ancient Rome in a number of European countries from the late eighteenth century to the end of the Second World War. Rome has been made to stand for literary authority, republican heroism, imperial power and decline, the Catholic church, the pleasure of ruins. The studies offered here examine some of the sometimes strange and unexpected places where Roman presences have manifested themselves during this period. Scholars from several disciplines, including English Literature and History of Art, as well as Classics, bring to bear a variety of approaches on a wide range of images and texts, from statues of Napoleon to Freud's analysis of dreams. Rome's seemingly boundless capacity for multiple, indeed conflicting, signification has made it an extraordinary fertile paradigm for making sense of – and also for destabilising – history, politics, identity, memory and desire.

Catharine Edwards is a Senior Lecturer in the Department of Classics and Ancient History, University of Bristol. From 1993 to 1996 she was Senior Research Fellow in the University of Bristol's Leverhulme-funded research project 'Receptions of Rome in the nineteenth and twentieth centuries'. She is the author of *The politics of immorality in ancient Rome* (1993) and *Writing Rome: textual approaches to the city* (1996). With Michael Liversidge she edited *Imagining Rome: British artists and Rome in the nineteenth century*.

Contents

Illustrations

(between pp. 148 and 149)

Contributors

STEPHEN BANN is a Professor at the University of Kent at Canterbury, where he is director of the Centre of Modern Cultural Studies and chair of the Board of Studies in History and Theory of Art. His books include *The clothing of Clio*, *The inventions of history*, *Romanticism and the rise of history* and, most recently, *Paul Delaroche: History painted.*

CHLOE CHARD teaches history of art at Wimbledon College of Art. She is the author of *Pleasure and guilt on the Grand Tour* and the editor (with Helen Langdon) of *Transports: travel, pleasure and imaginative geography 1600–1830.*

CATHARINE EDWARDS is a Senior Lecturer in the Department of Classics and Ancient History at the University of Bristol. Her work includes *Writing Rome: textual approaches to the city* and (edited with Michael Liversidge) *Imagining Rome: British artists and Rome in the nineteenth century.*

VALÉRIE HUET teaches archaeology and history of art at the University of Paris VII. She has published a number of articles on the reception of Roman monuments.

DUNCAN F. KENNEDY is a Senior Lecturer in the Department of Classics and Ancient History at the University of Bristol. He is the author of *The arts of love: five studies in the discourse of Roman love elegy* and is completing a book on Lucretius and the rhetoric of natural science.

VOLKER LOSEMANN teaches ancient history at the University of Marburg. His numerous publications are concentrated on the modern reception of classical antiquity and include *Nationalsozialismus und die Antike. Studien zur Entwicklung des Faches Alte Geschichte.*

JOHN LYON is a Senior Lecturer in the Department of English at the University of Bristol, who works on Shakespeare, the novel and aspects of influence. He has edited Henry James's *The Sacred Fount* (Penguin 1994) and is currently working on an edition of James's short stories (Penguin).

JAVED MAJEED teaches in the South Asia Department at the School of Oriental and African Studies, University of London. He is the author of *Ungoverned imaginings: James Mill's* The history of the British in India *and orientalism.*

CHARLES MARTINDALE, Professor of Latin at the University of Bristol, is the editor of *Virgil and his influence, Ovid renewed, Horace made new* (with David Hopkins) and, most recently, *The Cambridge companion to Virgil.* He is also author of a book on the importance of reception theory for classicists, *Redeeming the text: Latin poetry and the hermeneutics of reception.*

ELIZABETH PRETTEJOHN teaches history of art at the University of Plymouth. She contributed substantial sections to the exhibition catalogues *Imagining Rome: British artists and Rome in the nineteenth century* and *Sir Lawrence Alma-Tadema 1836–1912*. She is also the author of *Rossetti and his circle.*

MARLA STONE is Assistant Professor of History at Occidental College, Los Angeles, California. In addition to a number of articles on Fascist culture and politics, she is the author of *The patron state: art and politics in Fascist Italy.*

FRANK M. TURNER is the John Hay Whitney Professor of History at Yale University where he served as Provost from 1988 to 1992. He is the author of *Contesting cultural authority: essays in Victorian intellectual life* and editor of *John Henry Newman, the idea of a university.*

NORMAN VANCE is Professor of English at the University of Sussex. His works include *The sinews of the spirit* and *The Victorians and ancient Rome.*

MARIA WYKE is Senior Lecturer in Classics at the University of Reading. She has published widely on Roman love poetry and co-edited a volume of essays on *Women in ancient societies.* She is also the author of *Projecting the past: ancient Rome, cinema and history.*

Preface and acknowledgements

The essays in this interdisciplinary book set out to explore some of the ways, often strange and unexpected, in which ancient Rome's presence may be traced in a range of European cultural contexts from the late eighteenth century to the end of World War Two. The idea of Rome can be made to stand for both permanence – which may be reassuring or oppressive – and vertiginous discontinuities. But however it is understood, Rome with its weighty past remains a potent place in Europe's symbolic landscape.

This collection of essays developed out of a series of seminars which formed the central part of a three-year research project (funded by the Leverhulme Trust) on receptions of Rome in the nineteenth and twentieth centuries, carried out from 1993 to 1996 in the Department of Classics and Ancient History at the University of Bristol. First thanks are due to the Leverhulme Trust itself, without whom the project would not have been possible. We would also like to express our gratitude to Professors J. B. Trapp and T. P. Wiseman who wrote in support of our application for funding. Many people from a wide range of disciplines and geographical areas participated in these seminars and the resulting collection should be seen as very much a collaborative effort. In particular, thanks should go to the Leverhulme Project Steering Committee which included: Derek Duncan, Ted Freeman, Duncan Kennedy, Michael Liversidge, Peter McDonald, Charles Martindale (Project Director), John Whittam, Martin White (all of the University of Bristol), Susanna Morton Braund (now at Royal Holloway, University of London), Thomas Wiedemann (now at the University of Nottingham) and our external advisers Christopher Stray (University of Wales, Swansea) and Maria Wyke (University of Reading). A very significant complement to the research project was the exhibition *Imagining Rome: British artists and Rome in the nineteenth century* organised jointly by the University's History of Art Department and the Bristol City Museum and Art Gallery (with accompanying catalogue edited by Michael Liversidge and Catharine Edwards).

The early stages of editorial work, to establish the focus of the volume, were carried out by an editorial committee which included, besides myself,

Charles Martindale, Duncan Kennedy and Peter McDonald. Others have played an important part in the debates from which this volume developed, as well as (in a number of cases) contributing more practical assistance. In addition to the contributors themselves, it gives me great pleasure to thank Robyn Asleson, Mary Beard, J. W. Burrow, Anthony Copley, Linda Dowling, Wolfgang Ernst, Rowena Fowler, Phil Freeman, Thomas Habinek, Richard Jenkyns, Ellen O'Gorman, Thomas Osborne, Riccardo Santangeli Valenzani, Sam Smiles, Christopher Stray, Jennifer Wallace, Tim Webb, Dick Whittaker and Romke Visser. Jo Kear, Eleanor Tollfree and Jennifer Oster made valued contributions to the smooth running of the seminars. Conversations with Elizabeth Speller prompted me to rethink a significant part of the introduction to the present collection of essays.

Chloe Chard would like to thank the Centre for Cross-Cultural Research at the Australian National University, Canberra for paying some of the photograph and permission fees for illustrations to her essay. The Arts Faculty Research Fund of the University of Bristol also contributed to the cost of illustrations for this volume.

Particular thanks are due to Charles Martindale whose enthusiasm for and expertise in receptions of Rome gave the research project its initial impetus and did much to sustain it over its three-year duration. As director of the project he deployed his customary intellectual rigour to ensure high standards of debate in seminars and beyond. His vigilant critical eye has been invaluable in the final stages of the book's composition. Pauline Hire of Cambridge University Press has, as ever, been wonderfully supportive and encouraging.

Introduction: shadows and fragments

Catharine Edwards

. . . This Rome where the past lies weltering
In the blood of the present[1]

1944. An army advances towards the heart of Rome – in ruins like so many other cities all over Europe. Yet here the ruins, or at least most of them, predate the war, this war at any rate. Indeed the ruins themselves, as ruins, are being fought over. For the previous twenty years Mussolini had been laying claim to Rome's imperial heritage, integrating the remains of ancient monuments into a new vision of the city. Yet German and Allied leaders also claimed a particular entitlement to these stones; a letter of Eisenhower, the Allied Commander-in-Chief, dated 29 December 1943 and addressed to all commanders, instructed them to respect Italy's historical monuments wherever possible, for they 'by their creation helped and now in their old age illustrate the growth of the civilisation which is ours'.[2] On each side, army leaders urged their men to save Rome from the barbarians. Italians might identify either force as descendants of earlier invaders; in June 1944, shortly after the Allies had taken the city, a Roman aristocrat congratulated their commander: 'Yours is the first barbarian army in history to have taken Rome from the south.'[3]

In the 1930s and 40s, when probably the majority of British officers and maybe German, too, would have had a significant classical element in their education, Rome was still – or perhaps again – a very potent symbol.[4] In exploring the growing sense of cultural crisis in the interwar years, writers from Britain, Germany and other countries found parallels with the decline

1 Cecil Day Lewis, 'A letter from Rome' lines 38–9, in *An Italian Visit* (London 1953). The poem was written after Day Lewis visited Rome in 1948.

2 Appendix 'C-1' to Report 20345/0/MFAA. In fact considerable damage was inflicted by Allied Troops. I am grateful to Elizabeth Speller for drawing these documents to my attention.

3 Wiseman (1992) 12.

4 On the place of the classics in British education see Stray (1998). In Germany the dominant position of the Gymnasium (whose curriculum included a significant classical element) was under threat in the interwar years, yet it was still viewed as the most prestigious form of secondary education (Marchand 1996).

of imperial Rome increasingly suggestive.[5] Roman history became a renewed and central concern; Walther Rehm commented, in a major book on the theme of the decline of Rome in western thought published in 1930, that this subject was an especially insistent one, 'when an age was itself stirred and disquieted by a sense of decadence, when it desired to obtain certainty about the historical and spiritual position it occupies in its life'.[6]

Rome has long had a special place in western thought in part because it is always already familiar. Augustus Hare's literary guide, *Walks in Rome*, first published in 1871 but many times reprinted and read by countless travellers to Rome in the late nineteenth and early twentieth centuries, opens with the following observation:

> An arrival in Rome is very different to that in any other town in Europe. It is coming to a place new and yet most familiar, strange and yet so well known. When travellers arrive at Verona, for instance, or at Arles, they generally go to the amphitheatres with a curiosity to know what they are like; but when they arrive at Rome and go to the Coliseum, it is to visit an object whose appearance has been familiar to them from childhood, and long ere it is reached, from the heights of the distant Capitol they can recognise the well-known form; – and, as regards S. Peter's, who is not familar with the aspect of the dome, of the wide-spreading piazza, and the foaming fountains, for long years before they come to gaze upon the reality?[7]

We visit Rome knowing already that this is the city of the Colosseum, the city of St Peter's. Hare echoes the words of many earlier travellers, Gibbon, Goethe – and countless others whose responses are less often quoted. Soldiers in the Allied force entrusted with the capture of Rome in 1944 were issued with guidebooks to ensure that the most important sites remained undamaged, where possible – and that these visitors, too, should recognise the monuments of their own cultural heritage.[8]

Rome is the eternal city whose durability can also offer a more general reassurance.[9] Byron provides the best-known English version of a medieval saying attributed to the Venerable Bede:

> While the Coliseum stands, Rome shall stand;
> When falls the Coliseum, Rome shall fall;
> And when Rome falls – the World.
> (*Childe Harold's Pilgrimage* IV stanza 14, lines 1297–9)

The Colosseum, though crumbling, still stands. Rome can and often does signify permanence, order, authority; speaking in 1904, the distinguished

[5] Ziolkowski (1993) esp.6–26.
[6] *Der Untergang Roms im abendländischen Denken: Ein Beitrag zur Geschichtsschreibung und zum Dekadenzproblem* (Leipzig 1930) vii, cited by Ziolkowski (1993) 15.
[7] Hare (1871) 1. [18] I am again endebted to Elizabeth Speller for this information.
[9] On the association of Rome with eternity even in antiquity see Edwards (1996a) 86–8.

classicist J. W. Mackail reminded the Classical Association (a society composed of academics and teachers, as well as those with a general interest in the classics): 'Law, order, reverence for authority, the whole framework of political and social establishment, are the work of Rome on the lines drawn once for all by the Latin genius.'[10]

But the *pax Romana*, the Roman peace, ultimate gift of a city-state founded on fratricide, was sustained through bloodshed. The figure of the Colosseum, so often used to stand for Rome, reveals something of our ambivalence to the Roman empire. Is it possible to think of the Colosseum, that symbol of Rome itself, without thinking of the blood that flowed there, the brutal enactments of Roman power over the animal world, over conquered barbarians, over offenders against Roman justice, over Christian martyrs?[11] Indeed Byron's own descriptions of the Colosseum played a significant part in sustaining the sinister associations of the ruined arena – associations inextricably bound up with visitors' responses to this monument in particular and to Rome in general.

What did (and does) Rome stand for? The high culture of Cicero and Virgil – so long staples of the curriculum for later European elites? The resolute republican heroism of Horatius defending the bridge (vividly evoked in Macaulay's Lays) or Regulus (celebrated by Kipling) who returned to certain and horrific death at his enemies' hands rather than break his word – noble examples to soldiers of later centuries? Or perhaps the pernicious decadence of the emperors Nero and Heliogabalus – a terrible warning of the consequences of tyranny – or even of empire itself? And we cannot forget that other Rome, the city of St Paul and St Peter. Though Romans are often thought of as the enemies of the early Christians, it was precisely through the web of the Roman empire that Christianity was able to spread so rapidly. And it is Christianity which ultimately preserved its old enemy, though in a new form. For Christendom, stretching out from the eternal city, has served only to reinforce the old association of Rome with empire.

Rome's seemingly boundless capacity for multiple, indeed conflicting, signification makes it an extraordinarily fertile paradigm for making sense of – and also for destabilising – history, politics, identity, memory and desire. Rome is at once as familiar as a dog-eared school text-book and as alien as the terrible cult of the priest of Nemi with which J. G. Frazer opened his seminal work of social anthropology of 1889 *The Golden Bough*.

[10] Quoted by Vance (1997) 200. Mackail and his audience, of course, had a vested interest in justifying the increasingly embattled place of classics in the curriculum.

[11] On the associations of the Colosseum, see Vance (1989) I: ch. 2; Quennell (1971). There is no definite evidence that the Colosseum was used for the execution of Christians.

Scope of this volume

This book will explore responses to Rome from the late eighteenth century to the end of the Second World War. We see our project as a distinctive exercise in the writing of cultural history. The essays which follow engage with a wide range of questions relating to the receptions of ancient Rome during this period in the history of Europe. They also offer a variety of strategies for exploring uses of the past both public and also more personal. Some of what the contributors have to say might also be applied to receptions of other periods in history – the Italian Renaissance or classical Athens, for instance. Yet we also wish to argue that Roman antiquity has a very particular place in European culture. This is, of course, generally accepted for Rome's impact on earlier times but is perhaps rather less commonly acknowledged for the nineteenth and twentieth centuries.[12] Even the new edition of *The legacy of Rome* (1992) pays surprisingly little attention to more recent periods.[13]

One aim of this collection is to re-evaluate the received idea that in the late eighteenth and early nineteenth centuries ancient Rome was displaced from its position of dominant cultural authority, as a passion for ancient Greece swept over Europe. Certainly many leading writers and intellectuals looked to ancient Greece for inspiration. Comparisons were drawn between Greek and Roman literature and society which were often to the disadvantage of the Romans. 'We are all Greeks. Our laws, our literature, our religion, our arts have their root in Greece', Shelley wrote in 1821 in the preface to *Hellas*, crediting Rome merely as a means of spreading Greek civilisation.[14] But the importance of Rome was also brought into new relief by events such as the French occupations of the city in 1798 and 1809. Coleridge, for instance, lamented bitterly the fate of the place 'which, in ancient times was the civil, and in modern times, the spiritual metropolis of Europe, which is endeared by so many recollections and associations to the statesman, the soldier, the admirer of the arts, and the man of letters; of which the name alone calls before our imagination every sort of literary and martial glory'.[15]

Rome may have fallen out of favour with some writers and intellectuals of the early nineteenth century, yet to focus on Romantic Hellenomania as the dominant element in responses to classical antiquity is to privilege the disposition of certain representatives of 'high' culture over the responses of other interpretative communities. In Britain, for instance, Greek was only

12 Though see now Vance (1997), as well as Vance (1989) vol. I and Patterson (1984).
13 Cf. Wiseman (1992) 11.
14 Cf. Jenkyns (1980) ch. 1; Clarke (1989). This was, of course, a contestatory claim.
15 Cited by Webb (1996) 24–5.

ever studied at a small number of exclusive schools.[16] Of the Victorian 'classical' painters, Sir Lawrence Alma-Tadema, whose subjects were so often drawn from the Roman world, enjoyed considerably greater popularity than the Hellenophile Lord Leighton.[17] In the field of British architecture, the Greek revival of the early nineteenth century was a short-lived phenomenon; Rome, however, remained important throughout the century (and in the early years of the twentieth) as a model particularly for public buildings associated with imperial administration.[18] Greece may have been a more exotic and exclusive destination for wealthy travellers but those who could not afford to travel abroad could still share in the growing interest in material traces of the past by studying local antiquities which often included Roman remains.[19]

The studies offered here explore a number of the sometimes strange and unexpected places where Roman presences have manifested themselves in recent times. Rome has been a pervasive presence, often playing a significant role – as, for instance, in T. S. Eliot's *Waste Land* (discussed by Martindale) – even where it receives little explicit mention. Contributors to this volume are drawn from a range of disciplines and approach their material in sometimes very different ways. An emphasis on the variety of modes and contexts in which ancient Rome has been used over the past two centuries is itself a significant aspect of our project. Kennedy's essay, which follows this introduction, raises a number of general themes in relation to some central texts which are explored further in later papers. The order of the rest of the volume is largely chronological (with some exceptions in the interests of thematic continuity).

The influence of ancient Rome over the past two centuries is a vast topic. This collection of essays does not seek to be comprehensive. Several essays (Bann, Huet, Prettejohn and Stone, in particular) explore Rome's presence in the visual arts of France, Britain and Italy.[20] Music and theatre have, however, been largely omitted.[21] The place of Roman studies in school and university teaching (discussed in two important recent studies) is not covered here.[22] Classical scholarship plays a relatively minor role in our discussions, while no attempt is made to offer a complete survey of the influence of ancient Roman authors on great writers of the last two centuries (in any case, these are areas which have received extended scholarly

16 Cf. Stray (1998). 17 Cf. Prettejohn in Becker et al. (1996) 101–8.

18 See Metcalf (1989) and Port (1995).

19 Cf. Vance (1997) esp.14–18, 243–6. On increased preoccupation with the concrete in responses to the past in the nineteenth century, see Bann below.

20 Other recent work in this area includes Jenkyns (1991); Becker et al. (1996); Liversidge and Edwards (1996).

21 For some discussion of Roman themes in plays and opera see Vance (1997) esp.41–9.

22 On these topics see Stray (1998) and Marchand (1996).

treatment in recent years).[23] Reasons of space have obliged us to omit the large and complex question of responses to ancient Rome in the United States of America (we do, however, include Henry James and T. S. Eliot who made their homes in England).[24] The majority of essays concentrate on British responses. Among other western European countries, only France, Germany and Italy are discussed in any detail. Nevertheless, the comparative element is crucial to this collection of studies.

Retrieving Rome

Significant Roman traces may be discerned in the work of two writers of the late nineteenth and early twentieth centuries, Sigmund Freud and J. G. Frazer, who have played a vital role in the formation of modern sensibilities. Freud was fascinated by both the literary and the archaeological remains of antiquity and had an intense but ambivalent attitude to Rome itself.[25] In his essay of 1930, 'Civilisation and its discontents', he famously offers the city as an analogy for the human mind:

> Now let us by a flight of imagination, suppose that Rome is not a human habitation but a psychical entity with a similarly long and copious past – an entity, that is to say, in which nothing that has once come into existence will have passed away and all the earlier phases of development continue to exist alongside the latest one.[26]

Freud goes on to describe the appearance of Rome in different historical periods – manifestations of the city which are to be imagined as simultaneously visible. This arresting description of a synchronous, palimpsestic city, often cited by scholars, repays further consideration. In Freud's image, all of Rome's past is at once present; only a slight change in perspective is needed to glimpse each different version of the city. Each phase both is and is not Rome. Rome is a totality and one which necessarily defies the imagination (having set out at some length his image of Rome as an analogy for the human mind, Freud ultimately sets it aside as unsatisfactory).

Rome has often served as the embodiment of time – a place where the survivals of different historical eras are visibly layered upon one another. As the eternal city, it has also been made to stand for the transcendence of time. Freud's suggestive image, in making all Rome's pasts simultaneously fully present, collapses these two aspects. Several essays in this collection (Martindale's, in particular) explore tensions between approaches to Rome

[23] On classical scholarship see collections of essays ed.Christ and Momigliano (1989) and ed. Gabba and Christ (1989 and 1991). On individual authors, see particularly Martindale (1984) and (1988), Hopkins and Martindale (1993), Turner (1993), Ziolkowski (1993), Vance (1997).

[24] American responses to Rome are admirably discussed in Vance (1989) I.

[25] On Freud's familiarity with the ancient world in general see Mitchell-Boyask (1994).

[26] (1930/1985) 257–8. This passage is quoted at greater length in Kennedy below.

which could be described as 'historical' – seeing the city under the aspect of time – and those which are rather 'archaeological' – seeing it under the aspect of eternity. How far must we make a choice between, on the one hand, telling stories, framing narratives about Rome's past and, on the other, making sense of Rome through surveying its surviving fragments, mapping their current relationships?

The complexity of Freud's relationship with the city also highlights a number of issues relating to identity which will be central to the present collection of studies. Despite his lifelong fascination with Rome, Freud did not visit the city until 1900. In *The Interpretation of Dreams*, he writes of a series of dreams based on 'a longing to visit Rome'.[27] This failure to visit the city Freud himself associates with the incompleteness of his own participation in European identity. Rome, for Freud, symbolised western culture, but a Christian culture to which he, as a Jew, could never fully belong. As he became increasingly aware of anti-semitic feelings among his school-fellows, he came to identify with Rome's great enemy, Hannibal, leader of the semitic Carthaginians.[28] Leonard Barkan suggestively comments: 'Rome, with its own appropriated past, is . . . a Family Romance for those who identify themselves with Western culture. . . . For Freud personally, Rome was an object of unfulfilled but ambivalent desire.'[29] As we shall see from a number of the essays which follow, the idea of Rome has for many people served to articulate questions of identity in a similarly insistent manner.

Roman antiquity is invoked at the very beginning of *The Interpretation of Dreams*; the epigraph Freud chose for his book is taken from Virgil's *Aeneid*: *flectere si nequeo superos, Acheronta movebo* – 'If I cannot persuade the powers above, I shall move those below' (7.312). This quotation, he wrote to his friend Willhelm Fliess, was meant to hint, in psychoanalytical terms, at repression.[30] Rome, the city he had dreamed of but not yet seen,[31] could offer a suggestive and culturally resonant model for the exploration of uncharted areas of human existence. Virgil offered guidance to the underworld of the psyche.

This choice is interestingly in tune with one made by Freud's contemporary J. G. Frazer.[32] The classical allusion of *The Golden Bough*'s title and the work's initial discussion of the cult of Nemi in ancient Roman Italy served

27 (1900/1976) 282. Notes added by Freud in 1909 and 1925 indicate that he subsequently became a 'constant pilgrim to Rome'. On the complexity of Freud's relationship with Rome, see Schorske (1991). 28 (1900/1976) 282. Cf. 285.

29 (1991) 16–7. Note also Margaret Ferguson's discussion in Patterson (1984).

30 Quoted by Ziolkowski (1993) 3.

31 See (1900/1976) 282 for an account of one of Freud's dreams of Rome which drew on 'a well known engraving of the city'.

32 Freud himself, of course, drew extensively on Frazer's work (cf. especially his essay 'Totem and taboo' first published 1913).

in general to legitimate Frazer's unfamiliar methods and claims through an appeal to the authority of Roman antiquity. More particularly, as Mary Beard has recently emphasised, the title presented Frazer's work as itself enabling the reader to explore the murky and dangerous world of primitive rites and superstitions and emerge unscathed – like Aeneas visiting the underworld in Virgil's *Aeneid*, whose ability to come back to the upper world is guaranteed by his golden bough.[33]

In other respects, too, Frazer's vast synthetic work (which enjoyed enormous popularity with the reading public) can be seen as drawing on habits of thought bound up with the classical education the author shared with so many of his peers.[34] The extreme comparativism of his work was itself an approach which one might see as, in part at least, conditioned by the central place of the, one might argue, intrinsically comparative discipline of classics in nineteenth-century British elite education.[35] Majeed's essay later in this volume explores the comparative approach and the use of references to ancient Rome in British discussions of the administration of India. *The Golden Bough* itself served, in its exploration of a multitude of exotic practices drawn from a huge geographical area, to provide for Frazer's readers an inspiring image of the British imperial project.

National, political and religious identities

Freud found the Christian associations of Rome alienating. Others have found Rome appealing for its non-Christian associations. Pagan Rome has often been drawn on as a source of authority prior, and in opposition, to that of divinely sanctioned kingship.[36] Rebelling against the *ancien régime* of church as well as monarchy in the late eighteenth century, French revolutionaries took as names for themselves Cato, Gracchus and Brutus. Karl Marx in the *Eighteenth Brumaire* writes of the power of invocations of the past to mediate radical change: 'Just when they seem engaged in revolutionising themselves and things, in creating something that has never yet existed, precisely in such periods of revolutionary crisis they anxiously conjure up the spirits of the past to their service and borrow from them names, battle cries and costumes in order to present the new scene of world history in this time-honoured disguise and this borrowed language. Thus . . . the Revolution of 1789 to 1814 draped itself alternately as the Roman republic and the Roman empire.'[37] The routing of the Tarquins and the

33 Beard (1992).
34 Frazer also wrote a lengthy commentary on Ovid's *Fasti* published in 1929.
35 The study of comparative philology which originated in the late eighteenth century focussed particularly on classical European and Asian languages. For the more general intellectual impact of this discipline, see Dowling (1986).
36 Cf. Gay (1967).
37 (1967) 10. Cf. the comments made by Chateaubriand, cited by Vidal-Naquet (1995) 102.

assassination of Caesar – those two emblematically anti-monarchical moments from ancient Roman history, happily conflated in the name of Brutus – made clear the political intentions of those who invoked them, while also appealing to the authority of antiquity.[38]

The more conservative American predecessors of the French revolutionaries, rebelling against British rule, also figured themselves as Romans, founders of new republican institutions.[39] George Washington, for instance, lacked a classical education (unlike many of the leaders of the American revolution) but claimed his favourite play was Addison's *Cato* (1713) – a story celebrating the self-sacrifice of a Roman republican hero. America's first president, recalled from his rustic retreat, was himself hailed as a new Cincinnatus. The rule of a foreign monarch overturned, the political classes of the thirteen states declared they would follow the examples of Brutus, founder of the Roman republic, and Publius Valerius Publicola, another semi-mythical figure crediting with initiating key elements in Rome's constitution. Their new balanced constitution, they claimed, was based on that of ancient Rome as described by Cicero and Polybius. Rome could offer Americans dissatisfied with British rule an alternative model of government sanctioned by centuries of tradition – and associated with the classical education which remained a prime marker of elite status in the American states.

Rome then could function in the late eighteenth century as a revolutionary alternative to the existing order – a model familiar to all educated persons yet distant enough in time to allow latitude of interpretation. Here, as in other very different contexts, appeals to ancient Rome could help to articulate developments perceived as new and shocking. Rome could offer examples of republican (as well as autocratic) government – though conservative critics were quick to appropriate Roman parallels for their own purposes. In a sense, the revolutionary moments in America and, particularly, France can be seen as marking a turning point in the influence of Rome. Soon Athenian democracy was to become the preferred model for the advocates of more extensive popular participation.[40]

Rome, especially in its association with the Catholic church, but also because of the extent of its empire in antiquity, has often served as a symbol of cosmopolitanism (a habit of thinking exemplified in Macaulay's

38 Invocations of Brutus are discussed by A and J. Ehrard (1989). On appeals to Rome generally in the context of European revolutions, see Vance (1997) ch. 2 and Vidal-Naquet (1995) ch. 5.

39 See Richard (1994) and Sellers (1994). Both argue against the older view that the Roman flavour of constitutional debate in the 1770s and 80s was merely superficial.

40 See Turner (1981) esp.187–263 and Vidal-Naquet (1995). The example of Rome was still invoked in discussions of later European revolutions but usually as a negative model. Cf. Vance (1997) 24–53.

response to St Peter's, discussed by Edwards later in this volume). For many centuries Latin was the common language used by scholars and churchmen. Champions of vernacular literature constructed Latin as the supranational other against which local identities were to be defined. Mme de Staël's novel *Corinne, ou L'Italie* (1807), whose heroine was presented as offering her aristocratic British lover an emotional as well as historical guide to the sites of Rome (before going on to Naples, Venice and other cities), accompanied countless visitors to Rome in the nineteenth century and exercised an extraordinary influence over their responses to the city.[41] Yet *Corinne*'s author also played a key part in developing ideas of nationalism which could be seen as heralding the demise of Roman cosmopolitanism as a European ideal.[42] The novel's eponymous heroine could herself be read as embodying Italy (an Italy at that time united only by language – and French conquest);[43] the contrasting qualities of northern and mediterranean national characters are stressed throughout the work (as they would be, too, in de Staël's important study of German identity, *De l'Allemagne*, of 1810–13).[44] Corinne's spontaneous and yet learned responses to the remains of antiquity are presented as an integral aspect of her (ostensibly) Italian nature. Corinne's Rome, then, despite its appeal to visitors from many European countries, is Italian rather than cosmopolitan. De Staël's vision of Italy was in direct opposition to that of Napoleon, who occupied Rome from 1809 to 1814 (following an earlier French occupation in 1798), when it briefly held the position of second city in a new empire – that of France.[45]

Later in the nineteenth century, champions of Italian nationalism sought to appropriate the remains of Roman antiquity for their own cause.[46] Yet it is not only Italians who have exploited appeals to ancient Rome for nationalistic purposes. A key issue for several contributors to our collection is the different ways in which ancient Rome has been used to articulate national identities in Britain, France and Germany also. Here too one may trace a profound tension between different uses of Rome – in this case between Rome's association with particular national characteristics (Roman in opposition to Carthaginian, Greek or barbarian) and Rome's association with the law, language and culture held in common by diverse peoples.

41 Guide books, such as Hare (1871), quote from it repeatedly.
42 Cf. Marchand (1996) 158–60.
43 Cf. McGann (1984) 93. For further discussion of *Corinne*, see Kennedy and Chard below.
44 This work began by emphasising the distinctive characters of the northern nations which had resisted the tyranny of Rome. Cf. Isbell (1994).
45 De Staël's opposition to Napoleon led to her exile from France. Her influence as his opponent was so great that one contemporary observed: 'People said that in Europe one had to count three Great Powers, England, Russia and Mme.de Staël', cited by *ibid.* 6.
46 For appeals to Roman antiquity in the context of Italian nationalism, see Springer (1987) and Vance (1997) 49–53.

Different nations have competed sometimes to identify themselves with Rome, sometimes to impose a Roman identity on others. In his youth, Napoleon, like many involved in the French revolution, had identified with Brutus, later with Caesar. When he became emperor, however, Augustus was a more appealing model. The trappings of the new French court, its designs on Egypt, its European empire were uncompromisingly Roman (Napoleon's uses of Roman precedent are discussed by Huet later in this volume). As we have seen, however, Napoleon's invocation of Rome's imperial precedent brought with it cosmopolitan aspirations which were directly in conflict with the developing nationalist movements in other countries.

Even before the revolution, France had been seen as closer to Roman traditions than some of its neighbours. British writers sometimes concurred in this identification (Daniel Defoe in 1728 had praised Carthage as, like Britain, a great trading nation: 'It had been much happier for Mankind in general, but especially for the Trading Part of the World, if *Carthage* had stood, and the *Roman* Empire had been destroy'd').[47] Occasionally, however, even the French might be identifed with Rome's Carthaginian enemies. Two paintings by J. M. W. Turner, *Dido building Carthage: or the rise of the Carthaginian empire* (1815; London, National Gallery) and *The decline of the Carthaginian empire* (1817; London, Tate Gallery) painted before and after Waterloo, have often been read as commenting on the rise and fall of Napoleon. Implicitly Britain plays the role of Rome (in the time of the republic, naturally) triumphing over despotic Carthage.[48]

Partly in response to the increasingly assertive French appropriation of Rome in the early nineteenth century, there was a romantic vogue in northern Europe for local Celtic and Teutonic traditions – the traditions of Rome's barbarian enemies.[49] The early nineteenth century also saw a passionate devotion to things Greek among many Germans and British (and Americans too).[50] The desire to identify with the ancient Greeks fitted with new movements in politics, towards democracy (at least in Britain and America). In Germany, Prussian emphasis on Greece served, in part at least, to weaken the symbolic value of Rome on which the Holy Roman Empire – and later the Habsburg empire – had drawn for legitimacy.[51]

[47] *Atlas Maritimus et Commerialis* (London 1728) cited by Weinbrot (1993b) 183. This sentiment is interestingly echoed by Benjamin Constant in 1814, celebrating the essential modernity of Carthage as opposed to Rome (cited by Vidal-Naquet (1995) 115). Napoleon himself can even be found identifying with Hannibal in J. L. David's *Napoleon crossing the St Bernard* of 1801 (Musée du château de Versailles).

[48] See Liversidge in Liversidge and Edwards (1996) 83.

[49] See Weinbrot (1993a); Smiles (1993). This development should also be related to the development of nationalism.

[50] See for example Butler (1935); Jenkyns (1980); Turner (1981); Habinek (1992). Greece was also invoked by French revolutionaries. Cf. Vidal-Naquet (1995).

[51] Cf. Marchand (1996) 152–5. On German ambivalence to the Greek association with democracy, see *ibid.* 141–2.

In literature, the primitive grandeur, the rugged originality of Homer were celebrated by influential romantic thinkers such as J. G. Herder in Germany. As the romantic preoccupation with primitivism, sincerity, originality and imagination came to dominate European tastes, Rome was often characterised as overrefined, derivative, prosaic and out-of-date – indeed one might see the romantic notion of 'Greece' as essentially dependent on such a construction of 'Rome'. F. M. Turner has recently explored early nineteenth-century hostility to Virgil as a function particularly of burgeoning admiration for Homer. Virgil was too closely associated with the Augustan English poets against whom many romantics wished to rebel.[52] Such condemnations of Rome were, however, often qualified – Wordsworth's favourite ancient poet was no Greek but the Augustan Horace.[53]

Identification with the Greeks was all the more inviting in religious terms for Protestants, as Rome continued to be the symbol of Catholicism.[54] Northern visitors to the city often commented on the close link between the decadent popery of their own day and the vices of the ancient pagan Romans.[55] The religious associations of Rome shifted somewhat with the efflorescence of new and intense forms of Christianity in early nineteenth-century Europe. Turner's essay in this volume discusses some of the ways in which historical novels used the Christianised Roman Empire to explore doctrinal issues – and appropriate the authority of the early church for the author's own denomination. Such novels allowed ample scope for attacking the attractions of Catholicism in particular (which was acquiring some distinguished converts amongst the Anglican clergy in the middle years of the nineteenth century).

The 'otherness' of the Romans, their cruelty, their materialism, their lack of originality, their decadence, came to be represented with some frequency in the novels and paintings of the nineteenth century. Edward Bulwer-Lytton's *Last Days of Pompeii* (1834) presented its ancient Italian characters as vulgar, petty, cruel and materialistic, while its Greek hero and heroine were exemplars of sensitivity and refinement.[56] Even where Britain, for instance, might seem obviously to resemble Rome, as in the rule of an empire, the dissimilarities were often emphasised in the writings and speeches of politicians and administrators, as the peacefully trading Britons were contrasted with the aggressively military Romans.[57] The example of an empire which eventually collapsed through corruption and

52 Turner (1993) 290–312

53 On the critical fates of various Latin authors in the nineteenth century see the works cited in note 23 above.

54 Cf. Marchand (1996) xxiii.

55 See, for instance, Rev. J. J. Blunt, *Vestiges of ancient manners and customs, discoverable in modern Italy and Sicily* (1823).

56 Cf. Jenkyns (1980) 84–5.

57 Cf. Colley (1992) 168; Weinbrot (1993b) 176–84.

decadence, whose origins might be traced even back to the early phases of imperial expansion, was repeatedly held up as a negative model.[58]

Contrasts between immoral Romans and the virtuous early Christians whom they persecuted have been particularly favoured in novels set in antiquity and in cinematic representations of the ancient world (often based on those novels). *The Last Days of Pompeii*, *Quo vadis?*, *Ben Hur*, as Turner emphasises below, could include lurid scenes of luxury, sex and violence. In films, too, the evil but seductive Romans eventually lose out to the rather drab but nevertheless virtuous Christians. The victory of Christian morality validates the more cinematically impressive display of pagan luxury.[59] Such examples may serve, also, to point up the particular fascination ancient Rome continued to exert.

Since the days of the early Church Fathers (not to mention the moralists of pagan Rome) the ancient Romans have been notorious for their decadence – a decadence with which moralists, offering detailed denunciations, have of course been complicit. In the later nineteenth century, as Vance and Prettejohn describe later in this volume, decadence became fashionable, and with it features of Roman antiquity previously subject (at least in public contexts) to unqualified disapproval.[60] Des Esseintes, the hero of J. K. Huysmans' 1884 novel *A Rebours* (described as 'the breviary of the Decadence' by Arthur Symons) has a passion for Latin literature, particularly favouring authors whose style was considered corrupt by respectable scholars. Lavish paintings of decadent scenes, such as Alma-Tadema's images of the Roman baths or the imperial court, might be read as denunciations – or as celebrations – of Roman vice.[61] Embracing decadence could serve also as a strategy for identifying others as philistines or barbarians.

For some, however, the straightforward virtues of Roman soldiers and administrators themselves exercised an appeal. By the latter part of the nineteenth century, Rome was coming to seem a more attractive model to those who sought to emulate the Roman sense of public duty and the administrative efficiency of Rome's empire. *The Times* in 1878, for instance, celebrated Britain's provision of a 'Roman peace' in India.[62] British statesmen wrote elaborate comparisons of the British and the Roman empires. Here, too, however, Roman parallels might prove unsettling. Majeed, later in this volume, explores the ways Roman models were used to articulate anxieties about the dilution of British identity as a consequence of empire.[63]

58 Cf. Turner (1993) 231–61.
59 For recent discussions of Rome on film, see Mayer (1994), Wyke (1997).
60 On the link with developments in philology, see Dowling (1986) esp.84–103.
61 See Prettejohn (1996). 62 Cited by Read (1979) 193.
63 Similar anxieties were expressed concerning the threat posed by empire to Britain's linguistic identity. Cf. Dowling (1986) ch. 2.

An increased interest in Roman history on the part of Britain's educated elite derived enormous stimulus from the German scholarly tradition, which was especially associated with B. G. Niebuhr and, later in the nineteenth century, Theodor Mommsen.[64] German historiography became professionalised early in the century.[65] Caught up in the Rankean project to map all past human experience once and for all, those who saw themselves as professional historians shifted away from the exploration of explicit analogy and towards a purportedly scientific history of technical subjects – no longer great men but institutions were the business of history.[66] In some senses, at this time, narrative history lost its rationale among professional historians. This move away from narrative was another means by which they were differentiating themselves from more popular writers who continued to reach large audiences through more traditional literary-historical forms. Nevertheless, the professional historians' concern with the mechanisms of Roman imperial administration overlapped with concerns of statesmen in Germany, Britain and elsewhere charged in the late nineteenth century with the administration of growing empires.

An address made in 1903 to an audience of ancient historians by Professor Eduard Meyer, which severely criticised recent attempts to play down the role of the individual in history, may be seen as marking a turning point in German perspectives on the ancient past.[67] The quest for objective, scientific history among professionals was to some degree abandoned in favour of a return to the celebration of great men. Historians of the twenties and thirties in Germany were increasingly preoccupied with issues of national identity (though even for Mommsen, the question of the relationship between the German and the Roman had been of great importance). Oswald Spengler, writing in 1918, identified strongly with ancient Rome: 'Romanism – with its rigorous sense of factuality, lacking in geniality, barbaric, disciplined, practical Protestant, Prussian – will always provide us in our search for analogies with the key to understanding our own future.'[68] Hitler himself was a great admirer of the Romans, in particular of the monumentality of their remains. Albert Speer, the leading architect of Nazi Germany, is said to have boasted that: 'he and his collaborators had learned how to build in a more Roman manner than the Romans themselves'.[69] At the same time, many Germans were concerned not to promote ancient Rome at the expense of ancient Germany, while the fall of the Roman Empire was seen as a consequence of racial miscegenation.[70] Here, too,

64 On the background to Mommsen's interest in Roman imperial history see Wiedemann's intro. to Mommsen (1996). 65 Cf. Marchand (1996). 66 See Dowling (1985).
67 'Kaiser Augustus' in Meyer (1910) I 44–92. 68 Cited by Ziolkowski (1993) 12.
69 See Scobie (1990) ch. 2.
70 An emphasis on race in references to Rome can also be found in Italian Fascist literature, as Wyke points out below.

ancient Rome was viewed with mixed feelings, as Losemann shows later in this volume.

German ambivalence to ancient Rome was in part a response to the thoroughgoing appropriation of Roman antiquity taking place in Mussolini's Italy. Ancient Rome had become an increasingly important reference point for Italians since the reunification of the peninsula (as Wyke shows later in this volume). The Fascist regime, building on this tradition, made extensive, if heterogeneous, use of the Roman past. Mussolini took over many of the trappings of Roman imperial power (the *fasces* in antiquity symbolised a magistrate's power to punish). Proclaiming a new Italian empire in 1936, he also claimed to be following ancient precedent. Perhaps his most spectacular appropriation of Roman antiquity was his transformation of the city of Rome.[71] Enormous sums were spent on excavating ancient Roman monuments and integrating them into the fabric of a new Fascist city of even more grandiose dimensions. Stone, later in this volume, discusses some aspects of these changes.

The frequent and various use of Rome in negotiating national identities makes it particularly important to examine receptions of ancient Rome from a comparative point of view. The material we examine here reveals Britons at times identifying with Rome's enemy Carthage, at times with Rome, at times with the Celtic inhabitants of the British isles under the threat of Roman invasion. Some French writers were keen to emphasise the credentials of their own country as the true heir of Latin culture.[72] Others chose rather to characterise Paris as a new Athens, intellectual and sophisticated in contrast to London's wealthier – but more philistine – Rome (a comparison which served in part to articulate anxieties about the growing strength of the British empire).[73] Germans are to be found raising statues to the barbarian Arminius who defeated a Roman general, yet also choosing to build in the style of Rome's imperial monuments.[74]

Rome seems to stimulate a desire for analogies. Yet this handful of examples illustrates the slipperiness of all such identifications, whether with Romans, Greeks, Carthaginians or barbarians.[75] Freud, as we have seen, identified with Hannibal, Rome's Carthaginian enemy, an outsider – yet Hannibal nevertheless became an integral part of Roman history. In a sense Rome's empire continues to be irresistible. Rome still absorbs contradiction, includes resistance.

71 Cf. Manacorda and Tamassia (1985).
72 Cf. the example of Péladan discussed by Vance below.
73 I am endebted to Claire Hancock for showing me her unpublished work on this subject.
74 On the history of Arminius in Germany see Fansa (1994).
75 Not surprisingly Italians have identified more consistently with the ancient Romans – though regionalism in Italy has also stimulated identification with non-Roman peoples within the peninsula, such as the Etruscans.

Memory, desire and the pathos of distance

For some visitors to Rome in the early nineteenth century, the ruins of the city served not to call forth great figures from the ancient world (as they had done for Gibbon and many other visitors of the previous century) but as a reminder of the unbridgeable gulf between past and present. Bann, later in this volume, argues that perspectives on the past were transformed by the French revolution and its aftermath, so that all of Rome's previous history could be described as 'Ancient Rome'.[76] The paintings of Granet, he suggests, bring to bear the painter's feelings of intense nostalgia for the pre-revolutionary period in their representations of the recent Roman past, a past which had been so marked by continuities with far earlier periods.

Rome in its ruined state could also be taken as a sign of the irrecoverability, the illegibility of the past.[77] The Rome of *Childe Harold's Pilgrimage*, for instance (another book which accompanied innumerable visitors to Rome later in the nineteenth century), despite Byron's interest in the movement for Italian nationalism, was merely a ruin – a ruin whose mysterious allure might be compromised by excessive knowledge. The precise history of the column of Phocas in the Roman forum had recently been revealed by excavations, yet Byron referred to it as a 'nameless column' rendered eloquent precisely through its lack of specific identity.[78]

Such a model at the same time facilitated the incorporation of fragments of antiquity into personal time, as ruins become a medium for the exploration of subjectivity; Byron termed himself 'a ruin amidst ruins' (canto IV, stanza 25, 217–18). Another strategy for coming to terms with the mysterious strangeness of the ancient past was to gender it as feminine. Chard's essay in this volume explores this development in a number of texts of the late eighteenth and nineteenth centuries (including the work of Byron) which characterise antiquity as a feminine – and disruptive – force. Antiquities – like women – could be seen as intrinsically resistant to understanding. The characterisation of antiquities as feminine was also provoked by – and stimulated – their power to arouse desire. Wilhelm Jensen's novel *Gradiva* (1903), discussed by Chard below, explores an archaeologist's erotic obsession with a bas-relief of a young woman (the novel is the subject of a rather better-known essay by Freud).

Rome, as we have seen, played a particular part in Freud's own self-conception – Barkan speaks of Freud's 'unfulfilled but ambivalent desire' for

[76] See, too, Bann (1995). [77] See McGann (1984).

[78] Cf. Springer (1987) 6. Springer follows interpretation offered in notes to Byron's work by his friend and contemporary J. C. Hobhouse. One might also read the lines as refering to Trajan's column. On Byron's responses to Rome, see also Janowitz (1990) esp.40–52.

the city. Others too have drawn on Roman antiquity to explore troubling aspects of their own identity. Prettejohn's essay in this volume discusses the painter Simeon Solomon's use of Roman antiquity to articulate sado-masochistic homosexual desires in a work exhibited in the Royal Academy exhibition of 1865.[79] Antiquity, here, may be seen not so much as licensing but as enabling the exploration of 'deviant' sexuality. This example, in particular, renders problematic any attempt to characterise ancient settings as a mere mask for modern realities or to separate 'public' from 'private' uses of antiquity.

Rome attracted an increasing numbers of visitors over the period covered by our study. The city had been the culmination of the aristocratic Grand Tour. Despite the romantic tendency to eschew urban life for wild nature, Rome as the city of ruins was a favourite destination for the romantic traveller.[80] In the course of the nineteenth century, it was, with the development of tourism, to become the goal of many less grand travellers too. It is always *other* visitors who are 'tourists'; describing the resurgence in travel to Italy after the defeat of Napoleon in 1815, a commentator in the *Westminster Review* of 1825 observed: 'the inundation of Britons, like a second irruption of Goths, poured down upon Italy'.[81] Narratives of travel, both those claiming authenticity and those offered as literary fictions, present the traveller's response to places, buildings and works of art as a revealing marker of education, sensibility – and, implicitly, social status.[82]

Many visitors experienced unease at the dauntingly resonant mass of Roman sites. Rome frequently provoked feelings of 'touristic shame', as visitors felt the inadequacy of their own emotional and intellectual responses.[83] Often seen as an inspiration and stimulus to creativity in earlier periods, Rome's legacy could also feel somewhat oppressive.[84] Visitors often struggled to articulate a response to that much visited city which might seem fresh and distinctive; apparently personal responses to Rome are always necessarily mediated through earlier receptions of the city in art and literature (a point emphasised in Kennedy's essay). Lyon's study in this volume of responses to Rome in the work of Henry James explores an especially rich example of one writer's profound ambivalence to Rome's complex and contradictory associations.

[79] For the use of ancient precedents to construct and at the same time legitimate what were perceived as 'deviant' sexualities, see Dowling (1995).

[80] See McGann (1984) and Webb (1996).

[81] Cited by Buzard (1993) 83–4.

[82] See Pemble (1988); Buzard (1993); Chard and Langdon (1996); Edwards (1996b); Chard (forthcoming 1999).

[83] MacCannell (1976) 10.

[84] For invocations of Rome as a stimulus to creativity, see Greene (1982) and Ferguson (1984); also Lowenthal (1985) 74–87. Earlier periods, too, had sometimes found Rome's legacy an uneasy burden.

Conclusion

The parameters we have chosen for this book are roughly marked by the French revolution of 1789 and the end of the Second World War in 1945. Both these dates can be represented as turning points in European political history or even as epistemic shifts in the Foucauldian sense. How far does Roman influence come to an end in 1945? Do the catastrophes of Auschwitz and Hiroshima, for which Rome can offer no analogies, finally reveal Rome's limit? Or does Rome still have its uses? T. S. Eliot observed: 'We are all, so far as we inherit the civilization of Europe, still citizens of the Roman Empire.'[85] It is perhaps appropriate that the treaty marking the foundation of the European Community, latest successor to the empire of Rome, should have been signed in Rome itself. The majority of modern Europeans still live by some form of Roman law. Many speak a dialect of Latin. We write in the letters of the Roman alphabet. Some elements of Rome's legacy are so pervasive we can scarcely see them. And Roman cosmopolitanism may still, on some level, offer an alternative to the darker consequences of nationalistic emnity.

[85] Eliot in 'Virgil and the Christian world' of 1951, in (1957) 130.

1 A sense of place: Rome, history and empire revisited

Duncan F. Kennedy

A 'sense of place' is, I suspect, a notion more often invoked than investigated, but Rome seems a pre-eminent case for consideration. Rome has been seen as the destination *par excellence*, and all roads proverbially lead there. The entry under *voyage* in the French *Encyclopédie* of 1765 observes that one makes a journey to Paris, but one makes *the* journey to Italy; it is definitive.[1] The fervour expressed by travellers to Rome like Goethe or Henry James is one of desire and expectation fulfilled, presented to us as at least in part intellectual, and figured as *re*cognition as much as cognition. Goethe exclaims: 'All the dreams of my youth have come to life; the first engravings I remember – my father hung views of Rome in the hall – I now see in reality, and everything I have known through paintings, drawings, etchings, woodcuts, plaster casts and cork models is now assembled before me. Wherever I walk, I come upon familiar objects in an unfamiliar world; everything is just as I imagined it, yet everything is new' (*Italian Journey*, p. 129).[2] Goethe goes on to allude to the story of Pygmalion's statue of Galatea to suggest the way that Rome was for him fashioned as the destination of his desire through representation before it achieved 'reality' (figured as coming to life) in the fulfilment of that desire. The evocation of place often involves an appeal to authenticity, but authenticity is evoked precisely in and through notions of representation and recognition. Rome visited is always in some sense Rome revisited. Though we may fashion fables of an originary visit to virgin ground (Virgil's narrative of Aeneas' visit to the site of the future Rome in Book 8 of the *Aeneid* aspires to something of that quality), depictions of place are always already implicated in structures of representation, and often overtly appeal to them. As Jonathan Culler has remarked, 'the existence of reproductions is what makes something an original, authentic, the real thing'.[3] But the logic shuttles both ways, for the 'reality' no less serves to authenticate the representation, and its mode. On his first evening in Rome, Henry James wrote to his brother William: 'At

[1] Van Den Abbeele (1992) vii.
[2] Page references for Goethe are to the translation of Auden and Mayer (1970).
[3] Culler (1988) 160.

last – for the first time – I live! It beats everything: it leaves the Rome of your fancy – your education – nowhere. It makes Venice – Florence – Oxford – London – seem like little cities of pasteboard. . . . The effect is something indescribable.' But describe it is what he does: 'For the first time I know what the picturesque is.'[4]

James' biographer, Leon Edel, describes his exuberant rhetoric as understandable: 'the romantic spirit was strong in him, and to be in Rome was to visit History itself, to feel not only his own passion at the moment but the passions of the centuries'.[5] Such sentiments occur to many travellers to Rome, and the convention straddles travel literature and fiction. Goethe remarks: 'the entire history of the world is linked up with this city' (p. 148) and later explains:

> What I want to see is the Everlasting Rome, not the Rome which is replaced by another every decade. . . . It is history, above all, that one reads quite differently here from anywhere else in the world. Everywhere else one starts from the outside and works inward; here it seems to be the other way around. All history is encamped about us and all history sets forth again from us. This does not apply only to Roman history, but to the history of the whole world. From here I can accompany the conquerors to the Weser and the Euphrates, or, if I prefer to stand and gape, I can wait in the Via Sacra for their triumphant return.

Rome not only has a history but is identifed with History, and Rome visited is always in some sense History revisited. 'After the brief narrow experience of her childhood', George Eliot's Dorothea Brooke in Chapter 20 of *Middlemarch* 'was beholding Rome, the city of visible history, where the past of a whole hemisphere seems moving in funeral procession with strange ancestral images and trophies gathered from afar'. Travel is a metaphor for thought, and 'investigation' involves following in the footsteps of those who have gone before, a search that is at the same time *re*search. More generally, of course, theories of meaning and interpretation are framed in spatial terms. A conceptual destination often revisited is a *locus communis* or *topos*, a commonplace; a 'convention' is a textual point at which many come together. Citation is the textual counterpart of travel and shares its characteristics. Conversely, therefore, descriptions of places may be seen as encoding assumptions of various sorts; more precisely, 'place' will be configured in particular discourses by the particular epistemological interests involved. In his *Essai sur l'étude de la littérature* of 1761, Edward Gibbon wrote of the philosophical spirit that it 'consists in the power to go back [*remonter*] to simple ideas, to seize and combine first principles. The view [*coup d'oeil*] of one who possesses it is accurate but at the same time extensive. Placed on a height, he takes in a vast stretch of countryside,

[4] James (1974) 160. [5] Edel (1977) 256.

forming an image both distinct and unique, while minds as accurate but more limited discern only a part.'[6] In a famous account to which I shall return, Gibbon was to describe himself as climbing a particular hill, the Capitoline in Rome, and there conceiving the idea of writing the decline and fall of the city. If space exists in three dimensions, place, perhaps, can only exist in four. The evocation of a sense of place is, arguably necessarily, implicated in a sense of history and of time, and this is one of the factors that transforms 'space' into 'place'.

But history, and time, can be configured in more ways than one. The past is a foreign country, we are told, at least by those investigators to whom history means difference and discontinuity rather than similarity and continuity. If descriptions of place encode assumptions about the past and its relationship to the present, a city of seven hills can afford a variety of prospects, none of which is self-evidently superior to the rest. At the beginning of 'Civilisation and its discontents', Freud offered a summary of what 'historians tell us' about the phases of physical development of Rome, but then spins a fantasy of what Rome would be like if it were not a physical entity but a psychical one, 'in which nothing that has once come into existence will have passed away':

> This would mean that in Rome the palaces of the Caesars and the Septizonium of Septimius Severus would still be rising to their old height on the Palatine and that the castle of S. Angelo would still be carrying on its battlements the beautiful statues which graced it until the siege by the Goths, and so on. But more than this. In the place occupied by the Palazzo Caffarelli would once more stand – without the Palazzo having to be removed – the temple of Jupiter Capitolinus; and this not only in its latest shape, as the Romans of the Empire saw it, but also in its earliest one, when it still showed Etruscan forms and was ornamented with terracotta antefixes. Where the Coliseum now stands we could at the same time admire Nero's Golden House. On the Piazza of the Pantheon we should find not only the Pantheon of today, as it was bequeathed to us by Hadrian, but, on the same site, the original edifice erected by Agrippa; indeed, the same piece of ground would be supporting the church of Santa Maria sopra Minerva and the ancient temple over which it was built. And the observer would perhaps only have to change the direction of his glance or his position in order to call up the one view or the other.[7]

Malcolm Bowie sets this amongst the many appeals Freud makes to archaeological images as a favourite means 'whereby this redoubtable theoretician of a timeless unconscious sought to endow his discoveries with the resonance and prestige of history'.[8] We should resist the temptation to be seduced by Freud's contrast of his image with what 'historians tell us' and his disclaimer that his fantasy 'leads to things that are unimaginable and

[6] Cited and translated by Carnochan (1987) 48–9. [7] Freud (1930/1985) 257–8.
[8] Bowie (1987) 17–18.

even absurd'. Freud's configuration of a Rome in which there is no sharp or categorical distinction between past and present, rather than being ahistorical, can be viewed as a meditation on history, and I shall suggest that the topographical simultaneity of Freud's fantasy is precisely correlated to psychoanalysis' projection of its master analytical terms and methods *as* timeless and transcendent. The associations of Rome with timelessness and transcendence are crucially relevant to the impact of Freud's fantasy, and I shall analyse these associations in due course. But first, let us pursue the implications of the boundaries, or lack of them, between past and present – and future.

In a poem dated February 1837, 'A l'Arc de Triomphe', Victor Hugo writes of the landmark, planned by Napoleon for his new Rome but only recently completed, that three thousand years hence, when people will talk of Napoleon in the same way as they now do of Cyrus, when the Seine will be choked with stones, and all Paris except Notre Dame, the Vendôme column and the Arc de Triomphe has fallen into ruin, a man resting on a hill at dusk when the mists have begun to fall will be lost in wonder at the scene and then the monument will truly at last have what it now lacks.[9] Hugo's appeal to authenticity mobilises conventions of representation familiar, for example, from Claude's capricious depiction of the Arch of Constantine and the Colosseum standing isolated in an idyllic landscape. We might think also of Hubert Robert's 1796 depiction of the Great Gallery of the Louvre in ruins a full century-and-a-half before the building was completed, or John Michael Gandy's picture of Soane's rotunda of the Bank of England as a ruin (1832) *(fig. 2)*. The convention persists, arrestingly for the modern viewer, in the sequence *Scenes of the future* by the Soviet emigré artists Vitaly Komar and Alexander Melamid (1974–84), in which buildings such as the TWA terminal at Kennedy Airport, Dulles Airport, the Guggenheim Museum and the Museum of Modern Art are depicted ruined against idealised landscapes.[10] Although appropriated for Paris, London, New York and Washington, the convention seems particularly associated with Rome. As Mme de Staël's heroine Corinne prepares to leave Rome, she goes up to the cupola of St Peter's to bid farewell to the city:

> As she drew near, her first thought was to picture the building as it would be when its turn came to fall into ruin, an object of admiration for centuries to come. She imagined the columns now standing, half lying on the ground, the portico shattered, the vault open to the sky. But even the obelisk would still reign over the new ruins, for the Egyptians who created it laboured for eternity on earth.[11]

Similar thoughts occur to Walter Pater's Marius as he listens to Marcus Aurelius addressing the Senate:

9 Hugo (1967–70) V 573–83. 10 See Ratcliff (1988) 93. 11 De Staël (1987) 286.

There was a certain melancholy grandeur in the very simplicity or triteness of the theme: as it were the very quintessence of all the old Roman epitaphs, of all that was monumental in that city of tombs, layer upon layer of dead things and people. . . . The grandeur of the ruins of Rome, – heroism in ruin: it was under the influence of an imaginative anticipation of this, that he [Marcus Aurelius] appeared to be speaking. And though the impression of the actual greatness of Rome on that day was but enhanced by the strain of contempt, falling with an accent of pathetic conviction from the emperor himself, and gaining from his pontifical pretensions the authority of a religious intimation, yet the curious interest of the discourse lay in this, that Marius, for one, as he listened, seemed to forsee a grass-grown Forum, the broken ways of the Capitol, and the Palatine hill itself in humble occupation (p. 147).[12]

These representations, both verbal and visual, involve the superimposition of *a* 'future' on *a* 'present'. What a place means, they suggest, is what it will have meant. Such a narrative device occurs also in Book 8 of Virgil's *Aeneid* in the description of Aeneas' 'originary' visit to the place where the city of Rome will one day stand. Aeneas is guided across a site described to him by its present inhabitant, the Arcadian king Evander, in terms of its past history, but the epic narrator's voice superimposes on the site terms of description which cannot be known to Aeneas, but are familiar to the narrator and his audience:

hinc ad Tarpeiam sedem et Capitolia ducit
aurea nunc, olim silvestribus horrida dumis.

From here [Evander] leads [Aeneas] to the Tarpeian seat and the Capitol, golden now, but in other times bristling with forest thickets. (8.347–8)

talibus inter se dictis ad tecta subibant
pauperis Euandri, passimque armenta videbant
Romanoque foro et lautis mugire Carinis.

Conversing thus amongst themselves, they approached the dwelling of the humble Evander, and they saw the cattle everywhere, lowing in the Forum of Rome and the chic Carinae. (8.359–61)

The narrative's 'present' is the time of Aeneas, centuries before the foundation of the city, but these lines look 'forward' to a 'future' which also happens to be the narrator's 'present'. What we have here is a narrative transposition to the 'past' of the idea that what a place means is what it will have meant, involving the simultaneous projection of of a view 'forwards' from one point in time to another accompanied by a view 'backwards' from the latter point to the former. Character and narrator each have their 'present', which from each other's perspective will be regarded as the

12 Page references are to Pater (1985).

'future' or the 'past'. Thus Marius' 'future', a grass-grown Forum, is the narrator's 'present'; and in a similar, though slightly more complex fashion, Corinne momentarily takes on the role of narrator as, in a comparable moment of imaginative anticipation, she projects a 'future' which an implicit character, an observer of the ruined St Peter's, will inhabit as the 'present', and from which he or she will view Corinne's time as the distant 'past'.

The effect is to see the same place at two different times, in the cases we have been looking at, times enormously separated, and the place is observed by two sets of eyes. However, narrative time is infinitely elastic. An enormous span of years can be embraced in a single utterance ('three thousand years hence'). Conversely, a single moment can be expanded infinitely, and the boundaries between times designated 'past', 'present' or 'future' can be manipulated in all kinds of ways, or even collapsed entirely, as Freud collapses multiple 'pasts' into a moment of simultaneity experienced as the 'present'. Those eyes may belong to the same person, but be viewing a scene again after an interval of time, as the narrator Charles Ryder does in the prologue to the novel significantly entitled *Brideshead Revisited*:

> 'There's a frightful great fountain, too, in front of the steps, all rocks and sort of carved animals. You never saw such a thing.'
> 'Yes, Hooper, I did. I've been here before.'[13]

Indeed he had, 'first with Sebastian more than twenty years ago on a cloudless day in June'.[14] The house and park of Brideshead are disfigured by its wartime occupation by the army, and as Ryder now surveys the scene, his elegiac description is framed as the superimposition of a 'past' (though not, in this case, his past) on the 'present':

> The woods were all of oak and beech, the oak grey and bare, the beech faintly dusted with green by the breaking buds; they made a simple, carefully designed pattern with the green glades and the wide green spaces – Did the fallow deer graze here still? – and, lest the eye wander aimlessly, a Doric temple stood by the water's edge, and an ivy-grown arch spanned the lowest of the connecting weirs. All this had been planned and planted a century and a half ago so that, at about this date, it might be seen in its maturity.[15]

Ryder's description conjures up a character, the planter and planner of a century and a half ago, who looks forward from his present to a future which is the present from which the narrator looks back to a moment emphatically characterised as one of vision and inception. The sense of fulfilment, the park seen in its planned maturity, gives to this picture a powerfully teleological effect. The house has, in Hooper's words, 'a sort of R.C. Church attached',[16] reopened during the war by an evacuated priest, and

[13] Waugh (1962) 22. [14] *Ibid.* 23. [15] *Ibid.* 21–2. [16] *Ibid.* 22.

the attendance of troops at it ('surprising lot use it'),[17] and the 'small red flame'[18] burning once more in the art-nouveau lamp before the altar are a glimmer of hope in the midst of spiritual darkness. Brideshead is thus the repository of a faith that transcends time and ruin and bears the name of 'Rome'. Other aspects of Brideshead carry associations of place that are, in some sense, 'Roman'. In Virgil's narrative, what preceded Rome was a settlement peopled by migrants from Arcadia. That important primal visit to Brideshead, more than twenty years ago, is narrated in a section entitled 'Et in Arcadia Ego'. The fountain carries some of those associations of Arcadia and Rome as well: 'such a fountain as one might expect to find in a piazza of Southern Italy, such a fountain as was, indeed, found there a century ago by one of Sebastian's ancestors; found, purchased, imported and re-erected in an alien but welcoming climate'.[19] Frank Kermode has suggested that, even from these early moments in the novel, the house becomes an emblem of the Augustinian City of God,[20] and we might recall at this point the way that 'Rome' has been inscribed into providential models of history, both pagan and Christian. Conventions of representing a sense of place, no less than the fountain at Brideshead, have survived their translation, freighted with associations that are not so much topographical as expressive of particular ideological configurations of history.

What a place means, I have suggested, is what it will have meant. A phenomenon gains historical shape, order and meaning only when it can be viewed from the vantage point, the *coup d'oeil*, of the point deemed to be its end. 'End' may be figured principally as a moment of fulfilment, as in the cases of that first visit to the site of Rome by Aeneas, or the park envisioned by the planter and planner of Brideshead, or as demise, as in the pictures of Robert, Gandy and Komar and Melamid. Typically, however, there is a dialectic of fulfilment and demise, of persistence and change, and of eternity and transience. Thus for Hugo, the Arc de Triomphe achieves its fulfilment in the ruin of the city around it; and for Corinne, the obelisk would still reign over the new ruins of St Peter's, 'for the Egyptians who created it laboured for eternity on earth'. For one enmeshed in time and circumstance, for one in history, any phenomenon can only be historicised by just such an imaginative anticipation of its end. The end, it should be noted, is not a historical date, but the prerequisite for something's becoming history. As of places, so of ideas. The prerequisite for the historicity of the Roman empire is its end (which, it may be stressed once more, is not a historical date), and ancient texts offer various adumbrations of that end. A Sibylline oracle written in Greek detects Rome's end in its name:[21] 'Samos

[17] *Ibid.* 326. [18] *Ibid.* 331. [19] *Ibid.* 78–9. [20] Kermode (1962) 172.

[21] *Sibylline Oracle* 3: 363–4, cited by Siegert (1994) 303, to whom some of the following points are indebted. The Greek text of the oracle may be found in Geffcken (1902) 67.

too will be a pile of sand (*ammos*), and Delos will disappear (*adelos*), and Rome (*Rome*) will be a narrow street (*rume*);[22] for all oracles come to fulfilment.' The very name (*nomen*) of Rome is a foreshadowing (*omen*) of its end This topos occurs often elsewhere. In his apocalyptic sixteenth *Epode*, written in the midst of Rome's civil wars, Horace foresees the destruction of the city, and associates the name of Rome with the Latin verb *ruere*, etymologically the source of the word 'ruin':

> Altera iam teritur bellis civilibus aetas,
> suis et ipsa *Roma* viribus *ruit*.

> A second generation is being worn down by civil wars, and Rome herself through her own strength is tottering. (1–2)

Within this convention, the conferring of a name inscribes a deferral that gives a space its identity as place only in virtue of its prospective end. That end may be figured as demise, but also as goal, as *telos*. Against these pessimistic fantasies which work to foreground end as demise, Virgil's *Aeneid* offers an image of the end of the Roman empire as fulfilment, fulfilment infinitely deferred, figured in Jupiter's prophecy to Venus in Book 1 as power (*imperium*) without boundaries of space and time:

> his ego nec metas rerum nec tempora pono:
> imperium sine fine dedi.

> On [the Romans] I place neither limits of realm nor time: I have granted dominion without end. (278–9)

This historicisation of the Roman empire seeks to make it synonymous with history itself. Its end infinitely deferred, it offers no point beyond from which it may be viewed. The role of the historian, however, is one of determination, of imposing boundaries, beginnings and ends. Where stands, then, the historian of the Roman empire thus defined? The only position is one of transcendence, outside history, a God's-eye view. If the end of empire is a prerequisite of its historicity, but its end is infinitely deferred, then its demise (and indeed its inception) cannot be a date in history, nor *a fortiori* can the causes of its decline and fall be historical. Within this definition of empire, an event such as the sack of Rome by Alaric in 410 CE marks not demise of empire, but opens up the discursive opportunity to speak of Rome as a historical episode within the continually and ever-receding horizon of empire. Rome, from being identified, perhaps, with that empire, becomes, by the postulation of that (or any other) event as a historical date signifying rupture or discontinuity, its type or *figura*. This underlies the doctrine of *translatio imperii*, whereby Rome acts as a figure for whatever now represents this notion of empire, whether

[22] The meaning of *rume* is uncertain. Macleod (1979) 220–1 argues for the sense 'ruin'.

it be its identification with the City of God by St Augustine or with secular formations which seek to describe themselves as 'empires'. When empire is transferred in this way, what Rome is thought to represent historically is felt to be more authentically experienced elsewhere, whether it be Napoleon's Paris or London at the zenith of the British empire. Henry James alludes to this sensation on the opening page of *The Golden Bowl:*

> The Prince had always liked his London, when it had come to him; he was one of the Modern Romans who find by the Thames a more convincing image of the truth of the ancient state than any they have left by the Tiber. Brought up on the legend of the City to which the world paid tribute, he recognized in the present London much more than in contemporary Rome the real dimensions of such a case. If it was a question of an *Imperium*, he said to himself, and if one wished, as a Roman, to recover a little the sense of that, the place to do so was on London Bridge, or even, on a fine afternoon in May, at Hyde Park Corner.

Such transference can invoke and set against each other the two aspects of empire, the one transcendent and so eternal, the other secular and so subject to demise, and Rome can be the type of both. It is thus for those enmeshed in time, circumstance and history that Brideshead in its decay can represent the City of God, and so Macaulay, in reviewing Ranke's *History of the Popes*, can conjure up a scene of the future reminiscent of those we have looked at so as to meditate upon the durability of the Roman Catholic church: 'and she may still exist in undiminished vigour when some traveller from New Zealand shall, in the midst of a vast solitude, take his stand on a broken arch of London Bridge to sketch the ruins of St Paul's'.[23] 'Rome n'est plus à Rome', as Baumgarten famously remarked; but if Virgil's definition of empire seeks to make 'Rome' synonymous with history, then the historian would be well advised to return to 'Rome', and to Virgil.

Historical accounts often represent themselves as going over the ground again, as investigation, as research, as review. Narratives and the analyses made of them characteristically operate by invoking a distinction between 'story', an idealised sequence of events in a notionally sequential order, and 'narrative', the emplotment of those events in an actual telling. An easy assumption is that 'story' definitively pre-exists its 'emplotment' in 'narrative'; indeed, a word such as 'emplotment' already presupposes this order. However, this relationship emerges as more complex, and open to manipulation. Virgilian narrative seems to offer itself as the representation, the telling, of a pre-existing story. The famous plunge *in medias res* (the storm which shipwrecks Aeneas on the shores of Carthage provides the narrative with its opening incident) and the consequent flashbacks, such as

[23] Macaulay (1898) IX 288. Macaulay's responses to Rome are discussed further by Edwards later in this volume.

Aeneas' own retrospective account of the fall of Troy, constitute the narrative's 'present' as the wanderings of Aeneas and his arrival in Italy, and help to create this sense of the 'story' the poem tells as itself already determined, as simply a matter of report or passive transcription. The effect is to suppress the agency of the narrator: the narrative is represented as already there, and simply handed down to the poet, rather than as being shaped by him, as is signalled in the poet's appeal to the Muse to 'recount to me the causes' (*Musa, mihi causas memora, Aen.* 1.8). In the *Aeneid*, however, as well as flashbacks from the narrative's 'present', a view 'forwards' from that 'present' into the 'future' is provided by means of the supernatural, primarily prophecy in various guises. Jupiter's speech to Venus in Book 1 foretelling for the Romans empire without limits of time or space is one such scene which looks 'forwards' from the moment chosen as the narrative's 'present' beyond the incident with which the narrative closes, the death of Turnus, to the age of Augustus as its end, in the sense of both finishing-point and goal, its fulfilment or *telos*. For a character within such a narrative (Aeneas, for example), events will appear contingent, their shape or goal, their *end*, uncertain. When Aeneas is shipwrecked, Venus prompts her father's prophecy by demanding 'what end do you set to these travails, great king?' (*quem das finem, rex magne, laborum?*, *Aen.* 1.241). No such character can normally see into the future, and for that reason, the view 'forwards' is usually occluded in most narratives (although we should not make the mistake of believing that it is therefore absent). It is the explicit representation in the person of Jupiter within the narrative of the poem of the view 'forwards' (of the 'future' from the narrative's 'present' as *known*, its significance already *determined*) that has made the *Aeneid* the paradigm of teleological narrative; and the association of the view 'forwards' with the god Jupiter makes the view not only prospective but, in the fullest sense of the term, providential. Unlike the other characters, Jupiter enjoys a point of view from which he can view the end of these events, precisely a god's-eye view. Knowing the end of the sequence of events he prophesies, he can view that sequence not only prospectively but retrospectively at the same time as well. From this we get the trope of destiny, when the end is achieved which has been foreseen from the moment of vision and inception, when the sequence of events can be seen to have reached its anticipated destination. But that destination, of course, is the narrator of the *Aeneid*'s own time, and it is he who has chosen the story elements and constructed the sequence, its beginning and end points and order of presentation, and thus furnishes the narrative with its view 'forwards'. The view 'forwards' from the *narrative's* 'present' thus corresponds to the the view 'backwards' from the *narrator's* 'present'. The 'story' which the *Aeneid* purports to narrate emerges as a suprapersonal, providential order of history, named in the

Aeneid as *fatum* ('an utterance'), and articulated in the utterances of Jupiter. It is thus no less possible to view fate, destiny or history as an *effect* of narrative and the narrator's agency than, as the narrator of the *Aeneid* seeks to suggest, to see it as its *cause*.[24]

A major implication of what I have been saying is that *all* narratives (indeed, all utterances) have a teleological and a providential aspect *by virtue of having a narrator,* although this will only be apparent if the view 'forwards' is in some way rendered explicit, as it is in the figure of Jupiter in the *Aeneid,* or of the planter and planner of the park at Brideshead in Ryder's account; and if the end is a vital constitutive element in the act of historical understanding, no less so is the moment chosen as the beginning, the moment of forward vision, the moment of planting and planning. For there to be a shape or order to history, the 'future' (seen from whatever constitutes the narrative's 'present') must, at some level, be *known*. 'How it was' always involves 'how it was-to-be': we are asked not only to look back to a point in the past, when that point was the 'present', but also to look forward from that point to the *telos* of the moment which is the focus for the interests and desires which motivate the narrative act, and which the narrative act seeks to satisfy. It is from this shuttle, simultaneously backwards and forwards, that historical representations derive their sense of closure and fulfilment. What I have analysed as the view 'backwards' and the view 'forwards' are totally separable in theory, never in practice. However, the *Aeneid,* which identifies Empire and History and simultaneously sees itself as a type of both, can serve as a dramatic allegory of the act of narration and of historical understanding. The complex of perspectives involved in any act of historical narration are resolved into, and enacted by, the poem's characters, and Jupiter, the one character who enjoys perspectives both forwards and backwards, who knows the significance of the story he is telling because he knows its end, becomes the type or figure of the narrator, the epic poet transcribing history – even down to the description he offers of his own articulation of fate in terms of reading a book already written: 'I will unroll and bring to light the secrets of fate' (*volvens fatorum arcana movebo*), he says (*Aen.* 1.262), as he reveals the 'future' to Venus.

Whilst the view forwards to the future is normally associated with the supernatural, the narrator of the *Aeneid* himself explicitly provides the prospective view to his own present in the scene in Book 8 in which Aeneas makes his inaugural visit to the site where Rome one day will be. Just as a place means what it will have meant, so events have meaning only if their significance is simultaneously already, but not yet, known – already to Jupiter, or the narrator, not yet to Aeneas. In more conventional historical

24 These points are explored further in Kennedy (1997).

representations, the retrospective aspect is explicit, whilst the prospective view from the moment chosen as the narrative's present to the narrator's present, which gives to the act of historical judgement its teleological character, is occluded. The scenes from the future gain their surprise from the way they render explicit this prospective aspect of any historical representation. When Pater's Marius is travelling to Rome in Chapter 10 of *Marius the Epicurean*, he journeys through a landscape which from Marius' perspective seems headed towards demise: 'Meantime the farms were less carefully tended than of old: here and there they were lapsing into their natural wildness: some villas were also partly fallen into ruin' (p. 126). The narrator's next comment suggests a different perspective: 'The picturesque, romantic Italy of a later time – the Italy of Claude and Salvator Rosa – was already forming, for the delight of the modern romantic traveller.' Already for Pater; not yet for Marius, who cannot see the new end of fulfilment which the narrator has substituted for Marius' sense of impending demise. When Marius seems to forsee a grass-grown Forum, the broken ways of the Capitol, and the Palatine hill itself in humble occupation, it is the narrator's backward glance from the end which gives to this 'imaginative anticipation' its sense of historical fulfilment. The character Marius is represented as looking forward over a sequence of events to the end from which the narrator looks back. The effect is to place Marius 'within' history, trying to historicise the phenomena he experiences by imagining their ends, and the narrator, from the vantage point of the end, 'outside' it, enjoying that god's-eye view which can see events in terms of their ends, which may (whence a sense of inevitability) or may not be (whence irony) the ends which those 'within' history have envisaged.

When a scene is revisited, a textual topos re-employed, a citation enacted, or all of these, a further perspective is superimposed. In his *De varietate fortunae* of 1448, Poggio Bracciolini depicted himself and a companion climbing the Capitoline hill in a self-conscious reprise of the tour of Evander and Aeneas. In Gibbon's account of the passage in the final chapter of his *Decline and Fall*, they 'reposed themselves among the ruins of columns and temples' and what they viewed from 'that commanding spot' was 'the wide and various prospect of desolation'.[25] The previous end, the Virgilian narrator's 'present', becomes in the new account the 'past', and Poggio's 'present' supplies a new 'end' beyond the previous one, suggesting that the perspective Virgil offered is now superseded. The 'wide and various prospect' afforded by relating past to present from that 'commanding spot' now looks not towards fulfilment, but 'desolation'. Rather than being the transcendent view of history from 'outside' it had claimed to be, the

[25] Cited from the edition of Womersley (1994) III 1062.

Virgilian perspective is now relocated within the history the new account offers, and from narrator, Virgil has become character – like his Aeneas, consigned to his own 'present', and afforded a view of the past only from the perspective of that 'present'; and if he has any inklings of the future, they can only be in the nature of an 'imaginative anticipation', without that sense of fulfilment that only the retrospective view from the end can give. From the new narrator's privileged perspective, the past is reconfigured in the light of the new end, and a new order is imposed on history. The effect is to create a series of typologies. Frank Kermode explains:

> Strictly speaking, a type is distinguished from a symbol or allegory in that it is constituted by an historical event or person (as Christ makes Jonah the type of his resurrection, and St. Paul the crossing of the Red Sea by the Israelites a type of baptism). A type can therefore be identified only when fulfilled by its antitype, a later event in a providentially structured history; the Old Covenant is a type of the New. . . . Types are essentially what Auerbach has in mind when he speaks of *figurae*, events or persons that are themselves, but may presage others. Their purpose, to put it too simply, is to accommodate the events and persons of a superseded order of time to a new one.[26]

Thus we have seen how 'Rome' can become the type of empire, made such in various narratives by whatever is asserted to be its antitype, say, the British empire or the City of God. However, as we have seen, all narratives have a providential aspect by virtue of having a narrator. In the case of Poggio's narrative, typologies can be seen to operate on at least a couple of levels. Poggio makes Aeneas the type of his visit to Rome, but also makes Virgil the type of narrator, presaging Poggio's own role as the narrator of the history of Rome.

Gibbon's citation of Poggio serves to enclose his narrative in turn within one with a further end, forging one more link in this chain of typologies and making Poggio in turn the type of the historian of Rome. But there is one further dimension we must observe. In the stories we tell about ourselves, we are *both* character and narrator: we create a character in a narrative 'present' which is never entirely identical to the narrator's present, and whose perspective on events from within the story is never quite the same as that of the narrator, who can view them in the light of their 'end'. In a letter, Gibbon described his *Decline and Fall* after its completion in terms of a journey: 'I look back in amazement on the road which I have travelled, but which I should never have entered had I been previously apprized of its length'.[27] From the narrator Gibbon's position at the end, the character Gibbon's imaginative anticipation 'within' history is seen to fall far short of what transpired. If the end is a vital constitutive element in the act of

[26] Kermode (1983) 89–90. [27] Cited from the edition of Norton (1956) III 107.

historical understanding, not least in the narratives we tell of ourselves, no less is the moment chosen as the beginning, the moment of forward vision, the moment of planting and planning, the moment at which we set out in the direction of our anticipated destination. In Gibbon's own account, this road notoriously began in Rome. A couple of the variant versions of the conception of his great work Gibbon gave in his *Memoirs* will bear another citation.[28] Draft 'C' reads as follows:

> Yet the historian of the decline and fall must not regret his time or expence, since it was the view of Italy and Rome which determined the choice of subject. In my Journal the place and moment of conception are recorded: the fifteenth of October 1764, in the close of evening, as I sat musing in the Church of the Zoccolanti or Franciscan fryars, while they were singing Vespers in the Temple of Jupiter on the ruins of the Capitol.

We have a particularly striking example of the collapse of the distinction between past and present here as the Church of the Zoccolanti friars – the name redolent of the 'enthusiasm' and 'barbarism' which for Gibbon were crucial factors in the decline and fall of the Roman empire – occupies the same space on the Capitol as the Temple of Jupiter Optimus Maximus. The Capitol was, of course, the symbolic centre, and Jupiter the sovereign god, of the Roman empire.[29] The modern archaeological consensus is that Gibbon was mistaken in his belief about the exact location of Jupiter's temple on the hill, but since he is unembarrassed to speak of ruins on the Capitol (true perhaps in Poggio's day, though not in his own), realism of topographical representation seems hardly the main concern of this description. Draft 'E' of the *Memoirs* points this up even more clearly:

> It was at Rome on the fifteenth of October 1764, as I sat musing amidst the ruins of the Capitol while the barefooted fryars were singing Vespers in the temple of Jupiter, that the idea of writing the decline and fall of the City first started to my mind.

The friars are still there, though the references to their order and their church have disappeared; but the Temple of Jupiter amidst the ruins of the Capitol preposterously persists, the more to emphasise the simultaneity in the present of a number of pasts. David Womersley points to an interesting parallel to the phraseology of the *Memoirs* in the final volume of the *Decline and Fall*:

> It was on the twenty-seventh of July, in the year twelve hundred and ninety-nine of the Christian era, that Othman first invaded the territory of Nicomedia, and the singular accuracy of the date seems to disclose some foresight of the rapid and destructive growth of the monster.

[28] Cited from the edition of Bonnard (1966) 136. Gibbon's various accounts of the conception of *The Decline and Fall* are also discussed by Bann later in this volume.

[29] See Edwards (1996a) 69–72.

Womersley points out the ironic resonances this has for the expansion of Gibbon's history beyond its planned dimensions (it was, we may recall, to be a history of the *city*), and he comments: 'The singular accuracy of the date of the conception of *The Decline and Fall* may also disclose if not foresight, at least retrospective knowledge of the history's rapid and destructive, but also enriching and emancipating, growth.'[30] Retrospective knowledge (from the narrator's perspective at the end) *and* foresight (from the character's viewpoint), I should say, and the irony emerges in the mismatch of the two. Gibbon's narrative of the conception of his work presents us with a character who, at the moment of setting out, looks forward in the direction of the destination from which Gibbon the narrator looks back. The effect is discreetly teleological, and the coincidence of character and narrator serves to occlude the providential aspect of the narration. It has become a commonplace to describe Gibbon's historical perspective as 'Olympian'.[31] But as Gibbon presents himself as musing on that memorable spot where Aeneas stood and Poggio spoke (of the vicissitudes of Fortune, a configuration of history that would seek to eschew the notion of providence), the presence of the Temple of Jupiter is a typological reminder of the divine narrator of an exploded 'providential' history of a city expanding into an empire without boundaries of space or time which this historian of the Roman empire claims to supplant.

This by no means exhausts the typological functions of Jupiter. As we have seen, it is only from 'outside' history that factors such as 'decline' and 'fall' can be plotted. Configuring this position 'outside', the 'god's-eye view', with its capacity to look forwards, as well as backwards, from any moment designated 'the present', is one in which (unlike for those 'within' history) there is no firm boundary between 'past', 'present' and 'future'; and in which factors (like decline and fall) or terms of analysis (like Freud's unconscious) are projected as historically transcendent, and not subject to the same historical determination as the phenomena which they are used to explain. Simultaneities of past and present, as in Gibbon's or Freud's configurations of Rome, are explicit signs of the claim to that position of transcendence implicit in, and constitutive of, any historical utterance, from which the historian can range over time and space, and texts (of whatever 'date'), at will, and make the past, or many pasts simultaneously, 'present'. Conversely, to represent history 'realistically' or 'archaeologically' (in Freud's phrase 'as historians do') is to occlude, though not to escape, this position; Rome can never be simply a physical entity, it must be a psychical one also. That position of transcendence may be represented in terms of space no less than of time. Goethe seeks to capture in the imagery

30 Womersley (1988) 227.

31 See the passages assembled by Carnochan (1987) 51–2.

of imperial conquest the shuttle there and back again which constitutes (in a structure which is typological no less than topological) the points thereby joined as the 'margins' and the 'centre' – the movement out to the boundaries, and then back again in a triumphal procession that leads along the Via Sacra and up the Capitoline Hill to the Temple of Jupiter. It is a space so configured that provides the commanding spot from which one can see the Everlasting Rome, and not just the Rome which is replaced by another every decade.

2 Envisioning Rome: Granet and Gibbon in dialogue*

Stephen Bann

Few passages in the autobiography of a historian have been so resonant as the one with which Edward Gibbon announced the genesis of his vocation:

> It was at Rome on the fifteenth of October 1764, as I sat musing amidst the ruins of the Capitol while the barefooted fryars were singing Vespers in the temple of Jupiter, that the idea of writing the decline and fall of the City first started to my mind.[1]

The scene is one which we may at the present day have some difficulty in recapturing, since the location is a veritable palimpsest of historical buildings superimposed upon one another. The convent church which Gibbon's editor, Lord Sheffield, identified as 'the church of the Zocolants, or Franciscan friars'[2] and we call Santa Maria d'Araceli, still stands adjacent to the Roman Forum, although its attached convent was destroyed with the building of Mussolini's Piazza Venezia. Changes in ground levels have however isolated it from the site of the present Capitoline Museum, which stands in the place of the Temple of Jove, just as the Franciscan convent was held to occupy the site of a Temple of Juno.

Yet Gibbon's repeated retouchings of this famous sentence, noted recently by Claude Rawson,[3] should alert us to the point that topographical accuracy is hardly the issue at stake. Nor is it profitable to view Gibbon's anecdote merely as a piece of autobiography. What Gibbon succeeds in refining, in the course of his successive versions, is a verbal representation of Rome in rhetorical terms which has the form of a *catachresis*, or collocation of inappropriately matched terms. Six years before the recounted episode, he had made a similar formulation in a cancelled section

* I am glad to acknowledge the indispensable help which I received in the preparation of this essay from M. Bernard Terlay, of the Musée Granet, Aix-en-Provence. Among the audiences who have usefully commented on earlier versions, I would like to mention in particular the members of the Department of History of Art at Johns Hopkins University.

[1] Gibbon (1966) 160. [2] *Ibid.*

[3] See Rawson (1995) 3. There are a number of different versions of the statement, which indicate Gibbon's desire to adjust the different terms in view of a specific rhetorical effect. For the purposes of my own argument, however, the variations are not specially significant. On these variations, see also Kennedy above.

of a work written in French: 'On érige la croix sur les débris du Capitole'.[4] The different versions of the event supposed to have taken place on 15th October 1764 rework this piquant contrast and make it memorable. 'Barefooted fryars' might be no more than a literal translation of 'Zoccolanti' (a term derived from the Italian word for 'clog'). Juxtaposed with 'Jupiter', however, it aroused the image of an incongruous humility in the house of the thunderer.

As a description of the germination of *The Decline and Fall of the Roman Empire*, moreover, this rhetorical opposition becomes a clue to the character of Gibbon's narrative style. What he will write of Rome is emplotted from the start, to use Hayden White's term,[5] in the ironic mode. That is to say, it implicitly sets up the later history of the Empire, with its effete and incompetent rulers and its disruptive Christian communities, in relation to the model of its original, effulgent greatness. This is a functional irony since (as Lionel Gossman has so well explained[6]), it has the objective of singling out its own enlightened audience, whose values will coincide with those advocated on a secondary level by the philosophical author. But it cannot fail to be, in addition, a device which attracts our attention to the personal investment of the English gentleman who has condescended to note the existence of such undignified and ludicrous happenings. One might say that the autobiographical anecdote quoted here exactly mimes the see-saw movement between the representation of past events, and the enunciation of subjective states and intentions: 'It was at Rome . . . as I sat musing . . . while the barefooted fryars were singing vespers . . . the idea . . . first started to my mind.'

Much has already been written about the new historiography of the early nineteenth century, which was concerned precisely with reformulating the kind of contract with the reader which Gibbon's attitude takes for granted. To Leopold von Ranke, for example, the task of the new historian was one of sloughing off the 'philosophical' discourse of the previous century and showing the past 'wie es eigentlich gewesen' – as it really happened.[7] I have no intention of going over this well trodden ground once again. But I would like to use the indubitable contrast between the aims of the ironic historian and those of the new historian of the Romantic generation in order to pose a different sort of question from the one which is customarily asked. On a simple and obvious level, Gibbon is using his reminiscence of 15 October 1764 to draw a picture – one in which the context (Temple of Jupiter) and the actors concerned (barefooted friars) are disjoined for rhetorical effect. In what sense is Gibbon's 'picture' related, or not related as the case may

[4] Rawson (1995) 3. [5] See White (1973) esp.53–5. [6] Gossman (1981).
[7] See Bann (1984) 8–14.

be, to prevalent ways of picturing the Roman palimpsest in the period when he is writing?

This question has, of course, a further implicit agenda. It is to ask whether the received notion of 'ancient Rome' may not be understood as a rhetorical construct specially, though not exclusively, intelligible in visual terms – one to which Gibbon's word-painting demonstrably refers. But here we arrive at the second, more important question for the purposes of this chapter. This is to ask if the shift in historical orientation which has been briefly evoked in connection with Gibbon and Ranke might not also be analysed in terms of a conclusive difference between modes of visual rhetoric. In other words, what Ranke's phraseology can only convey by hints, might well be evident in a much more conclusive manner in the production of his visually innovative contemporaries: in particular, those who took as their privileged subject matter the representation of Rome from a historical point of view. This is not simply an arbitrary exercise undertaken for interdisciplinary effect. As Frank Ankersmit has recently argued, it may make more sense, philosophically speaking, to analyse historical discourse in terms of the creation of pictures, than to perpetuate well-nigh exhausted methods used traditionally by philosophers of history.[8] This implies that pictorial representations of the past might not be secondary and inessential accompaniments to the grand protocol of historical narrative, but primary evidence for what Lord Acton called 'historical-mindedness'.[9]

Before I introduce specific pictorial examples – from the century preceding Gibbon's vision in the Forum, and from the period half a century later when the French painter François-Marius Granet began to paint his radically new images of Rome – I would however like to emphasise the more precise agenda of this chapter. It is not simply a matter of comparing one visual rhetoric with another. In contrasting the seventeenth-century images of Claude, or the early eighteenth-century images of Vanvitelli, with the work of Granet, we can discern a qualitative shift of significant proportions. It is not that Vanvitelli and Granet represented 'ancient Rome' differently, but that Granet was possibly the first artist to represent Rome *in its ancientness*. That is to say, he addressed, over a long period, the specific issue of rendering the 'pastness' of the past. Although on one level, this was obviously a matter of technical and compositional innovations which set his work apart from that of his predecessors, it was on a psychological level the index of a new investment in the notion of the past as a lost domain, only to be recovered through representation. Thus it becomes necessary to reconstruct the pattern of Granet's personal and psychological

8 See Ankersmit (1995) 212–40.
9 For further discussion of the concept of 'historical-mindedness' in the context of nineteenth-century culture, see Bann (1995).

experience in order to appreciate the values which were embedded, for him, in the historical milieu.

The resonance of the term 'ancient Rome' can serve as a kind of talisman for gauging the transformation to which Granet contributed. What may we suppose the 'ancient' to have meant to the foreign visitors who were already flocking to Rome in the mid seventeenth century? For one of them – the collector and traveller John Bargrave – the use of the term falls in with a simple binary coding to which very little significance is attached. The bronze objects which he brought back to England from Rome were classified in his otherwise prolix catalogue in terms such as the following: 'very ancient', 'if not ancient, yet cast from ancient', 'supposed to be modern but cast from ancient'. Also indeed: 'The antiquarian that sold it to me avowed it to be truly ancient; but thousands may daily be made.'[10] Not much resides in the discrimination, we may infer, except a slight cash premium. It would be hazardous to argue from a single usage like this to momentous conclusions about mentality. But, in focussing on the new coding of the antique which we find in the paintings of Granet, I am implicitly arguing that they betoken a cast of mind not in evidence before. What people thought about the past – or Rome as the epitome of past history – in the eighteenth century and before is a question not easily susceptible to analysis. But the extent to which they possessed discourses for framing their awareness of the past, in the period Granet helped to inaugurate, can be measured more easily, since the discourses survive still in different modes of representation.

My argument takes for granted, indeed, the basic schema which Michel Foucault proposed in *Les Mots et les choses*: that the intensified historical consciousness of the early nineteenth century was a form of concrete compensation for the widespread experience of loss or (as Foucault expresses it) 'dispossession' which was registered in this spectacularly turbulent period of modern history.[11] There is no lack of further corroboration of the fact that, in France particularly, the sense of the revolution as forming a rupture in historical continuity endowed the directly prior period with a uniquely enhanced historicity. Prosper de Barante, one of Napoleon's sub-prefects who had been a mere child at the time of the revolution, was already, before the end of the empire, writing the history of the Vendée wars as, 'le dernier testament de la vieille France'.[12] He had himself been alive whilst the conservative nobles and peasantry of north-western France defied the revolutionary armies, and one of his own rela-

[10] See Bann (1994) 100–1.

[11] See Foucault: 'l'homme s'est trouvé comme dépossédé de ce qui constituait les contenus les plus manifestes de son Histoire' (1966) 380.

[12] Baronne de Barante ed., *Lettres de Prosper de Barante à Mme. de Stäel* (Clermont Ferrand 1929) 340.

tives had been involved. But, from the historian's point of view, the wars of the Vendée already constituted an episode discontinuous from the present day, yet maintaining continuity with the earlier centuries of French history.

A further point may be made about the universal habit of referring to pre-revolutionary France, from an early stage, as the '*ancien régime*'. Of course the French term 'ancien' has a different semantic value from the English 'ancient', and the origins of this habit of referring to monarchical France can no doubt be discerned as an attempt to neutralise and demythologise 'the former regime'. But it was not long before the romantic generation of the Restoration were able to integrate this usage into a discourse of repossession and rehabilitation of the previously devalued past. When, in 1825, Victor Hugo wrote his passionate tirade, 'On the destruction of the monuments in France', he called his fellow-countrymen to the colours with the rousing sentiment: 'there must be a universal cry to summon the new France finally to the help of the old [*l'ancienne*]'.[13]

It is within this general context that I shall be maintaining what, at first sight, may seem a dubious claim: that the 'ancientness' of Rome could be, not simply registered, but adequately represented in this period only by a Frenchman. Granet brought to his vision of Rome, as we shall see, a fund of early experiences which predisposed him to interpret the cityscape of Rome in the novel way that he did. His status as a visitor sharpened his eye, and allowed him to draw upon a fund of previous experiences and essays in representation, whilst confronting and transforming the existing pictorial tradition. Curiously but – as I shall argue – quite logically, his most conclusive and popular rendering of historical Rome was to be founded on a relatively minute difference of time. It portrayed a state of affairs only recently (and, indeed, temporarily) brought to a close. But it was this stimulus, precisely, that enabled him to draw on all his previous experience as an artist and a Frenchman, and elevated his work to a more than merely personal validity.

Born just over a decade after Gibbon experienced his illumination 'amidst the ruins of the Capitol', on 17 December 1775, François-Marius Granet was to spend a large part of his active life, between 1802 and 1824, for the most part as a resident in Rome. The son of a master mason from Aix-en-Provence, he began his artistic education in his home town, and contracted a lifetime friendship with the Provençal aristocrat, Auguste de Forbin, whom he was to follow first to the studio of David in Paris, and later to his lengthy period of residence in Rome. There can be few artists of any period who have so exhaustively chronicled Rome's historical sites, and yet, of

[13] Hugo (1967–70) II 569. See also Bann (1988) 240–59.

course, it is not the sheer volume of Granet's production that is important, but the distinctive quality of his vision. My hypothesis is that his Roman work in general, and one great series of paintings on the same theme produced between 1812 and 1819 in particular, enables us to appreciate the moves which were necessary to counteract the Gibbonian irony. The fact that a painter was pre-eminently qualified, by virtue of his medium, to achieve this feat is, in my view, significant, since it leads us to ask to what extent the nineteenth-century culture of 'historical-mindedness' was not dependent, in some essential way, on the type of concreteness which only the image can convey.

Yet in proposing this antithesis between Gibbon and Granet, I am not simply initiating a *dialogue des sourds*. The point is not simply that Granet's rapidly executed, *plein-air* sketches of Rome and its environs concretised a vivid response which Gibbon's stately prose could not achieve. This would be a banal conclusion. In effect, I would argue that Gibbon's own rhetorical juxtaposition of the old Rome and the new was itself expressive of a convention which had occupied the attention of artists from the early seventeenth century onwards. Gibbon's description of the 'barefooted friars . . . singing vespers in the Temple of Jupiter' can itself be regarded as a version of the trope of Rome old and new being revealed in a single vista which had developed over this period. Granet does not simply provide an innovatory medium; he refashions the rhetoric of place.

How was Rome to be represented in visual terms? In confronting this problem, the topographic artists of the eighteenth century had to take into account the signifying dimension of the Roman scene, as well as its variegated appearance. The visual texture of the city offered an almost inextricable weave of buildings and parts of buildings from all periods of its existence. In particular, it exhibited the pagan temples of imperial Rome in close juxtaposition with the great basilicas of the Christian era, sometimes to the point of being indistinguishable. From the Renaissance onwards, Italian painters had been in the habit of displaying ruined classical colonnades as a background to scenes such as the Nativity, to indicate the coming of the new law and the withering away of the old.[14] As their seventeenth-century successors began to feature more specific renderings of landscape and townscape, they remained mindful of this symbolic loading.

Thus, when Claude painted *A view in Rome* in 1632, at the beginning of his artistic career, he juxtaposed a realistic view of the church of Santa

[14] A good example is the *Madonna and Child*, formerly attributed to Verrochio, and part of the collection of Ruskin's Guild of St George (Fitzwilliam Museum, Cambridge). The conjunction of broken columns and toppling architecture with stages of the Nativity can already be observed in medieval manuscripts which illustrate the Fall of the Idols as a backdrop to the Flight into Egypt. See Camille (1989) 1–5.

Trinità dei Monti, possibly as seen from the rooftop of his home in the Via Margutta, with a fanciful image of a pagan temple which occupied the right foreground.[15] The fact that the splendidly sited church was occupied by a community of nuns no doubt added piquancy to the decision to people the temple with ladies of easy virtue, who are selling their favours to the male passers-by. Claude has indeed, in the parlance of art history, devised the fictive temple as a *repoussoir*, that is, a device for 'pushing back' the main subject of the painting into an appropriate distance. But he has supplemented his formal concern with symbolic charge: the modern, Christian church glows all the more splendidly in the sunlight because the pagan temple lurks lasciviously in its benightedness.

This early work forms an exception in Claude's career. For the most part, it is the landscape of the Campagna, rather than an urban vista, that forms the background of his idealised compositions. By the early eighteeenth century, however, the type of the Roman *veduta* has become established. A Northern painter like Gaspar van Wittel (whose name was conveniently italianised as Vanvitelli) produced numerous versions of his view of the dome and façade of St Peter's, seen across the Tiber, with the great bulk of the Castel Sant'Angelo looming in the right foreground. As Denis Coutagne has argued, this juxtaposition was loaded with historical and political meanings:

> Castel Sant'Angelo allied to St Peter's is one of the most well-known panoramas, since ancient Rome brought out in Hadrian's Mausoleum and modern Rome expressed by Michelangelo's dome associate the two Romes in a single picture, with the second taking over – but not destroying – the first. This is what is asserted by all the official accounts, whether they be historical or theological. It is also true in painting: the dome springs up as a full synthetic form whilst the mausoleum shows itself to be incomplete, time having gnawed away at the brickwork. The bridge, which is always present in this type of composition, recalls that there is not rupture, but passage and continuity from one monument to another, from one period to another, from one significance to another. Here ancient Rome and modern Rome achieve their profound unity.[16]

It is this concern for harmonious visual transitions, which subsume a view of history as a cumulative fulfilment, that Gibbon's choice of phrasing subjects to the corrosion of irony. The Rome of the pagan gods and the Rome of the barefooted friars are not integrated: they are separated by a jarring rhetorical effect. Whilst the artist's bridging devices constitute connective tissues of meaning, Gibbon's sub-clause collapses one world into another:

15 The painting (in the National Gallery, London) bears Claude's signature with the added inscription I. V. F.: 'in urbe fecit' (made in the city). Although the church looks much the same as in Granet's later work, the hillside beneath was transformed after Claude's time by the building of the Spanish Steps.

16 My translation from Coutagne in Néto-Daguerre and Coutagne (1992) 222.

it becomes the mythic prelude to half a lifetime of scholarship which will express the truth of history not in terms of the triumph of the Christian era, but in terms of the pagan empire's protracted and irrevocable decline.

In this connection, the importance of Granet lies not in the fact that he revived the traditional suavity of Roman *vedute*. As has been stated before, no one was more faithful and assiduous a devotee of Rome's historical sites. But the pictorial mechanisms which Granet employed cannot be merely assimilated to the conventions of his predecessors, any more than his soft and subtle oil techniques can be confused with the dry, meticulous facture of a van Wittel. What I am arguing is that the full significance of Granet's work becomes clearer if we relate it not only to the tradition of the Roman *veduta*, but also to the corrosive irony of Gibbon. For Gibbon wishes us to experience the modern viewpoint as an anomaly: how absurd that those barefooted friars should stand where they do! Granet, on the other hand, views the Christian past of Rome with a special predilection. For the first time, perhaps, it becomes the vehicle of a specifically historical nostalgia and reverie.

The evidence of Granet's innumerable promenades through Rome suggests that he swiftly emancipated himself from the conventions of the earlier generation. He paints Santa Trinità dei Monti many times, but it is to show not a pagan temple but a Christian church in the right foreground. (This may possibly be a building completed in the later seventeenth century, but if not, it is worth thinking of the very forceful substitution which Claude engineered.) However, Granet's originality is not to be summed up simply by the practice of the *plein-air* sketch, with its topographical accuracy and informality. In a number of works, Granet deliberately arranges prospects through the architectural vestiges of the ancient world in such a way that they focus attention on the monuments of Christianity. In some cases, the great arches of the Colosseum become the frame through which such a building in the middle distance is glimpsed. As Denis Coutagne has commented, the Church of Santa Francesca Romana becomes as a result of this focalisation a 'signal, standard, trophy or lighthouse' *(fig. 4)*.[17] Admittedly, Granet sees the great arch as more than just a framing device. The weight of the cyclopean stones is powerfuly conveyed by the soft tonal gradations, unrelieved by direct light. But there can be no doubt that the medieval church is the privileged object of attention.[18]

[17] *Ibid.* 281.

[18] It would be foolhardy to assert that Granet was the first painter to tackle such subjects, particularly as there is no satisfactory way of dating the majority of Granet's Roman works. However, it seems likely that Granet's approach was well established by 1810, when he had already spent eight years in Rome. A similar focalisation of a church tower through a classical arch by the English painter John Goldicutt, who spent the years 1815–19 in Italy, might well be in response to a knowledge of Granet's work. See his *Ruins of the Basilica of*

This inclination comes across even more fully when Granet begins to paint interior as well as exterior views of Roman churches. Granet was not alone among French painters of his generation in choosing to represent cloisters, crypts and choirs. The artists of the Lyons school, usually dubbed in a misleading way the 'peintres troubadours', were similarly inclined. Indeed Granet, who knew them well, is often regarded as an honorary member of the school.[19] But Granet was the only artist of his time to investigate the fertile terrain of Rome, with the consequence that the ecclesiastical interiors recreated by his brush have a special intensity, and a special sense of triumph over discordant elements. His own description of one of the expeditions in which he completed studies of such a scene, the *Crypt of San Martino in Monte*, is highly revelatory in its sensory details, and the impression which it gives of a dangerous sortie into a subterranean world:

> The walls [of the crypt of San Martino] are covered over with a greenish down produced by the humidity, and this endows this interior with a colour which can hardly be imagined. This spot suited my tastes well; so my mind was made up straight away, although my monk assured me that I would not be able to work in a place like that . . . all this reasoning was powerless. I could see my picture in my mind's eye. My decision once taken, the very next day I was down with my corpses who were the only residents of this vast tomb.[20]

The church which is now usually called San Martino *ai Monti*, in the vicinity of Santa Maria Maggiore, was indeed an interesting choice for Granet to make, as it incorporated not simply a ninth-century crypt but a further, substantial space on a lower level whose outside walls were in part formed by massive blocks of *tufa* from a nearby Roman monument. Into this lowest level Granet penetrated, despite the warning from a monk that he would catch a fever; and from it he was forced to regain the surface, and the hot sun of a Roman summer, before he could return to complete his work. An undoubted outcome of this perilous expedition was the fine painting in the Musée Fabre, Montpellier, where one of the 'dead' to whom Granet refers can be seen to be laid out beneath the greenish brick walls *(fig. 3)*. But it

Constantine, Rome (Victoria and Albert Museum), illustrated in Liversidge and Edwards (1996) 97.

Of course, the precondition of such interest in Christian antiquities was, to a great extent, the existence of contemporary writings such as Chateaubriand's *Génie du Christianisme* (1812), published shortly after Bonaparte as First Consul had signed a Concordat with the Papacy. But Granet's originality lies in giving such intuitions a plastic rather than a literary form. It is worth noting that Girodet's famous portrait of Chateaubriand, dated 1808, shows him musing in front of the ruins of the Colosseum. No Christian monument is to be seen.

19 See Chaudonneret (1989) 91.

20 My translation of a passage quoted in Néto-Daguerre and Coutagne (1992) 84, 86. There is no full published version of Granet's *Mémoires*: the extracts used in this catalogue, and quoted here, are taken from the version based on three manuscript sources which is included in Néto-Daguerre (1991).

seems likely that another sketch in the Musée Granet, Aix-en-Provence, is also a record of the submerged space below the choir of San Martino. The lighting suggests that the viewpoint is towards the north, away from the focus of the Montpellier picture, and the absence of specific subject matter makes the covering of mould even more directly palpable to the viewer.

It is not difficult to see how this little ritual of representation was the expression of Granet's sense of the past. He had descended to the lower depths, and the result was painting. In this respect, he had testified to the new connection between concrete notions of spatiality and sensory affect, on the one hand, and the new vision of history which was to become more and more widely diffused throughout the period of his career. As Nietzsche was to put it graphically at a later stage in the century: 'The antiquarian breathes a mouldy air.'[21] Here then is the antiquarian painter, or at least one of the first to be worthy of the name, drawn irresistibly to the place of the dead, and confident at the same time of the representational means which are necessary to communicate his vision ('I could see my picture in my mind's eye.') Yet I will make no further special claims for the significance of this incident. Granet's works at San Martino, like his framed view of Santa Francesca Romana, are simply contributory elements in my argument, which relies especially on a further series dealing with a church interior. This is the group of works showing the *Choir of the Capuchin Church in the Piazza Barberini*, begun around 1812, and forming without doubt the high-point of Granet's entire career *(fig. 1)*.

A brief chronology is needed to set this series in context. On 17 February 1810, the troops of Napoleon occupied Rome, and the religious orders were suppressed. Granet records the devastating moment in his *Mémoires*: 'This beautiful town had changed in appearance, and lost all its religious character. The men of war had taken the place of prelates, cardinals and religious orders; the drum had silenced the sound of canticles and prayers.'[22] At this very point, Granet's professional life received a new impulsion: he became associated with the great connoisseur and member of the Bonaparte family, Cardinal Fesch. Early in 1812, and in pursuit of purchases for the Cardinal's art collection, he was in Paris, where he met the antiquarian Alexandre Lenoir, creator of the famous Musée des monuments français in the former conventual buildings of the Petits-Augustins on the Left Bank of the Seine. In the summer of the same year, he was officially designated 'peintre de paysage historique' to Caroline Murat, Queen of Naples.

It seems virtually certain that the original purpose of Granet's *Choir of the Capuchin Church* was to satisfy his new royal patron. But the subsequent

[21] Nietzsche (1978) 20. [22] Néto-Daguerre and Coutagne (1992) 142.

history of the commissions associated with the project develops with a complexity rarely paralleled in the history of painting. As the kaleidoscope of history was thoroughly shaken up in the years immediately preceding and following Napoleon's downfall, Granet's work developed a wider and wider market among the crowned heads of Europe. In the summer of 1814, the first version is exhibited in the salon of the French embassy at Rome, and reserved by Lady Conyngham, wife of an English ambassador and mistress of the Prince Regent. Only in 1819 does the large version now held in the National Museum of Wales, Cardiff, finally reach the Paris salon, where it acquires an instant celebrity. According to Bénézit, Granet was constrained to repeat his work no less than sixteen times, in varying sizes and with different collections of figures on each occasion, to satisfy imperial and royal clients who importuned him for their own versions. The future George IV insisted on having one for Carlton House. The Tsar of Russia would not be dissuaded. The French King, Louis XVIII, who himself wanted a version but had to be content with one being allocated to his relative, the Duc de Berry, remarked on the occasion of presenting Granet with the Cross of the Legion of Honour in 1819 (so Bénézit recounts): 'Monsieur Granet, someone tells me he has just heard one of your Capuchins sneeze.'[23]

Of the eagerness to acquire this specimen of Granet's talents – first of all, among the grandees of the terminating imperial regime, and later among the sovereigns of post-Napoleonic Europe – there can be no doubt. Yet how was it that this peaceable painter, living far away from his native land and up to that point eclipsed by the achievement of other, more public-minded members of the school of David, had sprung to prominence? It is a truism to say that Granet's work had caught the mood of the times. What needs to be shown is why this particular painting struck his contemporaries as a congenial and at the same time wholly novel image. To do this, we must look more closely at the particular conditions of its conception. Lenoir's Musée de monuments français, which Granet saw in 1812, achieved its unprecedented effect by grouping historical sculpture and architectural fragments which had survived the iconoclasts of the revolution in a series of 'century rooms'. Different periods were therefore reconstructed in terms of syntagmatically related sets of objects. But here was a historical interior represented in terms of its ritual practices, which had ceased only in the very recent past, and of course begun again after a relatively short interruption. In what way was this vision of Christian Rome qualified to rank as 'historical' at all, let alone a representation of the 'ancient'?

To answer this question, it is necessary to look once again at Granet's

[23] The reference is from Granet's *Mémoires*, and is quoted in *ibid.* 168.

illuminating *Mémoires*, where the circumstances in which the work was conceived are sedulously described. Curiously, it is with a phrase reminiscent of Gibbon's 'barefooted friars singing vespers' that Granet epitomises the effect of the French occupation: 'the drum had silenced the sound of canticles'. But in Granet's case, the effect of this interruption of the daily round of religious ritual is to devastate the present, and throw him back on the resources of memory:

I could no longer find my quiet Rome; all in her that charmed the artist had disappeared; so the days seemed long to me. I sought in vain the sweet peace that I had enjoyed in the monasteries. With this in mind I betook myself to the convent of the Capuchins in the Piazza Barberini; but the good Capuchins were no longer there. At the door where I had hoped to find the venerable Brother Felice with his beautiful white beard covering his breast, his sweet saintly face and his unaffected manners, I saw a totally different man; he no longer wore the monastic habit, he was rigged out in a kind of sack of unbleached linen, whose shape was neither religious nor worldly. One could see that he had been a member of the order of Saint Francis, but with his beard shaven and dressed in this fashion, the man was a kind of farce. . . .

In spite of this loneliness, my thoughts [in the convent] turned to all the friars whom I had seen in earlier times. I rediscovered the places that had been occupied by the young novices, whose brows were calm and resigned at having bid farewell to the world, and the old men with harsh heads and noble faces which bore the traces of the austerities engraved there by time.

My mind was so vividly taken over by all these thoughts that I resolved to make a larger picture out of them . . .[24]

Granet's vivid account leaves us in no doubt that the painting, or rather the series of paintings, which were to establish his reputation, found their origin in a precise psychological motive: that of recovering by substitution the 'sweet peace' which he had (as he puts it) 'possessed' in a Rome peopled by living and working religious communities. It would be unnecessary to underline the relevance of this perception to Foucault's analysis of the logic of possession and dispossession which initiates the nineteenth-century regime of historical-mindedness. Granet painstakingly reconstructs an entire milieu in order to recover a state of mind which he sees as being irretrievably lost, in so far as it was tied to a historically based culture which has abruptly vanished. The comparison with Gibbon is also instructive, since it suggests a kind of inverse symmetry. For Gibbon, the 'barefooted friars' are the modern anomaly which distorts the vision of the ancient city and empire, whose 'decline and fall' must become the object of a narrative exfoliation if it is not to be perceived in the guise of a vivid catachresis. For Granet, it is precisely the Capuchin friars who metonymically represent the 'ancientness' of Rome: however recent the discontinuation of their ritual practices, they epitomise the unbridgeable gulf between present perceptions

[24] *Ibid.* 142, 144.

and a mythic past which has to be reappropriated through representation: in this case, not the creation of a narrative history, but that of a series of paintings so compelling as to restore the sense of perceptual plenitude – to make us hear the Capuchins sneeze.

But Granet's achievement can only be effectively analysed if we take note of the place which these paintings hold in the history of representational modes – if we consider their specific code of visuality within the evolving tradition of picture-making. Obviously they have nothing in common with the tradition of the Roman *veduta*; their antecedents lie instead with the Northern tradition, in the first place with the genre of the church interior as it was practised in seventeenth-century Holland by an artist like Pieter Saenredam. However, this comparison immediately brings out the very real differences between the Dutch genre and Granet's resourceful refashioning of it. The Dutch painters show us large, luminous, Gothic interiors, peopled with tiny figures whose scale enhances the overall aesthetic impression of spatiality: it is no part of their concern to represent religious practice. Granet, on the other hand, offers a dramatically back-lit, relatively small and undistinguished space, whose function is simply to support the coherent performance of the religious rites.

This difference can be further explored with reference to the techniques of perspectival painting, and their epistemological consequences. Martin Kemp has carefully analysed, with the help of original drawings, Saenredam's outstanding painting of *The Church of St Bavo, Haarlem* (National Galleries of Scotland, Edinburgh). He has shown exactly how the drawings enabled the artist to work from a freehand sketch to a spatial projection, in such a way as to accentuate the height and length of the building, with the figures in the side-aisle being deliberately diminished in order to corroborate this impression. There is certainly a precise point of view from which the church is surveyed, obliquely, so as to obtain the maximum simultaneous presentation of breadth, height and depth. But this is not identifiable as a position from which the viewer might participate in the religious practices taking place in the building which are (as has been stressed) very rarely featured.[25] In Granet's case, on the other hand, the maximum

[25] See, for example, the paintings by Saenredam discussed in Schefer (1995) 49–55. Although the first of these works is identified as an *Interior of St Bavo* 'with a catholic baptism' (Glasgow Art Gallery), the ceremony does not appear to have begun. Martin Kemp analyses the drawings related to the large *Church of St Bavo* in Kemp (1984) 30–37.

Walter Melion has rightly pointed out to me that, in many respects, the specific school of church interiors which anticipates Granet's works is that of Antwerp, which is associated with the Neeffs family (Peeter I, 1605–56/61 and Peeter II, 1620–after 1675). Mention might also be made of the various anonymous paintings of the *Interior of the Quire of Canterbury Cathedral* (Yale Center for British Art, New Haven and Canterbury City Council Museums: both *c.*1710–15), which derive from the Antwerp School. These works unquestionably focus more clearly on religious ceremonies, but from a high and distant viewpoint: they do not approach the back-lit intensity of Granet's scenes.

use is made of the capacity of perspective to offer a vicarious place to the viewer, along the lines which Hubert Damisch has sketched out:

> Perspective is not a code; but it has in common with language the fact that, in it and by it, is instituted or constituted, by means of a point, an instance analogous to that of the 'subject' in language, of the 'person', always placed in relation to a 'here' or 'there', with all the possibilities of passing from one position to the other which derive from that.[26]

In the *Choir of the Capuchin Church*, the spectator is indeed invested with the role of a person capable of passing from 'here' to 'there'. This transition is, however, made doubly effective by Granet's insistence that it should be a temporal, as well as spatial displacement. We are meant to feel that this is indeed a lost world, to which our only access is through the devices of representation. The psychological effect corresponding to this motivation is surely what Michael Fried has analysed with reference to the term 'absorption'. That is to say, we are drawn into the enticing spectacle of a coherent and compelling ritual taking place, so to speak, before our very eyes, only to realise as a secondary but irrefutable perception that we ourselves are completely excluded from the scene. No one is looking at us. To put it more strongly, the powerful markers of 'absorptive' attentiveness, etched in the profiles of the individual participants, highlight our alienation from the scene in just the same measure as they draw us in.[27]

This way of looking at Granet's work inevitably raises the more general question: at what stage does the tradition of 'absorptive' painting, traced to the mid eighteenth century by Fried, become available not simply for a spatial but for a specifically historical effect of displacement? My own view is that Granet's series of the *Choir of the Capuchin Church* has a crucial place in this process. But it is a place which can only be adequately assessed if we look at these works in relation to the multiple range of forms of historical representation which began to proliferate in the 1820s: historical stage-settings, dioramas and historical museums such as the Musée de Cluny. In all of these cases, we have more concrete forms of spatiality, sometimes incorporating real objects from the past. However, the common feature of all of them is that the spectator/participant should have learned to shift from present to past, in response to a precise set of representational effects and stimuli. In this respect, the back-lit scene of the Capuchin church, already anticipating the powerful manipulation of natural light

[26] My translation of Damisch (1987) 62.

[27] See Fried (1980). I have also been able to note the relevance to my theme of Fried's concept of a mode of 'absorptive closure' which he calls 'cloistering'. Although applied to the prominence of religious painting among the Realist circle of French painters in the 1860s, this point clearly applies retrospectively to the achievement of Granet. See Fried (1996) 254ff.

which is to animate Daguerre's diorama, proposes a new mode of subjective investment for the Romantic public to adopt.

What still needs to be considered, however, is the striking paradox that Granet's versions of the *Choir of the Capuchin Church* embodied, in representing the past as irreversibly lost, but chronologically very near. Here it is important to look rather more closely at Granet and the artistic milieu to which he was related. It seems realistic to suppose that Granet's reaction to the occupation of Rome in 1810 was grounded in his earlier experience of ruptures within historical continuity: in other words, that it concretised and condensed a whole series of similar experiences to which a Frenchman who had reached the stage of adolescence in 1789 would inevitably have been exposed. Furthermore, it seems reasonable to hypothesise that the innovations associated with the painters of the Lyons school, whose relation to Granet has already been mentioned, were not only technical achievements which they happened to share with Granet, but the consequence of a shift in pictorial conceptions which was also rooted in a certain form of historical experience. Marie-Claude Chaudonneret has convincingly placed the work of the Lyons painters in relation to the devastating experience of the citizens of that city during the revolution, when they suffered exemplary punishment at the hands of the Parisian authorities – even to the elimination of the very name of Lyons, and its replacement by the humiliating term of 'Ville Affranchie'.[28] There can surely by no difficulty in understanding, *grosso modo*, why such painters developed new types of pictorial space and a historical iconography strictly divorced from the neo-classical pieties of David's more orthodox followers.

In Granet's case, we have perhaps a less dramatic case of the experience of the injustices of history, but a more coherent example of the strategies which were necessary, over a period of time, to build up the imaginative reserves eventually utilised for the *Choir of the Capuchin Church*. We are told that Granet lived, as a student in immediately post-revolutionary Paris, in the disaffected convent of the Capuchins where his studio bordered those of Ingres and a number of other pupils of David. Like them, he worked in a building whose religious life had been cut off by the revolution; unlike them, he used the scenography of deserted cloisters as his subject matter, when he sent a painting, *Intérieur du cloître des Feuillants*, to the Salon of 1799. It is hard to resist the conclusion that, in resurrecting his recent experience of the Capuchin church in the Piazza Barberini, he was also reactivating the feelings which he had conceived during his stay in the disaffected Parisian convent where, in the most literal sense, the painters had come upon the scene bereft of its religious brethren. Of course, there is

[28] Chaudonneret (1989) 27–41.

no need to give special status even to this earlier bout of experience, except in so far as it must also have helped to concretise other perceptions of historical rupture which had accompanied his adolescence in pre-revolutionary France.

A general point about memory is implied here. And it has been investigated in a uniquely persuasive way by Freud, in his work on 'screen memories'. This is the point that 'memories' appear to represent not a direct trace of an original perception, but a secondary elaboration, which subsumes but also 'screens' the original experience, in such a way as to make it virtually irrecoverable. Freud used the concept particularly in relation to the idea that early experiences of a sexual nature can only approach the level of conscious recollection in so far as they have been transformed, often through the superimposition of an image that would be indecipherable to anyone but the trained psychoanalyst. Leonardo's recollection of the kite flying down and rudely placing its tail between his lips is an instance of Freud's purported diagnosis of a 'screen memory'. What Leonardo could not call to consciousness, in Freud's view, was the experience of maternal seduction which he had undergone as a very young child.[29] But Freud also speculates that the 'screen' effect may be a feature of all recollection, since childhood memories characteristically bring with them the subject's consciousness of self-involvement: 'the subject sees himself in the recollection as a child, with the knowledge that this child is himself; he sees this child, however, as an observer from outside the scene would see him.' This leads Freud to the following observation:

> Whenever in a memory the subject himself appears in this way as an object among other objects this contrast between the acting and the recollecting ego may be taken as evidence that the original impression has been worked over. It looks as though a memory-trace from childhood had here been translated back into the plastic and visual form at a later date – the date of the memory's arousal.[30]

I do not think that it is fanciful to draw a close analogy between this process, as Freud describes it, and the process which leads to the series of the *Choir of the Capuchin Church*. Granet is re-enacting a type of ceremony which has just been discontinued, on the first level: this is the manifest content of the painting. But he is also elaborating upon a former practice of representing disaffected religious buildings, which dates back at least to his student days, and can be taken to have substituted, even then, for a more diffused sense of the dispossession of the past which oppressed him during the revolutionary epoch. By giving the vision of the Capuchins 'plastic and

29 See Freud (1910/1985) 172. As is well known, Freud makes the mistake of translating the Italian word 'nibio' as vulture, rather than kite. However, this has no bearing on the relevance of this example.

30 Freud (1989/1962) III:231.

visual' form, he places himself as author and first spectator in the position of an observer simultaneously involved in the scene and detached from it, with more conviction than his youthful efforts had managed to display.

Where then did the new conviction spring from? The only answer must be that Rome provided Granet with the totally sustaining milieu within which such a fantasy of repossession could be brought to fulfilment. Rome offered the experience of temporal strata displayed in concrete form, in such a way as to satisfy the precise requirements of Granet's vision. I have already mentioned the specific configuration of the church of San Martino ai Monti, which required him to descend not simply to one, but to a second, lower crypt where the dead were laid out in a mould-covered chamber shored up by blocks of Roman *tufa*. The Church of the Capuchins in the Piazza Barberini also has a triple configuration which Granet explored. The Choir which he painted is separated off from the main church, darkened with its heavy wooden panelling and lit mainly from the light source above the main altar which causes the dramatic silhouettes to emerge in the series of paintings. Beneath this double church, however, stretches the celebrated cemetery of the Capuchins, containing the bones of thousands of fathers of the order which had been placed there from 1528 onwards. Granet could not have failed to be aware of the proximity of the remarkable site, where mummified remains were arranged in standing and recumbent positions, in expectation of their resurrection. His own recreative scenario is played out close by, as he sets up his easel in the Choir. From this confrontation with absence flows the sustained sequence of lively paintings, soon to be diffused throughout the whole of Europe.

Any discussion of the expanded historical consciousness of the Romantic period must confront, at some level, the problem that specific and innovatory artistic practices were recuperated with great rapidity in this period. But perhaps it is not in any way surprising that the many people who had experienced the turbulence of historical change could rapidly recognise the achievement of the few in finding a rhetoric to represent its particular dynamism. Just after two decades from his commencement of the *Choir of the Capuchin Church* series, in 1833, Granet was nominated by King Louis-Philippe as the person responsible for the huge gallery of historical paintings which was being commissioned for the Château de Versailles. He himself contributed works like the grand crusading episode: *Godefroy de Bouillon dépose dans l'Eglise du Saint-Sépulchre les trophées d'Ascalm (fig. 5)*. The medieval knights and monks who swirl around this vast composition indicated a new and generalised confidence in the use of historical costume. But the circular church plan of the Holy Sepulchre recalls Granet's Roman period, and his painstaking recreation of the Mass as it takes places in *The interior of the Church of Santo Stefano Rotondo at Rome (fig. 6)*. It is as if Granet's Roman residence did indeed qualify him to perform a kind of transubstantiation, not of bread and wine but of the equally humble materials of his craft. Only in Rome could the painter discover the complex spaces, both interior and exterior, that would yield the appropriate dividend in historical recreation. But once the lesson had been learned, it could be applied in other contexts, and indeed transferred by Granet's contemporaries into the domain of spectacle, by a range of new techniques. For Granet, and for those who reacted to his work – artists and members of the public – Rome was indeed a moveable feast.

3 Napoleon I: a new Augustus?*

Valérie Huet

Even before the French revolution, a fashion for the antique, prompted in part by the discovery of Pompeii and Herculaneum, was again developing in Europe. It was Johann Joachim Winckelmann's work above all which lay behind the particular value which came to be attached to classical Greek art as the 'Beau-Idéal' (though one should note that the distinction he put forward between Greek art and Roman was largely based on his study of Roman copies of Greek works).[1] But the French Republic marked a turning point in the influence of Rome as Rome came to be perceived as a source of political example. The two famous Brutuses – the Brutus who revenged the rape of Lucretia and drove out the Etruscan King Tarquin, and the Brutus who was spurred by Julius Caesar's hunger for power to plot his assassination – were models for the Republican citizen. The ancient biographer Plutarch's accounts of the lives of prominent Romans were much read. But, in the latter days of the French Republic, a more appealing Roman political model emerged: Augustus, who, having absorbed the lesson offered by Caesar's assassination, devised instead a new mode of rule which, while respecting the forms of the Roman Republic, established a very different kind of government: the Principate. This Roman lesson was rapidly understood by another new man: Bonaparte, who, instead of attempting to restore the monarchy, appropriated the Republic by becoming Napoleon, Emperor of the French, in 1804.

In a book published in 1959, David L. Dowd offered undergraduates a range of source texts to equip them to formulate an answer to the question posed by the book's title: *Napoleon: was he the heir of the revolution?* But no one has ever raised the question: Napoleon: was he the heir of Roman emperors? of Augustus? Is such a question not, however, implicit in the kind of art produced under Napoleon (the well-known 'empire style')?

* This chapter would never have seen the light of day without the extreme patience of Catharine Edwards. I thank her very much for having invited me to take part in Bristol's Leverhulme project and for having tried to correct my French awkwardness in English. I would also very much like to thank all the conference participants who heard a first version of this paper, and especially Andrew Laird, Michael Liversidge, Charles Martindale, Onno van Nijf, Jonathan Walters, Jo Weeks, Dick Whittaker, Greg Woolf, Maria Wyke.

[1] On the historiography of art history, see for instance *Winckelmann* (1991); Brendel (1953).

The question of the influence of Roman antiquity on Napoleon I seems at first unproblematic. Any reader will acknowledge its existence; there seems no need to discuss it further. This assumption appears to lie behind most recent books concerning Napoleon.[2] Napoleon's politics and his extensive use of classical antiquity in the decorative arts prove beyond doubt, apparently, that Napoleon is a modern Roman emperor.[3]

I shall suggest, however, that we are reluctant to examine further those uses of Roman antiquity by Napoleon which construct him as the 'natural heir' of Roman emperors because of our understanding of Napoleon as a myth. There is the myth of Napoleon and there is Napoleon as a living myth. There is also Napoleon's creation of his own myth through the use of images for propaganda. My aim is to sketch out, through some specific examples, what this phenomenon was, its form, the elements from which it was constituted and the extent to which it was the result of the conscious or unconscious will of Napoleon himself. In brief I would like to deconstruct our myth of Napoleon.

Napoleon I as a Roman emperor: evidence and assumptions

First, it is worth stating the obvious about Napoleon as a Roman emperor. The obvious starts with politics.[4] In December 1799, three provisional consuls were elected in accordance with a new constitution: the constitution of *L'An VIII*. The first consul had executive power and was assisted by a consul of peace and a consul of war. Not surprisingly, Bonaparte was the first consul. What is striking about the constitution is the use of terminology drawn from the Roman Republic. There was a tribunate (which debated laws without voting on them) and a senate which could revise or complete the constitution by a *senatus-consulte*. Bonaparte appointed the three consuls for ten years. But in 1802, after the Peace of Amiens (6 Germinal *an* X, 27 March 1802) and the Concordate,[5] Talleyrand and

[2] E.g. Boime (1990) who discusses in three chapters (chs.1, 2 and 10) Napoleon's image and influence, announces the "fact" that Napoleon is a classical hero, but then shows him to be also drawing on a fantastical medieval past such as that of Ossian, as well as Egyptian antiquity; the image of Napoleon as a classical hero vanishes: what matters is that all iconographic images convey more or less the message of Napoleon's 'Grandeur' and particularly his role as a world saviour; no clear analysis of Napoleon's use of Roman antiquity is provided. Ridley, in his excellent book *The eagle and the spade* (1992), devotes only three pages of his introduction to 'Roman influences in French culture during the revolutionary and Napoleonic periods': he recognises that Napoleon gave a 'new, heightened meaning' to the Roman influence seen under the Republic but does not explain what this meaning might be.

[3] See for instance *Napoléon* (1969); *Napoléon Ier, 1802* (1952).

[4] See the historical research undertaken by Tulard (1989). Cf. too the introduction by J. Billiet in *Napoléon Ier, 1802* (1952).

[5] Connected to the Concordate was the restitution of a number of art pieces by the Museums of the Louvre and of Versailles to a number of Parisian churches. According to Boyer (1969b), Daru reported the will of Napoleon but Denon was reluctant in obeying.

Cambacérès proposed to the Senate that Bonaparte be offered the consulate for life, which, after discussion, was reduced to ten years in addition to the seven years Bonaparte had still to run. Bonaparte refused, claiming that it was up to the people to grant this extension. This was a tactical move used several times by Augustus, for instance, in September or October 37 BCE, when he, not yet Augustus but Octavian, refused to rule as a triumvir for the second time without the consent of the people and when, in 36 BCE at the end of the civil wars, he proposed to Antony that they should surrender their triumviral powers. Antony's refusal worked to Octavian's advantage. Octavian's progressive 'handover' or restoration of power to senate and people, mainly from 28 BCE onwards, led these latter to offer Augustus a succession of honours and new forms of power which served to constitute the Principate, while at the same time Augustus could claim to have restored the Roman Republic.[6] Bonaparte's decision helped to reassure the mass of citizens that the legitimacy of the French Republic was not contested and that the republic was still in operation. Bonaparte, just as Octavian had done, required a power which was legitimate. Thus the State Council ('Conseil d'Etat') was in charge of the consultation. The question was: will Napoleon Bonaparte be a life consul? ('*N.B. sera-t-il consul à vie?*'). Of the 3,577,299 who took part 3,568,855 voted in favour. The results were proclaimed by a *senatus-consulte* 10 thermidor *an* X, 29 July 1802: 'Le peuple français nomme et le Sénat proclame Napoléon-Bonaparte, Premier Consul à Vie.' In this formulation, one may readily recognise the familiar formula SPQR (*Senatus Populusque Romanus*) of the Roman Republic, and later the Principate. 15 August, the birthday of Bonaparte, was declared a national feast, just as Augustus' supposed birthday,[7] along with the anniversaries of Augustus' victories in Actium and Alexandria, had been celebrated from 30 BCE. Then the constitution of *L'An XII* (28 Floreal, 18 May 1804) proclaimed Bonaparte Emperor of the French (under the name Napoleon I) to be succeeded by his heirs. Once again the people were consulted and there was even less opposition to the plebiscite. On 2 December 1804, Pius VII came to crown Napoleon at Notre-Dame de Paris.

What emerges from this summary? That Bonaparte certainly knew his Roman history well and had understood the difference between Caesar and Octavian-Augustus. After revolution, there can be no king,[8] no one can aspire to be *rex* or murder will follow, as it did for Julius Caesar on the Ides of March. Octavian's brilliance had lain first in prolonging his consulship, then in becoming *imperator* for life, an Augustus. The genius of Bonaparte

6 For a clear and concise analysis of the subtle way in which Octavian became Augustus and created the Principate, see Jacques and Scheid (1992) 1–109. 7 See Barton (1995).

8 That is, of course, not true for England – but according to the French, England is always a good counter-example.

was to redeploy this model but not in every particular: first a consul for life, then emperor for life with the full meaning implied by the title 'emperor' *after* centuries of imperial Roman power. Another slight difference is that Augustus did not give the appearance of having hereditary power at the beginning, while the hereditary nature of Napoleon's power was clear in the constitution of *l'An XII* (though, curiously enough, the first Augustus and the first Napoleon seem to have encountered similar anxieties in securing the transmission of their power).

Their strategies for securing their positions above all other citizens were also similar: they won their first place thanks to military victories but also thanks to claims of 'divine' inheritance; Augustus, through his adoptive father Caesar, inherited Julian ancestry: the lineage of Romulus, Mars, Aeneas and Venus; Napoleon encouraged the perception of a close parallel between himself and 'Charlemagne', presented then to the French as the great successor of Roman emperors (Holy Roman Emperor from 800 to 814),[9] responsible for the formation – and for the idea – of France.[10]

The other obvious fact about Napoleon as a Roman emperor concerns his use and abuse of Classical antiquity in the arts: city planning, architecture, interior decoration, furniture, silverware, china, jewellery – all emphasised the connections between Napoleon and Roman antiquity: the style of the Consulate and the Empire is thus easily distinguished from the style of the Directoire. But what is striking in the taste expressed for Roman antiquity is the interest of the artists in eclecticism: Roman copies of Greek art[11] or Egyptian symbols are part of Roman art and truly express the spread of Roman power over the world; in the same way, Egyptian civilisation,

[9] One might notice that the principal period of Bonaparte-Napoleon's rule was from 1800 until 1814, one millennium after Charlemagne. This coincidence contributed to the fusion of the myths of the two great men. See for instance the quite 'fantastic' and unhistorical book of Deslys, *L'Héritage de Charlemagne* (1887), who in his 'epilogue' wrote: 'Mais une dernière tombe est restée muette . . . regarde encore. . . . Un autre Charlemagne en sortit, un empereur au profil antique, au front puissant, au regard d'aigle. D'une voix brève, et comme faite pour commander à l'univers, il ne dit que ce seul mot: "Napoléon!" Et tout en traversant la grotte, il toucha du doigt le manuscrit des Capitulaires de Charlemagne, sur le vieux parchemin desquels on entrevit aussitôt resplendir, en caractères de feu, ces deux lignes:

Empire Français
Code Civil . . .' (415)

One should also note that Charlemagne's statue was the only war booty Napoleon gave back: it was returned to Aix-la-Chapelle, but a medal showing the two profiles of Charlemagne and Napoleon was minted in 1806 after a drawing by Denon.

[10] The 'mythic' argument was that Charlemagne, ruler of the 'Francs', created France and thus could be considered as truly French; he could to some extent be compared to Romulus, the founder of Rome.

[11] See nevertheless the problem raised by the arrival of the Apollo Belvedere at the Museum of the Louvre: Visconti had to defend it as a masterpiece by saying that it was an 'improved' version of an earlier Greek bronze. On that subject, see McClellan (1994) 153–4.

though studied for itself in the Napoleonic period, is considered as belonging once again to the ruler who has assumed the legacy of the 'Roman empire', that is to say to Napoleon as a Roman Emperor. Therefore, Napoleon's models must be Caesar, known for his fascination with Egypt, and Augustus, who conquered the country. Just as there were 'nilotic scenes' in Roman mosaics and paintings,[12] artists reinterpreted a mix of Egyptian symbolism and Roman art to create the 'empire style'. The overwhelming presence of Roman classical antiquity in any palace decorated for Napoleon (for instance, Malmaison, Fontainebleau, the Louvre) delivers a message clear even to one who is specialist neither in Roman antiquity nor in Napoleon: Napoleon is a modern Roman emperor. This 'fact' is reinforced for any French pupil by his/her knowledge of the Roman roots of Napoleonic *Code Civil*[13] and by his/her understanding of the creation of the sanitary system of Parisian sewers built on the orders of Napoleon and on the model of the ancient Roman sewer system. Napoleon is a true 'Roman' in his strong sense of the practical and prosaic. Beauty – that is to say, the 'ideal beauty' of the ancient Greeks – is not put first; plans for utilitarian urbanism were preferred by Napoleon.[14]

But when we identify Napoleon as 'obviously' a Roman emperor, a 'natural heir', we enter into Napoleon's myth – our own myth of Napoleon, the creator of myth through his use of images for propaganda. I would like to argue that our use of the words 'myth' and 'propaganda' is so broad that it prevents us from making any further attempt to understand the phenomenon: the notion of the myth of Napoleon positions us as outside, external, looking on, producing, using and deploying 'it'.[15] Not only we are external to it, we also do not want to know about Napoleon's myth. We feel uneasy about it, uncomfortable and at the same time fascinated by it: a kind of fatal attraction that we try to deny. Moreover, in analysing the myth of Napoleon as a Roman emperor, we are confronted with other problems: the problem of the myth of classical antiquity and of the myth of Roman emperors ('good' emperors, 'bad' emperors). We feel anxious that Napoleon's use of classical antiquity is clearly focussed on Rome and not Greece. He made the wrong choice. Since he took his political model from Rome, we cannot see him as anything other than a Roman emperor. Our contemporary scholarly Hellenocentrism has the result of making us suppress the myth of Napoleon as a Roman emperor. I intend here to take a different course: to enter the myth and to investigate its origins. What did

[12] See, for instance, those in the Archaeological Museum of Naples.

[13] It became law on 21 March 1804 and is still of great importance in French law.

[14] This emerges clearly from the diverse articles of the journal *Les Monuments Historiques de la France* 15, fasc. 4 which was devoted to Napoleonic urbanism and decoration.

[15] I am making use here of Beard's analysis of 'Greek myth' versus 'Roman myth' (1996) 84.

Napoleon know about Roman antiquity? How did he acquire his knowledge? From what sources was it drawn? What did he use from it? What was at stake when he used it? Why did he use it? And was it really Napoleon who commissioned the images or was he given persuasive advice by someone with a specialist knowledge of art? Of course, I do not intend to answer all these ambitious questions here; but I would like to explore the 'reality' of Napoleon's Roman inspiration by looking at some specific, if limited, examples taken from art.

Napoleon and Canova: the problematic image at Apsley House

The relationship between Napoleon and the sculptor, Antonio Canova (1757–1822), has been defined as ambiguous, Canova being both an admirer of Napoleon and a critic, resenting his invasion of Italy, and even more his seizure of Italian masterpieces of art.[16] Curiously enough, it was Canova who, having been appointed head of the Accademia di San Luca in Rome in 1810 thanks to Napoleon, was the agent sent by Pius VII in 1815 to bring back all the masterpieces taken by Bonaparte.

Canova's first French customers[17] were Julliot, then Murat and Joséphine. It was she who, in August 1802, bought Hebe and Love and a standing Psyche. She asked Canova to create twelve statues for her gallery representing either the twelve months or the twelve gods; this project was never realised. It was clearly through her that Bonaparte was made aware of Canova's work. In September 1802, on Bonaparte's behalf, Cacault asked Canova to come to Paris to do a portrait and a statue of Bonaparte. Canova's first reaction was a refusal. Then he accepted, arriving in Paris at the end of September (his second trip to Paris was in 1810). The bust was completed and presented by 21 November 1802 (it is now in the Palazzo Pitti, Florence). It was criticised for not being a close enough resemblance. Canova defended himself by saying that he was not a specialist in portrait busts but rather in statues. Canova's real project was a colossal statue of Bonaparte. We know that Bonaparte gave Canova *carte blanche* in the design of the statue and is reported to have declared 'On n'impose pas de loi au Génie!' Work started on the statue in Rome in 1803 and it was

[16] See Boyer (1937a) who quotes Canova's letter to Antonio d'Este, dated February 1797: 'Ne valait-il pas mieux donner 10 millions de plus que de perdre les chefs d'oeuvre si riches d'enseignement qui attirent ici les étrangers de toutes les nations et forment la gloire de Rome? Les millions peuvent revenir, mais ces chefs d'oeuvre, Dieu sait le destin qu'ils auront!'

[17] We should remember that Canova was not held in much esteem by French artists in the 1780s. Though he was a friend of the painter David, and they were both influenced by antiquity, his art was criticised and its success disparaged: he was accused of casting his statues directly from human bodies and of being too Greek. 'Canova c'est un sculpteur vénitien traduit en grec' is the alleged comment of a French artist, Swasy (certainly a nickname), about whom nothing else is known.

finished 3 September 1806. The cost was 60,000 francs. But there was a problem in transporting it from Rome to Paris and Napoleon did not see it until 1811. In 1810, before Napoleon had seen the original, Eugene, viceroy of Italy, ordered a small replica in bronze for himself (now in the Brera Gallery in Milan). Clearly, Eugene meant to please and honour Napoleon by this gesture – just as rich Roman senators did when, all over the Roman Empire, they commissioned statues and busts of their emperor. At the same time there was the project to place an exact replica in the middle of the Roman Forum between the arch of Titus and that of Septimius Severus. But Napoleon's reaction when faced with the actual statue was reported to be mixed: he commented that the execution was worthy of praise, that the aspect was impressive and majestic but that the form was too 'aesthetic' and the attitude not sufficiently cool, that the torso was too long and that there were problems with the joint of the arm holding the Victory.

The statue *(fig. 7)* represents Napoleon as a Roman divinity: the god Mars on a 'colossal' (over-lifesize) scale. Napoleon is nude (a vineleaf conceals his genitals, just as antique statues had had theirs hidden by the modern addition of a leaf in order to protect viewers[18]), a *paludamentum* or chlamys on his left shoulder; his weight on his right leg, he looks toward the small statue of Victory (*Nike*) 'dancing' on a globe, which he holds in his right hand, while his left holds a spear.[19] Behind his right leg is a tree-trunk and a sword. The ensemble in its attitude and its attributes resembles a Roman copy of a Greek statue. The addition of the tree-trunk, ostensibly to support the statue, seems to suggest the ancient translation of a statue originally cast in bronze into a version carved in marble. But the face is without doubt that of Napoleon with his characteristic coiffure, perhaps a little rearranged in order to evoke that of Augustus. The idea of presenting Napoleon, a great warrior, as Mars, the god of war, has many precedents: in Roman antiquity, the representation of a human being in the form of a divinity became very widespread from the first century CE;[20] it was common under Louis XIV and the aristocrats of the French court often appeared in the guise of divinities in paintings of the eighteenth century. However, Napoleon as Mars cannot be properly understood by a viewer unfamiliar with the statues Canova created of other members of

18 These 'restored' vineleaves are still kept in the Vatican museums.

19 In the Museum Revoltella in Trieste, there is a sketch by Canova representing the spear crowned by the eagle, but there is no Victory on the globe.

20 See for instance, portraits of the emperor Claudius with the attributes of Jupiter, partially nude with a mantle draped around his lower body (the best-known example is in the Vatican Museum). There are a number of nude images of Antinous, the lover of Hadrian, commissioned by the emperor after his death. Some show Antinous as Mars. There are also versions of two unknown Roman citizens portrayed as Mars and Venus, one in the Museum of Louvre in Paris, the others in the Capitoline Museum in Rome and at the National Museum of Rome (see Kleiner (1992) 131–5, 280–2, figs. 106–9, 207, 248–9.

Napoleon's family. The titles speak for themselves: 'Madame Mère' as Agrippina (1808),[21] Pauline Borghese as Venus Victrix (1804), Marie-Louise as Concordia (1810–11). Canova was very much the official sculptor of the Bonaparte family and was reportedly called 'Caesar's friend' by Napoleon.

So why did Napoleon not like his portrait as Mars? The symbols and the propaganda were clear: as a divinity and thanks to his qualities as a warrior which led to victory he dominated the globe, the world. What Napoleon criticised in the statue could perhaps be summed up in one thing: his uneasiness at the sight of his own nudity. And it was precisely his nudity that was felt to be problematic, even shocking.[22] But how did Canova come to have the odd idea of representing Napoleon as a nude divinity? To answer that question, we must be introduced to Quatremere de Quincy. This man was a friend of Canova and a number of letters have survived which might make us reassess our view of the *carte blanche* Napoleon gave Canova. As early as 1802, Quatremere de Quincy emphasised to Canova the necessity of representing Bonaparte in a Greek rather than a Roman style: for a colossal statue neither Roman nor contemporary dress could be contemplated, he stresses. Indeed, another statue should be executed at the same time, a statue *à la romaine*: Canova should create an equestrian statue of Bonaparte in bronze, a modern composition on the lines of Marcus Aurelius' statue on the Capitol. A number of ideas were exchanged for some years between Quatremere and Canova about this latter project, but, as they could not agree about the details of the statue, it never was completed.[23] It is of course Quatremere who reports Napoleon's reaction to Canova and one might suspect that Napoleon's own disappointment was perhaps not so strong nor expressed in such a manner but that this reaction was rather that of Quatremere himself, when he finally saw the statue he had imagined so clearly. What strikes me in this story is the role Quatremere seems to have played as a mediator between Napoleon and Canova. Was he commissioned by Napoleon to play this part or was it his own initiative? The colossal statue does not seem to have changed the relationship between Napoleon and Canova. However, as Albert Boime points out, it was

[21] The disagreements between Napoleon and his mother have long been known; her absence from Joséphine's coronation is a strong indication of the tension between them. Nevertheless, to compare her with Agrippina, bearing in mind the latter's relationship with her son Nero, might seem to be rather 'bad taste', or at least to indicate a cynical sense of humour, unless one supposed it was a warning from Napoleon to his mother. . . .

[22] Hubert: 'Canova est son préféré, mais la nudité héroïque et colossale de sa propre effigie en Mars pacificateur, due au maître italien, le choque au point d'en ordonner la mise en réserve et d'interdire qu'on en parle'(1969) 6. I disagree here with Boime (1990) 640–1, who explains the 'failure' of this statue as a reflection of Canova's ambivalence towards Napoleon which led him to undermine 'the traditional projection of heroism'.

[23] See the engravings of Napoleon I's equestrian statue by Canova in Moses (1824–8).

sequestered in the Louvre until 1816, when it was purchased by the English government and given as a souvenir to the Duke of Wellington. I would be very interested to know what it meant to the English at that time to own the much criticised nude representation of Napoleon. Why did they buy it? Was it because its lack of success was an announcement of Napoleon's failure or was it again a fatal attraction to the myth of Napoleon and the pleasure of mastering it?

Napoleon and the Borghese collection

A consideration of the role Napoleon may have played in the acquisition of a famous antique collection – that of the Borghese family – may also throw light on Napoleon's attitude to Roman antiquity. Did the idea for the sale come from Prince Borghese, from Napoleon himself or from one of the latter's advisers? F. Boyer[24] emphasises that Camillo Borghese naturally had many good reasons for wanting this sale – particularly his permanent state of financial crisis. Nevertheless the initiative seems to come from Napoleon himself – and Boyer draws attention to a note which is supposed to have been dictated by the Emperor to his *Intendant Général* on 14 May 1806: 'Je désire que M. Daru, très secrètement et en demandant le plus grand secret à M. Denon et à M. Visconti, fasse une évaluation de tous les chefs d'oeuvre de la maison Borghese: combien puis-je en donner en supposant que le Prince veuille les vendre? Comment les transporter et les placer à Paris? Les Galeries du Musée seraient-elles suffisantes et, dans le cas contraire, ne pourrais-je pas les placer à la Magdelaine?' On the other hand, Boyer also stresses the major role Vivant Denon, the director at that time of the Napoleon Museum, had in influencing Napoleon as regards the purchase of antiques. He thinks that Denon was very much Napoleon's adviser in everything concerning antiquities. In fact we have a number of letters from Denon to Napoleon dating from 1806 which seem to confirm this: they invariably begin by praising the great actions and ideas of Napoleon before suggesting, as a casual aside, how to improve the situation still further. In his letter dated 31 January 1806 (Arch. Nat. AF IV-1050),[25] Denon writes: 'Tout ce que fait votre Majesté a le même cachet de grandeur et Votre Destinée amène la confection de tout ce qu'elle entreprend. Je savais et je n'osais presque me dire à moi-même que qui aurait rassemblé l'Hercule Farnèse, le Gladiateur Borghèse, l'Apollino de Florence, 100 morceaux de second ordre et 200 de troisième ordre qui existent dans les collections Farnèse, Borghèse et Florentine, aurait fait un musée comparable au Musée Napoléon. Ce que Votre Majesté vient d'arrêter d'y ajouter

[24] Boyer (1937b). [25] See Vauthier (1911).

ne laisse aucune possibilité d'entreprendre et d'espérer rien d'égal. . . .' But then Denon adds a quite specific reference to the antiquities currently in the Kingdom of Naples, (that is to say the Farnese collection), which had recently become available following Napoleon's defeat of the Bourbons. One should notice that this letter precedes Napoleon's supposed note quoted above. A similar suggestion is made in December 1807 concerning works of art, including a number of antiquities, kept in Florence. Why not bring them back to Paris? is the subtext. Thus it appears that Vivant Denon was the person behind the idea of buying the Borghese collection without actually having formulated it explicitly – in order, presumably, that Napoleon would think it was his own idea. I would even suggest that Denon knew how to manipulate Napoleon just as far as our 'hero' was willing to be manipulated. I suspect he did not need to be pushed very far when the issue was the display of conquered art in Paris.[26]

Space does not permit an examination of all the details of the valuation of the Borghese collection. Denon's first estimate was five million francs – but in view of who the vendor was, he argued, it would be reasonable to pay twice as much (Camillo Borghese was the husband of Pauline, Napoleon's sister). The other expert valuation was carried out by E. Q. Visconti, curator of the antiquity department at the Napoleon Museum. It is an extremely detailed evaluation, including a ranking of the pieces of art. The total estimate was rather less than four million but Visconti stressed that it depended whether Napoleon planned to buy the whole collection or individual pieces. The price could be raised. Visconti specified also that the actual owner was in no great hurry to sell them. A new valuation was ordered (carried out in June 1806), this time by the two experts together. They valued the collection at a little less than four million but felt that it could be bought for five million. The actual papers relating to the purchase were not signed until 27 September 1807 (at Fontainebleau). We do not have any clear evidence for the causes of the delay: historians have suggested that the military situation in Prussia and Russia could have been a factor or else perhaps resistance from the Prince Borghese. At any rate the price paid was nothing like five million: it was thirteen million – a fact which led Boyer to conclude his article: 'Il ne faut donc pas s'étonner si, malgré les réclamations assez inattendues de Camille Borghèse en 1815, ces antiques ne reprirent pas le chemin de Rome comme les marbres tirés du Vatican. Elles avaient été cédées par leur propriétaire par une transaction tout à fait banale; il n'y avait d'anormal peut-être que le prix qui lui fut payé!'

[26] Hubert writes: 'Napoléon se montre . . . très prudent dans ses jugements sur les arts plastiques, au moins sous le Consulat. Il s'en remet alors volontiers à Denon, directeur du musée Napoléon, chargé des Salons, de la 'création artistique', du décor des monuments' (1969) 5.

It is difficult to imagine this wonderful museum of antiquities in Paris – a kind of ideal dream for a French classicist, whatever ideological and ethical problems it may raise. One of the main concerns was how to display the antiquities. According to Andrew McClellan's account of Napoleon's museum,[27] the first plan was to display the antique sculptures by grouping at least some of them iconographically but that classification was subordinated to the desire to showcase the famous marbles and to achieve a decorative ensemble.[28] With the arrival of Visconti as curator, statues were grouped roughly according to subject, as they were in the Museo Pio-Clementino in the Vatican. But what mattered most was not respect for a chronological historical order but for the high prestige of 'universal aesthetic value'. Boyer may, I suspect, have underestimated Visconti's role as Napoleon's adviser in antiquities. I would argue that both Vivant-Denon and Visconti played an active role in the construction of Napoleon as a Roman emperor and as a man of taste.

Napoleon and Trajan's column – or the birth of the Vendôme column

As I have elsewhere argued,[29] the story of the drawing and casting of Trajan's column seems to be repeatedly connected with French monarchs: François I, Louis XIV, Napoleon I and Napoleon III. According to some sources, Napoleon I wanted to transfer the column itself to Paris and it was an extremely complex and time-consuming process to dissuade him. His advisers argued that the Italians and the Romans in particular would never forgive this spoliation. But as a consolation, Napoleon was offered another toy, an even better one: a French contemporary adapted a version of Trajan's column on the same scale as Trajan's column to be erected in the middle of a square: the Vendôme column. Instead of Trajan, Romans and Dacians, there would be Napoleon and his enemies. He could also enjoy a goldsmith's replica of the 'real' Trajan's column in miniature (created by Valadier).[30] According to other sources, Napoleon's idea was not his own fantasy but had been suggested to him. What scholars agree, however, is that it was extremely difficult to make Napoleon change his mind.

In fact, the history of the Vendôme column is more complex and I shall summarise it here very briefly.[31] After Campo-Formio and the Egyptian campaign, Bonaparte inaugurated a competition in which artists would

27 McClellan (1994) 148–54. 28 *Ibid.* 151. 29 See Huet (1996) 9–24.

30 See Settis, La Regina, Agosti, Farinella (1988) 596, fig. 91. Another small replica in gilded bronze was made in a Roman workshop before 1819 and is now in the Museum of Modern Art, Palazzo Pitti, Florence (illustrated in *ibid.*, 112–3).

31 See for instance Bergé (1969), Biver (1963).

design columns celebrating each department, to be erected in each department capital (*chef-lieu*) in France; in Paris, a column celebrating the department would be erected in Place Vendôme, while, on the Place de la Concorde, a column would be erected for the entire French nation. The projects were to be examined by a commission of three famous artists: the painter David and the architects Percier and Fontaine,[32] two friends who were known by the sobriquets 'Castor and Pollux'. One should remember that when they were both studying in Rome before the revolution, Fontaine was made to provide architectural drawings of the arch of Septimius Severus,[33] and Percier was obliged to devote himself to drawings of Trajan's column. Though Molinos' project won the competition for the Vendôme column, it was never executed. On 1 October 1803, Bonaparte requested (by an *arrêté*) for this square a column on the model of that of Trajan. The architect Thierry's first project was a column in iron with allegorical reliefs representing the 108 departments of France. After Austerlitz, Vivant Denon suggested to Napoleon that a column be erected to the glory of the *Grande Armée*, the reliefs realised in the bronze melted down from the canons taken from the enemy during the battle. Lepère and Gondouin were in charge of its construction, but a pupil of David, Bergeret, designed the sculpted panels, to ensure their stylistic unity, and, finally, Napoleon advised on the choice between different drawings and scenes. A statue of Napoleon in his coronation robes, his head crowned with laurel, was executed by Chaudet to be placed at the top of the column.[34] This summary highlights two convergent influences in the making of the Vendôme column: that of Vivant Denon and that of Napoleon himself.

What interests me in this account is the way Roman art was used: it was literally transposed into modern terms; it asserted a direct filiation from a Roman emperor, Trajan, and at the same time it marked Napoleon's difference, since he was portrayed as a modern hero, a living legend and not as a fake of Roman antiquity. Napoleon was the true reincarnation of a Roman emperor. The Vendôme column was not an echo of Marcus Aurelius' column,[35] a much discussed and contested 'work of art'. It expressed Napoleon's triumph, celebrating his *Grande Armée* just as Trajan's column had commemorated the victories of Trajan and of his Roman soldiers, and at the same time it displayed Napoleon's superiority

[32] On the architectural history of France, Hautecoeur's great work has never been superseded: cf. Hautecoeur (1953).

[33] This arch is the model for the Arc du Carrousel in Paris.

[34] This statue was according to Napoleon forced on him by the admiration of his public. It seemed to have been Denon's idea, but one should note that Trajan's column was crowned by Trajan's statue. The role of triumphal columns in Roman antiquity was, it seems, to function as a base for the statues of great men! On this Napoleonic discussion, see e.g. Pérouse de Montclos (1969) 70.

[35] See Huet and Scheid (forthcoming).

to all French citizens just as Trajan had dominated both Roman citizens and barbarians.[36] Moreover, the process by which the Vendôme column was designed, with a number of artists involved in the work and Napoleon himself making political interventions, closely resembles the process of creation of Trajan's column as our contemporary art historians have imagined it.[37] And, when Napoleon was defeated, the same symbol had to be used: the erection of a column in the middle of a square – hence Nelson's column in Trafalgar Square in London. But there could no longer be a sculpted *volumen* wound around the column, for that had become the symbol of absolute power. Napoleon III showed his filiation to Napoleon I by ordering a cast (actually galvanoplasty) of the 'real' Trajan's column which he initially intended to erect on a square in Paris (this plan was never carried but it was displayed in pieces in a museum). Napoleon III, then, followed Napoleon I's original idea; he could not compete with the highly complicated duality of symbolism expressed by the Vendôme column.

The presence of Roman antiquity in paintings exhibited in the salons, 1800–1815

The last example I would like to discuss is that of the subjects of paintings exhibited at the Salons – official works of art, that is to say. I will be brief: classical antiquity inspires many paintings (I shall not here consider landscape paintings of classical ruins – most of which showed the remains of ancient Rome rather than ancient Greece). The problem is to determine how far Napoleon's personality and desire to 'be' a Roman emperor influenced artists in their choice of subjects. Another consideration is the kind of antiquity which was invoked. Was the model Greek or Roman? (Here too we should remember that this period saw the beginning of Hellenomania.) Were artists inspired by the antiques displayed at the Louvre? Which source texts did they use? Plutarch,[38] Livy,[39] Ovid[40] and

[36] Cf. Veyne (1991).

[37] See, for instance, the suggestion that a 'Master' would have devised the scheme of the whole 'volumen' of sculpted reliefs – a figure whose role would correspond to that of Bergeret; the possible intervention of Trajan's architect Apollonios of Halicarnass could have its equivalent in Denon; and finally the political survey of the column's propaganda by Trajan himself would be followed by Napoleon. On the conception of Trajan's column, see Settis (1985) and (1988).

[38] For instance, the second supplement of the guide to the Salon held in 1802 gives under no. 731 *Thésée apprend le secret de sa naissance*, a painting by Firmin-Hyppolite Beaunier, an extract of a French translation of Plutarch, *Life of Theseus*, VI.

[39] See e.g. the painting by Lemonnier entitled *Les ambassadeurs de Rome demandant à l'Aréopage communication des lois de Solon, l'an de Rome 300* exhibited under no. 386 at the Salon of 1808 which refers to Livy, III, 31.

[40] E.g. painting no. 270 of the Salon held in 1810, *Circé* by Jean-Philibert Dumet, which claims according to the guide to have taken its subject from Ovid's *Metamorphoses*.

Virgil (especially Eclogue VI)[41] were referred to in the titles of some paintings. How did Napolon's influence operate? Perhaps painters were inclined to tailor their works to Napoleon's interests, even if he did not explicitly request it, in order to please him?

But from the list of painting titles, one forms rather the impression that the focus on antiquity is not specifically on Rome and that the continuity of a French tradition is predominant. What distinguishes great painting (*La grande peinture*) from other painting in the French tradition even before the revolution is that the chosen topics are either Christian or classical and that they are executed on vast panels. In fact, there do not seem to be more paintings during Napoleon's reign concerned with the classical world than there had been in the revolutionary Salons.[42] In the wake of the French revolution's rejection of Christianity, one of the problems painters of great painting had to face was the legitimacy of subjects drawn from the Bible. Thus they were left with mythological and classical historical topics. There are some paintings depicting stories from Roman history; but there are also some depicting Greek subjects. Thus there is no obvious contrast in terms of the classical subjects of paintings between the revolutionary Salons and those of the Napoleonic period. But one may nevertheless detect Roman influence at work in the representation of Napoleonic subjects. Napoleon's great innovation in the field of painting was that he managed systematically to elevate contemporary historical events to the status of great painting.[43] In fact the painters who portray the life and actions of Napoleon are the same ones who depict or who used to depict classical subjects – the most obvious example being of course David. Napoleon made the same request as regards painting as he had in the case of Trajan's column. His fascination for Rome, its power and its strategies of display in art made him choose it as his model: Napoleon as a living Roman emperor had to use the same process; he had to have his 'historical' actions depicted. So there was a transposition from Roman antiquity to Napoleonic modernity. But instead of the so-called 'Roman historical reliefs', Napoleon's preference – he had no real choice, for in French culture the art of painting was always ranked first – was for 'history painting'. And in some paintings and even within the choice of the topics, one can detect Roman influence: there are for instance

41 For example, no. 590 in the Salon of 1814, a painting by Le Barbier the elder: instead of giving a title, the guide says: *Sujet tiré de la sixième églogue de Virgile*. Napoleon's interest in Virgil is clearly reflected in the subject of a painting by Nicolas-Antoine Taunay exhibited at the salon of 1810 (no. 757): *Hommage à Virgile. L'Empereur, à Pétiole, près Mantoue, se fait présenter le dessein de la colonne qu'il veut faire ériger sur l'emplacement de la maison où Virgile est né.*

42 See Heim (1989) which should be compared with Heim and Huet (forthcoming).

43 On this topic see now Prendergast (1997) which appeared too late to be fully taken account of here.

a number of paintings representing Napoleon in the act of *adlocutio*, addressing his men. Other examples depict Napoleon's triumphal entrance into vanquished cities where he can display his *clementia*, acknowledging his enemies and recognising his soldiers' bravery by distributing to them gifts or medals (such as the *légion d'honneur*), or his reception of foreign embassadors, and other such scenes. In fact, the viewer may rapidly form the impression that a careful inspection of a painting's composition, the attitudes, the gestures represented within it, would often reveal, for instance, a modern transposition of a scene from Trajan's column or the panels of Marcus Aurelius.

I shall briefly focus on a few select examples of scenes of Napoleon triumphant and demonstrating his *clementia*. The painting by Antoine-François Callet entitled *L'arrivée du premier consul à Lyon* – exhibited at the Salon of 1804 (no. 77) and known only by its preparatory drawing *(fig. 8)* – clearly presents Bonaparte as a modern triumphator: his chariot is led by Minerva, Bonaparte is crowned by a *Nike* and is encircled by allegories including, as we are told in the *livret*, Secrecy, Strength, Peace and Law; flying above the horses are allegories of Fame. In front of the triumphal chariot sit the personifications of the two rivers of Lyons, the Saône (the lying woman naked on the left) and the Rhône (the frightened old man on the right); a woman walking towards Bonaparte begs for mercy from the triumphant leader with the gesture of her hands and her naked breasts (the presence of two lions on her right means that she is an allegory of the town of Lyons). Such figures reveal the painter's familiarity with the art of ancient Rome; his only 'mistake' seems to be in the representation of the chariot. Of course, this kind of allegorical representation of a great man's victorious entrance into a city is part of a long tradition drawn from Roman models. Nevertheless the imploring allegory of Lyons is very close to the figures of barbarian women imploring Roman emperors. What strikes me is the discrepancy between the short description of the painting on the *livret* and my interpretation of the attitudes and gestures: according to the author of the *livret* the two rivers share in the general admiration while I see their expressions as suggesting feelings of defeat and fear. One can perhaps assume that the painting differed from the preparatory drawing, as some other details in the commentary seem to stress. However, to take another example (among many), it seems one may find a similar discrepancy in the interpretation of gestures: it depends on whether the reader relies primarily on the short commentary offered by the Salon guide or on their own familiarity with the language of gestures in ancient Roman art. The use of gestures in the painting by Charles Meynier, *Entrée de S. M. l'Empereur et Roi dans Berlin* exhibited at the Salon of 1810 (no. 570) and now at the Museum of Versailles *(fig. 9)*, may be considered nicely ambiguous:

according to the text of the guide, the crowd expresses its admiration towards Napoleon; according to the language of Roman historical reliefs, the gestures expressed by the crowd are those of beseeching and acclaiming, while Napoleon's gesture both acknowledges the crowd's acclamation and concedes *clementia*. Two diverse types of *clementia* are displayed in the following examples. The painting by François-Henri Mulard, *S. M. l'Empereur fait présent d'un sabre au chef militaire de la ville d'Alexandrie en Egypte*, presented at the Salon of 1808 (no. 443), and now held at the Museum of Versailles *(fig. 10)*, presents a typical attitude of *clementia*: a standing Napoleon gives to a kneeling 'barbarian' – the military chief of Alexandria as we are told by the guide[44] – a sabre. A more tragic and dramatic moment of *clementia* is displayed in the painting by Guillaume François Colson entitled *Trait de clémence du Général Bonaparte envers une famille arabe lors de l'entrée française à Alexandrie* exhibited at the Salon of 1812 (no. 219), now at the Museum of Versailles: 'barbarian' women, holding an infant, throw themselves at the feet of Napoleon riding his horse, in order to save the man of their family *(fig. 11)*. Napoleon holds up his right hand to call a halt to the execution;[45] here we are not far from the expression of *supplicatio* leading to *clementia*.

In brief, I want to argue that, despite the general judgement that Napoleon did not really intervene in the art of painting but rather in architecture and urbanism, his influence, inspired as he was by Roman antiquity and in particular the Roman Empire, is clearly revealed in his desire to be commemorated in his own actions: a well-known painting such as *Le sacre de Napoléon* by David shows the shocking moment when Napoleon himself crowned Joséphine in front of Pope Pius VII, but its title glosses over this fact in order to show deference to the pope. The 'truth' of the scene offers the viewer the opportunity to identify the characters, but one figure has been added for conventional political reasons: Napoleon's mother. The 'historical' scene has thus been rearranged for the purpose of political 'propaganda'. These 'rearrangements' were also current in Roman historical reliefs: the procession shown on the Ara Pacis, the Altar of Peace constructed under Augustus, provides a good example; Agrippa, Augustus'

44 The entire commentary published in the booklet is as follows: 'Après la prise de cette ville, les principaux habitans se rendirent au quartier général de S. M. qui, voulant honorer la valeur avec laquelle ils avaient défendu leur ville, fait présent d'un sabre à leur chef militaire. Pénétré de la reconnaissance du vainqueur, il le reçoit à genoux, jurant sur sa tête de ne s'en servir que pour la cause des Français.'

45 The livret comments: 'Lors de l'entrée de l'armée d'Orient dans Alexandrie, les habitans firent du haut de leurs maisons un feu très meurtier sur les colonnes. Les soldats indignes escaladèrent la maison de l'un d'eux qui s'étoit fait remarquer par une résistance désespérée; ils l'en arrachèrent et alloient le faire périr, lorsque sa famille éplorée, apercevant l'Empereur, s'élance au-devant de lui, implore sa clémence, et obtient de sa Majesté que la vie lui soit conservée.'

son-in-law, though dead at the time of the procession, is nevertheless portrayed on the relief. Napoleon and his artistic advisers understood the use of Roman imperial images perfectly: their great innovation was to transpose these Roman conventions into the representation of Napoleon's own times.

4 Translating empire? Macaulay's Rome*

Catharine Edwards

Where fur-clad hunters wander
    Amidst the northern ice;
Where through the sand of morning-land
    The camel bears the spice;
Where Atlas flings his shadow
    Far o'er the western foam,
Shall be great fear on all who hear
    The mighty name of Rome!

T. B. Macaulay, 'The prophecy of Capys', lines 281–8,
(from 'Lays of Ancient Rome')

T. B. Macaulay's magnificent evocation of heroic early Roman history in the 'Lays of Ancient Rome', published in 1842, rapidly captured the public imagination and was to remain a very popular work. In the first twelve years 23,000 copies were sold in the United Kingdom alone.[1] The British Library Catalogue lists sixty-three editions published between 1842 and 1939. Many of these were texts intended for schools; only with the Second World War did the Lays retreat from their entrenched position in the curriculum. Macaulay's evocation of ancient Rome appealed strongly, it seems, to the tastes of the British reading public and indeed offered many people their first significant encounter with Roman antiquity.[2]

Each of the four Lays develops a story from early Roman history (mainly taken from Livy and Dionysius of Halicarnassus), presenting it as it might have been told in later years by a popular bard. 'Horatius' tells the story of the defence of Rome against Etruscan incursions in the earliest years of the republic (when Horatius and two others heroically held a bridge until their compatriots could demolish it, then swam to safety). 'The

* Thanks to Norman Vance, Javed Majeed and Peter McDonald for bibliographical suggestions and to the late Dr Robert Robson for helpful advice and for allowing me to see his typescript of Macaulay's journal. I am also endebted to Charles Martindale, Anthony Copley and Fernando Cervantes for perceptive comments on earlier versions.

[1] Edwards (1988) 54–5.

[2] The preface of the 1899 Cambridge edition, for instance, envisages as its readership those 'who have not yet commenced the study of Latin and Roman history' (1899) v.

battle of lake Regillus' recounts a victory of the Romans over the Latins, allegedly with the supernatural aid of Castor and Pollux, generally dated to the early fifth century BCE. 'Virginia' offers an account of a father of plebeian family who, in order to save his daughter from the lustful advances of the patrician Appius Claudius, kills her – an incident which precipitated the end of exclusively patrician rule in Rome (this story, too, is traditionally dated to the early fourth century). 'The prophecy of Capys', set in the time of Romulus, Rome's founder, makes an ancient seer tell of future victories, culminating in that over King Pyrrhus in the early third century BCE.

Macaulay believed these stories to be largely fictitious; his principal interest lay in exploring the contexts in which such legends originally circulated. Each bardic voice is different in tone and located in a different context. Macaulay made clear that the narrative voices of the poems were intended to represent particular types from early Roman society. The Lays are framed and qualified by Macaulay's scholarly general preface and introductions to the individual poems. In the general preface he sets out the theories of the seventeenth-century scholar James Perizonius, more recently revived by B. G. Niebuhr, emphasising the universality of ballad traditions. The prefaces to the individual poems weigh up, with a great deal of erudite commentary, the different versions of the stories to be found in later Roman and Greek writers. He makes clear that the versions he has chosen to present in the Lays are not necessarily the most truthful but the representations of the past one might expect from bards of a particular background in particular political circumstances. Thus Macaulay distances himself by a number of strategies from the vivid language and rousing sentiments of the Lays themselves.

'The prophecy of Capys' is the last of the four Lays and relates events latest in time. The other three, though the perspective from which they are recounted is conditioned by the later periods in which Macaulay locates their narrators, are focussed on early Rome. The chronological shifts of the final Lay are more complex. The Lay, which tells of a prophecy made in Romulus' time, is to be imagined as composed for the celebration of the Roman victory over the Hellenistic King Pyrrhus – the first significant encounter between Roman troops and those of the Greek east. This was seen by later Romans as an important beginning to Rome's imperial expansion. Thus at the time of the victory over Pyrrhus, Rome's empire did not yet include the distant regions listed in the last stanza. The prophet Capys, however, is made to look still further forward in time, well beyond the defeat of Pyrrhus, to a period when Rome's empire will have encompassed vast and diverse regions extending to the margins of the known world. This is the only example in the Lays of an anticipation of events which were to take place *after* the occasion on which the Lay is presented as having been composed.[3]

This device in significant respects echoes the prophecy made in Virgil *Aeneid* 6 by Anchises to his son Aeneas in the underworld. Any reader familiar with this text (regularly set in schools and universities) would have recognised the close parallel particularly between stanza xxi of Macaulay's poem and Anchises' proclamation: *tu regere imperio populos, Romane memento* | *(hae tibi erunt artes), pacique imponere morem* | *parcere subiectis et debellare superbos* – 'Remember, Roman, these will be your arts, to rule, to make peace customary, to spare the conquered and cast down the proud' (*Aen*.6.851–3). Macaulay's seer is made to proclaim:

Thine, Roman, is the pilum:
Roman, the sword is thine,
The even trench, the bristling mound,
The legion's ordered line;
And thine the wheels of triumph,
Which with their laurelled train
Move slowly up the shouting streets
To Jove's eternal fane . . .

Macaulay himself draws attention to the parallel in his preface to the Lay (we are to imagine Virgil's version as inspired by the tradition of which this allegedly 'earlier' example formed a part). In both texts imperial rule is Rome's destiny and Rome's talent for conquest is contrasted with other nations' artistic achievements, though Macaulay's formulation is significantly more belligerent – no mention here of 'sparing the conquered' or the arts of government. Only later would Rome (like Britain, perhaps?) develop a more civilised form of imperialism.

A number of commentators have emphasised the different ways in which the political views of the Lays' narrators are at variance with those Macaulay himself expresses in his other writings relating to English history or contemporary politics. Macaulay's description of the narrator of 'Horatius' presents a character whose political views, as a plebeian pining after 'good old times which had never really existed' (in Macaulay's words), might be thought quite antithetical to those expressed elsewhere by Macaulay himself.[4] The endorsement of political violence at the end of 'Virginia' seems at odds with Macaulay's lifelong concern with pre-empting revolution through reform.[5] Macaulay might well have deplored the triumphalism of 'The prophecy of Capys'. Yet at least some readers will have

[3] For a suggestive discussion of such shifting temporal perspectives as a literary trope particularly associated with the teleology of imperial Rome, see Kennedy above.
[4] Edwards (1988) 63. [5] *Ibid.* 77.

been quick to see parallels between Capys' vision of Rome's future and Britain's own imperial mission.[6] Britain, too, after all, laid claim to territories as vast and diverse as those listed in the poem's closing stanza (quoted at the beginning of this chapter). And the British too, like Anchises' Romans, were at times self-conscious about the inferiority of their own artistic achievements in comparison with those of other nations.[7]

The author of the Lays

Macaulay was a prolific and influential author, not only of the Lays but also of literary criticism and history.[8] In addition to the city of brave Horatius, there were for Macaulay other Romes too: the conquering Rome of the empire (sometime occupier of Britain indeed), the present-day ruins of the ancient capital of that empire (which he visited in 1838) and also the Rome of the Catholic church, head of a successor empire. The rest of this chapter will explore some aspects of these multiple Romes, looking particularly at the sometimes uneasy relationship between them. Finally the connection between Macaulay's various conceptions of Rome and his perspective on Britain's government of its empire, in particular, India, will be briefly considered. For Macaulay himself was a prominent MP and, later, colonial administrator, being intimately involved in the East India Company administration, most famously in debates about education policy in India under British rule.

Macaulay's responses to Rome, which developed at least in part from his extraordinarily wide reading, are not perhaps wholly representative of those of his generation. While his other Romes may not have exercised so great an influence as that of the Lays, in their complexity they reflect something of the ambivalence of early nineteenth-century British attitudes to Rome and in particular the Roman empire.

Macaulay had an exceptional command of ancient languages and was a voracious reader of Greek and Latin. During his years in India (1834–8), especially, he read a staggering quantity of classical literature, regularly spending four or five hours a day on Cicero, Lucretius, Thucydides, Homer and innumerable others. Many authors he read two or three times over

6 For examples of the appropriation of Greek and Roman literature for patriotic purposes in educational institutions (a move which also served to reinforce elite identity), cf. Colley (1992) 167–9, 180–2.

7 An insistent concern, for instance, in debates of the 1830s and 40s about the decoration of the new Palace of Westminster. See Boase (1954).

8 Macaulay's collected essays (mainly from the liberal *Edinburgh Review*) appeared in 1843, while his mammoth *History of England from the Accession of James II* came out between 1848–55 (with postumous additions of 1861). References here are, where possible, to the 1898 edition of the *Complete Works*.

during this period.[9] Reading was a compensation for what Macaulay felt to be a lack of variety in his daily life in India; it was also a consolation, when he was devastated by news of the death of his favourite sister.[10] Indeed one might see his immersion in classical literature as a form of escapism both from grief and also from life in India, which he saw as a kind of exile, necessary to secure the financial future of himself and his remaining siblings.

His particular literary enthusiams are described in some detail in letters to his old friend and fellow classicist T. F. Ellis.[11] From these letters, Macaulay's pattern of preferences emerges. He was a decided Hellenophile, vastly preferring Homer to Virgil – he was moved to tears on country walks by reading the *Iliad* – and rating Thucydides superior to Tacitus, Demosthenes to Cicero.[12] In an article written in 1826 (on the foundation of University College London), he observed: 'the Latin language is principally valuable as an introduction to the Greek',[13] while in an essay on Dryden Macaulay wrote: 'The literature of the Romans was merely a continuation of the literature of the Greeks. The pupils started from the point at which their masters had, in the course of many generations, arrived. They thus almost wholly missed the period of original invention. The only Latin poets whose writings exhibit much vigour of imagination are Lucretius and Catullus.'[14] When Macaulay visited Rome in 1838 he lamented the fact that almost all visible remains were of buildings from the imperial period of Roman history: 'How very little there is among all these ruins which belongs to the most interesting age of Rome.'[15] Macaulay professed himself to prize vigour, imagination and originality in literature, associating these qualities with the Greek rather than with the Roman and, within Latin literature, with works written under the republic rather than those written under the empire. In these respects his tastes were in line with those of many of his contemporaries (though he was by no means a

9 His reading is described in his letters (ed. in 6 vols. by Pinney 1974–81).

10 In a letter to T. F. Ellis 30 December 1835, he writes: 'Literature has saved my life and my reason'. Cf. comments in essay on 'Lord Bacon' of 1837 (1898:VIII 496–647 at 498): 'Time glides on; fortune is inconstant; tempers are soured; bonds which seemed indissoluble are daily sundered by interest, by emulation, or by caprice. But no such cause can affect the silent converse which we hold with the highest of human intellects. That placid intercourse is disturbed by no jealousies or resentments. These are the old friends who are never seen with new faces, who are the same in wealth and in poverty, in glory and in obscurity'.

11 E.g. 15 December 1834, 29 May 1835, 25 August 1835, 30 December 1835.

12 On Macaulay's tastes in general, see Clive (1973) 79, 498; on his classical reading, Williams (1993) esp. 208–11. For his response to Homer, see e.g. letter of 19 August 1851 to Margaret Trevelyan.

13 'Thoughts on the advancement of academical education in England', *Edinburgh Review* 43 (1826) 315–41, at 331.

14 (1898) VII 133.

15 Journal, 17 November 1838 (some parts of the journal are published in Macaulay (1880)).

thoroughgoing admirer of the romantics, acquiring notoriety for his dislike of the poetry of Wordsworth).[16]

The element of Romantic taste which can be seen as informing Macaulay's preference for the Greek over the Roman, for the earlier over the later, may also be traced in his enthusiasm for Celtic ballads – an enthusiasm directly relevant to the composition of the Lays. In the later eighteenth century, a passion for Ossian swept through literary circles throughout Europe. This was the primitive Highland cycle of prose poems newly discovered, indeed, as it turned out, actually composed by James MacPherson. By Macaulay's day, MacPherson's fraud was generally acknowledged as such (Macaulay, when he discusses the ballad tradition in his prefaces to the Lays, makes no explicit reference to Ossian) but it had nevertheless played a significant part in forming tastes. Sir Walter Scott's painstaking collection of Highland ballads and indeed his immensely popular compositions in the same vein need to be seen in the context of the cult of Ossian. Macaulay explicitly praises Scott for preserving fragments of the songs of the border minstrels both in his preface to the Lays and in his *History*.[17] Owen Dudley Edwards has suggested Macaulay himself was also directly influenced by the oral traditions of the Highlands (his father's family came from the Western Isles of Scotland).[18]

Owen Dudley Edwards describes Macaulay as setting out 'to continue in English the work of the Celtic bards'.[19] Nevertheless when Macaulay undertook the attempt to write 'primitive' verse in the ballad tradition, he chose not ancient Scotland but ancient Rome for its setting. This might seem a strange choice. Rome was often seen as the enemy of the Celts; the figure of Calgacus in the Roman writer Tacitus' *Agricola* was frequently taken as an emblem of brave Celtic resistance to Rome.[20] Fingal, one of the heroes of the *Ossian* cycle, was also celebrated for holding off Roman encroachments.[21] Eighteenth-century constitutional history had come to stress the contrast between the Roman tradition (particularly as exemplified in modern France) and the Germanic tradition. Montesquieu, for instance, writing in 1748, saw represented in Tacitus' *Germania* (a treatise on the barbarian tribes of Germany) the source of the English idea of political government – 'This beautiful system was first invented in the woods.'[22] For those who admired the northern barbarians, in the words of Weinbrot, 'their primitive vigour defeats decadent Rome and provides the true model for modern British political freedom'. Macaulay himself, as will

[16] Cf. Turner (1989). [17] *History*, ch. 13 'State of the Highlands' (1898) IV.
[18] Edwards (1988) 71–4. [19] *Ibid.* 74. [20] Cf. Weinbrot (1993b) at 180.
[21] Cf. Weinbrot (1993a) at 532 – though this important book is somewhat partial in downplaying the classical elements. [22] *L'Esprit des lois* quoted by Weinbrot (1993b) 179.

be discussed below, regularly proclaimed his attachment to specifically British political traditions. We might well expect a corresponding distaste for Roman ones. Indeed in the opening pages of his *History of England*, Macaulay stressed that Britain, unlike, for instance, France, was unmarked by Roman occupation (a passage to be returned to).

Yet late eighteenth- and early nineteenth-century perceptions of Romans and barbarians were not as clear cut as all this might imply. MacPherson himself, in his historical writing, drew a sharp distinction between 'Sarmatians' (a category including Angles, Saxons, Teutons, Goths and Vandals) – the violent barbarians who had destroyed the Roman empire – on the one hand and the Celts on the other, stressing an ethnic connection between the Celts and the Romans. The Romans, for MacPherson, were an 'illustrious nation' who 'derived their blood from the Celtae' as well as other sources, although they were responsible for breaking the spirit of the Celts and leaving them vulnerable to conquest by the Sarmatian tribes, such as the Anglo-Saxons.[23] In MacPherson's account, the relationship between Celts and Romans is profoundly ambivalent. As H. D. Weinbrot puts it: 'To the degree that Rome was Celtic, Celts share Roman achievements and civilisation, while, as Roman victims, avoiding blame for Roman depredations.'[24]

Macaulay's Lays reveal a similar ambivalence to ancient Rome (though how far he shared MacPherson's view of the relationship between the Celts and the Romans is not clear). Certainly Macaulay seems, like so many of his contemporaries, to have shared MacPherson's sense of the cultural importance of Celtic bards, and Macaulay assumes that bards must have had an equivalent importance in early Roman society. Here he was also following the theories of Perizonius and Niebuhr, that the stories of early Roman history known to later ages were essentially the creations of bards, which were preserved for a number of centuries through the medium of bardic verse, only much later to be incorporated into written records.

The weight of scholarship paraded by Macaulay in his presentation of the Lays may be seen as functioning particularly to legitimate an attempt to rescue Rome for a particular strand of Romantic sensibility – as well as to distance Macaulay himself from the sentiments expressed in them. In the general preface to the Lays Macaulay stresses the derivative nature of surviving Latin literature: 'The Latin literature which has come down to us . . . consists almost exclusively of works fashioned on Greek models.' What he hoped to recreate was – paradoxically – something more authentically

[23] (1773) 307. Cf. Weinbrot (1993a) 516–25. Admired Roman writers, such as Virgil, were sometimes recuperated by attributing to them Celtic ancestry.

[24] (1993a) 521. On the complexities of eighteenth- and nineteenth-century attitudes to Celts, see too Smiles (1993).

Roman. 'There was an earlier Latin literature, a literature truly Latin, which had, indeed, almost wholly perished long before those whom we are in the habit of regarding as the greatest Latin writers were born. . . .' He went on: 'To transform some portions of early Roman history back into the poetry of which they were made is the object of this work.' Macaulay explicitly cited Sir Walter Scott as a source on which he had drawn in composing the Lays: 'It would obviously have been improper to mimic the manner of any particular age or country. Something has been borrowed, however, from our own ballads, and more from Sir Walter Scott, the great restorer of our ballad poetry.' Homer, however, was, Macaulay noted, a still greater influence. In the Lays, then, 'Homer' meets Sir Walter Scott to recreate the 'authentic' spirit of early Rome.

By no means all readers warmed to Macaulay's Lays. Their status as poetry was disputed by a number of literary critics. A distinguished Victorian Hellenist, R. C. Jebb, in a lecture on Macaulay delivered in Cambridge in 1900, suggested a parallel between Macaulay and Kipling: 'The vast and enduring popularity of the "Lays" does not indeed prove that they are poetry but it proves that they are heart-stirring. Macaulay shows in them the same kind of power which we see in Mr Rudyard Kipling's best poem – as many people deem it – the "Recessional"; that is rhetorical power, kindled into poetry by the kind of emotion which great national events or causes stir in poetically-minded men.'[25] Jebb's hesitation in terming Macaulay's Lays poetry is in line with the reponses of other nineteenth-century critics. Matthew Arnold in an essay 'On translating Homer' of 1860 claimed to hear the 'ring of false metal' in the Lays,[26] while Leslie Stephen, whose views received wide circulation through the *Dictionary of National Biography*, described Macaulay as 'no more a poet . . . than a metaphysician or a scientific thinker. In common phraseology, he is a Philistine.'[27]

Looked down on by more refined critics as rousing verse rather than poetry, the Lays nevertheless were, as was noted above, to become one of the most often read texts in the schools of imperial Britain and indeed educational institutions in the empire.[28] The parallel drawn by Jebb between Kipling and Macaulay is a suggestive one. What was admired in them both as suitable for inspiring the young was their promotion of, in the words of the editor of a late nineteenth-century edition of the Lays intended for schoolchildren: 'the nobler spirit of Roman heroism, – absolute devotion to

25 (1900) 96. 26 (1860/1960) 97–216, at 211.

27 (1899) 362. Cf. *Dictionary of National Biography s.v.* T. B. Macaulay. See Edwards (1988) 55–8.

28 The Lays figure in the syllabus of, for instance, Alexander Duff's Free Church Institution in Calcutta in 1852 (cf. Viswanathan (1990) 54).

the state'.[29] The Rome of Macaulay's Lays (unlike Kipling's Rome) is explicitly not yet imperial – indeed it springs precisely from Macaulay's dissatisfaction with the extant literary remains of imperial Rome. Yet the ease with which Macaulay's work was appropriated as literature suitable for British imperial education may suggest perhaps a surreptitious sympathy for imperial undertakings on the part of the author.

Other Romes

The Lays were probably the best known of all Macaulay's works, as Owen Dudley Edwards comments.[30] Yet they form only a tiny proportion of his vast literary output, most of which was concerned with the politics, literature and history of Britain. G. O. Trevelyan, in his little book *The marginal notes of Lord Macaulay* (London 1907), remarks: 'twelve or fifteen paragraphs [on the Phalaris controversy] and the prefaces to the Lays of ancient Rome are the sole visible fruit of the thousands of hours which he spent over the classical writers during the last thirty years of his life' (p. 38). It is, I think, legitimate to examine Macaulay's life and writings for other less visible fruits of his extended engagement with ancient Rome.

In early nineteenth-century British politics, the word Rome was liable to evoke first and foremost the Catholic church. Despite concern, especially on the part of Tories, that Catholics owed their first allegiance to pope rather than country, intense debate eventually culminated in a bill for Catholic emancipation in 1829. This debate lent particular significance to discussions of seventeenth-century British history.[31] Macaulay's own *History of England* argued against the Tory position which presented the 'glorious revolution' (replacing the Catholic James II with the Protestant William and Mary) as brought about largely by anti-Catholic feeling. A number of his essays, too, explored the historical development of sectarian controversy in Britain with some sympathy for the Catholic protagonists: Queen Mary was praised for her sincere attachment to her faith, Queen Elizabeth criticised for her cynical attitude to religion.[32]

Macaulay's family had strong evangelical links; he himself was certainly Protestant in his faith (though not as fervently so as, for instance, his brother-in-law Charles Trevelyan, who set his heart on the conversion of India to Christianity). However, he was also a strong supporter of the movement for Catholic emancipation.[33] Later, he suffered political martyr-

29 J. H. Flather in Macaulay (1899) v. 30 (1988) 55. 31 Burrow (1981).

32 Edwards (1988) 96–8. Note in particular his essay of 1828 reviewing Hallam's history, (1898) VII 221–326.

33 His concern for religious toleration is revealed particularly in his maiden speech in the House of Commons in 1830 which was against the civil disabilities affecting Jews.

dom – the loss of his parliamentary seat in 1847 – defending Catholics over the issue of the grant to Maynooth College in Ireland.[34] Macaulay seems then, from his political activities as well as from his writings, to have felt a sympathy for Catholicism which went beyond a concern for civil liberties.[35]

Visiting Rome in 1838, Macaulay took a lively interest in the remains of the ancient city (sometimes with particular reference to details of the Lays which he was then in the process of composing).[36] He was, for instance, profoundly stirred by the Colosseum: 'There may be greater delicacy and grace about some Greek remains. Greater stateliness and majesty, – a more imperial air no edifice can have than I find in the Colosseum' (18 November 1838). But what most drew him – the place he hurried to on first arriving in Rome and which he seems to have visited daily during his six-week stay – was St Peter's: 'I never in my life saw, and never I suppose shall see again, anything so astonishingly beautiful. I really could have cried with pleasure', he writes on his first day (15 November). Having visited St Peter's again the day after, he writes: 'I was struck by observing the confessionals for all the nations of Europe, with the inscriptions Lingua Hispanica – Lingua Anglica – Lingua Germanica – &c. – There is something very imperial, very metropolitan in this' (16 November 1838). He attended mass repeatedly and was, he records, moved to tears by the *Stabat mater*.

Macaulay's fascination with Catholicism finds its most extended expression in a review of the English translation of Ranke's history of the popes, published in 1840 (that is to say, after his journey to Italy – though he had read the book before or during his visit).[37] The sympathy towards Catholicism suffusing this piece was later to be used against Macaulay by his political opponents.[38] The Catholic church, for Macaulay, inspires awe at its antiquity and at the hold it exercises over so many people; he notes the great successes of the Counter Reformation in reversing many of the gains of Protestantism, as well as the triumphs of Catholic missionaries in Africa and other non-Christian areas.

Macaulay begins his lengthy essay with a discussion of the Catholic church as heir to the Roman empire: 'The history of that Church joins together the two great ages of human civilisation. No other institution is left standing which carries the mind back to the times when the smoke of sacrifice rose from the Pantheon, and when camelopards and tigers

34 Edwards (1988) 42–5

35 *Ibid.* 33–4. Though he could also be critical of both Catholic theology itself and what he perceived as the cultural impact of Catholicism. Cf. his letter of 7 February 1849 to Sir James Stephen.

36 'Back by the Colosseum then off towards the river – got to the Ponte Rotto – looked about to see how my Horatius agreed with the topography. Pretty well – but his house must be on Mount Palatine – For he could never see Mount Coelius from the spot where he fought.' (Journal, 17 November 1838).

37 (1898) IX 286–334.

38 Edwards (1988) 116.

bounded in the Flavian amphitheatre.'[39] We have seen how he was impressed on visiting St Peter's by the church's imperial sway over the peoples of many nations; the church is here presented as a direct link with the empire of ancient, pagan Rome. The two images he chooses are striking ones. The smoke of sacrifice rises from the Pantheon – in ancient times a pagan temple but in the seventh century converted into a Christian church, one of the very few ancient buildings in Rome to have remained intact, thus symbolising most effectively the power of Roman continuity. The exotic creatures disporting themselves in the Colosseum conjure up not only that structure – which, as we have seen, Macaulay considered the most imposing relic of Roman antiquity – but also perhaps the martyred Christians, allegedly mauled in the same arena by other exotic felines. The Catholic church forms a living link with the ancient Roman empire, once its oppressor, which it then subsumed. Despite Macaulay's declared preference for early Rome, the attraction of glittering, metropolitan, imperial Rome, living on through the Catholic church, is hard to resist.

Roman Britain

The role of Rome, for Macaulay, need not always be played by Rome itself; most of his adult life was devoted to the politics of another imperial city, London. And a later passage in his review of Ranke anticipates a time when, though London may be in ruins, the Catholic church will flourish yet: 'and she may still exist in undiminished vigour when some traveller from New Zealand shall, in the midst of a vast solitude, take his stand on a broken arch of London Bridge to sketch the ruins of St Paul's'.[40] The power of secular Rome has come and gone; thus may the secular power of London ebb away, leaving nothing but picturesque ruins in a desert like that of the Roman Campagna.

This seductive and memorable fantasy is a reworking of a passage which appears in the journal he wrote during his visit to Italy: 'Yet – to indulge in a sort of reflection which I often fall into here, the day may come when London, then dwindled to the dimensions of the parish of St Martin's and supported in its decay by the expenditure of wealthy Patagonians and New Zealanders may have no more important questions to decide [than the wording on the tomb of a baker's wife]' (22 November 1838). Macaulay looks at Rome and thinks of London. The slippery relationship

39 (1898) IX 287.

40 *Ibid.* 288. The dust-cover of the present volume shows an engraving by Gustave Doré, clearly inspired by this passage from Macaulay. Macaulay's famous fantasy may well, as N. Vance suggests (1997, 34) owe something to Comte de Volney's widely read work of 1791, *Les Ruines: ou, méditations sur les revolutions des empires.*

between these two imperial powers in Macaulay's writings repays some consideration.

Britain (or most of it) had once been a province of the Roman Empire. At the start of his *History of England*, however, Macaulay comments on Roman remains in Britain: 'Of the western provinces which obeyed the Caesars, she was the last that was conquered, and the first that was flung away. No magnificent remains of Latin porches and aqueducts are to be found in Britain' (*Complete Works*, vol. I, p. 4). Thus is the cultural independence of Britain established, with a rather striking refusal to acknowledge such substantial Roman remains as, for instance, Hadrian's wall. Instead, in Macaulay's *History*, classical culture comes to Britain to stay during the Renaissance, freely chosen not imposed.

Britain, for Macaulay, need not be awed by the civilisations of antiquity; his attachment to the monuments of British tradition was deep. He wrote, in a review of 1828: 'We have classical associations and great names of our own which we can confidently oppose to the most splendid of ancient times. Senate has not to our ears a sound so venerable as parliament. We respect the Great Charter more than the Laws of Solon. The Capitol and the Forum impress us with less awe than our own Westminster Hall and Westminster Abbey.'[41] Macaulay's *History of England* is shot through with pride in the development of vernacular British political institutions (though we should note that in the passage quoted here Greco-Roman antiquity is the measure against which subsequent civilisations are tested).

But Britain had not always been a civilised place. The Saxon inhabitants of Britain, Macaulay suggests in his *History*, came to civilisation first of all through their participation in the supranational organisation of the Catholic church. Pilgrimage widened their horizons. He writes: 'Travellers, to whom Livy and Sallust were unintelligible, might gain from the Roman aqueducts and temples some faint notion of Roman history. The dome of Agrippa, still glittering with bronze, the mausoleum of Adrian, not yet deprived of its columns and statues, the Flavian amphitheatre, not yet degraded into a quarry, told to the rude English pilgrims some part of the story of that great civilised world which had passed away.'[42]

Indeed – to consider briefly a very different medium – Macaulay's perspective on the uncivilised nature of earlier Britons may well have played a significant part in determining the decorative scheme planned in 1847 for the central corridor of the new Houses of Parliament (he was elected to the Commission responsible for this in 1844).[43] Six subjects were selected for frescos. 'In three Britain appears sunk in ignorance, heathen superstition

[41] (1898) VII 167–220, at 188–9. [42] (1898) I 9–10.

[43] As Smiles has suggested, (1993) 147–8. For a full account of the plans for decorating the new Houses of Parliament, see Boase (1954).

and slavery; in the other three she appears instructing the savage, abolishing barbarous rites and liberating the slave.'[44] The six subjects were: the Phoenicians in Cornwall, a Druidical sacrifice, Anglo-Saxons on sale as slaves in Rome, and then, Captain Cook in Tahiti, English authorities stopping a Suttee sacrifice (in which a widow would be sacrificed on her husband's pyre) in India and, finally, the emancipation of black slaves. The civilising roles played by Britons in the latter three pictures, are played by Romans (and Carthaginians) in the first three. The ambiguities of this scheme of images are well explored by Sam Smiles. We might also note Macaulay's personal interest in at least the last two in the series. Bentinck, the Indian Governor-General who had approved Macaulay's controversial Education Minute (to be discussed below) was also responsible for the decision to impose a ban on the practice of Suttee, while Macaulay's own father, Zachary, had been a prominent figure in the campaign to abolish slavery.

For Macaulay, civilisation was larger than the individual nation. It is, I think, legitimate to see a connection between the profoundly cosmopolitan nature of Macaulay's conception of civilisation – a conception which had important implications for his attitude to the government of India – and his intimate and long-standing familiarity with classical literature (though the universalist views of the utilitarians, too, may well have influenced his thinking).[45] In a letter to his father of September 1819, when he was an undergraduate at Cambridge, Macaulay had written: 'My opinions, good or bad, were learnt not from Hunt or Waithman [contemporary reformist politicians], but from Cicero, from Tacitus, and from Milton. They are the opinions which have produced the greatest men that ever ornamented the world and redeemed human nature from the degradation of ages of superstition and slavery.' Cicero and Tacitus, of course, found slavery at least perfectly acceptable. What is significant, however, is that Macaulay saw classical writers as fundamental to his own political and cultural outlook.

India

After his time as an undergraduate, it was particularly during his years in India that Macaulay immersed himself in the literature of Greece and Rome (it was in India, indeed, that he conceived the project of writing the Lays[46]).

[44] Quoted by *ibid.* 341.

[45] Cf. Majeed (1992) 30, 97. Macaulay was however critical of certain aspects of utilitarianism, cf. his review of 1829, James Mill's *Essay on government* (1898: VII 327–71).

[46] 'The plan occurred to me in the jungle at the foot of the Neilgherry hills; and most of the verses were made during a dreary sojourn in Oootacamund [*sic*] and a disagreeable voyage in the Bay of Bengal', he wrote to his friend Henry Hallam in a letter of October 1842. See Clark (1967).

Macaulay's deep familiarity with classical antiquity can, I think, cast light on his activities as Legal Member of the Supreme Council for India (the governing body of India under the East India Company until 1857, when control of India was directly subsumed by the British Government). Especially relevant here is Macaulay's contribution to the so-called Orientalist-Anglicist debate about education.[47]

First, however, it is worth considering Macaulay's general views on the future of India under British rule. In a speech made to parliament before he went to India, during the debate on the 1833 renewal of the East India Company's Charter (10 July 1833), he dismissed the possibility of representative government in India under current circumstances, but he made clear that, in his opinion, this situation might be temporary, concluding as follows:

> It may be that the public mind of India may expand under our system till it has outgrown that system; that by good government we may educate our subjects into a capacity for better government; that, having become instructed in European institutions, they may, in some future age, demand European institutions . . . such a day . . . whenever it comes . . . will be the proudest day in English history. To have found a great people sunk in the lowest depths of slavery and superstition, to have so ruled them as to have made them desirous and capable of all the privileges of citizens, would indeed be a title to glory all our own.[48]

Thus Macaulay, unlike many of his contemporaries, anticipated with approval the day when Indians would acquire sufficient knowledge of western democratic practices for self-government. Macaulay certainly emphasised the commercial profit to be derived from trading with a more westernised and prosperous India (*Complete Works*, vol. XI, p. 584). Yet the emphasis in his speech is not entirely on profit. There is, for him, something good in itself about the prospect of the people of India adopting western institutions.[49]

The education debate, in which Macaulay became involved on arrival in India, focussed most immediately on the interpretation of a passage in the Act of Parliament of 1813 renewing the East India Company's charter, which set aside a sum of money: 'for the revival and promotion of literature, and the encouragement of the learned natives of India, and for the introduction and promotion of a knowledge of the sciences among the

47 The other main facet of his role when in India was (almost exclusive) responsiblity for the new Indian penal code. Cf. Clive (1973) ch. 14. Other aspects of his continuing involvement in the administration of India are discussed by Majeed below.

48 A speech on the government of India, delivered House of Commons, 10 July 1833 (1898: XI 543–86, quotation from 585–6).

49 Cf. Majeed (1992) ch. 1 on the conservative agenda of some of those who wished to leave Indian institutions unaltered.

inhabitants of the British territories'. So-called 'advanced' learning, that is to say western science and philosophy, was felt by British politicians and administrators to be desirable for Indians, while all parties (at least all British parties) agreed that vernacular languages in India were not sufficient in scope as media for such education. The question was whether ancient Indian languages should be supported as they had been for a number of years (and important works of western literature translated into these languages) or whether the money should rather be spent on instruction in English. The former view was particularly associated with Orientalist scholars, such as the Sanskritist Horace Wilson, while the latter view was espoused particularly (though not exclusively) by Evangelical Christians.[50]

Macaulay himself, as we have seen, devoted thousands of hours to reading the literature of vanished civilisations. In the article of 1826 on UCL in the *Edinburgh Review*, he had expressed unease at the dominance of classics in British education and argued that academic courses should be more varied and practical.[51] In 1854, however, he was chair of the committee which recommended success in classical examinations as a good indication of the fitness of individual Britons to govern India.[52] It may seem curious that someone so devoted to classical European literature should be so hostile to the idea of continued government support for the teaching of Sanskrit and Arabic to Indians.[53] Yet Macaulay, it appears, made no attempt to familiarise himself directly with Sanskrit and Arabic literature. Instead, his Education Minute of February 1835 reveals an ill-informed contempt for Indian (particularly Hindu) culture; he argued against support for the inculcation of, what he termed, 'medical doctrines which would disgrace an English farrier, astronomy which would move laughter in girls at an English boarding school, history abounding with kings thirty feet high and reigns thirty thousand years long, and geography made of seas of treacle and seas of butter'.[54] Such literature, he felt was (particularly perhaps because of its religious authority) incompatible with modern learning.

Rather than sponsoring the ancient languages of India, Macaulay claimed (as did a number of others) that the British authorities should support English teaching. 'Improvement' in India was to be attained by

50 Some Evangelicals were concerned that promotion of the classic texts of Indian literature would inevitably involve the promotion of traditional Indian religions. On this controversy see Cutts (1952–3) and Viswanathan (1990).

51 Clive (1973) 377–8. In his article on UCL, he wrote, 'though we are sensible that great advantages may be derived from the study of the Greek language, we think they may be purchased at too high a price' (1826) 333.

52 Discussed by Majeed later in this volume. See, too, Symonds (1986) 186.

53 Though cf. Majeed below on the contrasting roles attributed to western and to Indian classical literature in the work of Alexander Duff and others.

54 (1862) 111. Cf. comments on 115.

teaching the native 'those foreign languages in which the greatest mass of information [has] been laid up and thus putting all that information within his reach'.[55] To teach the entire population of India English would of course be impractical but Macaulay envisaged the education of a limited class who, in his words: 'may be interpreters between us and the millions whom we govern – a class of persons Indian in blood and colour, but English in tastes, in opinions, in morals and in intellect. To that class we may leave it to reform the vernacular dialects of the country, to enrich those dialects with terms borrowed from the Western nomenclature, and to render them by degrees fit vehicles for conveying knowledge to the great mass of the population.' Macaulay's Minute persuaded Sir William Bentinck, the Governor-General, and the decision was implemented.[56]

Anglicisation left a long and problematic legacy but what I wish to concentrate on here is the nexus of ideas informing Macaulay's contribution to the debate. His vision of a class of Indians with English tastes, opinions, morals and intellect bears a strong resemblance to the class of Romanised provincial inhabitants of the Roman empire described by Cicero and Tacitus.[57] Though the Roman government had not provided free instruction in Latin (except informally through the medium of the Roman army), substantial inducements, not least Roman citizenship, were offered to provincials willing to Romanise. It was through the co-operation of these local elites that the Roman government was able to exercise domination over a large part of the world with a relatively small number of administrators. Charles Trevelyan, another supporter of Anglicisation and Macaulay's brother-in-law, with whom he shared a house for most of his time in India, drew an explicit analogy between the learning of English in India and the learning of Latin in the Roman Empire. Indian youths, he commented, 'educated in the same way, interested in the same objects, engaged in the same pursuits with ourselves . . . become more English than Hindus, just as the Roman provincials became more Romans than Gauls or Italians. . . . The Indians will, I hope, soon stand in the same position towards us in which we once stood towards the Romans.'[58] This analogy was plainly also propagated within educational institutions in India. An essay by an Indian student at Hooghly College observes: 'The English are to us what the Romans were to the English; and as the English are the children of modern

[55] *Ibid.* 111–12.

[56] For the debate about the extent to which Macaulay himself was responsible for this education policy see Clive (1987) 421. For an account of the wide range of criticisms made of the policy, see Viswanathan (1990) 114–17, 142–65.

[57] For instance in Cicero's *Pro Balbo* and Tacitus' *Agricola.*

[58] Trevelyan (1838) 190–6. This vision of assimilation was, especially in the aftermath of the 1857 Mutiny, largely displaced by an emphasis on the intrinsic differences between British and Indians. Cf. Metcalf (1994) esp.28–65.

times, and command more resources and power than the Romans, we derive the greater advantage.'[59]

Macaulay however resisted making this analogy himself, insisting in discussions of the British presence in India, that there were no earlier parallels.[60] For him, the analogy with militaristic, exploitative Rome was perhaps too uncomfortable to articulate directly.[61] The closest analogy he offered was that of classical learning in the English Renaissance. English, he observed, would seem no more difficult to young Indians than Latin and Greek to schoolboys in Renaissance England (*Minutes on education*, p. 115). 'What Greek and Latin were to the contemporaries of More and Ascham, our tongue is to the people of India' (p. 111). Latin here models for English but only once it has been removed to the safer context of Renaissance humanism, where it no longer symbolises the political dominance of an outside power.

Trevelyan, as John Clive observes, regarded the allegedly forthcoming collapse of Indian religion in the face of British instruction as a triumph of Christianity over idolatry. Macaulay, however, saw this process as rather the triumph of civilisation over barbarism.[62] Macaulay (perhaps in deference to the views of his father) had supported the Evangelical clauses in the 1833 Act renewing the East India Company's charter, thereby widening the scope for missionaries (who had only been permitted to operate within the Company's domain since 1813). Yet religion played remarkably little part in Macaulay's plans for the enlightenment of India as articulated in his Education Minute.[63] In the end Macaulay's notion of civilised values may be said to owe most to his humanist education.

Macaulay's cultural paradigm was in some ways exceedingly narrow, even compared with the views of some among his contemporaries such as Horace Wilson who had devoted many years to familiarising themselves with the classical literature of India. He saw little value in learning about eastern cultures; the best Indians could hope for, in his view, was to become experts in the superior culture of the west. But his notion of 'progress', though tied to an inflexible cultural paradigm, was not tied to a particular national context. The science and learning of Britain (and other western countries) had absorbed and then overtaken the achievements of Greece and Rome. 'The literature of England is now more valuable than the literature of classical antiquity', as he observed in his Education Minute.[64] His

59 Essay by Nobinchunder Dass included under Appendix N, Hooghly College essays, *Great Britain Parliamentary Papers* (1852–3) 32:594–5.
60 'The government of India', (1898) XI 559.
61 The militarism and exploitation of the Roman Empire was often held up as a negative model. Cf. Weinbrot (1993b) 176–84. 62 Clive (1973) 412.
63 Cf. Viswanathan (1990) 144–5. 64 (1862) 111.

advocacy of Anglicisation implicitly suggested that, in a similar manner, Indian science and learning might one day overtake that of Britain. Macaulay's vision of London in ruins, too, might be read as implying an acceptance that individual civilisations come and go, that the sun might indeed set on the British empire, that inhabitants of Britain's sometime colonies and dominions might one day outdo the achievements of the British, just as the Britons and Gauls had gone beyond the achievements of their sometime Roman masters (though Macaulay imagines the future visitor to ruined London as a New Zealander rather than an Indian).[65]

Rome in Macaulay's writings is a slippery and multivalent term. There was much about ancient Rome and about Latin literature that he disapproved of, in part at least, under the influence of Romantic literary fashion. Yet, while professing a preference for the primitive Rome of his own imagination, he nevertheless seems to have felt a strong attraction for imperial Rome too – an attraction that was most clearly articulated in his response to the Catholic church. The surreptitious presence of Rome in Macaulay's approach to empire did nothing to enlarge his sympathy for Indian culture, yet it did perhaps help Macaulay to envisage for the short term an Indian administration in which Indians would play a major part, and in the long term, a world in which cultural and political predominance might have shifted from Britain to Britain's sometime imperial possessions.

65 On Macaulay's cyclical view of civilisation see Clive (1973) 78–9 and Burrow (1981) 41–3.

5 Comparativism and references to Rome in British imperial attitudes to India

Javed Majeed

This chapter considers the extent and character of references to ancient Rome in British imperialist discussions of India in the late nineteenth and early twentieth centuries. Allusions to ancient Rome can be divided into a number of related areas: the general European classical heritage, Latin paired with Greek as part of the Indo-European family of languages, Roman law and the history of the Roman Empire. The purpose here is to outline the role which these allusions played in the general comparative perspective which characterised British imperial attitudes to India.

Introduction

In his 1911 inaugural address to the Society for the Promotion of Roman Studies, Professor F. Haverfield began by referring to the cynical view that learned societies are of interest to specialists alone. He countered this claim by pointing to the way in which such specialised areas as Roman studies were in fact relevant to 'larger issues'.[1] He outlined the influence of Theodor Mommsen's work in making the study of Roman history an increasingly complex and technical area, for which the 'old looseness of phraseology' was no longer tenable. At the same time, he was careful to balance this with a detailed consideration of how Roman history 'was the most instructive of all histories'.[2] Here he concentrated on the way in which the Roman imperial system 'lights up our own Empire, for example in India, at every turn'. The comparisons and contrasts between the two empires were particularly valuable when considering the processes of assimilation of imperial subjects and their 'denationalisation', the question of the defence of frontiers, and the problems of decline. All these issues, Professor Haverfield argued, 'come very closely home'.[3]

[1] Haverfield (1911) xi–xx. [2] *Ibid.* xviii.

[3] *Ibid.* (1911) xviii–xix. On the question of decline, Haverfield refers in an anecdote to two opposing views in *The Clarion* as to the causes of Roman decline. It is perhaps instructive to place this anecdote in the context of such works by J. M. Robertson and J. A. Froude on the decline of the Roman empire. For a discussion of these works, see Betts (1971) 149–59.

Thus, in the context of showing how the study of Roman history was becoming more technical as a subject in its own right, its existence was at the same time justified on the grounds of its general relevance to the history of the British empire itself, and in particular, to the part of it which related to India. Haverfield's argument here points to a genre of works on the Roman and British empires in the late nineteenth and early twentieth centuries, in which, in the words of one scholar, allusions to Rome had become a 'heuristic reinforcement' in British imperial thought.[4] In general, while focussing on the areas which Haverfield had delineated in his address, these works also indicate how comparisons and contrasts with the ancient Roman empire sometimes clustered around problematic areas of race and identity, in which allusions to Rome are more anxious than reinforcing. This chapter will deal with two instances of this genre of writing, namely C. P. Lucas' *Greater Rome and Greater Britain* (1912) and James Bryce's *The Ancient Roman Empire and the British Empire in India. The Diffusion of Roman and English Law throughout the World* (1914). Like Haverfield, both authors refer in particular to British India in their comparative arguments. Bryce explains that British India is the most useful area for comparison with the Roman empire because the Dominions are not subject territories, but rather 'new Englands' which reproduce the constitutional features of the mother country's government, while the Crown colonies are too scattered and diverse in character to admit of any useful comparisons with Rome. British India, on the other hand, is a single and compact subject territory, governed by the same principles and methods, which encompasses an area more populous than the Roman empire.[5]

The extent to which the comparative perspectives of these books were a part of British imperial thought can also be measured by analysing the style and content of the examinations for the Indian Civil Service from the late 1850s to the early twentieth century. The role which European classical learning played in the syllabus for these examinations is considered here, especially in comparison to what were defined as the Indian classical and vernacular languages. The scheme of marking is one indication of the relative values attached to each subject area in the examination syllabus. The type of questions asked in the papers on history and jurisprudence provide evidence as to whether or not the candidates were encouraged to take comparative perspectives in these subject areas, and if so, the extent to which allusions to ancient Rome played a role in these perspectives. Also of importance are some of the books on the reading lists for the candidates, such as Henry Sumner Maine's *Ancient Law* (1861), in which comparisons

[4] Betts (1971) 158. [5] Bryce (1914) 5.

between Roman law and the laws of other cultures were a significant strand in the overall argument.

The style of British comparative attitudes to India

It is possible to see a comparative perspective built into British attitudes to India from the late eighteenth century onwards, when the British began to establish their hegemony in the subcontinent. Such a perspective was especially evident in the work of Sir William Jones, who arrived in Bengal as a Supreme Court judge in 1783. Jones' scholarly work was not just an important index of the comparativist nature of British attitudes to India in this period; it also played a crucial role in the emergence of such disciplines as historical and comparative linguistics and jurisprudence. The most famous instance of this perspective was his comparison of Sanskrit with Greek and Latin in 1786, which laid the foundations of the study of Indo-European languages as a family.[6] Jones' work on Hindu and Muslim law in the 1790s played an equally significant part in laying the foundations of historical and comparative jurisprudence, but his methodology had already been evident in his earlier *An Essay on the Law of Bailments* (1782). Here comments from and parallels with Roman law and other ancient and modern legal systems were woven into his discussion of English law, for the purposes of comparison and as a means to elucidate English law itself. Furthermore, in the context of expressing his ambition to prepare a Digest of Hindu and Muslim law, Jones described himself as the 'Justinian of India'.[7] To a certain extent, then, Jones' stay in India provided him with both the means and the opportunity to refine and broaden the comparativist perspectives which were implicit in his earlier work. One might go even further and say that in the late eighteenth and early nineteenth centuries British work on India sometimes explicitly considered the nature of comparativism *per se*, and the kind of methodology which was needed to underpin it. In part at least, it might be fruitful to see aspects of James Mill's critique of Jones in the former's *The History of British India* (1817) in this light, that is, in terms of different approaches to the construction of idioms in which cultures could be compared, contrasted and criticised.[8]

The comparative perspective in British attitudes to India from the late eighteenth century onwards was thus evident both in the concern about what it meant to be comparative, as well as in specific comparisons and contrasts in the areas of linguistics, law and history. These comparisons and contrasts were made between historical eras, as well as between cultures in the same era, and sometimes both types of comparisons and contrasts were

[6] Jones (1788) 422–3. [7] Jones (1786) II 699.
[8] This argument is pursued in Majeed (1992).

conducted simultaneously. For example, in the context of explaining the differences between *contemporary* western and Indian society, what were perceived to be features of *contemporary* Hindu law might be used to help explain the development of aspects of *ancient* Roman law. This is sometimes the style of argumentation in Maine's *Ancient Law*.[9] Or the modernity of the European notion of race is highlighted by contrasting the British empire with the *ancient* Roman empire, while at the same time placing cultures in the *contemporary* world on a scale based on race, justifying this by reference to the differences between the 'races' conquered by the British and those conquered by ancient Rome. This is the style of argumentation in Lucas' and Bryce's work.[10] In other words, there is often a confusion between the diachronic and synchronic axes of comparison in these works on the Roman and British empires.[11]

Questions of language

One area in which the comparativist perspective of British attitudes to India was clearly evident is in the area of language, particularly in the analogies drawn between European and Indian classical languages, and their respective relationships with vernacular tongues and cultures. Jones' scholarly work in the late eighteenth century has already been referred to. These relationships and analogies were also at issue in the so-called Orientalist-Anglicist debate which was precipitated by T. B. Macaulay's infamous 1835 Minute on Education.[12] At the centre of Macaulay's Minute, which lay behind the general shift in the government's policy away from higher education in Indian languages, was a comparison between European literatures and Indian literatures to the detriment of the latter. In the wake of H. H. Wilson's attack on this policy, the Scottish missionary Alexander Duff made some 'illustrative remarks' in a paper which dealt with the issues raised by the 1835 Act.[13] These remarks are representative

9 Maine (1861/1968) 20–3 where the distinction between progressive and stationary societies is made on the basis of contemporary Hindu law and ancient Roman law, and 221–6 where a gap in the history of primogeniture in European legal history is filled by an examination of contemporary Hindu law.

10 For some details of Lucas' and Bryce's comments on race, see below, but for a good example of this sort of reasoning, see Bryce (1914) 68–70.

11 On diachronic and synchronic approaches in social theory, see Galtung (1990).

12 For this debate see Wilson (1836) 1–16, Duff (1853) 397–415, G and N. R. Sirkin (1972–3) 257 and Kopf (1969). Aspects of this are also discussed in Edwards' essay earlier in this volume.

13 H. H. Wilson (1786–1860) was the first incumbent of the Boden Chair of Sanskrit at Oxford in 1832, but he was also involved in education in India (see Sirkin (1972–3)). Wilson attacked the new education policy in his article 'Education of the natives of India' (1836). Alexander Duff (1806–78), who arrived in Calcutta in May 1830, was an ardent supporter of the use of English as the medium of higher education in India; see Laird (1972) 180–229 for Duff's work on Indian education.

of the ways in which allusions to the European classical languages were made in the context of such debates over policy. Duff argued that the usual Orientalist defence of the study of Indian classics 'on the grounds of its being analogous to the study of the Greek and Roman classics in Great Britain' is a 'fallacious analogy'. Whereas in Britain the study of Greek and Roman classics is only a part of collegiate education, in Indian Muslim and Hindu colleges, other than Arabic and Sanskrit 'little else has been taught'. Furthermore, he made a connection between religious morality and learning; in the case of the classical texts in Britain, any 'injurious impressions' formed on the mind by the perusal of classical texts were neutralised by the 'higher species' of Christian learning, whereas in India classical texts in Sanskrit and Arabic were not thus neutralised. On the contrary, these classical texts were part of living religions, whereas in Britain both teachers and students know that the 'religion of Saturn and Jupiter is not only false, but a *dead* religion'. [14]

The development of these analogies can also be traced in comments in the Indian Civil Service Commissioners' reports from the 1850s onwards, as well as in those parts of the Parliamentary Papers which dealt with the administration of India. The committee appointed in 1854 to inquire into the examinations of Indian Civil Service (ICS) candidates considered these issues carefully. In many ways, this committee was a crucible for defining the intellectual make-up and cultural identity of the British Indian service elite. The committee was chaired by Macaulay, and its recommendations defined the policy guidelines for the examination, training and selection of ICS candidates.[15] Such was the importance of its deliberations, that the Civil Service Commissioners' reports and various parliamentary papers invoked the spirit of Macaulay's Committee (as it came to be known) whenever any significant shift in policy was discussed.[16] Macaulay's Committee defined its priority as the recruitment for the East India Company's service of young Englishmen who would have 'received the best, the most liberal, the most finished education that [their] native country affords'.[17] In prac-

14 Duff (1853) 412.

15 For a detailed discussion of the education of members of the ICS, see Dewey (1973) 262–85.

16 For example, see *Fourth report of Her Majesty's Civil Service Commissioners, together with appendices. Presented to both Houses of Parliament by command of Her Majesty* (London 1859) xix–xx, xxiii, 228, 240; *Fifth report of Her Majesty's Civil Service Commissioners* (London 1860) 11, 18–9, 21–3, 25, 27; *Thirteenth report of Her Majesty's Civil Service Commissioners* (London 1868) xiv; *Twenty first report of Her Majesty's Civil Service Commissioners* (London 1877) 610; *Thirty-fifth report of Her Majesty's Civil Service Commissioners* (London 1891) 14, 16; *Forty-fifth report of His Majesty's Civil Service Commissioners* (London 1901) lxxvii–lxxix; and 'The selection and training of candidates for the Indian Civil Service' in *Parliamentary Papers* 55 (1876) 14–15, 38–9, 224–5, 306.

17 'Copy of the report, dated November 1854, from the committee who were requested to take into consideration the subject of the examination of candidates for the Civil Service of the East India Company', in *Parliamentary Papers* 40 (1854–5) 8.

tice this meant changing the qualifications of age so as to ensure that 'a considerable number of the civil servants of the Company should be men who have taken the first degree in arts at Oxford or Cambridge'. In accordance with this general aim, the syllabus of the examinations was to be 'confined to those branches of knowledge to which it is desirable that English gentlemen who mean to remain at home should pay some attention'.[18] The Committee argued that in Greek and Latin the examination should be 'not less severe than those examinations by which the highest classical distinctions are awarded at Oxford and Cambridge'.[19] Skill in Greek and Latin versification must have 'a considerable share' in determining the issue of the competition. The fact that great figures such as Fox, Canning, Grenville, Wellesley et al. excelled in this accomplishment, indicated how 'powers of mind . . . properly trained and directed, may do great service to the State'. On the other hand, one had to take into account the sorry state of affairs north of the border, where unfortunately 'the art of metrical composition in the ancient languages is very little cultivated'. Nonetheless, men such as Dugald Stewart, Horner, Jeffrey and Mackintosh, had all proved to be eminent figures, in spite of the fact that none of them were able to 'write a good copy of Latin alcaics or to translate 10 lines of Shakespeare into Greek iambics'.[20]

While Macaulay's Committee believed that the Indian vernaculars should not be subjects for examination, since these might perhaps be better acquired in India itself, a distinction was made between the Indian vernaculars and the 'classical' languages of India. Sanskrit and Arabic 'are by no means without intrinsic value in the eyes both of philologists and of men of taste'. Furthermore, Sanskrit's relationship to the vernaculars of India was analogous to Latin's relationship to French, Italian, Spanish and Portuguese, while Arabic, too, had contributed to the 'vocabularies' of the Indian vernaculars. This view was often echoed in subsequent reports.[21] It was also echoed by a number of Indians such as Saiyyid Ahmad Khan and Shiva Prasad, who were concerned with the development of Indian vernaculars. Furthermore, underlying the later parallel processes of the 'Sanskritisation' of Hindi and the 'Persianisation' of Urdu was the belief that Indian vernaculars were imperfect or corrupt versions of Indian classical languages.[22] Macaulay's Committee also argued that Sanskrit and Arabic were also important for the religion, jurisprudence and science of the high cultures of India, and conveniently, both were also studied at seats of learning in Britain itself. On this basis, the Committee proposed to include Sanskrit and Arabic in the list of subjects which could be taken at

[18] *Ibid.* 8–9. [19] *Ibid.* 10. [20] *Ibid.* 12.

[21] For example, see *Twenty-first report of Her Majesty's Civil Service Commissioners* (London 1877) 626–7. [22] King (1994) 88, 91–2, 174–5 and Shackle and Snell (1990) 23–78.

the examinations. It suggested allocating 375 marks to each, as opposed to 750 each for Latin and Greek.

This comparative map of the relations between the classical and modern European and Indian languages was a recurring feature of imperial attitudes to the Indian linguistic landscape.[23] It could be argued that this comparativist approach was initiated or at least facilitated by the central place of classical studies in the education of the British elite.[24] However, both Duff and Macaulay's Committee argued for the prime importance of English language and literature in education curricula, and in the case of the committee, this had much to do with the definition of cultural identity. This was made clear when the subject of English language and literature was deemed to include not just the works of poets, wits and philosophers but a knowledge of English history and the constitution as well.[25] The Committee suggested allocating to English language and literature 1,500 marks (500 marks each for composition, history and 'General Literature'); so that in terms of the allocation of marks, Greek and Latin came third on the scale with 750 marks each, after mathematics (1,000 marks) and English language and literature (1,500 marks). Sanskrit and Arabic were placed on an equal footing with modern European languages (French, German and Italian), which were also allocated a maximum of 375 marks each.

Thus while much space was devoted to extolling the value of classical learning by Macaulay's Committee, in terms of the marks allocated to classics its position in the syllabus was not completely pre-eminent. This slight anomaly between the Committee's stress on the value of classical learning and its actual place in the syllabus might tells us something about the character of allusions to the classical world generally in British imperial thinking. It is as though references such as those of Macaulay's Committee to the importance of Greek and Latin are needed precisely because classical learning was given third place to English and mathematics in terms of the scale of marks. There also might be the added problem that once an analogy is drawn between Greek and Latin, and Sanskrit and Arabic, this might actually open the way for an equal relationship between the two. As it is, it is possible to see the arrival of Sanskrit texts in Europe from the late eighteenth century onwards as having an unsettling effect on what might be described as 'Eurocentric' views regarding the universality of the Greco-Roman heritage.[26] Such allusions to the value of European classical learning as the Committee made were perhaps part of a ready-made rhetoric which could be called upon in those very contexts in which the place of that

[23] This is evident earlier in the century too. For example, see Gilchrist (1800) iv.
[24] I am indebted to Catharine Edwards for this point.
[25] 'Copy of the report . . .' *Parliamentary Papers* 40 (1854–5) 11. For the genesis of English as an academic subject, and its role in a newly defined sense of cultural identity, see Baldick (1983).
[26] A point forcefully made in Schwab (1984) 11.

learning was not clearly pre-eminent. In a sense, the sometimes uncertain role of classics in the ICS curriculum reflected some of the wider trends in English education at the time. Some historians have seen the development of English education in the nineteenth century as the story of the gradual displacement of classics from its position of total domination in the curriculum of public schools. Even in the early nineteenth century the dominant position of classics was not taken for granted but was subject to debate in such journals as the *Westminster Review* and the *Edinburgh Review*.[27]

There are a number of explicitly sceptical references in the Civil Service Commissioners' reports as to the value and importance of European classical and vernacular languages. Thus, Sir William Molesworth in his letter of 16 October 1858 to the Commissioners, argued that special attention ought to be paid to practical fields such as finance, accounts and engineering, as well as local languages.[28] Similarly a Minute by Lord Northbrook, dated 22 September 1875, strongly resisted the proposal that a knowledge of classical languages be made compulsory. The Viceroy opined that there was no reason 'why a young man who could succeed in the competition without any knowledge of the classical languages might not be perfectly well qualified for service in India'.[29] Even so influential a figure as Henry Sumner Maine questioned the apparently unshakeable belief in the value of classics. In his Minute of 12 November 1875 he wrote, 'though it be a vulgar and ignorant prejudice that Greek and Latin are useless, it is not the less certain that much of their hold on our Universities, Colleges, and schools is a "survival" from the fifteenth century'. He argued that as far as the value of certain subjects in the syllabus went, their inclusion reflected the continuing hold of a medieval curriculum on British universities.[30] More relevant to service in India were disciplines like political economy and jurisprudence, particularly if they covered such areas as the history of land tenure as established by the 'comparative method'.[31]

Maine's reference to the importance of political economy and jurisprudence for service in India is echoed elsewhere in official papers and reports. In particular, the inclusion of the latter subject in the syllabus for probationary candidates,[32] along with Indian languages, testifies to the regard in which they were both held. For example, for the further examination of July

27 Edwards (1994). I am grateful to Catharine Edwards for allowing me to see a copy of her unpublished paper.

28 *First report of Her Majesty's Civil Service Commissioners* (London 1859) viii. For the suggested scale of marks, see x–xi.

29 'The selection and training of candidates for the Indian Civil Service' in *Parliamentary Papers* 55 (1876) 227. 30 *Ibid.* 306.

31 *Ibid.* 307. Maine does not discuss what he means by the 'comparative method'.

32 Probationary candidates were those who succeeded in the open competition. They then had to undergo a series of further examinations during their probationary period, which varied from a year to two years during the period under consideration here.

1860, four subjects were compulsory: Sanskrit or the vernacular languages of India (a maximum of 500 marks and 350 for each of the latter), the history and geography of India (500 marks), general principles of jurisprudence and elements of Hindu and 'Mohammedan' (*sic)* law (1,000 marks), and political economy (500 marks).[33] The syllabus for the further examinations in succeeding years was more or less a variation of this one, but the one constant factor was the stress placed on knowledge of the Indian vernaculars of the district to which a candidate was assigned. Indeed, in contrast to the remarks about the value of classical learning, those about Indian vernaculars were markedly unequivocal. Even Macaulay's Committee, with its classical bias, emphasised that every probationer should acquire elementary knowledge of at least one Indian vernacular before arriving in India.[34] It was the *Thirteenth report of the Civil Service Commissioners* (1868) which first explicitly stressed the importance of Indian vernaculars. The Commissioners noted that since it is not possible for civilians to discharge their duties in India without 'a competent acquaintance with the vernacular tongues, we consider that at the "Final Examinations" no amount of proficiency in other subjects should be accepted as compensating for deficiency in this essential qualification'.[35] In some ways, this statement in the *Thirteenth report* became a reference point for later reports.[36]

At the same time, as already noted, the analogy between European and Indian classical languages opened the possibility of a more equal (though never completely so) relationship between the two. Thus, the *Thirteenth report* argued that the marks for Arabic and Sanskrit should be increased 'in expectation of a probable increase in the amount of proficiency in these branches of knowledge'.[37] Since the examinations were also open to Indian candidates (at least theoretically), the increase would cater for their training in these branches of knowledge.[38] As a result, the marks for Sanskrit and Arabic language and literature were increased from 375 each to 500 each. Modern European languages were allocated 375 marks each, and the

[33] *Fourth report of Her Majesty's Civil Service Commissioners* (London 1859) 241.

[34] 'Copy of the report . . .' *Parliamentary Papers* 40 (1854–5) 13–14.

[35] *Thirteenth report of Her Majesty's Civil Service Commissioners* (London 1868) xvi. See also Civil Service Commissioners (1859), Secretary of State to India to Civil Service Commissioners, 30 September 1858, 232.

[36] *Cf. Twenty-first report of Her Majesty's Civil Service Commissioners* (London 1877) 287 (footnote), and *Fifty-fifth report of His Majesty's Civil Service Commissioners* (London, 1911) 4.

[37] *Thirteenth report of Her Majesty's Civil Service Commissioners* (London 1868) xiv.

[38] *Ibid.* 277. However, the admission of Indians to the ICS was a highly problematic area. For a discussion, see Hogben (1981). The connection between raising the profile of Arabic and Sanskrit in the ICS examinations and the admission of Indians into the service was hinted at in the *Fourth report of the Civil Service Commissioners* (London 1859) xli.

language, literature and history of Greece and Rome 750 each. In fact, the development of the syllabus for the ICS examinations shows a steady raising of the profile of Arabic and Sanskrit *vis-à-vis* Greek and Latin, although a complete symmetry in the allocation of marks was never arrived at. Thus, in 1889 the Director of Examinations argued that, following the recommendation of the Public Services Commission, the marks for Sanskrit and Arabic should be raised again, since 'though these Oriental languages cannot be said to present to the candidates most likely to study them the same difficulties as are encountered by the students of Latin and Greek, they are nevertheless the classical languages of the East, and provide opportunities of mental culture analogous to those afforded by the literatures of Greece and Latin [*sic*]'.[39] However, in this case the marks for Sanskrit and Arabic remained at 500 each (Greek was allocated 600 and Latin 800 respectively), but a note was added to the effect that 'the standard of marking in Sanskrit and Arabic will be determined with reference to a high degree of proficiency, such as may be expected to be reached by a Native of good education'.[40]

The raising of the profile of Sanskrit and Arabic in the remarks of the Commissioners' reports was not reflected in any equal allocation of marks as such. It is also likely that Greek and Latin were viewed very much as a package, but this might also have been the case with other subject combinations, such as Arabic and Persian, or indeed Sanskrit and Arabic.[41] Instead, the syllabus and subdivisions of subjects became more complex. Thus, for the open examination of 1911, 38 subjects were on the syllabus. Of these Sanskrit and Arabic were allocated 800 marks each, while both Greek and Latin were allocated a total of 1100 marks each. However, for the latter these marks were distributed among four divisions of the subject; candidates only had to do two of these, so that in effect it was possible to manipulate the marking system in such a way as to allow Sanskrit and Arabic to have a greater allocation of marks than Greek and Latin.[42]

The equivocal remarks in the Commissioners' reports regarding the place of classical learning in the ICS syllabus, and the increasingly complex ways in which the place of Sanskrit and Arabic on the syllabus was adjusted

39 Director of Examinations, Civil Service Commission, to the Under Secretary of State, India Office, 11 November 1889, in *Thirty-fourth report of Her Majesty's Civil Service Commissioners* (London 1890) 23.

40 'Open Competition for the Civil Service of India June 1889' in *Thirty-fourth report . . .* (London 1890), 3–4.

41 Unfortunately, the Civil Service Commissioners' reports do not provide us with any information about the number of candidates who sat the various subject combinations of the ICS examinations, so we can only speculate on this matter.

42 'Regulations for the Open Competitive Examination for 1911' in *Fifty-fifth report of His Majesty's Civil Service Commissioners* (London 1911) 3–4.

relative to that of Greek and Latin, suggests that European classical learning was not always as clearly dominant in the syllabus as might be expected. In the contexts in which it was considered to be important, there was increasing pressure to give the classical languages of 'the east' their due measure as well. Nevertheless, the study of Greek and Latin did continue to hold a significant position.

Questions of law

To a certain extent, this situation is paralleled by the character of the questions in the ICS examination papers. Candidates were sometimes encouraged by the questions to take comparative perspectives. Roman history and law formed one component (among several others) in such a comparativism. The majority of the comparative questions occurred in the papers on jurisprudence and law. Candidates were invited to draw comparisons and contrasts between Roman, English, Hindu and Muslim law. The comparative mode behind such questions was similar to the general character of comparative arguments in British attitudes to India; that is, it operated diachronically and synchronically. As far as comparisons between Roman and English law were concerned, questions ranged from asking candidates to use examples from English and Roman law to elucidate their answers, [43] to questions directly comparing the two.[44] Sometimes there were questions inviting threefold comparisons; in one paper candidates were asked 'In what respects do the Roman law of Tutela and Curatela, and the English law of Guardian and Ward, coincide with, or differ from, Bentham's theory of a law of Guardianship?'[45] There were also a number of questions comparing Roman with Hindu law. One question of the 1890 examination paper on Hindu law asked candidates to compare the *familia* of Roman law with the joint family of Hindu law, while the paper on Jursiprudence included a question on the history of women's separate property in Roman and Hindu law.[46] These indications of comparativism in the

[43] For example, 'Within what limits may "superior need" or "anterior service" be recognised by law as founding a claim to receive services or advantages from others ? Give examples from Roman and English law.' Papers set at the final examination of candidates selected in 1866 in *Thirteenth report of Her Majesty's Civil Service Commissioners* (London 1868) 466–7.

[44] For example, on points of contrast between the English law of master and servant and the Roman law of guardian and ward. In other papers there were questions asking candidates to compare the respective positions of praetor and English chancellor, and Roman and English law as to the validity and consequences of marriage; see *Twenty-first report of Her Majesty's Civil Service Commissioners* (London 1877) 352.

[45] *Thirteenth report of Her Majesty's Civil Service Commissioners* (London 1868) 466–7.

[46] 'Final examination papers for 1890' in *Thirty-fifth report of Her Majesty's Civil Service Commissioners* (London 1891) 119, 113.

examination papers for the ICS also extended to questions inviting comparisons between Hindu and Muslim law.[47] As with some of the questions discussed above, the comparisons were sometimes threefold, as when candidates were asked about Hindu and Muslim law in relation to local law in British India.[48] The nature of the comparative questions in the papers of jurisprudence and law suggest not just that Roman law functioned as a point of reference (among others), but also that the comparative style of British imperial attitudes often spawned points of reference which by their very nature were mobile, given that the function they served depended on which other points they were related to.

The comparative strand running through such questions on jurisprudence and law in the ICS examinations was reflected in some of the texts which were on the reading list. This was especially the case with Maine's *Ancient Law*. Throughout the book, Roman law is compared and contrasted to what is perceived to be Hindu law, but for a variety of purposes. The overriding purpose is to demonstrate the superiority of Roman law, the study of which illuminates the differences between what Maine calls 'stationary' and 'progressive' societies.[49] The measure of Roman law's superiority is, according to the author, 'the fate of the Hindoo [*sic*] law'.[50] However, contemporary features of Hindu law and Indian society as a whole are used by Maine to fill gaps in the narrative of legal developments in Europe. For example, when considering the question as to why primogeniture became the custom of Europe, Maine resorts to what he describes as a 'valuable hint' from contemporary India.[51] Similarly, the author argues that as far as archaic institutions of joint property ownership are concerned, a study of Roman law does not yield any results. But the 'village community' of contemporary India provides an example of this lost institution of 'primeval society'.[52] Apart from these two important points in the argument, passing references made in a comparative style are scattered throughout *Ancient Law*. For example, the author compares the conception of law in Homeric poems with the conception of deity in Hindu law,[53] and the Roman law of adoption and of wills with Hindu customary law.[54] So, too, family rites surrounding a will or testament in Roman law are compared to the

47 'Contrast Hindu and Mohammedan [*sic.*] law in respect of a wife's power over her property, and power to enter the contracts' in 'Final examination papers for candidates selected in 1874', *Twenty-first report of Her Majesty's Civil Service Commissioners* (London 1877) 352. For some other examples, see examination papers for 1910 in *Fifty fifth report of His Majesty's Civil Service Commissioners* (London 1911) 32–3.

48 'How do the various enactments providing for the application of Hindu and Muhammadan Law in British India deal with the subject of local or family customs at variance with the ordinary rules of Hindu Law and Muhammadan law?' *Fifty fifth report* . . . (London 1911) 33–4.

49 Maine (1861/1986) 23.

50 *Ibid.* 19.

51 *Ibid.* 226.

52 *Ibid.* 251–2. The argument is pursued 253–9.

53 *Ibid.* 3–5.

54 *Ibid.* 6.

performance of those death rites in a Hindu context upon which the right to inherit the deceased's property turns.[55] At one point, there is even the suggestion of a comparison between Hindu law and the law of German tribes.[56] It is in fact scattered references such as these which give the book its flavour, rather than more sustained pieces of comparison. As with the ICS examination questions, one is struck by a comparative habit of mind, in which few subjects can be discussed without reference to another cultural or historical point of reference. The aim appears to be elucidation by means of comparison and contrast, but sometimes it is only the invocation of such a method, rather than any substantial rendering of it, which is more important. In such invocations, allusions to Roman law certainly had their place. In the case of Maine's treatise, Roman law had a central place and allusions to other laws were made to help it keep that place. However, there are one or two hints in the text of the author trying to break out of the comparative net of allusions he has woven around the development of Roman law, as when he questions the validity of the distinction between civilisation and barbaric tribes in Tacitus' *Germany*, [57] or when he interprets the Cyclops in the *Odyssey* in terms of the 'almost physical loathing which a primitive community feels for men of widely differing manners from its own'.[58] Although these hints remain undeveloped, they are suggestive of the shifting nature of the comparative framework, and of the ways in which the central place of Roman law in Maine's argument might be moved to a marginal position from the perspective of other points of reference.

Questions of race

This shifting character of the comparative framework is also reflected in the role of 'race' in British imperial ideologies. In the comparative framework of British perspectives on India, the map of Indo-European 'races' formed a counterpart to the Indo-European family of languages. Maine's observations on Roman and Hindu law are sometimes underpinned by references to this racial map.[59] The notion of the Indo-European races is also evident in some of the questions asked of candidates sitting the jurisprudence examination papers in the ICS competition. These questions referred explicitly to Maine's work.[60]

55 *Ibid.* 185–6. 56 *Ibid.* 221. 57 *Ibid.* 116–7. 58 *Ibid.* 121.

59 *Ibid.* 145, 260.

60 For example, 'Define a Family, a Sept, a Gens, a Tribe, and a Manor, as described by Maine, giving historical instances of each, from one or the other of the Indo-European races' and 'Point out the resemblances between different forms of legal remedies existing from the earliest times in different Indo-European nations, and state the special reasons which led Sir Henry Maine to refer them to a common original.' Both questions appeared in the final examinations of 1889; see *Thirty-fourth report of Her Majesty's Civil Service Commissioners* (London 1890) 111–12.

However, it was in Lucas' and Bryce's work that the theme of race was a recurrent one. The comparisons and contrasts between the British and the Roman empires tended to cluster around the issues raised by the question of race. Both authors depicted the eventual extension of Roman citizenship to all imperial subjects as a process of 'assimilation' and 'fusion' of different groups, both Roman and non-Roman. Lucas put the position crisply when he stated that in the Roman empire 'there was a perpetual opening out of citizenship. The tendency was all towards fusion and uniformity, and race imposed few or no barriers.'[61] He regarded Rome's 'great invention in politics' to be 'universal citizenship developed out of the citizenship of one'.[62] Both Lucas and Bryce further argued that in the Roman context religion also imposed no barriers to this process of assimilation.[63] This state of affairs was the 'natural result of polytheism', which only the arrival of monotheistic faiths with exclusive claims to revelation transformed.[64] In some ways, this process of assimilation was reflected in the development of Roman law itself, which effected a fusion between the various laws of the provinces and the law of Rome. As Bryce argued, it was in the development of a law applicable to both Italians and provincials that the Romans of the empire became 'almost a nation'.[65]

In contrast to this, and with equally broad strokes, both authors emphasized how in India a similar process of assimilation was not possible. In the case of Rome by the end of the fourth century CE the conquering and conquered groups tended to become 'substantially one in religion, one in patriotism, one in its type of intellectual life and of material civilization'. In British India such a 'fusion' of the conquering and conquered 'seems to be forbidden by climate and by the disparity of character and of civilization, as well as by the antagonism of colour and religion'.[66] However, this problem of race was not just confined to India; it was a global issue. The relation between the European races and the more 'backward races of a different colour' was an issue 'full of significance for the future', especially given the 'indisposition', as well as 'impracticability of fusion'. This is in contrast to Rome, where the fusion of the conquerers and conquered led to the creation of one type of Greco-Roman civilisation for all.[67] As might be expected, this contrast between the Roman empire and British India was reflected in the divergent courses which their laws had taken. While the work of codification which the British had done in India far surpassed anything Justinian did, English law itself had not been substantially altered in India: 'Had Rome not acquired her Empire, her law would never have

[61] Lucas (1912) 100. [62] *Ibid.* 95. [63] Bryce (1914) 64; Lucas (1912) 78.
[64] Bryce (1914) 50, 64–5. [65] *Ibid.* 123–4; see also 83–91.
[66] *Ibid.* 68–9. The question of colour is dealt with in some depth; see 59–62. See also Lucas (1912) 129–30 on the importance of paying regard to appearances in the context of race.
[67] Bryce (1914) 74.

grown to be what it was in Justinian's time. Had Englishmen never set foot in India, their law would have been, so far as we can tell, exactly what it is today.'[68]

What needs to be stressed here are the anxieties linked to the discussion of race in both Bryce's and Lucas' work. These anxieties can, in part at least, be related to the ideology of British rule in India, which was underpinned by what David Washbrook has called a 'sociology of multiple ethnicity'.[69] Central to official British perceptions of Indian society was the view that the racially heterogeneous society of India meant that only British rule could provide the subcontinent with a unified framework. It was also this heterogeneity which denied Indians the right to nationality, as well as the institutions of liberal democracy. With the development of Indian political activity in the late nineteenth century, and especially with the foundation of the Indian National Congress in 1885, this official British view of India solidified.[70] Some elements of this perspective are also to be found in Bryce's work. Thus while he argues that the fusion of the conquerers and conquered was not possible in India, he also claims that any fusion of the conquered 'races' into one people seemed also unlikely, because of their own racial, linguistic and religious differences.[71] Bryce also worries about the possible unifying effect of the British presence in India, for example, through the building of railways. He felt that there was some evidence that this would lead to the union of Indians 'into a body animated by one national sentiment', which might pose political dangers for the colonial state.[72] However, 'everyone admits in his heart that it is impossible to ignore the differences which make one group of races unfit for the institutions which have given energy and contentment to another more favourably placed'.[73]

Thus Bryce's insistence on the impossibility of 'fusion' in India because of reasons of 'race', as opposed to the success of fusion in the Roman empire, begins to appear politically convenient, rather than simply a matter of historical record. Kenneth Ballhatchet has pointed out in his classic study *Race, sex and class under the Raj* that 'the preservation of social distance [between British and Indians was] essential to the maintenance of structures of power and authority' in British India.[74] Unlike imperial elites elsewhere, the British official class in India never became a creole elite.[75] It was for this reason that Eurasians were regarded by British officialdom with

68 *Ibid.* 126–7. 69 Washbrook (1982) 157.

70 For a discussion of these official perceptions of Indian society and their political impact, see *ibid.* 143–81, and Sheikh (1989) 49–75. 71 Bryce (1914) 69.

72 *Ibid.* 21. See also 77 on the 'new dangers [which] may arise to threaten the permanence of British power' in India, caused by the possible disappearance of caste and religious differences under the impact of European rule. 73 *Ibid.* 32.

74 Ballhatchet (1980) vii. 75 Marshall (1988).

such unease, as they threatened to bridge the gap between the ruling British elite and Indians.[76] In other words, the category of 'race' was used in part to construct the defining differences between coloniser and colonised in British India. The category was also implicated in maintaining the distance between ruler and ruled upon which the preservation of imperial prestige and authority was seen to depend.

Ballhatchet has also shown that 'racial feeling' among the British became more explicit and aggressive in the course of the nineteenth century. He suggests that one reason for this was the establishment of competitive examinations for the ICS in 1855, which opened up the possibility of Indians joining the official elite.[77] Both Bryce and Lucas raise the question of race in the context of competition for posts in India. Bryce argues that before the actual extension of Roman citizenship to all inhabitants of the empire, the large majority of important posts were open to all subjects, as opposed to the case of British India, where the higher posts were reserved for men 'of European stock'. It is this contrast in imperial policies which 'goes down to the foundation of differences between English and Roman rule', differences which can only be explained in terms of race.[78] Similarly, Lucas also worries about the 'system of open competition, as applied to an Empire of multifarious races, like our own'. Such a system 'presents obvious difficulties and needs to be safeguarded'.[79] This is especially because it is difficult to define what British citizenship actually means. This is in contrast to the state of affairs in Greco-Roman times, when citizenship was quite clearly attached to persons and not the locations where they lived.[80]

Lucas' anxieties about British national identity were prefigured in the 1852 Report of the Select Committee of the House of Lords into Indian Affairs. A number of witnesses were asked about the admission of Indians into the Civil Service with reference to the 87th Clause in the 1834 Charter Act. This clause stated that 'no native of the said [Indian] territories, nor any natural-born subject of his Majesty resident therein, shall, by reason only of his religion, place of birth, descent, colour, or any of them, be disabled from holding any place, office, employment under the [East India] company'.[81] But as one witness pointed out this clause conflicted with the principle on which British civil administration in India rested, namely 'native agency, and European supervision and control'. This principle was maintained by the distinction between the covenanted and uncovenanted service. However, as another witness suggested, part of the problem was

[76] Ballhatchet (1980) 4, 96–122. [77] *Ibid.* 6. [78] Bryce (1914) 40–1.

[79] Lucas (1912) 99–100. [80] *Ibid.* 92.

[81] 'Report from the select committee of the House of Lords . . . for the better government of Her Majesty's INDIAN TERRITORIES', Session 1852, *Parliamentary Papers* (1840–52/3) 56–7.

that 'it was not very easy to explain to what extent the term "British subject" now applies'.[82]

The concern with race in the context of comparisons with Rome can therefore also be seen as reflecting problems of national and cultural self-definition. To a certain extent, the discussions of Macaulay's Committee as to how much scope might be given to the European classical heritage as opposed to English language and literature in the ICS syllabus can also be seen in a similar light. In this case, the problem addressed is that of defining the cultural identity of a class of ruling 'gentlemen' in an imperial context, and the fixing of different components of that identity in relation to each other.[83] That in the case of Bryce the concern with such problems might have gone deeper, is evident from the diction of some of his passages concerning the processes of 'fusion' and 'assimilation'. For example, he writes of how Rome passed her 'individuality' to the provinces; in the process of doing so, this 'individuality' was 'diluted' by their influence.[84] This sense of the loss of identity through 'fusion' comes across strongly in another passage, where Bryce observes that the way 'Rome effaced herself in giving her name and laws to the world suggests an inquiry into what may be called the retroactive influence of India upon England'. In the case of the Roman empire, the provinces 'avenged themselves upon their conquerors'. So much so, that in the end Rome 'ceases to have any history of her own, except in architectural history, so completely is she merged in her Empire'.[85] The contrasts with Rome, as far as the concept of race goes, were perhaps motivated not just by problems of cultural and national self-definitions, but also anxieties about the loss of identity itself in empire. In a sense, this oscillation between a rigid and a fluid category of race parallels the style of some works of colonial ethnology, particularly those which sought to classify caste. As Sara Suleri has argued, texts like *The people of India: a series of photographic illustrations with descriptive letter press of the races and tribes of India* (1868–75) attempted to 'interpret cultural systems as both highly rigid and highly fluid at the same time'.[86] This was also true of a work such as Herbert Risley's *The people of India* (1908), in which one stratum of caste unravelled into 'endless subdivisions of both casted and casteless groups, shifting with a dynamism that defied the stable grid upon which the British sought to read the very category of caste'.[87]

[82] *Ibid.* 53. The reference is to the covenants executed by which members engaged to subscribe to pension funds, not to accept gifts etc. Members of the uncovenanted service executed no such covenants; see O'Malley (1965) 83–4. See also *Thirty fourth report of Her Majesty's Civil Service Commissioners* (London 1890), Under Secretary of State, India Office, to the Secretary, Civil Service Commission, 24 July 1889, 11, on the clash between the Civil Service being open to Indians and its 'essentially English . . . character'.

[83] For some comments on the changing notions of a 'gentleman', see Dewey (1993), 215–16.

[84] Bryce (1914) 68. [85] *Ibid.* 70–1. [86] Suleri (1992) 18–19. [87] *Ibid.* 30.

It is worth stressing here that although the apparently ubiquitous concept of race had achieved a pseudo-scientific status by the turn of the century, the concept itself was far from being clear. On the contrary, it seemed to cover a variety of identities and loyalties which were not clearly differentiated from each other. In British India, for example, the term applied to a variety of caste, sectarian, tribal and ethnic identities.[88] The concept of 'race' which emerges from Bryce's and Lucas' work is clearly incoherent.[89] This reflects the generally vague use of the word in the period. Lucas writes of different 'types' of the same race, and admits that the question of the global relationship between races might not be as urgent as the relations between 'different groups of our own race'. Here Lucas refers explicitly to class, in terms which suggest that class identity in some ways competes with racial identity. Indeed, he hopes that in the end the 'race instinct' will prove the 'stronger force among the white citizens of the Empire'.[90] Similarly, Bryce also refers to 'five or six races which we call the European branch of mankind'.[91] This breakdown of the concept of race into other categories of community is suggestive of the fluidity of the category, as well as of its incoherence. While Bryce and Lucas recognise the modernity of the notion of race, both explain the contrasts between Roman and British policies of assimilation using the language of race. This language is seen to be applicable to Roman times, even though at one level the contrast between the British empire and the Roman empire lies in acknowledging the absence of any Roman notion of race. Thus, Lucas describes the 'greatest difficulty' in the British empire as the 'colour question', and he adds that this is a 'modern problem'.[92] At the same time, though, the ease of assimilation in the Roman empire is attributed to the relatively primitive nature of the 'races' of the western province. As Lucas puts it, the 'higher and more civilized races are, the more difficult they are to assimilate, because they are more stereotyped'.[93] Bryce also offers a comparative (although contrary) picture of the conquered 'races' of India and those of Rome. The races overcome and incorporated by Rome were either possessors of an advanced and old civilisation, such as the Greeks, or 'belonged to stocks full of intellectual force, capable of receiving [Rome's] lessons, and of rapidly rising to the level of her culture'. The communities of India, on the other hand, are lagging behind in material civilisation and are 'intellectually backward'.[94]

The tension between a recognition of race as a modern European concept, and its application to Roman times, is thus indicative of how the notion of race which emerges in the comparative framework of British

[88] Washbrook (1982) 157.
[89] For a recent argument by a scientist on this incoherence, see Jones (1993) 245–63.
[90] Lucas (1912) 19,129, 106–8. [91] Bryce (1914) 2. [92] Lucas (1912) 97.
[93] *Ibid.* 128. [94] Bryce (1914) 69–70.

attitudes is sometimes inchoate, and often oscillates between rigidity and fluidity. However, there is a method to Bryce's and Lucas' polemic about 'race' in the British and Roman empires. On one level, Bryce and Lucas are confronting the possibility of the dissolution of boundaries between coloniser and colonised in British India. This possibility, though, is neutralised by displacing it on to the Roman empire, whose uniqueness in terms of its policies of 'assimilation' and 'fusion' is presumed in order to forestall the possibility of any such creolisation of imperial culture in the British empire. In this way, the apparent fluidity of race in the Roman empire actually serves to reinforce the rigid modernity of the European and imperial category of race. On another level, though, the processes of 'assimilation' and 'fusion' in the Roman empire are presented in racial terms already. This serves to legitimise the modern notion of race by reading it back into the Roman empire, although by doing so, the modernity of the notion is thereby undermined.

The discourse of race in the British and Roman empires is thus indicative of the imperial anxieties surrounding the category of race. In general these anxieties related to the ways in which imperial and subordinate cultures needed to be demarcated from each other, and so to insecurities about national and cultural self-definitions. In particular, they also related to the growth of Indian nationalism and its challenge to British rule, and the need to preserve the ICS as a monopoly of European officers. We can conclude here that while on one level allusions to imperial Rome did serve as a 'heuristic reinforcement' in British imperial ideology,[95] on another level, they also served to unravel and confront much that was rigid about categories in imperial ideology.

'Ultra-Roman Britons and ultra-British Romans'[96]

However, lying behind Bryce's and Lucas' ambivalence towards the category of race is an ambivalence towards imperial Rome and classical European culture itself. Catharine Edwards has pointed to two apparently opposed views of the ancient European world. One is Thomas Arnold's, who argued that 'Aristotle and Plato, Thucydides and Cicero . . . are most untruly called ancient writers; they are virtually our own countrymen and contemporaries.'[97] The other is Lord Dufferin's, as reported by Kipling, in which the ancients 'were once people who didn't talk our tongue and who were very strong on sacrifice and ritual, particularly at meals, whose gods were different from ours and who had strict views on the disposal of the

[95] Betts (1971) 158. [96] Kipling (1924) 149.
[97] Edwards (1994) 2, citing Arnold's 1834 essay 'The use of the classics'.

dead. Well, you know, all that is worth knowing if you ever have to govern India.'[98] In this view, the ancients become exotic, and even merge into the exoticism of India, which is presented as a contemporary manifestation of 'all things ancient'.[99] This presentation of India as a form of contemporary ancientness is implict in the texts of Bryce and Lucas, and explicit in Maine's *Ancient Law*, in which ancient Roman institutions are compared to contemporary Indian ones. It also lies behind the confusion of synchronic and diachronic axes of comparison discussed above. In this way, the playing out of sameness and difference with the ancients mirrors relations of sameness and difference between British coloniser and colonised India.

To use current parlance, in the texts discussed above we see a colonial domestication of an exotic 'other'. This 'other' is represented by the merging of imperial Rome with colonised India, which points to a need to subjugate and domesticate the classical Greco-Roman heritage itself. Firstly, the question here becomes how does this 'pagan' but classical past become part of British cultural and historical identity, or to use Bryce's diction, how can it be 'assimilated' into that identity? In a sense, this question parallels Matthew Arnold's own reflections in his *Culture and Anarchy* on 'Hebraism' and 'Hellenism' as components of English identity.[100] Secondly, the European classical past, and imperial Rome in particular, can begin to overshadow the achievements of the British imperial present, in much the same way as the ancientness of India threatens to undermine the 'youthfulness' of British colonialism.[101] Thirdly, the policies of 'assimilation' and 'fusion' in the Roman empire become allied to the assimilative capacities of Indian ancientness.[102] Both need to be forestalled so that British national and cultural identity can be clearly demarcated from the colonised but assimilating India of the present and the past of the classical European world. The threat of assimilation is neutralised by the way in which present day India and ancient Rome merge into each other. This merging acts as a diversionary tactic which apparently leaves British imperial culture itself untouched by the dangers of assimilation. In this way, anxieties about the loss of identity in empire, or of what Bryce called the revenge of the provinces upon their conqueror, are assuaged.

There may be another level of complexity in this ambivalence towards ancient Rome. One of the questions implicit in these comparative maps of sameness and difference is that of identification. In his study of De Quincey, John Barrell has suggested that a simple binary model of self and other

98 Edwards (1994) 8, citing Kipling's *Book of Words*. 99 Suleri (1992) 33.

100 Arnold (1869/1965) 88–226. See also Shaffer (1975) ch. 6. 101 Suleri (1992) 32.

102 The theme of the assimilative capacity of Indian culture is central to Jawaharlal Nehru's *The Discovery of India* (1946), where it becomes the basis for a secular Indian national identity.

might not be adequate for thinking about the uses and dangers of the oriental to the western imagination.[103] He argues for a 'triangulation of ideas and images' which points to 'a continually reinvented third term which acknowledges that whenever two things have been "put together", something else has been pushed aside'.[104] Here there are a set of shifting relationships between a triad of imperial Britain, imperial Rome and colonised India. The British imperial project is linked with an earlier Roman one at the outset, one which is sometimes treated as an ideal, and sometimes as a cautionary tale.[105] In some ways, Britain is heir to an imperial Roman enterprise, but it also wants to distance itself from this earlier enterprise, particularly because of the dangers of assimilation it implies. However, there is a sense in which imperial Rome is also an adversary to be shaken off rather than a guide to be followed, and this lies in the occupation of Britain itself by imperial Rome. In other words, identification with imperial Rome is divided in that Roman Britain becomes too close for comfort to colonised India itself. As imperial Britain is identified with imperial Rome, and imperial Rome merges with colonised India, there is also a threatened identity between colonised Britain and colonised India. The distinction between coloniser and colonised is further muddied by the term 'assimilation', which allows either imperial Rome or colonised India to be understood as the assimilating force; both, it seems, have the fearsome capacity to assimilate British national identity on different levels.

Finally, it is not difficult to see in this ambivalence towards ancient Rome a rehearsal of the drama between the ancients and the moderns. In particular, an enthralment to the ancients conflicts with the narrative of history as progress which Robert Nisbet has argued 'reached its zenith in the Western mind in popular as well as scholarly circles [between 1750 and 1900]'. He asserts that 'from being one of the important ideas in the West it became the dominant idea'.[106] British rule in India was seen by some liberal thinkers, such as John Stuart Mill, as embodying the forces of progress, and so as playing out a narrative of history as progress.[107] Such a narrative would conflict with a view of the ancients as representing the high points in history, in which all that followed would be derivative of that originary excellence or an inferior type of it. The greatness of the British imperial present would begin to look like a mere shadow of the original imperial plenitude of ancient Rome.

It is also possible to see insecurity at the root of the classical revival in British Indian architecture during the first decade of this century. Both

[103] Barrell (1991) 8. [104] *Ibid.* 190, 10. [105] Betts (1971) 152.
[106] Nisbet (1980) 171–2.
[107] See Mill (1861) 164, 386 and Mill (1858). See also Bearce (1961) 282–5 on notions of progress used to justify British rule.

Thomas Metcalfe and Philip Davies have argued that the classical revival, evident in some of the designs in New Delhi, was an attempt to mask a growing insecurity in the assertively magnificent.[108] Thomas Metcalfe further argues that a classical architecture was suitable to the declining British empire in India, because the evocations of Roman glories were reassuring to a European audience.[109] Bryce and Lucas paid some attention to the decline of the Roman Empire, but both evaded the possibility of British decline. On the contrary, Bryce felt that British power in India showed no signs of weakness.[110] Decline, however, was the main theme of the masterpiece of the great Urdu poet, Altāf Husain Hālī's *Mussadas-e Madd o Jazr-e Islām* (The flow and ebb of Islam, 1879) and later of Nehru's *Discovery of India* (1946). British imperial attitudes to the Roman empire, and the issues these attitudes raised need to be placed alongside Indian texts such as the two above, in which indigenous classical notions were fashioned in historical narratives of decline and progress. This would help us to understand how points of reference multiply in a comparative framework, as cultures measuring themselves against each other in a colonial context, deployed overlapping sets of allusions for their own purposes.[111] This mobile quality of comparativism characterised British allusions to Rome in imperial attitudes to India, in which comparison and contrast were used to express and elucidate, as well as to conceal, political and cultural anxieties.

108 Metcalfe (1989)177, 236; Davies (1985) 215–41.

109 Metcalfe (1989) 247.

110 Bryce (1914) 76.

111 For a detailed treatment of Ḥālī's *Musaddas*, see Shackle and Majeed's edition of Ḥālī (1871/1997).

6 Decadence and the subversion of empire

Norman Vance

Did Rome really decline and fall, or was she pushed? There was no real doubt in the matter. Nineteenth-century imperial nations, particularly the French and the British, fascinated and appalled by the Roman example, were driven to cultural and social self-examination because it was hard to blame anyone except the Romans themselves for the eventual collapse of the western empire. The rot clearly spread from the centre: Rome subverted Rome and barbarism triumphed. If the process of imperial decay could be properly understood perhaps it would be possible to stop the same sort of thing happening again, if it was not already too late. Social and political moralists compulsively constructed narratives of Roman decadence, tracing a progressive falling away from earlier moral, physical and cultural excellence which could be seen as both cause and consequence of political misjudgement and failure. The political instability of nineteenth-century France and the sexual and emotional excess frankly celebrated in contemporary French literature perhaps prefigured the ominous shape of things to come in Britain.

But the gamy flavour of decay had its own slightly perverse attraction for connoisseurs of civilised life and art as well as of pheasant. Part of the fun was the annoyance such tastes could cause: unravelling moral fibre and casually flicking grains of incense in the face of insular philistines, particularly when the philistines sounded like Samuel Smith, the MP for Flintshire, who complained to the Commons in 1888 about Zola and obscene publications: 'Were they to wait until the moral fibre of the English race was eaten out, as that of the French was almost? Look what such literature had done for France. It overspread that country like a torrent. . . . France today was rapidly approaching the condition of Rome in the time of the Caesars.'[1]

This kind of obsession with decadence or the fraying of moral fibre coincided and collaborated with the *fin de siècle* concern with physical degeneration. Was Britain, were the British, still fit to rule, physically and mentally as well as morally? British concern about possible physical

[1] Quoted in Keating (1989) 241. The speech was republished as the pamphlet *Pernicious literature* (1889) by the National Vigilance Association.

deterioration and its wider implications, prompted by the experience of rapid urbanisation, had been simmering for some time. Similar anxieties in France had seemingly been justified by failure and defeat in the Franco-Prussian war of 1870 and indeed this prompted Frenchmen such as Baron Pierre de Coubertin to renewed interest in physical recreation which led ultimately to the modern Olympic movement. Public school games were being taken ever more seriously in England, a practical response to Juvenal's rather well-worn advice to pray for a healthy mind in a healthy body (*mens sana in corpore sano*, *Satires* 10.356).[2] Unhealthy minds were being studied more carefully than ever before. Throughout Europe the new science of abnormal psychology, applied variously to criminals (by Lombroso) and to writers and artists (by Max Nordau) intersected with post-Darwinian concerns with human evolution and regression and Galton's statistical studies of heredity to create alarm and despondency about what might be happening to the breed under the changing conditions of modern life.

Edward Gibbon had followed Tacitus in contrasting the puny breed of the Roman race with the fierce giants of the north, but had northern vigour now declined in its turn? Hugh Percy Dunn, a breezy Northumbrian eye-surgeon, tackled the question in the pages of *The Nineteenth Century* in 1894. Like many of his predecessors and contemporaries he was scathingly puritanical on the subject of the demoralising luxury or conspicuous consumption (a new term which had just been coined in America) which was traditionally included among the explanations of Roman moral and imperial decline. It is perhaps epitomised in the silk garments of the Emperor Heliogabalus to which Gibbon took such indignant exception as a symptom of imperial effeminacy.[3] It might not be entirely irrelevant to remember that the Gibbon family money came from wool. But perhaps none of this luxurious looming degeneracy applied to Britain? Dr Dunn briskly reviewed the causes of physical, moral and intellectual decline proposed in 1857 by the Viennese psychologist and degeneration theorist Benedict Morel and comfortably concluded that so far these factors were present only among foreigners. He noted the absence of reliable statistics but felt sure that British decline had not yet set in: as long as the British kept on exercising vigorously and playing games they would be all right.[4]

In the face of such wholesomeness the appeal of sloth, luxury and conspicuous consumption was almost irresistible. The fierce giants of the north were clearly the ancestors of the rugby-playing hearties and the fox-hunting country gentlemen described by Oscar Wilde's character Lord

[2] Discussed in Jordan (1993) 168–73; for French and English athleticism see Vance (1985) 11 and n.; 189–95. [3] Gibbon (1994) ch. 40, II 580. [4] Dunn (1894) 300–14.

Illingworth as the unspeakable in full pursuit of the uneatable.[5] Classically educated aesthetes in revolt against the manly and character-building English regime of the great outdoors and cold baths naturally favoured indoor luxury and the warm baths of Caracalla and of Pompeii. They identified with Greco-Roman civilisation and repudiated the barbarous Goths, ancestors or not, who could be represented as trampling on its ruins.

But the Goths had always had their defenders. Charles Kingsley, often sneered at as a muscular Christian, included not a fox-hunt but an ostrich-hunt in *Hypatia* (1853), his novel of fifth-century Alexandrian Christianity, and brought on a gang of exceedingly muscular and heterosexual Goths as a foil to the effete and luxurious civilisation of the malfunctioning late Roman empire and the ascetic celibate Christianity of the time. The historical Hypatia, a neo-Platonist philosopher, had been brutally murdered by Christian monks. For Kingsley, as for Gibbon before him, the fanatical murderers of Hypatia represented the enemies of civilisation, the wrong kind of religion, but for Kingsley the antidote was not a return to Roman virtue so much as an admixture of German virtue and the manlier non-celibate Christianity which would eventually develop in the Protestant north.[6]

But the story of Hypatia could be read differently. In the 1840s and 1850s the French Parnassian poet Leconte de Lisle, obsessed with metaphorical barbarians at the gates threatening French civilisation, alarmed rather than delighted by crude Gothic vigour, had seen in the doomed philosopher Hypatia and the old pagan tradition of classical civilisation she represented a symbol of the vulnerable beauty and truth to be embraced by the artist at all costs. Hypatia should sleep on in a world given over to ugliness, but she should still sing the melodious hymn of beauty in the heart of the poet.[7] The gendering of civilisation as female and physically vulnerable implicitly rebukes not only Kingsley's aggressive masculinity but the hearty game-playing philistinism associated with later Victorian commercial and imperial successes. Fragile sensitivities and fragile beauty could make the success and practical common sense of burly post-Roman barbarians such as the Prussians and the British seem rather brutal and just a little vulgar. Leconte de Lisle and Oscar Wilde were of one mind in this matter.

A similar point was being made in England even in Kingsley's heyday in the 1850s. Paul Falconer Poole's painting *The Goths in Italy* was exhibited at the Royal Academy in 1851 (it is currently in the Manchester Art Gallery) *(fig. 12)*. In the picture the vigorous invaders have reached a

5 Oscar Wilde, *A Woman of No Importance,* Act I, in Wilde (1966) 437

6 For a much fuller account of *Hypatia* and manly Christianity see Vance (1985), esp.116–20.

7 Leconte de Lisle, 'Hypatie' (1847), 'Hypatie et Cyrille' (1857) in Leconte de Lisle (1858) 3–6, 309–20.

Roman villa but remain outside it: there are classical columns in the background and a classical statue to the right in the foreground, tokens of classical order, but most of the foreground is occupied by dissolute Goths drunkenly lolling around a pool, representing the uncouth termination of classical civilisation.

But the motif of drunkenness and abandon seen against the unforgiving straight-up-and-down rectitude of classical architecture, particularly Roman columns, could be used differently. Roman satirists and historians from Juvenal to Procopius supplied ample evidence that the charge of being drunk and disorderly could apply at least as much to Romans as to Goths. A slightly earlier painting by the French artist, Thomas Couture, *The Romans of the decadence* (1847) *(fig. 13)*, rather indulgently showed Roman liberty degenerated into licence with statues of nobler Romans such as Germanicus and Seneca in the background, stonily disapproving but forever mute.[8] The painting was so popular that it provided the basis of an orgy scene interpolated into an otherwise lifeless production of Gounod's pallidly Ovidian opera *Philemon and Baucis* (1860) by a desperate theatrical management.[9]

Clearly 'Decadence' on the Roman model, peevishly deplored by some, could be perversely celebrated by others, a matter of sin or a matter of style. It overlapped with the contemporary cult of aestheticism or art for art's sake, privileging the cultivated life of the senses and accepting as a corollary a studied indifference to political and social concerns. Perhaps the difference between decadence and aestheticism was largely a matter of discretion: where the aesthete might discreetly avoid or smother with rosewater any whiff of corruption, moral perversity or cruelty underlying the aesthetic sensations he cultivated, the decadent would positively savour the scent as a piquant aspect of the experience.

Corrupt or not, this cultivated life of the senses, stimulated by Roman precedent, could provide the late Victorians with a means of escape from the more public and contested legacy of Rome, involving strong-arm 'Caesarism', militarism, imperialism and the noisy and tiresome controversies associated with the politics of the day. This preference could be spurned as itself effete or 'decadent', dodging the real issues, but for those who cared about such matters the personal, artistic and communal life of the later empire, progressively disclosed and interpreted by a newly rigorous classical archaeology and well represented by surviving artefacts, had its own fascination despite or because of its implication in the loss of political will, the alleged moral and physical degeneration which might have caused the Roman empire to crumble. In his late Victorian poem 'Ars

8 See Boime (1981)131–59, 176–9. 9 Walsh (1981) 115.

Victrix' Austin Dobson summed up the aestheticism which coexisted with the enthusiasm of empire:

> All passes. Art alone
> Enduring stays to us;
> The Bust outlasts the throne;
> The Coin, Tiberius.

The poem was not completely original, any more than the design of Roman busts or coins was completely original: it was adapted from the French of Théophile Gautier, prophet and high priest of the cult of 'art for art's sake' which spread to Britain from France. Gautier's poem was first published in 1857 and later included in his self-consciously artificial collection *Emaux et camées,* 'Cameos and enamels'. In Gautier's original, Dobson's coin is a medallion uncovered by a labourer and the Roman emperor is not named.[10] In Gautier's second-empire France, where monarchy and empire had failed in the recent past, the prospect of art outlasting an unspecified emperor was topical and subversive. In Britain, naturally wary of imperial aspirations when they involved either Napoleon, the novelist George Moore, writing in 1889, could assume a greater degree of public sympathy for his brilliant and decadent hero Mike Fletcher as he fantasises that he has deliberately rejected conventional greatness on the Franco-Roman model: 'there never was any one like me. . . . I could do anything, I might have been Napoleon or Caesar.'[11]

But the nineteenth-century cult of decadence ranged well beyond cultivated political indifference, and well beyond Rome, though Rome was a useful model as always. Nineteenth-century constructions and appropriations of specifically Roman decadence in art and life languidly savour purple moments from every century of the history of the empire in the west, from Augustus or Nero to Heliogabalus or Honorius, leaving it endlessly open to question at what point the rot set in, or when Rome attained that peak or plateau of assured civility and moral and literary excellence from which future decadence, decline and fall could be measured.

For Gibbon the high point had seemed to be the Rome of the Antonines, but what could be more decadent than the conduct of the promiscuous Faustina, consort of the Antonine Emperor Marcus Aurelius? Some of the fascination with Roman decadence had to do with moral deviance, and Algernon Swinburne, the pioneer English decadent, projected on to Faustina his own flamboyantly deviant fascination with sado-masochistic cruelty as an aspect of sexuality. Gibbon is knowing but laconic about

[10] Austin Dobson, 'Ars Victrix' p.205 in *Collected Poems*, 5th edn (London 1902). Gautier's poem was first published in *L'Artiste* in September 1857 and then included as the final poem in the expanded 1858 edition of *Emaux et camées*; see Gautier (1954) 132, 336.

[11] Moore (1972) ch. 8, 199.

Faustina in his text, observing only that 'The grave simplicity of the philosopher [Marcus Aurelius] was ill-calculated to engage her wanton levity, or to fix that unbounded passion for variety, which often discovered personal merit in the meanest of mankind.' The passion for variety and instinct for personal merit are less innocent and laudable than they seem. The Latin of Gibbon's footnote, quoted from the account of Marcus Aurelius in the *Historia augusta*, makes it clear to the *cognoscenti* at least that he is alluding to her reported habit of choosing lovers from common sailors and gladiators. The gilded opulence of the imperial court and the barbaric cruelties of the arena where Faustina might look for future lovers gave Swinburne his opportunity to fantasise, mingling lust and murderous relish with metallic art and heartless beauty:

She loved the games men played with death,
Where death must win;
As though the slain man's blood and breath
Revived Faustine.

The poet addresses Faustine directly:

You seem a thing that hinges hold,
A love-machine
With clockwork joints of supple gold -
No more, Faustine.

To compound the relished, aestheticised horror Swinburne vaguely invokes the nightmare-figure of Medusa, whose head was entwined with snakes. According to the *Historia augusta*, when Faustine was pregnant with twins she dreamt that she gave birth to serpents, and this was all Swinburne needed. He asks:

What adders came to shed their coats?
What coiled obscene
Small serpents with soft stretching throats
Caressed Faustine?[12]

Rome never used to be like that, or so it was claimed. Perhaps the rot set in with the empire itself, a view for which there was some support in antiquity. It was rhetorically essential to insist that there was once a time when stern political virtue was still respected and women, poetry and prose-style were chaste and seemly. In this austere imagined world despotism, moral irregularity and the decadent celebration of art for art's sake had no place. The anti-romantic French critic Désiré Nisard hated the idea of art for art's sake. He has been credited with introducing the phrase into English, in

[12] Gibbon (1994) ch. 4, I 108 and n.; 'Scriptores historiae Augustae *Marcus*' 19; *Commodus* 1; Algernon Swinburne, 'Faustine' stanzas 17, 36, 34, in *Poems and Ballads* (1866) included in Swinburne (1924) I 346–53.

1837, but that was only to warn the English against it.[13] Born in 1806, reared in the shadow of Napoleon's Europe, he played an important part in articulating the moralised cultural history which linked bad emperors, bad books and bad behaviour in a wholly negative version of the concept of 'decadence'. More positive versions of decadence make the same kinds of linkage, but in celebration rather than sorrow and anger.

Nisard's influential studies of the Latin prose of the decadence (*Etudes de moeurs et de critique sur les poètes latins de la décadence*), published in 1834, turn out to be about the poets who followed Lucretius, Virgil and Horace. The high point, on that showing, must have been the last days of the Republic and the earlier part of the Principate of Augustus. His epigraph from Seneca the Elder implies that the best of times was the time of Cicero, before luxury proved the death of genius. For Nisard the conditions essential to the production of great literature were individual liberty, a humanitarian spirit and political independence: in short, life under a democratic republic before emperors were thought of. When Greek liberty yielded to the sway of emperors there were no more writers like Sophocles. The Alexandrian school fostered only a minor, fastidiously self-conscious rhetorical art. When Roman liberty was lost under Augustus the great writers such as Virgil, cradled in the last glorious years of the Roman Republic, were soon succeeded by facile wordsmiths such as Ovid and Lucan who imitated the merely clever, merely erudite writers of decadent Alexandria.[14]

Contemporary parallels were just below the surface. Nisard and his brothers had manned the barricades during the July Revolution of 1830 to uphold republican ideals. Nisard's politics proved more flexible than his conservative literary taste. His early republican convictions were adaptable enough to safeguard his career as a senior civil servant at the Ministry of Public Instruction under the July monarchy and the Second Empire. But he did not mellow in his hostility to French Romanticism, distrusting facile writers and rhetorical fireworks, shrinking from romantic excess. It was not difficult to read his critique of later Roman writing as a coded attack on his contemporaries. His *Manifeste contre la littérature facile* (1833) had already hinted that the verbose Statius curiously resembled Lamartine and that tiresome Lucan was not unlike Victor Hugo. The romantic quarrel with French classicism and the romantic quest for strong and novel sensation were both closely associated with Hugo and both could be seen as morbid symptoms of neo-Roman decadence in French culture. The high point of French classicism, against which French decadence could be measured, was

[13] See Findlay (1973) 246–8.

[14] Seneca *Controversiae* 1, praef.7; Nisard (1834), esp.I 58–61; II 46–52.

the golden age of Louis XIV, of Racine and Boileau, and though Nisard tried to suggest that unlike Rome France had the capacity to rejuvenate itself and so keep decadence at bay this was not totally convincing.[15]

Wilhelm Sigmund Teuffel (b.1820) was a Tübingen professor rather than a careerist man of letters like Nisard, but his version of Roman cultural history was broadly similar. His authoritative and comprehensive *Geschichte der römischen Literatur* (1870), almost immediately a standard text-book in German universities, was promptly translated into English and French and repeatedly revised and expanded. Teuffel gave weight and authority to what was in any case a widely accepted view of Roman literary history already outlined by Nisard: the golden age of Virgil and Horace gave place to a silver age in the first Christian century, the period from Tiberius to Trajan. The second century witnessed a further decline in Latin literature, and matters were worse still from the third to the sixth centuries. Teuffel's narrative of deterioration, like Nisard's, began even before Tiberius, in the later years of Augustus, and had direct connections with the growth of despotism and the consequent extinction of independent intellectual life. The regime because 'wily [or 'insidious' – *tückisch*] and brutal, obtuse and mad'. Under these conditions naturalness and sincerity in literature were ill advised. It was necessary for everyone in the public eye, politicians and writers alike, to act a part in order to escape official censure or worse. The literary consequence was a morbid combination of servility and frenetic ostentation. Teuffel's references cite Quintilian (*c.*35–*c.*100 CE), the great exception to the literary corruption of his age, as a contemporary witness to what was happening. Quintilian had noted that Cicero had made a plea for clarity of language and recommended keeping faith with the idiom of ordinary speech and the common feeling of humanity (*De Oratore* 1.3.12), but now rhetoricians dismissed Cicero as ignorant and uncouth and sought to demonstrate their own genius through wilful obscurity decorated with figures and metaphors imported from the most decadent poets (*corruptissimo . . . poetarum*) (Quintilian, *Instituto Oratoria* 2.5.11; 8. Praef. 25.)

English scholars usually accepted this narrative of literary decline responding to the decline of political freedom. J. L. Strachan-Davidson, the Dean of Balliol, commented succinctly in 1879 that 'Art and literature, which so often flourished even amidst the most turbulent storms of a free commonwealth, withered away under the depressing influence of the cosmopolitan despotism.' This narrative easily assimilated a parallel narrative of moral and personal degradation illustrated by the debauched lives of the emperors: Strachan-Davidson added in a footnote 'A glance at the series of

15 Nisard (1834) II 252–4.

Roman coins from Augustus to Justinian gives a striking view of the process of decadence.'[16] But the moralised narrative of Roman political and literary decadence, historically dubious in any case since so many bad emperors and good books can be found in the politically successful first century, did not entirely harmonise with the tastes of nineteenth-century decadents. Catullus and Horace, poets who flourished before despotism and decadence really took hold, on Teuffel's theory, were remembered for lines and whole poems, distilled passions and moods which appealed to self-consciously effete and languid 'decadents' in the late nineteenth century. Aubrey Beardsley, controversial illustrator of perversely erotic subjects such as Wilde's Salome and Wagner's Isolde, contributed to the famously decadent journal *The Savoy* (November 1896) a sombre stylised illustration of Catullus 101, 'Ave atque Vale', accompanied by his own neat and romantically melancholy translation:

> By ways remote and distant waters sped,
> Brother, to thy sad grave-side am I come,
> That I may give the last gifts to the dead,
> And vainly parley with thine ashes dumb . . .
> Take them, all drenched with a brother's tears,
> And brother, for all time, hail and farewell!

Horace as the poet of transient pleasures assisted the process of transforming Romantic despair into accomplished, conspicuously formal verse in the work of 'decadent' poets such as Ernest Dowson. 'Non sum qualis eram bonae sub regno Cynarae', one of Dowson's titles (Horace *Carmina* 4.1.3–4), is perhaps more Horatian than the rest of the poem. Dowson's poetic personas look back from a degraded and hopeless present to evanescent passion and fulfilment represented by the conventionalised Horatian delights of young love and wine and roses, even though the roses belong to Alma Tadema's painting of Heliogabalus (1888) rather than Horace:

> I have forgot much, Cynara! gone with the wind,
> Flung roses, roses riotously with the throng
> Dancing, to put thy pale, lost lilies out of mind;
> But I was desolate and sick of an old passion,
>   Yea, all the time, because the dance was long -
> I have been faithful to thee, Cynara! in my fashion.[17]

The artistry of Catullus and still more of Horace commended itself as art for art's sake to men of taste, but tastes could be refined and varied. Despite the partly political disapproval of the dons it was possible to like

[16] Teuffel (1873) II 2–5; Strachan-Davidson (1879) 487.

[17] Beardsley's translation of Catullus was reprinted from *The Savoy* in Aubrey Beardsley, *Under the hill and other essays in prose and verse* (1904) and in Duckett (1925) 197–8. For Dowson's Horatian poems see Buckley and Woods (1965) 841–2.

late Latin, not just out of perversity like the Disraelian fop in *Sybil* who rather liked bad wine as a change from good wine. Such Latin often transgressed against the purity of Cicero's Latin so tediously commended by schoolmasters, but its extravagant vocabulary, stylistic virtuosity, wordplay, technical ingenuity and metaphorical audacity could commend themselves on their own terms, embodying a new aesthetic at variance with the rough-hewn virtues of manly simplicity claimed for earlier Roman life and letters.

Théophile Gautier's influential 'Notice' which prefaced the 1868 edition of Charles Baudelaire's *Les Fleurs du mal* had identified and praised 'le style de décadence' very much in these terms and had noted that Baudelaire treasured not the Latin of Virgil and Cicero but the later Latin of Christian writers such as Tertullian and the copious vocabulary of Apuleius, who was to be imaginatively incorporated in translation into Pater's *Marius the Epicurean.* Where Gibbon had sardonically noted the simultaneous advance of Christianity and decline of empire and of Roman civility, Baudelaire saw this as progress rather than simple decay and claimed that the language and what he regarded as the mysticism of the last Latin decadence passing over into the spirituality of Christianity provided an appropriate idiom to articulate the consciousness of modern man.[18]

His Latin poem *Franciscae meae laudes,* included in *Les Fleurs du mal,* ostensibly illustrates this point. The atmosphere is quasi-religious and the rhymed accentual verse certainly defies the exacting conventions of quantitative verse which prevailed in the time of Virgil and Horace. But Baudelaire's model is not so much the Christian verse of the late empire written by St Ambrose or Aurelius Prudentius Clemens in the fourth century as the medieval *Dies irae* written by Thomas of Celano in the thirteenth century. Baudelaire's emphatic triple rhyme responds subjectively and in a minor key to the terrible music of medieval dissolution. Where Baudelaire sings

> Piscina plena virtutis
> Fons aeternae juventutis,
> Labris vocem redde mutis!
>
> (Lovely pool that fills with virtue,
> Of eternal youth the fountain,
> Brings my silent lips to speech!)[19]

Thomas of Celano had intoned

> Rex tremendae maiestatis,
> qui salvandos salvas gratis,
> salve me, fons pietatis!

[18] Gautier (1915) 20–2. [19] French text and translation in Baudelaire (1993) 126–7.

(King of majesty tremendous,
Who dost free salvation send us,
Fount of pity then befriend us!)[20]

The agent of salvation and mystic renewal is not now the divine pity (*fons pietatis*) but human youthfulness (*fons . . . juventutis*).

This medieval rather than late imperial Latinity draws attention once again to the chronological vagueness of nineteenth-century constructions and appropriations of Roman decadence as a matter of style. But decadence may involve a certain vagueness of historical reference as well. Paul Verlaine famously impersonated and popularised Roman decadence in his languid but slightly tongue-in-cheek poem 'Langueur' (1883), beginning 'Je suis l'Empire à la fin de la décadence'. This too evoked the largely ahistorical myth of the empty literariness and political and moral torpor of the late Roman empire threatened by vigorous barbarians at the gates. Verlaine's poem lazily alludes to Latin poetry in the form of acrostics, the acrostics for which Des Esseintes was to praise Commodian in J.-K. Huysman's novel *A Rebours,* the 'Bible of the decadence', much admired by Oscar Wilde. The speaker of the poem also languidly involves one Bathyllus, beloved object of address in a Greek Anacreontic poem, but this hints at a homosexual eroticism that could relate to almost any period of Greek or Roman history.[21] A similar mood of stylish torpor characterises Mallarmé's early prose-poem *Plainte d'automne* (1864), translated by the would-be decadent George Moore in his *Confessions of a Young Man* (1889). The poem associates the speaker's emotional desolation 'Since Maria left me to go to another star', with the 'sad voluptuousness' of the last authors of the Latin decadence untouched by the 'rejuvenating approach of the barbarians'.[22]

This self-consciously effete identification with the alleged languors of dying Rome was more a mood than a movement. French intellectuals of the later nineteenth century often felt they were essentially Latin people, racially identified with the Romans and like them threatened within and without, exhausted and overshadowed by Germanic barbarians. They saw themselves as enfeebled victims of their own hyper-civilisation, leading to nervous prostration and irritability. A fifteen-novel sequence by Joséphin Péladan entitled *La Décadence latine* (1884–1900) was seen as the chronicle of the dying Latin race; the last line of the first novel, *Le vice suprême,* was FINIS LATINORUM, the end of the Latins. Péladan himself wrote in 1891 that he believed in the imminent collapse of Latin civilisation and of France.[23]

[20] Latin text in Raby (1959) 393; trs. W. J. Irons as 'Day of wrath and doom impending', no. 351 in *The English Hymnal* (London 1905).

[21] Paul Verlaine, 'Langueur', included in *Jadis et naguères* (1884) in the section entitled 'A la manière de plusieurs', Verlaine (1969) 314; discussed in Richardson (1971) 189–90.

[22] Moore (1972) 170. [23] Swart (1964) 164; see also Hemmings (1971) 210–16.

This doom-laden perspective was encouraged by the military defeat of the Franco-Prussian war in 1870. But it goes back before it. A novel by the brothers Goncourt, *Charles Demailly* (1868), attributes to a mental patient the malady of the Roman empire as it was indicated by the evidence of progressive physiological degeneration apparent in bronzes of (unspecified) Roman emperors (chapter 58). The novel implies that like the Romans of the later empire modern Frenchmen such as the Goncourts had an enervating anaemia calling for a life-giving transfusion of barbarian blood. Historical or not, French notions of Roman decadence and hyper-refinement struck a sympathetic chord with late Victorian aesthetes seeking deliverance from modern barbarians, the half-educated multitude and the lumpish inelegance and philistinism fostered by Victorian insular complacency – as they saw it.

For George Moore and Oscar Wilde and others the intensified consciousness and brilliant artifice of contemporary French poetry, the artistry and the new frankness of French novelists such as Flaubert and Zola, could expand imaginative horizons and literary possibility just as the intricate elegance and erudition of Hellenistic Greece had expanded the expressive resources of later Latin literature. Both Moore and Wilde were Irish, and Franco-Roman decadence provided them with a means, modest indeed in an era of dynamite outrages and political assassination, of subverting the empire of England.

The rich ambiguity of the Roman model conveniently permitted strategic alignment with Rome as a way of getting back at the mad dogs and Englishmen who sometimes saw themselves as neo-Roman world-rulers as well as the colonists of Ireland. Rome could be seen simultaneously as colonising oppressor and model of colonial administration, intermittently resented imperial power and type of future empires and monarchies. She could also be seen both as the persecutor and as the nurturer of early Christianity, an important but ambiguous model for Christian states. Rome as nurturer, keeping anarchy and darkness at bay, could be used to trump Rome as a persecutor and colonial oppressor. John Henry Newman, adapting a traditional Christian reading of Roman history which can be traced back to Tertullian, Thessalonians and the book of Daniel, had argued that in a prophetic sense Rome had not yet fallen: despite revolution and other disturbance there was still a more or less stable political order in European Christendom which served to postpone the coming of Antichrist and enshrined an essential continuity with the early church which had eventually been recognised and supported by the Roman empire.[24]

[24] Newman (1890) 50–1. See also Tertullian *Apologia* 32 (Migne. *Pathologia cursus, series Latina* 1.447); *De resurrectione* 24 (Migne, *Pathologia cursus, series Latina* 2.829–30); II Thessalonians 2:6–7; Daniel 2:44 and 7:27.

This essentially Catholic notion of benign Roman continuity could be audaciously secularised into a notion of essential aesthetic rather than civic or religious continuity with the Rome of the Caesars, and this was in effect what the originally Catholic Moore and the intermittently almost Catholic Wilde proposed. The point was not so much to identify with the enemies of Roman imperial authority, which would be too overtly political to be decadent, as to identify with imperial Rome as the guardian of an opulent tradition of art and civilised extravagance. This involved dissociating themselves as flamboyantly as possible from the conventional and very Protestant moralising critique of Roman civilisation under the empire. The Reverend F. W. Farrar, author of the juvenile spiritual cliff-hanger *Eric, or Little by Little,* later Dean of Canterbury, had tersely described this civilisation in 1882 as 'heartless cruelty, and unfathomable corruption', which was a promising point of departure.[25]

Moore, the translator of Mallarmé's 'Plainte d'automne', looked to French literary culture and 'decadence' partly as a way of distancing himself from despised but dominant English letters, circumscribed by the informal moral censorship exercised by the circulating libraries which eventually boycotted his novel *Esther Waters* in 1894. The moral atmosphere of Victorian England frankly discouraged the Romantic quest for untrammelled experience which had led John Keats to sigh for a life of sensations rather than thoughts and had given French literature from Victor Hugo onwards its purple hours of quasi-Roman luxury and excess, invoking amidst much else the magnificent beauty, the excitements and the vivid cruelty of the imperial court and the amphitheatre. In extravagant self-parody which seems to look back to the wilful perversities of Swinburne's 'Faustine' Moore makes himself exclaim defiantly: 'Oh, for the silence of marble courts, for the shadow of great pillars, for gold, for reticulated canopies of lilies; to see the great gladiators pass, to hear them cry the famous "Ave Caesar", to hold the thumb down, to see the blood flow, to fill the languid hours with the agonies of poisoned slaves! Oh for excess, for crime!'[26] Wilde carefully trod the path of excess while trying to confine crime to literature, not entirely successfully. When he came back from America in December 1882 he went to have his hair cut – in Paris. It had to be Paris, partly, no doubt, because the extravagant gesture would naturally outrage bourgeois insularity and economic prudence, but chiefly because he wanted it curled in the fashion favoured by the colourfully wicked emperor Nero, on the evidence of the busts of Nero preserved in the Louvre. According to Wilde he looked amazing and society was suitably amazed.[27] There was a Paris fashion for this sort of thing, at least among artistically minded women, which adds a

[25] Farrar (1889) 7. [26] Moore (1972) 125. [27] Wilde (1962) 148.

further dimension to Wilde's flamboyant behaviour: shortly afterwards (in 1892) the Paris-based Max Nordau described women's hair cut in the style of Roman busts in the Louvre, or of ladies in Renaissance paintings, as one of the symptoms of degeneration.[28] As far as he was concerned, Wilde was another symptom, characterised by a 'hysterical longing to make a sensation' and 'a malevolent mania for contradiction'.[29]

Wilde's haircut, and his choice of Nero as model, can be seen as particularly sensation-seeking and contradictory and, more importantly, as a symbolically transgressive act summing up and celebrating the idea of decadence. The church had always hated Nero, and with reason, sometimes associating him with Antichrist or identifying his name numerologically with the number of the beast, 666, in the Book of Revelation. A seventeenth-century Scottish divine described him as 'that monster of cruelty and filthiness' and Dean Farrar described his reign as 'wickedness raised to superhuman exaltation'.[30]

This transgressive sublime was irresistible. Ever since his Oxford days Wilde had been fascinated with Neronian Rome, Nero's 'terrible joy in all things evil and beautiful', and the colourful sins of the other bad Roman emperors and of Renaissance poisoners, as we know from an early notebook which groups them all together. Mischievously he argued that the moralising tendency of most historians distracted attention from the aesthetics of evil: 'Nobody with the true historical sense ever dreams of blaming Nero, or scolding Tiberius, or censuring Caesar Borgia. . . . They have passed into the sphere of art and science.' This aesthetic fascination with elegant and luxurious evil Wilde passed on to his creation Dorian Gray, who fantasised 'that he might really become to the London of his own day what to imperial Neronian Rome the author of the *Satyricon* had once been'.[31]

After his disgrace Wilde referred to his own extravagant heyday as his 'Neronian hours'. In a long letter to Lord Alfred Douglas written from prison in 1897 and known to us in the truncated form as *De profundis* Wilde offers the other side of the same transgressive coin: the wonder and the imaginative appeal of Christ's atonement lies in his shouldering not just past sins but those still to be committed in the years and centuries after the crucifixion, the sins of the emperors Nero and Heliogabalus, of Caesar Borgia and Pope Alexander VI.[32] In giving Wilde a Neronian haircut his Parisian hairdresser had helped him both to assert the primacy of style and to aestheticise the flowers of evil.

[28] Nordau (1896) 7–8. [29] *Ibid.* 319.
[30] Blair (1848) 16; Farrar (1889) 11. For the number of the beast see Revelation 13:18.
[31] Wilde (1989) 12; 'Pen, pencil and poison', Wilde (1966) 1008; *The picture of Dorian Gray*, ch. 11, Wilde (1966) 104. [32] Wilde (1979) 275; *De profundis*, Wilde (1966) 923.

Wilde may also have rather envied Nero, the self-promoting artist, poet, actor and musician, whose greatest triumph was not military or political success but the spectacular perversity of his life as performance. His greatest moment of theatre was when he allegedly played music against the backdrop of burning Rome. He also arranged for a carefully staged form of marriage entered into with a man called Pythagoras. As Tacitus puts it, 'The emperor, in the presence of witnesses, put on the bridal veil. Dowry, marriage bed, wedding torches, all were there. Indeed everything was public which even in a natural union is veiled by night.'[33] Decadence as perverse public spectacle or theatre had obvious appeal for the author of *Salome*.

Wilde the dandy could respond to a certain fastidiousness in Neronian decadence, in so far as it was governed by the judgement of Petronius, the role-model for Dorian Gray specifically invoked in the novel. The Petronius who was consul under Nero and Nero's supreme arbiter of taste (*arbiter elegentiae*) was usually identified with the Petronius Arbiter who wrote the *Satyricon*, a sub-pornographic (though probably satirical) account of Roman manners condemned by the Victorian historian of European morals W. E. H. Lecky as 'one of the most licentious and repulsive works in Roman literature'.[34]

Needless to say, neither Wilde nor Moore had any particular desire to appear either licentious or repulsive, or even to insist they were right. They were prepared to settle for being 'wrong but wromantic', in the language of *1066 and all that*, as long as people noticed. As cultural propagandists, compulsive self-publicists and Romantic rebels against the philistines they selected and annexed a partly French and Roman-inspired model of decadence, derived from historically dubious narratives of complex progressive decay, which was trans-historical and ultimately ahistorical. But it worked, and it still works to shock us out of conventional habits of thought and aesthetic complacency. Nero died exclaiming what an artist was lost. But there was a tradition in the east, alluded to by Tacitus and St Augustine, that in defiance of the normal rules of history, ancient and modern, Nero would come again.[35] In a sense he did, when Oscar Wilde had his hair cut, and he keeps returning in spirit every time the ruthlessly transcendent and subversive claims of art are debated. But do we really want to have him back?

[33] Tacitus *Annals* 15.37, Grant trs. (1989) 362. [34] Lecky (1897) I: 215n.

[35] Tacitus *Histories* 2.8; Augustine *City of God* 20.19.

7 The road to ruin: memory, ghosts, moonlight and weeds

Chloe Chard

Og of Basan

In one of the fictional biographies in William Beckford's *Biographical Memoirs of Extraordinary Painters* (1780), the painter Og of Basan travels down to Italy from northern Europe with his friend Andrew Guelph. (The two artists, in their respective inclinations towards wild 'solitude and gloom' and 'the humbler prospects of the valleys', evoke the established personae of Salvator Rosa and Claude Lorrain.) Their first stop is Venice, but Og leaves that city for Rome before Andrew, and lingers in the 'enchanted region' of Tivoli, embroiled in amorous dalliance with a 'young native'. At first all goes well: 'Many are the nights they passed together, and many the mornings when they ascended the cliffs, and beheld the sun rising behind the towers of Rome.' Then the hapless 'young native' learns the perils of an entanglement with a busy man: 'At length Og recollected, he was born not to spend all his days at Tivoli, and whilst his beloved nymph was sleeping by his side, he arose, and without venturing to cast one look behind, fled like a criminal towards Rome.'[1] When his lover realises what has happened, she throws herself into the river and dies.

In Rome, Og enjoys astounding success, under the patronage of the Cardinal Grossocavallo. Eventually, however, gloomy ideas are excited in his mind by 'the magnificence of the ancient Romans reduced to heaps of mouldering ruins, objects continually before his eyes'. 'The recollection of Tivoli', we are told, 'now stole insensibly into his mind'; after some terrifying dreams, he goes back there and learns of his lover's fate from her brother, who cries 'Avaunt, wretch!', and bitterly reproaches him: 'Og, terrified at the resolute aspect of the young man, and appalled by the lively sense of his wrongs, retired without making any reply, and remounting his horse, which he had led when he ascended the steeps of Tivoli, galloped away with astonishing swiftness, without determining where to direct his route.'[2]

[1] Beckford (1824) 30, 30, 43, 44, 45, 45. Dates given in the text refer to the first published edition of the works cited. [2] *Ibid.* 50, 51, 52, 52, 53, 54.

The painter at last stops near the tomb of Cecilia Metella, by the Via Appia *(fig. 14)*: 'throwing himself from his wearied horse, which he left carelessly to drink at a fountain', he 'sought the interior of the structure'. Disturbed by 'the screeches of noxious birds', he starts up and leaves the ruin 'with terror, as if he had been personally guilty of the murder'. Having spent 'half the night' in 'vain lamentations', he falls asleep only in 'the grey twilight' of dawn, and a distressing dream hovers 'before his fancy':

A fictitious city was stretched out before him, enlightened by a fictitious moon. The shade of her he loved skimmed along a colonnade, which cast its shadows on the plain, and then stood leaning on the lonely pillar, uttered a feeble groan and glided by his side. Her wet garments clinging round her delicate shape, her swollen eyes and drooping hands, announced a melancholy fate. She seemed to say, 'Why do my affections still linger on thee beyond the tomb! – Why doth my pale bosom still cherish its wonted fires! – How comes it that I do not appear riding on a sulphureous cloud, shaking a torch in my hand and screaming out Perjury! – No! my gentle nature forbids me to injure thee. But mark! Quit yonder fatal city; seek the islands of the south, and may'st thou expiate thy crime!' The form next shed some visionary tears, and seemed to mingle with the mists of the morning.[3]

Rome, in this narrative, initially seems to represent a masculine domain of work, worldly success and identification with authority, set in a relation of symmetrical opposition to the feminised domain of passion: Og is well received both by the Cardinal Grossocavallo and by the Pope, and shows his deference towards the masters in his own field by asking for 'permission to study the works of Raphael, dispersed in the apartments of the Vatican'. His lover knows that he is lost to her for ever the moment a peasant informs her that he has seen him 'at the first dawn on the way to Rome'.[4]

The reader might, at this point, expect ancient Rome, too, to be marshalled on the side of authority, order and masculinity, as it is in narratives such as Dr Johnson's account of Caesar firmly clamping down on undisciplined wandering – the same activity that Og engages in when he allows the delights of Tivoli to divert him from the road to Rome, and when he gallops away across the Campagna 'without determining where to direct his route'.[5] Censuring those who engage in 'capricious and casual' migrations, Johnson remarks, in his *Journey to the Western Islands of Scotland* (1775): 'When Caesar was in Gaul, he found the Helvetians preparing to go they knew not whither, and put a stop to their motions. They settled again in their own country, where they were so far from wanting room, that they had accumulated three years provision for their march.'[6]

Ancient Rome, however, within the life of Og, erupts as a force in opposition to the confirmatory paternal approval offered by the Pope and

[3] *Ibid.* 54, 55, 56, 56–7, 57, 57–8. [4] *Ibid.* 48–9, 46. [5] *Ibid.* 54.
[6] Johnson (1993) 198.

Cardinal, and enters into an affiliation with a version of the feminine. The 'young native' of Tivoli, on the periphery of the city, is introduced just after the observation that Og is 'very fortunate in his researches after antiquities', and is herself, Beckford suggests, qualified to play the part of a supplementary antiquity: 'Her form was perfectly Grecian, and the contours of her face exceeded those of the antique Julia.'[7]

When Og is installed in the Vatican, it is the sight of Roman ruins that drives him back to Tivoli, abandoning work, worldly success and identification with masculine authority: the ruins only assume their power over him – and revive the memory of the 'beloved nymph' – once he has finished writing, under the influence of the works of Raphael, 'a treatise upon his art, and a dissertation upon the plurality of worlds'.[8] He then seeks out the Tomb of Cecilia Metella – another site on the periphery of Rome, and one that is regularly presented in travel writings as a place where the antique and the feminine merge.

The antique, the feminine and the personal

Elisions between the antique and the feminine, of the kind established at such sites, supply a useful starting point for an analysis of ghosts and ruins as repositories of memory in travel writings – that is, in writings of any literary or non-literary genre that map out an imaginative topography of a particular region. My concern here is, first, with writings of the late eighteenth and early nineteenth centuries that map out an imaginative topography of Italy and the warm south as a region that bears the traces of the ancients, and, secondly, with later writings that incorporate some of the themes, concepts, assumptions and rhetorical strategies found in these earlier works.

Femininity, when it enters into affiliations with antiquity, within the discourses of travel, assumes at least three distinct roles. Both women and antiquities, in late eighteenth-century travel writing, are assumed to be in various ways resistant to understanding: women are seen as behaving in baffling ways within foreign customs such as cicisbeism, and antiquities are viewed as part of a remote past that can never be entirely recovered.[9] Selecting objects of commentary that bear the imprint of both the feminine

[7] Beckford (1824) 43, 43–4, 44. [8] *Ibid.* 49.

[9] Cicisbeism was the practice by which, in eighteenth- and early nineteenth-century Italy, a married woman was expected to form a relationship with a *cicisbeo*; a male admirer, who escorted her to social events and spent much of his time with her. Both British and French travellers are often teasingly periphrastic in the explanations of this custom that they offer. See Cork and Orrery (1773) 116: 'Upon the whole, we may pronounce equitably this sentence, that if the *Lady* is chaste, she has great virtue; if the *Chichisbee* is chaste, he has greater.' See also Dupaty (1788) I 82–3, for an account of cicisbeism in Genoa which is phrased almost entirely in the form of questions.

and the antique, therefore, supplies a useful strategy for affirming that the topography does in fact offer the mysterious otherness that is expected and demanded of it.

At the same time, however, traces of the feminine, imprinted upon ancient ruins, can also serve to define the specific form of alterity that the traveller confronts as one which, however intriguingly it resists investigation, is nonetheless not utterly beyond the reach of all attempts to understand and assimilate it, and may in fact prove surprisingly accessible to a more artlessly intuitive approach. In Canto IV of Byron's *Childe Harold's Pilgrimage* (1818), the narrator, contemplating the Tomb of Cecilia Metella in a less frenzied state than Og, and explaining at great length how little we know about its inhabitant, eventually feels that his relationship with her has reached a point where he can proclaim, with some satisfaction: 'I know not why – but standing thus by thee | It seems as if I had thine inmate known, | Thou tomb!'[10]

Feminised ruins also supply an especially useful means of transmuting historical time into personal time, a task that travel writing constantly sets itself, from at least the middle of the eighteenth century onwards. By defining an ancient fragment or ruin as the site of a ghostly female presence, the traveller, implicitly invoking an established elision between the personal and the feminine, makes the vestige of antiquity more easily transportable into a private domain of emotional intimacy – as in the lines by Byron just quoted, where a failure in public, historical memory is succeeded by a triumph of intuition. For Og, the process of moving antiquity into personal time is already under way in Tivoli, where he and his lover indulge their shared taste for 'the ruins that lay scattered over her country':

> She would often lead him to meadows of greensward, where she had observed some sculptured marble overgrown with flowers; when the sun had cast his setting gleams on the Sybil's temple, she would hasten to her love and conduct him to a grove of cypresses, and sing under their shades till the moon dimly discovered the waterfalls to her view.[11]

A similar *mise-en-scène* of gentle pastoral eroticism, deploying a woman as a means of shifting ancient history into an intimate, private world, is set up in Charles Dupaty's *Lettres sur l'Italie* (1788), when the traveller and his companions are served their dinner in the Temple of the Sybil at Tivoli, and relish the combination of 'de l'appetit, des mets sains, le sentiment toujours présent du lieu où nous étions'. Their delight is further enhanced not only by the antique architecture and natural scenery around them, but also by 'l'arrivée imprévue d'une charmante Tivolienne', who brings them milk

[10] Byron (1980–92) II 159; stanza 104, lines 1–2. For a useful discussion of Romantic concepts of the feminine, see Ellison (1990) 11.

[11] Beckford (1824) 44.

and strawberries. The travellers align the woman with the ruin by their eagerness to leave their own imprint on both: they first cause the woman to blush, through their smiles and glances, and then proceed to carve their names on the masonry. The final summary of their enjoyment again emphasises the equivalence that the 'Tivolienne' and the antiquity assume, by listing both amid 'tous ces plaisirs réunis' – the pleasures of this 'dîner champêtre', ' which together provide, for Dupaty, 'un des moments les plus doux de ma vie.'[12]

Antique femininity proves disruptive

Dupaty's 'charmante Tivolienne' arouses no disturbing memories. Og's 'beloved nymph', on the other hand, despite her own reference to her 'gentle nature', manages to propel the artist into a wild and reckless course of action: 'Og, awakened by the sun-beams, recollected his dream, and without even taking leave of the Cardinal Grossocavallo, in whose care he had deposited a coffer containing the rewards of his pencil, heedlessly took the road to Naples, resolving to pass into Sicily, and end his days in that island.'[13]

He does in fact die in Sicily, plunging into an abyss, as his betrayed lover has. In an ekphrastic invocation of Salvator Rosa's painting of Empedocles throwing himself into the crater of Etna, Beckford assigns Og the same dramatic death as the philosopher; some local peasants see him 'fall from the cliff, wrapped in a blue flame'.[14]

In other accounts of visits to ruins, too, the alliance between the antique and the feminine shifts antiquity not merely into a domain of the personal, but into a domain of destabilising passion. Germaine de Staël, in her novel *Corinne; ou, l'Italie* (1807), invests the Tomb of Cecilia Metella with a power to disrupt the lives of those who view it – or, at least, a power to reinforce processes of disruption that are already at work. As in Beckford's narrative of Og, the description of one of the characters raises at the outset a possibility that the ancient world might enter into elisions with contemporary life. When Corinne herself, the half-Italian heroine, makes her first appearance, as she is about to be crowned on the Capitol in recognition of her talents as an *improvvisatrice*, her beauty is described as resembling that of ancient sculptures ('sa taille grande, mais un peu forte, à la manière des statues grecques, caractérisoit énergiquement la jeunesse et le bonheur'). The narrator observes, moreover, that 'elle donnoit à la fois l'idée d'une prêtresse d'Apollon, qui s'avançoit vers le temple du Soleil, et d'une

[12] Dupaty (1788) I 255–6, 256, 256, 257. [13] Beckford (1824) 54, 55, 58.
[14] *Ibid.* 86.

femme parfaitement simple dans les rapports habituels de la vie'. Corinne is dressed in the costume of Domenichino's *Sibyl,* and later proclaims further affiliations with one of the Sibyls through her choice of a spot very close to the Temple of the Sibyl at Tivoli for her 'maison de campagne' *(fig. 15)*.[15]

Corinne visits the Tomb of Cecilia Metella in the company of her lover Oswald, Lord Nelvil, a Scotsman on the Grand Tour. For the heroine, the military arms sculpted on the tomb exude emanations of mingled innocence and valour that remind her of Propertius' elegy on Cornelia. This elegy, in turn, prompts her to see a distinction between her own life and that of the two ancient women of the tomb and the poem, and causes her eyes to fill with tears: 'qu'il est digne d'envie,' she muses, 'le sort de la femme qui peut avoir ainsi conservé la plus parfaite unité dans sa destinée, et n'importe au tombeau qu'un souvenir.' Oswald evinces some consternation at this inadvertent confession that Corinne's life will not be marked by the memory of one man alone – that in the past, as she delicately puts it, 'mon imagination a pu me tromper sur l'intérêt qu'on m'inspiroit!'[16]

The allusion to Propertius' elegy, in which a woman speaks from beyond the grave, emphasises the spectral nature of memory: its ability to haul the past into a lurking, shadowy visibility. Earlier in the narrative, a more general reference to ghostly repositories of memory anticipates this resurgence of the past in the deserted Campagna. During her improvisation on the Capitol, the heroine catches sight of Lord Nelvil, in mourning for his father, and speaks of the painfulness of personal memories; she then immediately presents Rome as a city that offers unusual opportunities to spectral beings: 'Ailleurs, les vivans trouvent à peine assez de place pour leurs rapides courses et leurs ardens désirs; ici, les ruines, les déserts, les palais inhabités laissent aux ombres un vaste espace.'[17]

Ghosts

One particular aspect of 'Andrew Guelph and Og of Basan' – the intervention of a ghost in a conflict between passion and work (more specifically, between passion and a devotion to work that is channelled into scholarship) – invites comparison with a much later narrative: the story of Gradiva, as told by Wilhelm Jensen, in *Gradiva: ein pompejanisches Phantasiestück* (1903), and elaborated by Freud, in his essay 'Delusions and

15 De Staël (1979) I 46, 46, 45 (Book 2, ch. 1), 216 (Book 8, ch. 4). For a useful account of Elisabeth Vigée-Lebrun's painting *Madame de Staël as Corinne* (1807), which includes the Temple of the Sibyl in the background, see Sheriff (1996) 239–61.

16 De Staël (1979) I 123, 123 (Book 5, ch. 1).

17 *Ibid.* 57 (Book 2, ch. 3); see also I 115 (Book 4, ch. 6).

dreams in Jensen's *Gradiva*' (1907). In the work that 'Delusions and dreams' analyses, a young archaeologist, Norbert Hanold, 'has surrendered his interest in life' – in particular, his interest in women – 'in exchange for an interest in the remains of classical antiquity'. He is, however, attracted to a bas-relief, which he has discovered, in the past, in a museum of antiquities in Rome; a plaster cast of this work hangs in his study in a German university town. The relief represents a young girl, lifting her flowing dress a little to reveal her sandalled feet, and stepping forward in a manner that he finds especially charming. He calls her 'Gradiva': 'the girl who steps along'. In a dream that fills him with terror, he sees her buried in ashes in Pompeii on the day of the eruption of Vesuvius in 79 CE, and he forms a conviction that this has in fact been her fate. His researches soon present him with a pretext for a journey to Italy. Moving restlessly on from Rome to Naples, he goes to Pompeii partly in order to avoid the swarms of honeymoon couples whom he meets on his travels, and who baffle and annoy him. At 'the "hot and holy" mid-day hour, which the ancients regarded as the hour of ghosts', he sees the Gradiva of the relief; in the series of events that follow, this figure is finally revealed to be not a ghost, as Hanold at first thinks, but a living woman, whom he has known well in the days before 'archaeology took hold of him and left him with an interest only in women of marble and bronze'.[18]

For both Hanold and Og, then, the ancient past merges with a version of the feminine that reinforces the claims of passion rather than work. The texts are nevertheless marked by some very striking differences. Some of these differences can be defined by reference to the distinction between the 'archive' and the archaeological that Jacques Derrida establishes when analysing 'Delusions and dreams' in his *Mal d'archive: une impression freudienne*. The archive, as Derrida defines it, is a concept that derives its meaning from the Greek *archeion*: the building housing the *archontes*, or superior magistrates, and the place where official documents are filed. It therefore provides a place of transition from the private to the public, and a place for gathering signs together, as well as unifying, identifying and classifying them. In an addendum to the book, Derrida defines the archive further, through a series of oppositions:

Ne faut-il pas commencer par distinguer l'archive de ce à quoi on la réduit trop souvent, notamment l'expérience de la *mémoire* et le retour à l'*origine*, mais aussi l'*archaïque* et l'*archéologique*, le souvenir ou la fouille, bref la recherche du temps perdu? Extériorité d'un lieu, mise en œuvre topographique d'une technique de consignation, constitution d'une instance et d'un lieu d'autorité . . . telle serait la condition de l'archive. Celle-ci ne se livre donc jamais au cours d'un acte d'anam-

[18] Freud (1907/1985) 36, 37, 59.

nèse intuitive qui ressusciterait, vivante, innocente ou neutre, l'originarité d'un événement.[19]

These oppositions are reiterated in the discussion of 'Delusions and dreams'. The structure of the archive, Derrida declares, is spectral: 'ni présente ni absente "en chair et en os", ni visible ni invisible, trace renvoyant toujours à un autre dont le regard ne saurait être croisé, pas plus que... celui du père de Hamlet.' The motif of spectrality, in other words, 'met bien en scène cette fission disséminante dont s'affectent dès le principe et le principe archontique, et le concept d'archive, et le concept en général'.[20] In 'Delusions and dreams', for example, Freud presents the truth as spectral and divided when he observes that a grain of truth remains within Norbert's delusion and his haunting by the supposed ghost.[21]

The archive, however, leaves us 'en mal d'archive': that is, drives us to a passionate pursuit of the archive that ends up by attempting to elude the inevitability of its structure of endless displacement: 'Etre *en mal d'*archive... C'est courir après elle là où, même s'il y en a trop, quelque chose en elle s'anarchive. C'est se porter vers elle d'un désir compulsif, répétitif et nostalgique, un désir irrépressible de retour à l'origine, un mal du pays, une nostalgie du retour au lieu le plus archaïque du commencement absolu.'[22]

Hanold, then, suffers from a 'mal d'archive': at the midday hour of ghosts, when Pompeii returns to life, he realises that he has gone there to revive the pressure or impression that Gradiva's foot has left in the ashes: 'Il rêve ce lieu irremplaçable, la cendre même, où l'empreinte singulière, comme une signature, se distingue à peine de l'impression. Et c'est alors la condition de singularité, l'idiome, le secret, le témoignage.' In other

19 Derrida (1995a) 14, 'Prière d'insérer' 2 (not included in Derrida 1995b): 'Should we not begin by distinguishing the archive from that to which it is too often reduced: in particular, the experience of *memory* and the return to the *origin*, but also the *archaic* and the *archaeological*, the memory or the excavation: in short, 'la recherche de temps perdu'? The exteriority of a place, the topographical setting-up of a technique of classification and assemblage, the constitution of an instance and a place of authority . . . these are the necessary conditions for the archive. The archive, therefore, never yields to an act of intuitive anamnesis that would resuscitate – living, innocent or neutral – the originarity of an event' (my trs.).

20 Derrida (1995a) 132; trs. in Derrida (1995b) 54 as: 'neither present nor absent "in the flesh", neither visible nor invisible, a trace always referring back to another whose eyes can never be met, no more than those of Hamlet's father, thanks to the possibility of a visor'; 'the spectral motif stages this disseminating fission from which the archontic principle, and the concept of the archive, and the concept in general suffer, from the principle on'.

21 Derrida (1995a) 136–7, referring to Freud (1907/1985) 103.

22 Derrida (1995a) 142; trs. in Derrida (1995b) 57 as: 'To be *en mal d'archive* . . . is to run after the archive, even if there's too much of it, right where something in it anarchives itself. It is to have a compulsive, repetitive, and nostalgic desire for the archive, an irrepressible desire to return to the origin, a homesickness, a nostalgia for the return to the most archaic place of absolute commencement.'

words, he seeks a unicity that is from the very start haunted by its imminent divisibility: the possibility of a split between the pressure and the impression. Freud too, in his commentary, Derrida suggests, is driven by a 'mal d'archive': he attempts to offer explanations more complete than those of the novelist, and strives to be 'un archiviste plus archéologue que l'archéologue'. In explaining the ghost who appears to Hanold by a logic of repression, 'Freud prétend encore mettre à jour une origine plus originaire que celle du spectre.'[23]

The purpose of this long summary, as far as the distinction between the haunting of Hanold and the haunting of Og is concerned, is to draw attention to two aspects of Beckford's biography, First, this biography resembles 'Delusions and dreams' in that it incorporates a critical commentary on the narrative. This commentary, however, is not explanatory but satirical: the subject of critical reflection, far from pursuing the archive to a point where the displacement of meaning might stop, cheerfully refers the reader back to the established conventions of travel writing, as sufficient explanation for the experiences undergone by the artist-hero. Fusions between the historical and the personal do not serve as starting points for reflections on the human psyche, but simply provide a means of satirising these conventions, by pursuing them to the point of hyperbole where they reveal themselves as ludicrous.

One object of satire in 'Andrew Guelph and Og of Basan' is the principle that in order to revive the ancient past – and so to demonstrate an ability to appropriate it, by transmuting historical time into personal time – the traveller first of all has to kill off that past: to insist on its irretrievable remoteness.[24] (Byron's account of the Tomb of Cecilia Metella, with its long account of our ignorance of the 'inmate', provides one example of a description that applies this principle.) Beckford kills off the 'beloved nymph' with a swiftness which emphasises that there is no time to lose if she is to claim the same power to resurge spectrally from beyond the grave as the long dead Cecilia Metella. The acceleration of personal time, as though in an attempt to catch up with centuries of historical time, becomes most conspicuous when the young woman hears that her lover has left for Rome. As she faints, the reader, discerning some hope in the support of an 'aged pine', finds that events are moving so fast that such support proves

23 Derrida (1995a) 151–2, 150, 149–50; trs. in Derrida (1995b) as: 'He dreams this irreplaceable place, the very ashes, where the singular imprint, like a signature, barely distinguishes itself from the impression. And this is the condition of singularity, the idiom, the secret, testimony' (61–2); 'he wants to be an archivist who is more of an archaeologist than the archaeologist' (61); 'Freud claims again to bring to light a more originary origin than that of the ghost' (61).

24 See Stewart (1993) 143 for some similar observations on yet another repository of memory, the souvenir.

disconcertingly irrelevant: 'She started: A cold tremor seized her whole frame: She would have fallen had not an aged pine sustained her. She opened once more her eyes, and casting a last look on the scenes of her former happiness, plunged headlong into the tide, and was seen no more.'[25]

The second aspect of 'Andrew Guelph and Og of Basan' that it is possible to clarify through a comparison with 'Delusions and dreams', and by reference to the concepts of the archive and the archaeological, is the lack of archaeological impulse displayed by Og himself, within his personal life: despite the spirit of enquiry that prompts him to pursue his researches in the Vatican, and to compose his treatise and dissertation, he shows very little desire to trace causes and discover origins in his dealings with the 'beloved nymph'. His dreams, it is true, in combination with Roman ruins, drive him back to Tivoli in search of her, but the journey southwards that he undertakes is a more or less aimless one, guided only by the ghost's vague suggestion that it might help him expiate his crimes. Og simply accepts that he has no hope of resolving the crisis into which his entanglement with the nymph has plunged him, and so remains entirely at the mercy of his memories, of the ghost and of the fusion of the feminine and the antique that has drawn him into this entanglement in the first place: he acts, in other words, as though recognising that his role is to take the strategy of transmuting historical time into personal time to the most breathtakingly uncompromising of extremes.

Destabilising travel and tourism

Og's acceptance of the impossibility of any resolution of his difficulties except in death is in sharp contrast to Hanold's attitude to his own disturbing state of mind: in undertaking a journey with investigatory fervour, however little he consciously anticipates the turn that his investigation will take, Jensen's archaeologist registers a desire not only to reach some point of origin but, at the same time, to reach some point of stability. One way of defining this difference between the two texts is by reference to two opposing approaches to the foreign, which begin to assume a place in travel writing from the late eighteenth century onwards, and still remain in a state of dramatic tension and interaction today: on the one hand, the approach which might for convenience be termed *Romantic*, and which regards the encounter with the topography of foreignness as potentially dangerous and destabilising, and, on the other, the approach recognisable as that of the tourist: an approach which also acknowledges an incipient danger within the experience of travel, but which seeks to keep danger and destabilisation at bay.

[25] Beckford (1824) 46.

Various permutations of romantic and touristic attitudes to travel, in their mid twentieth-century forms, are outlined at the beginning of Elaine Dundy's novel *The Dud Avocado* (1958). The novel recounts the adventures of Sally Gorce, a young American woman in Paris. Sally's fellow American Larry Keevil defines, for her benefit, two varieties of 'Disorganised' traveller and two 'Organised' types. Unsurprisingly, the former both adopt the destabilised approach, and the latter register a touristic determination to control and limit any destabilising forces that might beset them. The first 'Disorganised' traveller reaches a point in her relationship with foreign culture where 'all restraint is thrown to the wind and anything really *old* enough is greeted with animal cries of anguish at its beauty'. The heroine easily recognises herself in this: 'Blushingly I recalled a night not so long before when I had suddenly fallen in love with the Place de Furstenberg in the moonlight. I had actually – Oh Lord – I had *actually* kisssed one of the stones at the fountain, I remembered, flung my shoes off, and executed a crazy drunken dance.'[26]

The second variety of romantically destabilised traveller is one with whom Sally aligns herself yet more wholeheartedly (Larry, in fact, describes her as a mixture of the two):

> It's her first time free . . . and, by golly, she goes native in a way the natives never had the stamina to go. Some people think it's those stand-up toilets they have here. . . . After the shock of that kind of plumbing something snaps in the American girl and she's off. The desire to bathe somehow gets lost. The hell with all that, she figures. Then weird haircuts, weird hair-colours, weird clothes. Then comes drink and down, down, down. Dancing in the streets all night, braying at the moon, and waking up in a different bed each morning.[27]

The two types of travellers who adopt the strictly touristic approach, are 'first, the Eager-Beaver-Culture-Vulture with the list ten yards long' and, 'secondly, the cool suave Sophisticate', who 'stuffs her suitcases full of nylon, Kleenex, soapflakes, and DDT bombs': 'This babe . . . finds the hairdresser who speaks English, the restaurant who knows how she likes her steak, and the first foreign word she makes absolutely sure of pronouncing correctly is the one for drugstore. . . . If she's got enough money she's got no trouble at all.'[28]

Norbert Hanold, having initially plunged into a highly destabilised form of travel, makes a similar acknowledgement of the pleasures of experiencing the foreign at a safe distance when he suggests to the living Gradiva, Zoe Bertgang, that they should return to Rome and Pompeii on their

[26] Dundy (1988) 12, 12. The full appellations that Larry himself adopts, in referring to the two general categories of traveller, are (slightly confusingly in the context of my own opposition between destabilised travel and tourism) 'the Disorganised tourist' and 'the Organised tourist'. [27] *Ibid.* 14. [28] *Ibid.* 11.

honeymoon: he implies, in other words, that there is no longer anything in these places to disturb him, and that they can happily be deployed as congenial backdrops to the resolution of the tale of passion.

Other narratives of travel, from the late eighteenth century onwards, follow this same sequence, raising the possibility of destabilisation and then reimposing a state of stability. The whole plot is acted out with unusual swiftness in 'The sentimental baronet', a short story in *The English in Italy* (1825), a collection of sketches by the Marquis of Normanby. One evening at the Colosseum, by the light of 'the rising moon' *(fig. 16)*, an Englishman appears, 'muffled and mantled for the purpose of concealment', and walks off 'to pursue his meditations and perambulations . . . alone'. He is succeeded by 'a gay party, chiefly of ladies'. One of the party, Lady Watkins, is terrified by a sound which 'was . . . heard to issue from one of the dark recesses of the circular corridore, and reverberate through the amphitheatre'. The responses of her companions, however, reassure the reader that no destabilising forces from the past can hope to overcome such stolid contemporaneity:

> 'Boh!' cried the appalling voice from the recess.
> 'It is prodigiously like a calf,' observed one of the gentlemen that accompanied her Ladyship, 'I wonder how it could have strayed up here.'
> 'Oh, no,' said one of the young ladies, 'it is the ghost of Titus Oates, that built this theatre for his informations; so papa told me.'
> 'Boh!' cried the ghost of Titus Oates or Emperor, whilst Lady Watkins was nearly fainting.[29]

The ghost, in fact, when challenged by one of the party, proves to be 'the sentimental, mantled, muffled gentleman', who, recognised by his wife as Sir William Watkins, tells her that he has come to the ruin 'to frighten you, my dear'.[30]

A plot more often adopted, as a means of placing destabilising travel and tourism in a sequential relation to each other, reverses that of *Gradiva*: in many narratives, travellers at first seem to maintain a touristic distance, but are then radically destabilised, as dangerous elements erupt within their experience of the foreign. Such narratives also, in many cases, make use of elisions between the ancient, historical past, and the personal past of the individual. At the beginning of Edith Warton's short story 'Roman fever' (written in the early decades of the twentieth century but not published until 1964), two widowed, middle-aged women sit on the terrace of a restaurant in Rome, looking down 'on the outspread glories of the Palatine and the Forum, with the same expression of vague but benevolent approval', as their two daughters fly off to Tarquinia with some Italian aviators. The

[29] Normanby (1825) II 83, 85, 85–6. [30] *Ibid.* 86.

confessions that they make to each other about events that took place in their early youth, in the same city, soon dispel all vestiges of benevolence. Alida Slade reveals that in a mood of ferocious jealousy, knowing that Grace Ansley was in love with the man whom she herself was engaged to (and soon married), she wrote a note purporting to come from this man, inviting Grace to a secret assignation one evening in the Colosseum. Her motive was to ensure that Grace would wait in the malarial night air long enough for the 'Roman fever' to remove her temporarily from the scene of action. Grace however, reveals that she replied to the note, and that her friend's fiancé did in fact meet her at the ruin. In reply to Alida's crushing observation: 'After all . . . I had him for twenty-five years. And you had nothing but that one letter that he didn't write', Grace remarks simply – but chillingly – that she had her daughter.[31] The husband, like Gradiva and the woman in Og's dream, assumes a spectral presence in the story: half invisible, since he is now dead, half visible through the child of passion – who, unlike his legitimate daughter, inherits his brilliance of personality.

Moonlight and weeds

Whichever sequential relation between destabilising travel and tourism is adopted, the power of ancient sites to marshal the disruptive forces of personal memories is frequently reinforced, in narratives of visits to such sites, by moonlight. The ability of the moon to propel susceptible travellers into mildly unhinged behaviour is noted in Larry Keevil's listing of 'braying at the moon' among the symptoms of a frenzied impulse of self-destruction, in *The Dud Avocado*, and (in the specific context of the European past – as Larry puts it, of 'anything really *old* enough') in Sally's embarrassed recollection of her 'crazy drunken dance' in Parisian moonlight. Moonlight operates yet more forcefully as an agent of destabilisation in 'Roman fever'. Grace Ansley was reported to have made her fateful visit to the Colosseum 'to see the moon rise', and the story begins with Alida Slade frowning as the waiter reminds them that it will be 'a full moon night': unsurprisingly, 'Mrs Slade's black brows drew together, as though references to the moon were out-of-place and even unwelcome.'[32] In 'The sentimental baronet', the narrator raises expectations of a tale more unsettling than that which in fact unfolds through a long initial account of 'the rising moon, which now poured its ray upon the theatre of Titus'.[33]

During Og's fateful night at the Tomb of Cecilia Metella, too, the moon reinforces the effect of the ancient site in increasing the traveller's destabilisation, and leaving him a prey to the ghost. Just as Og is helping himself

[31] Wharton (1993) 9, 24. [32] *Ibid.* 19, 11. [33] Normanby (1825) II 82.

to some fruit, after 'the screeches of noxious birds' have driven him from the Tomb's shelter, 'the moon arose, and discovered faintly the desolate scene around'; amid the 'heaps of mouldering marbles', he himself reaches a degree of desolation at which he is 'on the very point of depriving himself of existence'. The ghost appears to him in his dream in the setting of 'a fictitious city . . . enlightened by a fictitious moon'.[34]

Plant life assumes a similar role in increasing the destabilising power of memory. Just before the visit to the Tomb of Cecilia Metella in *Corinne*, the discreet indication of a danger lurking within the situation is anticipated by the narrator's description of the plants that Corinne and Lord Nelvil observe in the Campagna, as they continue their tour after visiting the Fountain of Egeria – plants whose resistance to human control foreshadows the unruly passions that are to cause endless trouble in the narrative that follows: 'Ces plantes parasites se glissent dans les tombeaux, décorent les ruines, et semblent là seulement pour honorer les morts. *On diroit que l'orgueilleuse nature a repoussé tous les travaux de l'homme.*'[35] Byron's description of the Fountain of Egeria in *Childe Harold's Pilgrimage* is yet more explicit in using vegetation as a metaphor for disruptive passion *(fig. 17)*. Having described the 'fantastically tangled' plants around the spring, the speaker, speculating about the nymph Egeria's relationship with her mortal lover, first uses 'the deadly weed which cloys' as a metaphor for the 'dull satiety' that blights mere 'earthly joys' (as opposed to 'immortal transports'), and then introduces yet more weeds to represent the unhappy fate of 'our young affections':

> Alas! our young affections run to waste,
> Or water but the desart; whence arise
> But weeds of dark luxuriance, tares of haste,
> Rank at the core, though tempting to the eyes,
> Flowers whose wild odours breathe but agonies,
> And trees whose gums are poison; such the plants
> Which spring beneath her steps as Passion flies
> O'er the world's wilderness, and vainly pants
> For some celestial fruit forbidden to our wants.[36]

For Og, about to see the ghost in his dream, 'roots of fantastick laurels' form part of the scene of desolation in which he contemplates suicide; when

[34] Beckford (1824) 54, 55, 56, 56, 57.

[35] De Staël (1979) I 121 (Book 5, ch. 1; emphasis added). The proleptic role of the Campagna is vigorously affirmed, some pages later, when Lord Nelvil comments on the 'influence maligne' of the 'mauvais air' that blights the entire region: – 'J'aime, disoit Oswald à Corinne, ce danger mystérieux, invisible, ce danger sous la forme des impressions les plus douces' (I 132, 132–3; Book 5, ch. 3).

[36] Byron (1980–92) II 163, 164; Canto IV, stanza 117, line 1; stanza 119 lines 9, 8, 6, 4; stanza 120.

the reader is told that 'some branches loaded with fruit . . . offered themselves opportunely to allay his hunger', this edible aspect of the vegetation also offers itself opportunely to the reader, as a prolepsis of the fruits of faithless passion that Og is to reap in events that follow, and as a sad reminder of the need for some consolatory affection that both the beloved nymph and the Tomb deny him.[37]

Beckford's biography, then, teeming with agents of destabilisation, would seem to resist the very idea of approaching the foreign with the smug imperviousness of a tourist. While Og himself rushes on to his doom, however, the narrator's constant irony, in allowing his hero to pursue all forms of self-destructive behaviour so unreservedly, invites the reader to adopt a more sanguine approach to the possibilities and dangers of a journey into the imaginative topography of the antique. At one point in the narrative, when the artist summons Andrew Guelph to join him in Naples, such irony is converted into a positive suggestion that there might be a way of approaching the foreign that would leave the traveller less vulnerable. Andrew, we are told, 'had met with no damsel that died for love of him, and afterwards scared him in his dreams. He had whined away [*sic*] no months in shady retirements, nor wasted his youthful hours in sauntering through deserted galleries, or in moralizing upon the decline of empires.' Having devoted his own stay in Italy to making money, his attitude to such a mode of sightseeing is one of robust common sense: 'Andrew had heard of his friend's ridiculous conduct, and lamented his being carried away by the impetuosity of his imagination.'[38]

The reader, at this point, is left to choose between such common sense and the pleasures of an impetuous imagination. The same choice confronts travellers – and readers – in vast numbers of subsequent accounts of topographies of memory. In Elizabeth Bowen's novel *The Hotel* (1927), a young woman, reflecting on the past of a stretch of southern French coastline, near the establishment of the title, maps out the two options in terms that delicately indicate the disadvantages of maintaining too sensible and stable an approach:

> 'Wouldn't it be nice,' she said, suddenly smiling, 'if the Saracens were to appear on the skyline, land, and ravage the hotel? They all take for granted – down there – that there aren't any more Saracens, but for all we know they may only be in abeyance. The whole Past, for a matter of fact, may be one enormous abeyance. But I wonder,' she added, while a cloud of depression crept over her, 'how many of us they would really care to take away?'[39]

[37] Beckford (1824) 56, 55. Moonlight and weeds can both serve the purposes of touristic detachment as well as those of frenzied destabilisation; for an account of the equivocal role of these two devices in travel-writing see Chard (forthcoming 1999) ch. 5.

[38] Beckford (1824) 62–3, 63. [39] Bowen (1987) 35.

8 Henry James and the anxiety of Rome

John Lyon

In February 1916 Henry James was again in Rome, in search of his brother William, 'the one person in all Rome I want to see'.[1] Two and three months earlier, James had dictated various pronouncements, most usually addressed to his brother and sister(-in-law). Thus he had declared 'I feel sure I shall discover plenty of fresh worlds to conquer, even if I am to be cheated of the amusement of them.'[2] Recognising the 'first omens of defeat' in 'these days of cold grey Switzerland weather', he criticised those who, in 'the march of history', 'pluck in their terror handfuls of plumes from the imperial eagle, and with no greater credit in consequence than that they face, keeping their equipoise, the awful bloody beak that he turns round upon them'.[3] Truly dictatorial, he sent his brother and sister 'precious enclosed transcripts and designs for the decoration of certain apartments of the palaces here, of the Louvre and the Tuileries, which you will find addressed in detail to artists and workmen who are to take them in hand'. When they had reported such work 'fully settled', James assured his brother and sister that 'I shall require of you further zeal and further taste.' And he concluded, 'Please understand I regard these plans as fully developed and as having had my last consideration and look forward to no patchings nor perversions, and with no question of modifications either economic or aesthetic. This will be the case with all future projects . . .'[4] A subsequent dictation further assured his two addressees that, given their 'position as residents of our young but so highly considered Republic at one of the most interesting minor capitals', they 'must rise to each occasion'. And he warned 'any failure to push your advantage to the utmost will be severely judged'. And finally, returning to his own case, James recorded 'I never dreamed of such duties as laid upon me.'[5]

And all this was lovingly recorded by Henry James's amanuensis, Theodora Bosanquet, who saw in James 'a merciful Caesar or a benevolent Napoleon'[6] and again noted, after James's death, that '[s]everal people who

[1] Edel (1977) II 815. [2] James (1984a) 809. [3] *Ibid.* 810. [4] *Ibid.* 811. [5] *Ibid.* 812.
[6] Bosanquet (1924) 4.

have seen the dead face are struck with the likeness to Napoleon which is certainly great'.[7]

Such details of course comprise what James might call 'the possible other case, the case rich and edifying'. Actuality – once audaciously dismissed by James as 'pretentious and vain'[8] – is here, in late 1915 and early 1916, a dying James, bedridden in London, and debilitated by two successive strokes. William James, sought in Rome in 1916, and variously advised and instructed regarding his brother's grand plans, had in fact died in 1910.

What was in evidence in all this was the slow breaking up of a truly huge imaginative empire. The entire world – or more accurately perhaps *his* entire world – was continually dislocating and reforming in James's mind. He was in London at his own address, *and* also at the address of Lady Hyde. He was at a hotel remote from London . . . or in California . . . or in Rome . . . or Rye. Or in 'the strangest mixture of Edinburgh and Dublin and New York and some other place'.[9] At other times, he was literally at sea. He remarked on 'the curious annexation of Chelsea to Cork'.[10] Was Napoleon appropriating Henry James or James Napoleon? *Which* 'imperial eagle' is at issue in his dictations? And *which* 'young but so highly considered Republic'?

James' biographers typically smooth such details over into a narrative of pathos and elegy. Leon Edel, in particular, offering the conventional gloss that here James is engaged in a 'kind of heroic struggle to retain his grasp on reality' seems profoundly wrong.[11] On the contrary, James seems intent on retaining his grasp, *in spite of*, *in the face of*, reality. That '*grasping* imagination'[12] remained in evidence even in the sick room when James's hand 'would make the movements of writing'.[13] Old age and illness were finally mastering the Master. But the writer whose last great heroine had entered *The Golden Bowl* with the declaration 'Oh I'm not afraid of history!'[14] was also struggling against reality, actuality, history in the misshaping form of the Great War, the 'grand Niagara' which 'seems to me to *undo* everything, everything that was ours, in the most horrible retroactive way'.[15] And even in the face of this, he had advised Rhoda Broughton 'only sit tight, and invoke your heroic soul', while James himself had endeavoured to treat the war merely as an unspeakable social *faux pas*: '- but I avert my face from the monstrous scene! – you can hate it and blush for it without my help; we can each do enough of that by ourselves'.[16]

What is remarkable here is first the tenacity and internal coherence which remain in evidence in these expressions of James's fragmenting mind, and secondly, the continuity which such crazed extravagances exhibit with the

[7] Edel (1977) II 816. [8] James (1962) 222. [9] Edel (1977) II 803. [10] *Ibid.* 802.
[11] *Ibid.* 805. [12] James (1974) 252. [13] Edel (1977) II 806. [14] James (1985) 47.
[15] James (1984a) 713. [16] *Ibid.* 713–14.

Master at the height of his artistic powers, the James of 'the major phase', the James whom Stephen Donadio has yoked together with Nietzsche in a study of the 'artistic will'. James's deathbed fantasy of 'fresh worlds to conquer' is not very far from the devilishly imperial designs of the dying dove, Milly Theale, whom an anxious Mrs Stringham encounters atop the Alps. Mrs Stringham first fears that Milly is contemplating suicide, but she soon discovers,

> if the girl was deeply and recklessly meditating there she wasn't meditating a jump; she was on the contrary, as she sat, much more in a state of uplifted and unlimited possession that had nothing to gain from violence. She was looking down on the kingdoms of the earth, and though indeed that of itself might well go to the brain, it wouldn't be with a view of renouncing them. Was she choosing among them or did she want them all?[17]

Milly will die in Venice at the novel's close, but even here, in the curious Jamesian appropriation and transformation of notions such as that of death, it is the other characters who feel dead or deadened. And the fragile dove is revealed as a misnomer as, eagle-like, Milly spreads her wings 'wider', stretching them out until Kate Croy and Densher feel '[t]hey cover us'.[18]

Nor are James's mad Napoleonic designs too far removed from the American father and daughter, Adam and Maggie Verver, who, in the new *Imperium* of London, take possession of the 'loot' of Europe, including 'human furniture' in the shape of an Italian Prince, and Charlotte Stant, the latter finally enslaved with 'a long silken halter looped round her beautiful neck'[19] – a metaphor which some of James's readers have found all the more offensive precisely because of its opulence and aesthetic refinement. James's later novels exhibit a kind of aesthetic imperialism, creating worlds rarefied, remote, otherworldly, too readily ignoring of the recalcitrance of non-Jamesian realities, yet worlds which manifest exercises of ordering, shaping power and control that are quite breathtaking.

The young Henry James who walked from the Alps into Italy and made his first visit to Rome in 1869 – a year in advance of yet another momentous event in Rome's momentous history – was altogether less masterful. The letters which emanate from that visit have been much anthologised, and James's enthusiastically appreciative response – 'At last – for the first time – I live!'[20] – has been much remarked. What has received less attention is the curious instability, indeed the anxiety of those letters. Part of that anxiety is undoubtedly an awareness of the need of a young son and brother, alone amidst pagan and Catholic European culture, to assuage the

[17] James (1986b) 135. [18] *Ibid.* 477, 508. [19] James (1985) 43, 574, 523.
[20] James (1974) 160.

worries of his Boston family. And the repeated declarations of inarticulacy – 'Appreciate, but not express!'; 'The Coliseum is a thing about which it's useless to talk'; 'that simple and unutterable Pantheon'; the sculptures at the Capitol, 'all of them unspeakably simple and noble and eloquent of the breadth of human genius'[21] – are undoubtedly in part the rhetoric of the letter writer intent on conveying his excitement. But James seems involved – however light-heartedly such involvement is expressed – in some contest with Rome, and he seems unsure how that contest is to be negotiated.

Indeed James almost never made it to Rome. Prior letters from Florence reveal James fearing he will 'turn [his back] upon Italy altogether', to turn away 'at the very gates of Rome' and 'take refuge' in England again because of the recurrence, for six weeks, of 'an old trouble', an 'ancient sorrow'.[22] To his father he wrote bizarrely '[t]here will be no Rome and no Italy like the Rome and Naples of my getting really relieved of this dismal burden. They will be utterly vulgar in comparison.'[23] The plain, indeed vulgar but – according to Eve Kosofsky Sedgwick – never '*simple* fact' of Henry James's constipation has fascinated Henry James and his brother, psychoanalysts and queer theorists alike.[24] But in this case, the 'exquisite joy of final relief' which the arrival of a letter from William brings – the physiological, the psychological and the metaphorical are much confused in these curious letters – finally allows James to resolve to 'hurl myself upon Rome and fight it out on this line at the peril of my existence'.[25] The initial encounter with Rome which results, Henry 'reeling and moaning thro' the streets, in a fever of enjoyment', is 'something indescribable'.[26] And a week later, James, in a letter to his sister Alice, remained apparently helpless in the face of this city: 'And now as for this Rome, it seems a sadly vain ambition to give you any idea of its affect upon the mind. It's so vast, so heavy, so multitudinous that you seem to require all your energy simply to bear up against it.'[27] '[B]ear up against it' here is as distinctively Jamesian as his altogether more famous formulation which has Isabel Archer not confronting, but 'affronting her destiny'.[28] And later, I would suggest, James's relation to Rome will stabilise as an affront, a stand off rather than an engagement or confrontation, a wilful and imperious ignoring: Rome in Henry James is merely – and deliberately vaguely – background. But, in these early letters, from the twenty-six-year-old James's first visit, James is uneasy and embarrassed by the ignorance which he would later come to cherish. Thus, in the same letter to Alice, he is anxious about the superficiality of his touristic appreciation: '[y]our foremost feeling is that of your own ignorance' since '[a]t every step in some guise or other History

21 *Ibid.* 163, 163, 164, 167. 22 *Ibid.* 155, 157, 156, 155, 157. 23 *Ibid.* 157.
24 Sedgwick (1995) 224. 25 James (1974) 159. 26 *Ibid.* 160. 27 *Ibid.* 162.
28 James (1962) 48. The oddity of the latter phrase is discussed by Bell (1991) 80–122.

confronts you'.[29] And indeed James's 'want of [historical] knowledge'[30] has some narrow squeaks: 'All the Roman portraits give me a deep desire to plunge into Roman history – so that yesterday I narrowly escaped paying 22 frs. for an English publication on the subject. But to approach it, you must have a Roman will.'[31] Henry James's will, while strong to the point of tyranny, was never to be Roman and he was never to surrender to what he called 'the fatal futility of Fact'.[32] Just as James was content to found his greatest novel on the tiredest of Parisian clichés – 'the dreadful little old tradition, one of the platitudes of the human comedy, that people's moral scheme *does* break down in Paris'[33] – so he is content to draw opportunistically and casually on historical 'error', the chance survival of the equestrian statue of Marcus Aurelius, mistaken for a Christian, in order to give Roman Catholicism and its effete '*papalino*'[34] an energetic, gendered and Protestant drubbing. And in doing so, James is *creating* the juxtaposition, pursuing a paralleling of physical attitude and gesture which owes something to Nathaniel Hawthorne's prior noticing, and which serves James' own polemical ends:

> When you have seen that flaccid old woman waving his ridiculous fingers over the prostrate multitude and have duly felt the picturesqueness of the scene – and then turn away sickened by its absolute *obscenity* – you may climb the steps of the Capitol and contemplate the equestrian statue of Marcus Aurelius. This work, by the way, is one of the things I have enjoyed most in Rome. It is totally admirable – the very model of the *genre*: – so large and monumental and yet so full of a sweet human dignity – stretching out a long thin arm in the act of mild persuasive command – that affects you like an audible personal voice out of that stony Roman past. As you revert to that poor sexless old Pope enthroned on his cushions – and then glance at those imperial legs swinging in their immortal bronze, you cry out that here at least was a *man*![35]

In the letters emanating from his subsequent visits to Rome, James continues to give unstintingly of a rich rhetoric of appreciation and – his word – 'impressions', intermingled with occasional American frustrations. Yet that rhetoric rarely yields anything of distinctively Roman substance. We learn little of Rome, and much about Henry James. Indeed James's various visits allow him to meet the celebrated palimpsest of Rome, what James himself in *Roderick Hudson* called 'the infinite superpositions of history',[36] with a layering of his own history – the Jamesian Rome of 1869, the Jamesian Rome of 1872 and 1873, and so on, until the Jamesian Rome of 1907 – James using, in his letters, his attitude to Rome at any given time to measure and to convey *his* own present moods, and *his* own present state of health, physical, intellectual and creative. Thus for example to his brother and

[29] James (1974) 162–3. [30] *Ibid.* 162. [31] *Ibid.* 167. [32] James (1962) 122.
[33] *Ibid.* 316. [34] James (1995) 153. [35] James (1974) 165. [36] James (1986a) 108.

sister-in-law he writes in 1894: '[Rome] is "changed" immensely – as everyone says; but I find myself, I am afraid, so much *more* changed – since I first knew and rhapsodised over it, that I am bound in justice to hold Rome the less criminal of the two.'[37] What I have been describing as James' ignoring or displacing of Rome is given its most frank expression in that late biography which was a duty rather than a pleasure to write, *William Wetmore Story and his Friends,* where James is prepared to

> brave even the imputation of making a mere Rome of words, talking of a Rome of my own which was no Rome of reality. That comes up as exactly the point – that no Rome of reality was concerned in our experience, that the whole thing was a rare state of the imagination, dosed and drugged [. . .] by the effectual Borgia cup, for the taste of which the simplest as well as the subtlest had a palate.[38]

The James of the Roman travel writing is entirely continuous with the James of the Roman letters. The young aspiring professional writer may have embarked on his travel essays in the hope that his writings might serve as a guide for travellers – a hope echoed in the blurb for recent editions of such writing that they may serve 'a practical function for the modern traveler'.[39] But any acquaintance with these writings, even the early essays, soon reveals the hope as a forlorn one, with travellers better served – as James himself was not ashamed to be[40] – by their Murray, their Baedeker, the books of Augustus J. C. Hare – or indeed by the *Blue Guide*. James's Roman essays are exclusively aesthetic and descriptively impressionistic, diminishing from early to late writings in specificity and substance as they increase in style.

Nevertheless, the early travel essays – precisely because *that is what they are*, the genre releasing James from the burden of creative fiction – are, to a degree, exceptional. They belong to the phase of early James, where the author is prepared to be more attentive to history and to actuality – although, as Roslyn Jolly has shown in her recent study *Henry James: history, narrative, fiction* (1993), the characters of the *fiction* emanating even from this period are capable of plotting against and putting up considerable resistance to their narrators' scientific, historic and realist emphases. In James's early Roman essays all the sights – the Forum, the Colosseum, the Pantheon, St. Peter's and so on – are richly present, but that is what they are – *sights*, 'moments of direct visual experience',[41] appreciations rather than analyses. And if James uncharacteristically submits to his subject matter here – to the overwhelming *multiple* impressions of Rome, and their multiple 'reverberations and relations', then as the most extensive study of

37 James (1980) 478. 38 James (1903) II, 209.
39 James (1995) or – note the cautious adjective – as 'an unusual guidebook' (Kaplan (1994)).
40 James (1974) 162. 41 MacDonald (1990a) 2.

these works concedes, these 'reverberations and relations, it must be said, remain unnamed'.[42] These essays, heavy with a rhetoric of adoring, wondering inarticulacy, offer surprisingly little to a tourist standing on the spot; they serve instead to convey something of the *experience of being in Rome* to readers remote from the Eternal City.

And the larger development of James's travel writings confirms the characteristic development of James's writing generally, and of his fiction in particular, whereby the play of consciousness itself increasingly takes precedence over and indeed obscures the ostensible objects of that consciousness's attention. Thus Tony Tanner has remarked on James's Italian writing as something 'not dependent on accumulations of facts; rather it sedulously and sinuously avoids and evades the factual as if in tacit deprecation of that kind of impersonal information'.[43] And Tanner, presenting James as a travel writer avoiding history and specification, concludes that the writing offers '[n]ot only a *sense* of a place, or of the past [but . . .] a sense *of* that sense'.[44] Again the appreciating consciousness is privileged, and the place and the past are placed at a further remove.

James is famous – or notorious – for bringing America and Nathaniel Hawthorne together in a long list of what America lacked for Hawthorne – or any other American writer (though it is not merely to read James against the grain to detect a note of Emersonian pride and triumph in the energy of the ostensible condemnation):

> No sovereign, no court, no personal loyalty, no aristocracy, no church, no clergy, no army, no diplomatic service, no country gentlemen, no palaces, no castles, nor manors, nor old country-houses, nor parsonages, nor thatched cottages nor ivied ruins; no cathedrals, nor abbeys, nor little Norman churches; no great Universities nor public schools – no Oxford, nor Eton, nor Harrow; no literature, no novels, no museums, no pictures, no political society, no sporting class – no Epsom nor Ascot! [45]

And it is not difficult, regarding the apparently alluring subject of Henry James and Rome, to gather the critics together in an answering catalogue of omissions and vaguenesses (though this list too may be a measure of the Jamesian triumph over the challenge of Rome). Arguing for Jamesian literary theory's indebtedness to a classical education – a thesis which retains its plausibility only in direct proportion to its vagueness – Elizabeth Block admits Rome is present in James's writings 'only as a setting, an atmosphere, a mass of impressions' and not as 'specific images, detailed descriptions, still less historical facts';[46] it is 'a culture only vaguely grasped and recalled with deliberate vagueness' until, in later James 'the city sank almost beneath the surface of the prose'.[47] George Bisztray notes that '*Daisy Miller*

[42] *Ibid.* 40. [43] Tanner (1992) 159. [44] Tanner (1995) 17. [45] James (1984b) 351–2.
[46] Block (1984) 141. [47] *Ibid.* 142.

strikes the reader with a lack of any substantial description of Rome'[48] and that James uses Rome as 'a vaguely characterized social milieu'.[49] Bonney MacDonald argues that the 'magic' of James's Italian writing derives from the fact that 'James's love of Italy remained *beyond* the reach of words'.[50] Even that most thorough researcher of *The Museum World of Henry James,* Adeline Tintner, concedes that, from the 1880s on, James 'rarely uses Rome or France as a setting for his fiction, and when he does his interests are in social behavior in private houses, not in museum settings'.[51] And the formidable Agostino Lombardo must surely have taken some of the sweetness out of the 1988 New York international conference, the purpose of which was 'to pay tribute to Italy as a source of inspiration to American thought and imagination'[52] and the proceedings of which were subsequently published as *'The Sweetest Impression of Life': the James family and Italy*. Lombardo announced that of Italy James knew 'very little, as all the critics, who have touched on this subject [. . .] have convincingly demonstrated'. James's Italy is 'not a real country' [53] but is devoid of knowledge of social class, political problems and daily life, without Italian characters other than 'operatic' stock-types, and marked by near-ubiquitous misspellings. 'What exists is the Italy of the past – and not so much of the historical past [. . .] as of the artistic one.'[54] James's relationship with Rome, according to Lombardo, '[i]dentified as it is with the artistic experience, and even with the artistic text [. . .] produces all the anxiety, the strenuous effort, the struggle which the artist's job itself produces'.[55]

Perhaps because they chose not to engage with it in its artistic manifestation, Henry James's father and brother could express that anxiety more succinctly and bluntly than James himself. Henry James Senior responded to his son's first impressions of Rome by asserting '[t]he historical consciousness rules to such a distorted excess in Europe that I have always been restless there, and ended by pining for the land of the future exclusively. Condemned to *remain* there I should stifle in a jiffy.'[56] And William, with his brother in Italy, wrote to Alice James: 'Italy is a very *delightful* place to dip into but no more. I can't imagine how, unless one is earnestly studying history in some way, it can in the long run help injuring all one's active powers. The weight of the past world here is fatal, – one ends by becoming its mere parasite instead of its equivalent.'[57] But there was also near artistic kin, a fellow American novelist, who had not merely described that anxiety, but had fallen victim to it in what was to be for Henry James an edifying fashion. For if *The Marble Faun* does Rome in thorough if turgid

48 Bisztray (1991) 48. 49 *Ibid.* 50. 50 MacDonald (1990b) 130.
51 Tintner (1986) 62. 52 Tuttleton (1990) 5. 53 Lombardo (1990) 230.
54 *Ibid.* 231. 55 *Ibid.* 232. 56 Matthiessen (1980) 289. 57 *Ibid.* 291.

detail – for example borrowing much directly from Hawthorne's *Italian Notebooks* – then Rome does for *The Marble Faun* with a vengeance. Hawthorne writes of 'a vague sense [in Rome] of ponderous remembrances; a perception of such weight and density in a by-gone life, of which this spot was the centre, that the present moment is pressed down or crowded out, and our individual affairs and interests are but half as real, here, as elsewhere.'[58] Hawthorne offers in the character of Hilda the figure of the American artist who, in coming to Rome has 'entirely lost the impulse of original design' to become 'the best copyist in Rome'.[59] Subsequently '[i]nstructed by sorrow' Hilda learns, not greater artistic independence, but the realisation of 'something beyond almost all which pictorial genius has produced'[60] and learns moreover to descend from her virginal tower and embrace the role of wife. (So, complicating matters, Hilda is not in a straightforward sense a representative artist but a female one, and Hawthorne's representation of her is readily subject to feminist analysis.)

But *The Marble Faun* enacts the problem it describes. James Buzard has recently reminded us that it is anachronistic – indeed Jamesian – to dismiss, in the name of 'aesthetic-organic unity', a narrative which mingles fiction and travel.[61] But *The Marble Faun* is a case, not of mingling, but muffling. The set pieces, the elaborated descriptions, and the mass of ancient artefacts which weigh down such pages entirely sap the narrative energy and render the plot so vague that, notoriously, Hawthorne had to add a postscript, after first publication, to shed a little light. (James wrote of the novel that its 'action wavers between the streets of Rome, whose literal features the author perpetually sketches, and a vague realm of fancy, in which quite a different verisimilitude prevails'[62]). And Hawthorne's comprehensiveness and specificity in respect of Rome on the one hand and vagueness in respect of the novel's own story on the other is a relation which James would learn, in the main, to reverse.

In particular, *The Marble Faun* falls apart when it presses its most precise analogies between the novel's own actions and the events and scenes of Rome's cultural and historical past. Thus the sinister Model who pursues Miriam meets his death when Donatello throws him from the Tarpeian Rock, the sight of so many ancient traitorous plunges. And, in the immediate aftermath of the murder, Hawthorne takes us to the site of Pompey's forum for this self-thrillingly melodramatic dialogue:

> 'For there was a great deed done here!' she said – 'a deed of blood, like ours! Who knows, but we may meet the high and ever-sad fraternity of Caesar's murderers, and exchange a salutation?'

[58] Hawthorne (1990) 6. [59] *Ibid.* 56, 59. [60] *Ibid.* 375. [61] Buzard (1993) 240 n.31.
[62] James (1984b) 447.

1. François-Marius Granet, *Choir of the Capuchin Church, Rome*, 1817.

2. J. M.Gandy, *Soane's rotunda of the Bank of England as a ruin*, 1832.

3. François-Marius Granet, *The crypt of San Martino*.

4. François-Marius Granet, *View of Santa Francesca Romana through an arch of the Coliseum.*

5. François-Marius Granet, *Godefroy de Bouillon deposits in the church of the Holy Sepulchre the Trophies of Ascalm* (engraving after)

6. François-Marius Granet, *The interior of the Church of Santo Stefano Rotondo at Rome.*

7. Antonio Canova, *Napoleon*, 1806.

8. Antoine-François Callet, *L'arrivée du premier consul à Lyon*, c. 1804.

9. Charles Meynier, *Entrée de S. M. l'Empereur et Roi dans Berlin*, 1810.

10. François-Henri Mulard, *S. M. l'Empereur fait présent d'un sabre au chef militaire de la ville d'Alexandrie en Egypte*, 1808.

11. Guillaume François Colson, *Trait de clémence du Général Bonaparte envers une famille arabe lors de l'entrée de l'armée française à Alexandrie*, 1812.

12. P. F. Poole, *The Goths in Italy*, 1851.

13. Thomas Couture, *Les romains de la décadence*, 1847.

14. 'Tomb of Cecilia Metella'. An engraving in James Hakewill, *A Picturesque Tour of Italy, from drawings made in 1816–1817* (London 1820).

15. Elisabeth Vigée-Lebrun, *Madame de Staël as Corinne at Cape Miseno*, 1807–8.

16. Richard Wilson, *The Coliseum by moonlight*.

17. 'Fountain of the Nymph Egeria', from J. Merigot, *A Select Collection of Views and Ruins at Rome* vol. I.

18. Simeon Solomon, *Habet!*, 1865.

19. Dante Gabriel Rossetti, *Bocca baciata*, 1859.

20. Simeon Solomon, *The toilette of a Roman lady*, 1869.

21. Simeon Solomon, *Heliogabalus, High Priest of the Sun*, 1866.

22. 'The Roman mosaic discovered at Ain-Zara' from *L'Illustrazione Italiana* (14 January 1912).

23. The home of Cabiria's father in Sicily, from *Cabiria* (1914).

24. The sacrifice of children in the temple of Moloch in Carthage, from *Cabiria* (1914).

25. Otello Chiti, *La partenza*, 1936.

26. Filippo Sgarlata, *It is the plough that draws the sickle but the sword which defends it*, 1938.

> 'Are they our brethren, now?' asked Donatello.
>
> 'Yes; all of them,' said Miriam; 'and many another, whom the world little dreams of, has been made our brother or our sister, by what we have done within this hour!'[63]

Such meetings are indeed 'high', the events of the Roman past rendering the novel's own immediate actions merely laughable, as if Hawthorne 'were asking an army of glorious veterans to help him to arrest a peddler who has given him the wrong change'. That last simile is, of course, Henry James's, and comes from his recollection of his own struggle to write *The Portrait of a Lady* in Italy only to receive Italy's

> rather grim admonition that romantic and historic sites, such as the land of Italy abounds in, offer the artist a questionable aid to concentration when they themselves are not to be the subject of it. They are too rich in their own life and too charged with their own meanings merely to help him out with a lame phrase; they draw him away from his small question to their own greater ones; so that, after a little, he feels, while thus yearning toward them in his difficulty, as if he were asking an army of glorious veterans to help him to arrest a peddler who has given him the wrong change.[64]

Unlike Hawthorne, James learned to contain Rome to 'a little', just as he learned, more generally, to contain *any* idea or 'germ' of his fictions since 'anything more than the minimum [. . .] spoils the [creative] operation'.[65]

The first, somewhat laboured fictional fruits of James's encounter with Rome are salutary tales for academics, warnings to those who would, in the manner of science, appropriate Roman culture and comprehend Roman history. These tales are also crude and entirely literal attempts to bury the past. They are, moreover, rewritings of Hawthorne's Roman novel, a novel which James called by its English title, *Transformation*, in part because James sought to displace the marble faun of Praxiteles from its oppressive prominence: *The Marble Faun*, as title, 'completely fails to characterise the story'.[66] If James loved picturesque ruins – echoing Clough, he declares 'I *do* find Rome "*rubbishy*" – magnificently, sublimely so'[67] – then it would appear that he despised archives and archaeologists. One essay catches him at Siena in that characteristic gesture which registers his historical ignorance only to resist its remedy: 'I ought perhaps, for justification of the right to talk, to have plunged into the Siena archives. [. . .] I didn't descend into the pit.'[68] And if the archaeologist of the early tale, 'The Last of the Valerii'(1874) is anything to go by – 'an ugly little dwarfish man', 'a mouldy gnome of the under world'[69] – then such people's company is not to be cultivated. In this tale, the narrator's American god-daughter, Martha,

63 Hawthorne (1990) 176. 64 James (1962) 40–1. 65 *Ibid.* 119.
66 James (1984b) 444. 67 Kaplan (1994) 115. 68 James (1995) 234.
69 James (1978) 266.

marries Count Valerio, a man whose head is as round and his hair as curly as 'the familiar bust of the Emperor Caracalla'.[70] But the Count, in his sturdy, sensual simplicity, is much more closely related to Hawthorne's faun, Donatello, than to any Italian James might have encountered in Rome. Martha has money; the Count has good looks, a good nature, and 'a villa within the walls of Rome'.[71] And despite the misgivings of both the narrator and the Count himself, Martha's 'archaeological zeal' leads to a project for excavations at the villa with a find so exciting that, on first hearing of it, the narrator assumes they have found 'a Juno of Praxiteles at the very least!'[72] An 'incomparable Juno' it proves to be, identified first by the hand which has broken from the statue, and subsequently confirmed by the unearthing of the figure itself.[73] And in short, as a result of the find, the Count reverts to the paganism of his ancestors, and embarks on a worship of the Juno and the neglect of his wife. The solution is drastically and comically simple. The excavation of the 'monstrous heritage of antiquity' is halted.[74] Martha has a hole dug, and the Juno is lowered into it. Casting earth on the statue's breast, Martha announces 'May it lie lightly' – and then the common classical formula *sit tibi terra levis* takes a wonderful swerve – 'May it lie lightly, but for ever!'[75] And the Count, restored to his wife, is left with only the marble hand of his beloved Juno to hold.

In 'Adina', another tale published in the same year (1874), James again reveals a hostility to 'ample information', precision, learning, concern for historical accuracy and discrimination amongst the ruins of Rome: this is the story of our narrator and his acquaintance, the unpoetically named Sam Scrope, a 'punctilious classical scholar', who, in a further sadistic twist is revealed as 'very ugly', physically and psychologically 'crooked', '*common*', devoid of 'style'. To Scrope's 'learned allusions', 'capital memory' and 'rigid science', the narrator opposes 'loose sentiment', 'poetic sighs' and quotations not from the Classics, but from Byron.[76] These two encounter, on the Campagna, a young Italian, Angelo, in possession of a small, recently discovered, artefact. Scrope tricks Angelo into parting with the object for a pittance. On cleaning and restoring, the object reveals itself as a quite extraordinary topaz intaglio, 'the finest intaglio in the world'.[77] It is elaborately carved with imperial head, laurel crown, orb and sceptre encircled by 'warriors, and horses, and chariots, and young men and women interlaced in elaborate confusion'.[78] And it is inscribed: 'DIVUS TIBERIUS CÆSAR TOTIUS ORBIS IMPERATOR'.[79] But, however rich, this intaglio in James's tale represents a remarkable diminution and containment of the mass of ancient artefacts which clutter Hawthorne's novel, and a contain-

70 *Ibid.* 259. 71 *Ibid.* 260. 72 *Ibid.* 262, 268. 73 *Ibid.* 270. 74 *Ibid.* 278.
75 *Ibid.* 282. 76 *Ibid.* 348–9. 77 *Ibid.* 357. 78 *Ibid.* 356. 79 *Ibid.* 357.

ment of the matter of Rome, since a magnifying glass is literally required to see and to read it. Alert now to Scrope's deception, Angelo gets his revenge by making off with Scrope's fiancée, and marrying her. Scrope is left to return the topaz to 'the mouldering under-world of the Roman past'[80] by casting it into the Tiber, the river which James, on his first day in Rome, had seen 'hurrying along, as swift and dirty as history!'[81]

The early novel *Roderick Hudson* (1875) represents James's larger engagement with Rome, and with *The Marble Faun*. Here the Faun of Praxiteles, which initiates Hawthorne's novel, is, as it were, shipped back to Northampton, Massachusetts, to be refashioned as a new and entirely fictional sculpture, the work of the young Virginian, Roderick Hudson. Rowland Mallett's viewing of that sculpture, of 'a naked youth drinking from a gourd', entitled 'Thirst', precipitates his patronage of the sculptor, and Rowland's and Roderick's encounter with Rome, and with the 'knowledge, pleasure, experience' for which Roderick Hudson thirsts.[82] The novel charts Rome's destruction of the eponymous artist, Roderick finally leaving 'this terrible Italy'[83] to take a suicidal plunge from the Alpine heights which Milly Theale will later conquer. But *Roderick Hudson* is a busy novel, too busy a novel, in which James self-protectively takes a large swipe at the philistinism of the American tourist abroad; creates an initially amiable and stupid Italian Prince Casamassima who continues James's debt to Hawthorne's Donatello; discovers, in keeping with the novel of the late nineteenth century, the heroine as coquette in the figure of Christina Light, later to be the Princess Casamassima; and begins to extend his concern beyond Rome, his principal setting, to take in an altogether wider view of Europe. The writer's explicit concern with art, is, moreover, giving way in this novel to a concern with erotic intrigue – indeed, perhaps too much so, since there are so many women in a novel named for a male artist. So, for example, the reader struggles to follow the relationship between Rowland and Roderick, negotiated through so many of the novel's female characters, a relationship where the homosocial shades into the homosexual in ways not fully under James's control. Nevertheless, it is important to recognise that the dilemma of the American artist confronting Rome is being gradually written out of this novel, as James comes to recognise a rich and enabling theme, to be treated altogether more subtly in later works – of the young American woman confronting the amatory and ethical challenges of Rome, and of Europe more generally. The male writer's anxiety is being gradually transmuted, transformed or – to borrow a favourite Jamesianism – 'converted' into one of his great themes, to be centred on a role call of

[80] *Ibid.* 382. [81] James (1974) 160. [82] James (1986a) 59, 66. [83] *Ibid.* 344.

memorable Jamesian heroines. Even the coquettish Christina Light will gain, in *The Princess Casamassima*, a title of her own, in *two* senses.

The unlucky thirteenth chapter of *Roderick Hudson*, set in the Colosseum, is one of this novel's weakest: here, Hawthorne-like, setting overwhelms action and renders it weakly melodramatic. In this scene, Rowland Mallett accidentally eavesdrops on Christina and Roderick discussing whether Roderick can or cannot be an *amatory* conqueror. Attempting to prove his worth, Roderick seeks to scale a wall to secure a little blue flower admired by Christina, only to be prevented by the eavesdropping Rowland. And the effect of the scene is altogether more bathetic than James intended: straining for effect, James finds in the Colosseum a 'questionable aid'[84] which undermines rather than bolsters his writing.

When he returns to the Colosseum again, to treat of love and social and cultural conventions and mores in *Daisy Miller*, James's writing is now firmly under control. The tawdry clichés and over-used conventions which have accrued to the Colosseum are now the property, not of James himself, but of James's characters, and the interpretative drama of how such characters are to 'read' such clichés and conventions, and 'read' each other *through* them, is an altogether more substantial matter. In *Daisy Miller*, Winterbourne finds himself in the Colosseum murmuring 'Byron's famous lines, out of *Manfred*'.[85] And when Daisy herself announces 'he looks at us as one of the old lions or tigers may have looked at the Christian martyrs!' or declares "Well, I *have* seen the Colosseum by moonlight!',[86] the jokey gaucheness and the blustering, defensive naivety respectively are not James's but go towards the subtle and difficult characterisation of Daisy Miller herself.

'At last – for the first time – I live!' *Not* the spontaneity of a first impression, but coming in the *middle* of Henry James's long first letter to his brother from Rome, a statement strongly echoing, and indeed verging on a translation of Goethe in his *Italian Journey*. (Leon Edel is 'fairly certain' that, in walking into Italy, James 'carried Goethe with him'.[87]) And, as such, a statement altogether more knowing, literary, ironic – both self-deprecatory and self-possessed. Hawthorne, as we have seen, Goethe, Byron, Byron further filtered through Hawthorne, Stendhal, Taine, Ruskin, Gautier, Clough, George Eliot, Howells . . . to name but an incomplete list of those Roman writers who were most important to James: James's engagements with Rome are typically mediated through his revisions of the Roman writings of predecessors altogether nearer, and indeed of contemporaries. James diverts his contest with Rome into challenges to his more immediate precursors. And in his reworkings of *them*, where he goes

[84] James (1962) 41. [85] James (1984d) 197. [86] *Ibid.* 198, 199. [87] Edel (1990) 13.

further, writes more fully and with greater ironic inflection and awareness, James in a sense can be seen to master and *exceed* his originals, to correct and to complete, to retain a writerly self-possession, in ways that a more direct confrontation with the vast matter of Rome would have rendered impossible. Such a revisionary swerve, or deflection of point of focus, alleviates, indeed overcomes the anxiety of influence. And, moreover, the writer's aesthetic and historical anxiety is displaced or transposed into his theme, his characters' ethical dilemma in confronting an ambiguous Rome which is at once rich and alluring and corrupting and deadening.[88] Thus Rome is subsumed within the large and familiar Jamesian international theme of American and European, north and south, rendering Rome merely one of a range of possible narrative 'backgrounds' which, rich in atmosphere, nevertheless retains little that is specifically and significantly Roman (other than the one detail of the Roman summer's threat – prior to drainage and quinine – of malaria).

Too much excellent criticism has been written on James's most famous heroine, Isabel Archer, 'affronting her destiny' in the setting of Rome for much to be said here. But it is germane to my immediate argument that James's letters from Rome in 1872 and 1873 sustain dialogues with his correspondents about another great novel which honeymoons darkly in Rome. *Middlemarch* (1871–2) was clearly much on James's mind when in Rome, and in *The Portrait of a Lady* he extends Dorothea Brooke's unhappy brief visit to Rome into the long, seemingly sterile Roman marriage of Isabel Archer and Gilbert Osmond. And even Isabel's husband does not derive straightforwardly from any expatriate American encountered in the social gatherings of Rome, but has some of his origins among James's literary contemporaries. For, as Richard Ellmann has noted, the 'little sonnet' Osmond shows Isabel, 'Roman revisited', has an inverted relation to Oscar Wilde's 'Rome unvisited', and, in the characterisation of Gilbert Osmond, James is engaged in a contemporary quarrel about differentiating various kinds of aestheticism.[89]

For the larger part of *The Portrait of a Lady* James has learned, as it were, to abandon any contest with the guidebooks. He leaves Rome to Henrietta Stackpole who finds the pavements of Rome 'a good deal like New York' and who regards Julius Caesar as '"a cheeky old boy"',[90] and pre-eminently to Isabel Archer:

> I may not attempt to report in its fulness our young woman's response to the deep appeal of Rome, to analyse her feelings as she trod the pavement of the Forum or to number her pulsations as she crossed the threshold of Saint Peter's. It is enough

[88] See, for example, Maves (1973) and Fogel (1990). [89] Ellmann (1983) 215.
[90] James (1984c) 337.

to say that her impression was such as might have been expected of a person of her freshness and her eagerness [. . .] and she went about in a repressed ecstasy of contemplation, seeing often in the things she looked at a great deal more than was there, and yet not seeing many of the things enumerated in her Murray.[91]

Only as *The Portrait* approaches its close, a close which has notoriously perplexed its many interpreters, do Roman sites, and in particular the Colosseum of the fiftieth chapter, begin to crowd in on the novel as James gives in to the temptation of placing his heroine, somewhat sentimentally, among the ruins, much as Hardy seems to sacrifice his heroine at Stonehenge at the close of *Tess of the D'Urbervilles* (1891). And, as a consequence, James's novel perhaps finally succumbs to a Hawthorne-like fate: the generalised significance of historical setting occludes and overwhelms particular narrative significance, leaving the reader at the last baffled regarding the precise reasons prompting Isabel's final return to Rome.

A loose misprision of Harold Bloom has shadowed this discussion.[92] Any appropriation of Bloom, is of course, by his own definition, a misprision. And here the anxiety I have been describing is more overt and on the surface than the altogether less obvious, more repressed relations between ephebe and precursor which Bloom characteristically describes. Moreover, this anxiety involves not relations between individual *poets*, as Bloom's own notoriously individualistic focus does, but one novelist's encounter with an entire culture. But Bloom seems apposite here for a variety of reasons. Where traditional studies of influence and tradition had stressed veneration and celebration, Bloom admits the legitimate role of anxiety in creativity, and Bloom's own Freudian inheritance, with its psychoanalytic readings and reversals, allows the presence of anxiety even in the most seemingly affirmative declarations and venerations. The primacy of the aesthetic in Bloom's theory accords well with the predominantly aesthetic nature of Henry James's engagement with Rome. Bloom's revisionary ratios, with their talk of swerves, antitheses, deflations and truncations, afford a model, loosely appropriated, for the vocabulary to describe the particulars of Henry James's indirect tussles with Rome by way of Hawthorne, George Eliot and the like. Behind Bloom stands not only Freud but Emerson, and it is in its dealing with American writers and the burden of the past that Bloom's theory has often seemed most persuasive.

In *Poetry and repression* Bloom writes that '[n]ot merely rebirth, but the even more hyperbolical trope of self-begetting, is the starting point of the

91 *Ibid.* 336.

92 For two other Bloomian readings of James, very different from that proposed here – 'the American anxiety of influence' and 'the Victorian anxiety of influence' – see Rowe (1984) 29–83.

last Western Sublime, the great sunset of selfhood in the Evening Land'.[93] And, in a 1975 review, that 'America is the evening land, or the last phase of Mediterranean culture, and this late in tradition all reading (and writing) is heavily shadowed by the past.'[94] As an American tourist, James was often quite literally a latecomer. As Tony Tanner notes,[95] he preferred to arrive late in the afternoon, to enjoy his sightseeing when others had gone home, in the fading yet enriching light and the approaching dusk, and to savour what he described in an essay on Venice as 'the sense of having come too late – yet not too late, after all, for this glimpse and this dream'.[96]

If Henry James was a last man, he harboured an exorbitant dream of being a last emperor. James's biographer, Leon Edel, characterised that dream in Roman terms: 'He would create indeed a kind of *imperium* of letters, annex Europe to his native America, achieve a transatlantic empire larger than that of other novelists. And like Marcus Aurelius he would offer the world the countenance of a conqueror who was, as Arnold said, tender and blameless – *tendentemque manus ripae ulterioris amore*.'[97] One reader, hesitating in 1905 'before the magnitude of Mr Henry James's work' was persuaded of the Master's 'imperishable consciousness' and rose to a vision of the last artist-hero among the ruins:

> When the last aqueduct shall have crumbled to pieces, the last airship fallen to the ground, the last blade of grass have died upon a dying earth, man, indomitable by his training in resistance to misery and pain, shall set this undiminished light of his eyes against the feeble glow of the sun. The artistic faculty, of which each of us has a minute grain, may find its voice in some individual of that last group, gifted with a power of expression and courageous enough to interpret the ultimate experience in terms of his temperament, in terms of art.[98]

Such high-flown rhetoric is perhaps less easily dismissed when one recalls that the writer is Joseph Conrad.

In his later years Henry James himself finally became sufficiently confident of his aesthetic empire to appropriate or subjugate the matter of Rome as a metaphor for his own novelistic procedures. So, writing in the preface to the New York Edition of *The Golden Bowl* of his preference for masking his omniscient authorship behind a narrator or a narrating consciousness, James explains

> It's not that the muffled majesty of authorship doesn't here *ostensibly* reign; but I catch myself again shaking it off and disavowing the pretence of it while I get down into the arena and do my best to live and breathe and rub shoulders and converse with the persons engaged in the struggle that provides for the others in the circling tiers the entertainment of the great game. There is no other participant, of course,

93 Bloom (1976) 244. 94 Quoted in Allen (1994) 130. 95 Tanner (1995) 7–11.
96 James (1995) 70–1, quoted in Tanner (1995) 10–11. 97 Edel (1977) I 355.
98 Conrad (1924) 11, 13, 13–14.

than each of the real, the deeply involved and immersed and more or less bleeding participants; but I nevertheless affect myself as having held my system fast and fondly, with one hand at least, by the manner in which the whole thing remains subject to the register, ever so closely kept, of the consciousness of but two of the characters.[99]

Never more imperial than when he is disavowing to be so, Henry James finally deigns to occupy, for our entertainment, the arena of the Colosseum, but only on his own magisterial terms.

[99] James (1962) 328–9.

9 'The monstrous diversion of a show of gladiators': Simeon Solomon's *Habet!**

Elizabeth Prettejohn

In Simeon Solomon's *Habet! (fig. 18)*, six patrician women, accompanied by a female slave and a child of indeterminate sex, watch a gladiatorial combat from their marble seat in the amphitheatre. Audiences at the Royal Academy exhibition of 1865 would have understood the title, an exclamation used frequently in Victorian historical novels about ancient Rome: *Habet!*, 'he is hit', the cry of the crowd when a gladiator suffers the decisive blow. Viewers conversant with historical fiction might interpret the women's expressions as clues to the 'decadence' of this public spectacle: one faints in horror, another seems inured to such events, a third watches with cruel eagerness. The painting thus gives vivid visual form to a familiar scene in fictional narratives about Roman decadence. Lost from view until its recent rediscovery,[1] *Habet!* can now take its place among celebrated nineteenth-century images of ancient Rome, such as Thomas Couture's *The Romans of the decadence (fig. 13)*, Jean-Léon Gérôme's amphitheatre scenes,[2] and Lawrence Alma-Tadema's *The roses of Heliogabalus* (1888, private collection).

The picture also occupies a crucial position in the *oeuvre* of its painter, Simeon Solomon, whose career has often been figured as a story of decadence analogous to that of the Roman empire itself. According to a standard narrative that has only recently come under challenge, Solomon's career flourished briefly in the 1860s, a golden age followed by an extended

* My thanks to Whitney Davis, Colin Cruise and Rosemary Barrow for detailed and thought-provoking comments on an earlier version. I am grateful to the many Latinists who have attempted to decipher the inscription, and particularly to Peter Wiseman for his efforts both painstaking and imaginative. Eleanor Winsor Leach advised me on the Pompeian fresco in *The toilette of a Roman lady*, and Robyn Asleson made many valuable suggestions. Charles Martindale has been the most patient and sensitive of readers, ever vigilant about both content and style.

1 The picture was untraced after its sale from the collection of Charles P. Matthews at Christie's, 6 June 1891, until its rediscovery in a private collection in the early 1990s. The first twentieth-century account is by Elizabeth Prettejohn in Liversidge and Edwards (1996) 128–30.

2 *Ave, Caesar Imperator, morituri te salutant* (1859, Yale University Art Gallery); *Pollice verso* (1874, Phoenix Art Museum); *The Christian martyrs' last prayer* (1863–83, Walters Art Gallery, Baltimore).

period of decadence and decline ending with his pathetic death in a workhouse in 1905.[3] As in the case of the Roman empire, the putative cause is vice, since Solomon's decline is presented as the inevitable result of his arrest and conviction for illegal homosexual activities in February 1873, when he was just thirty-two. Many of Solomon's contemporaries unhesitatingly attributed the poverty and misery of his later career to sexual vice. More recent accounts moralise the story differently, locating the vice in Victorian society's cruel treatment of Solomon. But the simple narrative pattern of brief flowering followed by long decadence has proved too powerful to be easily dislodged.

In a sympathetic account by Arthur Symons, written shortly after Solomon's death, the decline in the painter's outward circumstances is traced palpably in his art, as a progressive loss of technical control: 'The drawing becomes more and more nerveless. . . . In the latest drawings of all, we see no more than the splintering wreck of a painter's technique.'[4] Solomon's failure, in this version, is a risk of genius, but other writers could present a more sinister morality tale. A closer contemporary and one-time friend of Solomon's, the painter William Blake Richmond, made the parallel with Roman decadence explicit. Writing after 1914, Richmond praised Solomon's early pictures, 'wholly inspired by the Hebrew Bible', but he continued: 'Unfortunately Solomon departed from his simple genius to accept an artificial and neurotic vein of late and debased Roman Art.'[5] Recent students of Solomon's work have rightly opposed the decline-and-fall storyline of accounts like Richmond's, which use the motif of Roman decadence partly as coded censure for Solomon's homosexuality. Nonetheless, there is something significant about the way Richmond locates Roman decadence at the intersection of Solomon's public career as an artist with his transgressive private life.

It is deceptively easy to divide Solomon's production into two antithetical categories: 'respectable' pictures designed to function in the public arena and 'illicit' pictures that circulated through more private channels. Conspicuous among the respectable pictures were Old Testament subjects and scenes of Jewish religious ritual, shown at the major London exhibitions of the 1860s and approved by art critics as appropriate to Solomon's Jewish background; that notion of decorum is still evident in Richmond's much later account.

However, Solomon also made drawings that were unequivocally transgressive, by contemporary standards. The most famous of these is *Love among the schoolboys* (1865, private collection), showing older and younger

[3] For a summary of the relevant sources see Seymour (1986) 1–11. Recent reinterpretations of Solomon's career include Cooper (1985–6); Cruise (1995); Dellamora (1990), esp.170–1.
[4] Symons (1906) 60. [5] Stirling (1926) 161.

boys engaged in mild flirtation. More often, Solomon chose subjects from ancient Greece for works of this kind, drawing on Victorian perceptions of ancient Greek society as sanctioning homosexuality and pederasty. In a watercolour of 1864, Solomon represented the Greek poets *Sappho and Erinna* in a scene of lesbian love (Tate Gallery); and a series of drawings from early 1865 dramatised the Diamastigosis, an ancient Spartan ritual that involved flagellating naked boys before the altar of Artemis.[6]

Drawings of this kind were never exhibited in public. Instead they were photographed by the skilled fine art photographer, Frederick Hollyer, and circulated on a special private market – an elite market, since Hollyer's photographs were high in quality and quite expensive. One set of photographs was purchased late in 1868 by John Addington Symonds, the author of two privately published theoretical discussions of homosexuality in the Greek and modern worlds, *A Problem in Greek Ethics* (written in the late 1860s, printed in 1883) and *A Problem in Modern Ethics* of 1891. However, Symonds had misgivings about Solomon's drawings. As he wrote in a letter, 'They rather please me, except that they are, I feel, the product of a distempered and radically vicious soul gifted with a sense of Beauty – *une fleur maldive*.'[7] Symonds' equivocations suggest that Solomon's drawings were functioning on the borderline between fine art and pornography.

The obvious parallel with the recent controversy over Robert Mapplethorpe's photographs makes it difficult to be condescending about this Victorian situation. Indeed, to divide Solomon's production between a respectable Hebraic category and an illicit Hellenic one is to subscribe to a simplistic model of the Victorian world as irrevocably sundered between a public face of moral rectitude and an underworld of private vice. This model, fashionable in the 1960s, has come under attack from the Foucauldian perspectives of more recent studies of Victorian sexuality.[8]

It is here that *Habet!*, and Solomon's few other pictures of Roman decadence, are of special interest: Solomon's Roman pictures destroy any notional boundary between public respectability and private vice. The pictures clearly functioned in the public realm; *Habet!* was prominent in press reviews of the Royal Academy exhibition of 1865. Nonetheless, *Habet!* and the other Roman pictures explore the same issues as the privately circulated drawings: sado-masochism and homoeroticism, to use the most convenient modern terms. Since the Roman pictures are much larger and more considered works than the drawings, it might be argued that they make more complex explorations of problematical areas in Victorian sexual morality.

[6] Two drawings with Diamastigosis subjects are at the Victoria and Albert Museum; another is known through a contemporary photograph. [7] Schueller and Peters (1968) II 27.

[8] See Mort and Nead (1996); Weeks (1981) ch 1.

But how was that possible within the context of Roman decadence, ordinarily the most simplistic of moral paradigms?

A preliminary answer might be that the morality of Roman decadence, or rather its immorality, was so firmly entrenched in Victorian minds that *Habet!* could pass for a straightforward denunciation of decadence. As noted above, the picture makes visible a stock scene found in Victorian historical novels about Rome; starting with the founding work of the genre, Edward Bulwer-Lytton's *The Last Days of Pompeii* of 1834, such fictions routinely included a scene describing the reactions of female spectators to a scene of gladiatorial carnage. One later commentator on *Habet!* went so far as to call it an illustration of a popular novel published just two years before its exhibition, G. J. Whyte Melville's *The Gladiators*.[9] The painting does not, in fact, correspond to a particular scene in Whyte Melville's novel. More significantly, it lacks specific clues to the moral censure for the gladiatorial games that is built into the plots, as well as the authorial interventions, of Whyte Melville's and other historical novels. Solomon might have provided an explanatory quotation of the kind frequently printed in Victorian exhibition catalogues, to guide the viewer's moral response; he chose instead to leave the circumstances unusually vague, by Victorian standards for narrative painting. There is no hint, for instance, that the fallen gladiator is worthy of the viewer's sympathy as a Christian or a slave from Britain, like many of the gladiators in historical novels; the inscription on the parapet, cut off by the lower edge of the picture, remains tantalisingly unintelligible.[10]

On the other hand, the close-up presentation of the women is enough to put the viewer in mind of the amphitheatre scenes in historical novels, conjuring up by association the context of moral censure that ordinarily accompanied such scenes. The press critics who reviewed the painting in 1865 unanimously supplied such a context, describing the depicted figures as if they were characters in a novel.[11] They identified the central woman as the highest ranking figure, often calling her the Empress; interpreting the standing figure at the rear as a slave, they constructed an orderly social hierarchy. They were also confident about reading the facial expressions and gestures of each of the women, to differentiate their responses to the scene

[9] Bate (1899) 65.

[10] No contemporary art critic mentioned the inscription. Since Victorian critics delighted in explaining such details, this suggests that the inscription baffled them as it does modern Latinists.

[11] The following remarks summarise notices in reviews of the Royal Academy exhibition of 1865 in the *Art-Journal, Athenaeum, Builder, Daily News, Daily Telegraph, Fortnightly Review, Fraser's Magazine, Globe, Illustrated London News, Pall Mall Gazette, Saturday Review, Spectator* and *The Times*.

of carnage they are witnessing. The Empress appeared 'blasée', too familiar with such spectacles to evince a reaction; the blond woman next to the right appeared 'bloodthirsty', baring her teeth and thrusting her thumb downwards. But the woman who has fainted in horror, on the left, seemed to many critics a redeeming touch of humanity.

It is noteworthy that all critics read the psychologies of the various figures in much the same way. The two critics closest to the artistic circles in which Solomon moved, F. G. Stephens of the *Athenaeum* and W. M. Rossetti of *Fraser's Magazine,* wrote longer and more enthusiastic accounts than most, but their characterisations of the figures were similar to those in reviews by critics who were unacquainted with the artist. Nor were there marked differences between critics whose general stances were progressive or conservative, or between journals addressed to elite or popular readerships. That occurred partly because Solomon was deploying fairly standard conventions for facial expression and gesture. Indeed, he altered the usual gesture of condemnation, in historical novels, from thumbs up to thumbs down, presumably because he thought the thumbs-down gesture would be more intelligible in the absence of a verbal explanation of the Roman custom; in the event, all critics read the gesture as a cruel refusal of mercy to the fallen gladiator.

The uniformity of the critical responses also indicates that critics were deploying standard conventions for their own verbal characterisations of the figures. To single out one figure, in this case the fainting woman, as a 'redeeming' touch of human 'sympathy' was a frequent technique in Victorian art criticism. Otherwise, critics stressed signs of deviation from normative female sympathy. Pretending merely to describe, they were interpreting. Repeatedly they singled out physical characteristics with pejorative vocabulary: the Empress's 'languid air' and 'heavy-lidded' eyes, the lip of the blond woman curled with disdain, the thumbs-down gesture of two of the figures.[12] These observations were highly selective, concentrating on signs of unfeminine cruelty but omitting any reference to the women's attractiveness. The only comment on the gleaming textures of the women's hair, for instance, criticised the fashion of hairdressing as over-elaborate,[13] and no critic used admiring vocabulary to describe the women's full red lips or their clear skins. The critical accounts encourage the reader to see the characterisations as censorious, and by extension to interpret the entire scene as a morality tale condemning the wickedness of the gladiatorial games in particular and Roman decadence in general.

Solomon's visual characterisations need not be read in so prescriptive a

[12] *Saturday Review,* 3 June 1865, 666 ('languid air'); *Fraser's Magazine* 71 (June 1865) 744 ('heavy-lidded'). Virtually all critics mentioned the thumbs-down gesture.

[13] 'The Royal Academy Exhibition', *Builder* (13 May 1865) 330.

fashion; indeed he was using physical features that were part of a pictorial vocabulary for female beauty, to be explored below. Nonetheless, critics could plausibly present their pejorative verbal characterisations, by drawing on conventional assumptions about the wickedness of Roman women promoted by contemporary fiction. Even the critic who complained that the picture was 'not very complimentary to the Roman ladies' presented this as a simple excess of 'realism': 'This indiscriminating love of historical accuracy leads [painters] into a realism that is quite offensive.'[14]

Although the press accounts might seem to have neutralised the picture's potential celebration of feminine evil, several critics nonetheless pleaded for a more thoroughgoing form of censorship: the subject, they wrote, was one which ought never to have been painted in the first place.[15] Such comments hint that despite all efforts to persuade the reader to draw a respectable moral from the scene, another, more dangerous, reading remained possible.

That response may well have amused Solomon's friend, the poet Algernon Charles Swinburne, since he had virtually predicted it even before the picture was painted. Perhaps the first adumbration of the general theme of *Habet!* is in the opening pages of the novel Swinburne wrote at the beginning of the 1860s, *A Year's Letters*. Here Swinburne attacks contemporary practices of both literary and artistic criticism, parodying the Victorian critic's propensity to value morally worthy subject-matter over beauty of style. Swinburne invents words for a fictional critic of moralising views: 'For our part, we prefer a badly drawn and faintly coloured picture representing an act of virtue – say a sister of charity visiting the sick – to the most gorgeous and laboured reproduction of a scene better forgotten – for instance, the monstrous diversion of a show of gladiators.'[16]

Swinburne was unable to find a publisher for his 'immoral' novel until late in the 1870s,[17] but the artists and writers in Swinburne's circle must have known the work well, given Swinburne's habit of reading his writings aloud to his friends. The passage makes the Roman gladiatorial games the quintessential example of a transgressive kind of subject matter; Solomon's choice of a gladiatorial subject, for his largest and most ambitious Royal Academy picture, might therefore be described as a kind of challenge. In the event, many real Victorian art critics concurred with Swinburne's fictional critic, describing *Habet!* in terms uncannily reminiscent of Swinburne's phrase: 'a scene better forgotten'.

Swinburne elaborated on the motif of the gladiatorial games in his poem 'Faustine', first published in the *Spectator* in 1862. The title anglicises the name of Faustina, wife of Marcus Aurelius and the most decadent of

[14] *Pall Mall Gazette* (3 May 1865) 10.
[15] *Ibid.*; *Illustrated London News* (13 May 1865) 451; *The Times* (8 May 1865) 8.
[16] Swinburne (1974) 8. [17] See *ibid.*, xi, xxv–xxxii.

Roman empresses, notorious for her reputed affair with a gladiator. Swinburne goes well beyond the story of the historical empress, to create a female archetype of magnificent cruelty and sensuality transcending any one historical location. Nonetheless, the most elaborate image is that of Faustine watching the gladiatorial games in the Roman amphitheatre:

> She loved the games men played with death,
> Where death must win;
> As though the slain man's blood and breath
> Revived Faustine.
>
> Nets caught the pike, pikes tore the net;
> Lithe limbs and lean
> From drained-out pores dripped thick red sweat
> To soothe Faustine.
>
> She drank the steaming drift and dust
> Blown off the scene;
> Blood could not ease the bitter lust
> That galled Faustine.

George Du Maurier's novel of 1894, *Trilby,* recalls the impact of Swinburne's poem on the young artists of the early 1860s, presenting the three fictional artists of his story as impressed by the poem:

> For Taffy was getting sick of 'this ghastly thin-faced time of ours', as he sadly called it (quoting from a strange and very beautiful poem called 'Faustine', which had just appeared in the *Spectator* – and which our three enthusiasts already knew by heart), and beginning to love all things that were old and regal and rotten and forgotten and of bad repute, and to long to paint them just as they really were. (Part Sixth)

Habet! would appear to carry Taffy's longing into practice. Although the picture is not an illustration in the earlier Victorian sense of reproducing the exact details of the literary text, it recapitulates the theme and tone of Swinburne's poem. Moreover, Swinburne's description of the physical appearance of his Faustine corresponds closely to the women in Solomon's *Habet!*:

> That clear hair heavily bound back,
> The lights wherein
> Shift from dead blue to burnt-up black;
> Your throat, Faustine,
>
> Strong, heavy, throwing out the face
> And hard bright chin
> And shameful scornful lips that grace
> Their shame, Faustine . . .

The physical features Swinburne stresses are exactly the ones most prominent in Solomon's later picture: heavy hair, strong throat, 'hard bright chin', 'scornful lips'. Although it is not inconceivable that Solomon had Swinburne's words in mind when designing the picture, the resemblance is principally due to the way that both Swinburne's words and Solomon's figures reproduce a female physical type particularly associated with their mutual friend Dante Gabriel Rossetti. The type first appeared in Rossetti's *Bocca baciata* of 1859 *(fig. 19)*, a picture to which Swinburne perhaps alludes in the final stanza of 'Faustine'. When Swinburne writes of Faustine's

> Curled lips, long since half kissed away,
> Still sweet and keen . . .

he echoes the line from Boccaccio that supplied the title for Rossetti's picture: 'the mouth that has been kissed does not lose its savour, indeed it renews itself just as the moon does'.[18] Rossetti's picture was something of a cult image in the progressive art circles of the 1860s, where it was seen as having initiated a new, overtly sensual female type; the line from Boccaccio epitomised the perceived import of the type, with its reference to promiscuity, echoed in the lines from Swinburne's 'Faustine'. Rossetti's deployment of the type was promiscuous in another way; he repeated and varied it in numerous subsequent pictures, certainly familiar to Solomon.

The public art critics of 1865 could not compare Solomon's figures to Rossetti's, since Rossetti resolutely refused to submit his pictures to the ordeal of public exhibition. However, art critics did recognise that a type was being employed for the female figures in *Habet!*; there were many complaints that all of the faces looked alike, and with considerable justice. All of the mouths are narrow from side to side, but full and red, with the same bow-like curve for the upper lip; all of the figures have the same pronounced jaw and bulging throat. When an exaggerated throat reappeared in Solomon's *The toilette of a Roman lady* of 1869 *(fig. 20)*, one critic characterised it as a distinctively Roman feature, a 'swelling throat' characteristic of the art of 'a period of decadence'.[19]

In the twentieth-century art historical literature, the exaggerated throat has been described more often as a peculiar mannerism of Rossetti's, frequently imitated, along with the other physical characteristics of the *Bocca baciata* type, by the artists in his circle, including Frederick Sandys and Edward Burne-Jones as well as Solomon. Indeed, the repetition and imitation of similar female types, among the artists in Rossetti's circle, has tended to embarrass twentieth-century art historians, addicted to the notion of originality. However, the non-originality of the types is precisely the point.

18 See Surtees (1971) I 68. Two virtually identical versions of the painting survive, in the Museum of Fine Arts, Boston, and in a private collection.

19 *Saturday Review* (5 June 1869) 744.

The pouting lips, luxuriant wavy hair, and bulging throat become standardised symbols, like the attributes of saints in traditional religious iconography. The pictures display the physical attributes as detachable symbols of desire, analogous to the exotic accessories that appear in the same pictures. Hair and lips share the intense colours of jewels, flowers and opulent textiles; colours that critics often likened to Venetian Renaissance painting, traditionally associated with the pleasures of the senses. Solomon's picture, too, uses glittering gold jewellery, based on Pompeian examples, and 'Venetian' colouring to intensify the sensuous immediacy of the image.

In *Habet!*, though, the standardised attributes characterise the women less as objects than as subjects of sexual desire. The spectator may choose to desire the depicted women, but the women are also presented as desiring the fallen gladiator who is under their inspection. At one level this merely reproduces a stock element in Victorian narratives of Roman decadence. Romances like that of Faustina, between patrician women and gladiators, were a commonplace in Victorian historical novels; the motif is prominent, for instance, in Whyte Melville's *The Gladiators*. Moreover, the amphitheatre scenes in novels often dwell on the female spectators' admiration for the gladiators' muscular and scantily clad bodies. In Bulwer-Lytton's *The Last Days of Pompeii*, the dialogue stresses the women's sexual excitement as they see the gladiators entering the arena. One of the characters asks her companion, 'But who is yon handsome gladiator, nearly naked – is it not quite improper? By Venus! but his limbs are beautifully shaped!' (Book V, ch. 2).

Bulwer-Lytton's context clearly prescribes censure for the decadent Roman women who lust after gladiators. However, a different reading is available for the same motif in Solomon's picture, if the spectator chooses to identify with the depicted women rather than despising them. Although this is a picture exclusively of women, the focus of their attention is a male body; one that is not seen, but implied by the direction of the women's gazes. Identification with a female subject of desire was a frequent motif in contemporary homoerotic literature. In his memoirs, Symonds reported that the first poem to capture his imagination, as a boy, was Shakespeare's 'Venus and Adonis'; Venus, as Symonds wrote, 'only expressed my own relation to the desirable male. She brought into relief the overwhelming attraction of masculine adolescence and its proud inaccessibility.'[20] The reference to 'proud inaccessibility' is poignant, given the prohibitions against same-sex desire in the Victorian period.

In Solomon's picture, the gladiator is certainly 'inaccessible'; he is not

[20] Grosskurth (1984) 63.

seen at all. In the public context of Royal Academy painting, it was difficult to represent the desired male body. Critical censure for the male nude in Frederic Leighton's *Daedalus and Icarus* of 1869 (Faringdon Collection, Buscot Park), and other depictions of idealised masculine beauty, suggests that the representation of the male figure as beautiful object made an unacceptable challenge to contemporary notions of active manliness. Solomon's picture takes a different approach, using the women to suggest a 'relation to the desirable male'; the women's gazes direct the viewer's imagination to the absent body of the gladiator. Moreover, Solomon's redeployment of the Rossettian features results in a more 'masculine' physical type, with the swelling necks, in particular, suggesting the male throat; the tendency towards androgyny, already evident in *Habet!,* would become more pronounced in Solomon's later figure types. Although the figures in *Habet!* are clearly women, the signs of physical strength in their faces and bodies perhaps reinforce the sense that they are assuming the active role associated with masculine subjectivity in contemporary writing on sexuality, in relation to a fallen gladiator whose role is passive and therefore feminine.[21]

Remembering the amphitheatre scenes in novels, it can be surmised that the unseen body of the gladiator is half-naked, athletic and probably beautiful. But the body is also mutilated. As the title indicates, the gladiator has received the blow that marks his defeat; the viewer is perhaps encouraged to imagine one of the celebrated classical sculptures of a wounded gladiator, such as the Capitoline Museum's nude Dying Gladiator. The women's gazes, then, are not only desiring, but sadistically so; two of them are gesturing for the gladiator's death. By indicating different shades of emotion among faces that all look rather alike, Solomon perhaps suggests the range of feelings that one person, or any person, might experience when witnessing a scene of extreme emotional intensity; as critics thought, the faces variously suggest pity, terror, anxiety, superiority, detachment. Nonetheless, the shades of feeling inflect a basic element of sadism. All of the figures are seated in the amphitheatre for the express purpose of watching a spectacle of hyperbolic cruelty, in which the usual outcome is a brutal death for at least some of the participants. Furthermore, the composition places the spectator in the masochistic position of the wounded gladiator himself, suffering the ruthless gaze of the women.

It is not anachronistic to use the terminology of sadism; Swinburne and Solomon read the works of the Marquis de Sade at the beginning of the 1860s.[22] Moreover, the sado-masochistic implications of the picture are

[21] See Sinfield (1994) 45–6. [22] Seymour (1986) 85.

stressed in the article Swinburne wrote on Solomon, and published in 1871 in the *Dark Blue*, a short-lived periodical with high-flown intellectual ambitions. The article culminates in an extravagant passage about the beauty of cruelty, weaving together a bewildering range of historical allusions, from Nero to St Theresa. Although the passage is so densely written as to verge on impenetrability, the references to sadism and masochism are impossible to miss. Swinburne described figures by Solomon:

> made beautiful beyond the beauty of serpent or of tiger by the sensible infusion of a soul which refines to a more delicate delight the mere nervous lust after blood, the mere physical appetite and ravenous relish for fleshly torture; which finds out the very 'spirit of sense' and fine root of utmost feeling alike in the patient and the agent of the pain.[23]

Despite the obscurities of Swinburne's writing, the final phrase is clear enough, with its reference to both the 'patient' and the 'agent' of pain.

When he wrote the passage, Swinburne was no doubt thinking partly of Solomon's drawings of subjects involving flagellation, Swinburne's own particular interest. However, he could scarcely describe those drawings in print, even in an elitist periodical such as the *Dark Blue*. When he comes to cite an example, he chooses, instead, a publicly exhibited picture, *Habet!*: 'The poignancy of this pleasure is patent and fervent in the face of the fair woman overlooking the fresh full agony in the circus.' In Swinburne's article, *Habet!* plays a crucial role; it can be openly described, but it can also serve as the prime example in the most subversive passage in the article.

Solomon returned to the theme of Roman decadence only twice after 1865, but both pictures are comparable to *Habet!* in complexity.[24] At the Royal Academy exhibition of 1869, Solomon showed *The toilette of a Roman lady*. Since the completion of *Habet!*, Solomon had made his first trip to Italy, including an extended visit to Pompeii; J. B. Atkinson, the critic for *Blackwood's Edinburgh Magazine*, was probably correct to stress the later picture's resemblance to 'the mural paintings of Pompeii'.[25] In pose and physical type, the principal figure recalls the seated female figure in the well-known fresco of *Hercules and Telephus* from Herculaneum. However, the

23 Swinburne (1871) 576.

24 A few other works by Solomon can perhaps be associated with ancient Rome: two unexhibited watercolours, of 1863 and 1865, both titled *In the Temple of Venus* and featuring female figures in semi-*déshabillé*; and the painting *Roman lady with a votive urn* of 1867, with an ambiguous setting, probably Italian Renaissance (although the subject of woman with funerary urn is strongly associated with ancient Rome). Most interesting are the two pictures of *Bacchus* (oil, Royal Academy 1867, Birmingham Museums and Art Gallery; watercolour, Dudley Gallery 1868, private collection); Swinburne associated Solomon's Bacchus pictures with Antinous (Swinburne (1871) 572–73), often represented in classical sculpture in the guise of Dionysus.

25 *Blackwood's* 106 (August 1869) 224.

conflation of the Rossettian and Roman physical types produces a figure also startlingly reminiscent of Solomon's contemporary pictures of male figures. Critical comments on Solomon's male figures leave no doubt that they appeared androgynous to contemporaries. The similar female figures, in *Habet!* as well as *The toilette of a Roman lady*, can perhaps be described as gynandrous by analogy. The possibility of oscillating gender is emphasised, in *The toilette of a Roman lady*, by the fresco on the rear wall, where the four figures mimic the grouping of the foreground female figures, but all appear to be male.[26]

The play on gender is the more intriguing since the subject matter represents the most stereotypically feminine of activities, one that corresponds to another stock scene in the historical novel. Beginning with *The last days of Pompeii*, historical novels about Rome routinely included a toilet scene, demonstrating the irredeemable vanity of the Roman woman, decking herself with make-up and attended by slaves. In Solomon's picture, the statuette of Isis, on the table to the right, suggests that the Roman woman is a devotee of a mystery cult, another standard element in the novelistic characterisation of the decadent Roman woman. Like *Habet!*, then, the picture uses the most commonplace elements from the contemporary mythology of Roman decadence to purposes that exaggerate their transgressiveness.

The toilette of a Roman lady is the only painting by Solomon to approach the dimensions of *Habet!* By virtue of size, and exhibition at the Royal Academy, these two Roman subjects must be called Solomon's major public works. Rather different is *Heliogabalus*, a watercolour of modest dimensions exhibited at the Dudley Gallery in 1868 *(fig. 21)*. Here the subject is drawn from the repertoire of historical, rather than fictional, paradigms of decadence: the depravity of the third-century emperor, already noteworthy in the classical account of his reign in the *Scriptores historiae Augustae,*[27] was reiterated in Gibbon's *Decline and Fall* and other eighteenth- and nineteenth-century texts. But Heliogabalus was also celebrated in antiquity for his personal beauty, expressed in Solomon's version through Rossettian facial features and a swaying pose with crossed feet that surely alludes to the ancient statue of a beautiful male nude, associated with Scopas and called *Pothos* or *Desire*.

Swinburne's account of the watercolour, in his *Dark Blue* article of 1871, emphasises Heliogabalus' dual role as 'Emperor of Rome and High Priest of the Sun', indicated in the watercolour by an array of gorgeously painted ritual accessories. Swinburne extends the idea into a series of dualities: 'symbolic in that strange union of offices at once of east and west, of ghostly

[26] The fresco appears Pompeian, but does not correspond to any particular example.
[27] 'Antoninus Elagabalus' 21.5.

glory and visible lordship, of the lusts of the flesh and the secrets of the soul, of the kingdom of this world and the mystery of another.'[28] These dualities are not necessarily reconciliatory. In his poetry, Swinburne used the pairing of priest and monarch to denote repressive authority, as in 'A song in time of revolution', published in the volume *Poems and Ballads* of 1866: 'The heart of the rulers is sick, and the high-priest covers his head.' Here, and in the political poems published in *Songs before Sunrise* of 1871, there is no moral ambiguity; kingship and priesthood are unequivocally to be hated, the enemies of freedom and happiness. As both emperor and high priest, Heliogabalus is indeed 'an embodiment of pure and unmodified evil', in the words used by Walter Pater, a friend of both Solomon and Swinburne, in 1874.[29] The emperor's decadence is not frivolous, but dangerous.

Yet Solomon's *Heliogabalus* is also eroticised and aestheticised. Writing of another work by Solomon, Swinburne referred to a still more basic duality, 'a supersexual beauty, in which the lineaments of woman and of man seem blended';[30] the phrase was perhaps intended to resonate through the description later in the same paragraph of Heliogabalus, the emperor who in Lemprière's words 'professed himself to be a woman'. Solomon's watercolour uses an androgynous version of the Rossettian type in an exploration of the (im)morality of decadence at least as radical as the eroticisation of pain in *Habet!* As tempting as it is to interpret *Heliogabalus* as a coded image of a sexuality gloriously free from the Victorian dichotomy between masculine and feminine, the sinister resonances of the subject cannot be ignored. The promise of sexual liberation is contradicted by the certainty of political cruelty in the representation of the emperor, no less than in that of the patrician women of *Habet!* Indeed, Solomon's pictures of Roman decadence might be described, in the words of his friend Pater, as implying a 'moral sexlessness',[31] a refusal to choose between good and evil. That suggests a bizarre parody of the conventional mythology of Roman decadence, with its black-and-white moral categories.

It might be argued that the more extreme implications of Solomon's Roman pictures were available only to an elite of classicists, aesthetes and the sexually sophisticated, while the majority audience remained content to read the pictures as straightforward denunciations of decadence. On that view, Solomon would be addressing both majority and minority audiences simultaneously, in the fashion hypothesised in recent research on the writings of Swinburne and Pater.[32] That interpretation, though, makes little advance on the old notion of a Victorian world polarised between public respectability and private vice, except in the limited sense that both respect-

28 Swinburne (1871) 574. 29 Pater (1973) 120. 30 Swinburne (1871) 574.
31 Pater (1867) 103. 32 See Morgan (1993).

able and illicit are wrapped into one image, rather than segregated between the realms of fine art and pornography.

On the other hand, the views of majority and minority audiences have points in common: both locate Solomon's pictures on the very borderline of the permissible, and in both readings it is Roman decadence that creates the potential for crossing the border. For most Royal Academy critics, the amphitheatre subject threatens to push *Habet!* beyond the pale. Swinburne approaches the border from the other side; in his account, *Habet!* serves as the case where sado-masochistic content can be brought within the realm of public discussion. It might be argued that the mythology of Roman decadence functions, in both readings, to keep the picture on the respectable side of the border, by invoking the moral context within which the Romans were conventionally censured for their depravity. However, it is the same mythology of Roman decadence that permits the picture's most extreme sado-masochistic implications; the perfectly conventional motifs of sexual attraction between patrician women and gladiators, and of the amphitheatre as paradigm of bloodshed for the sake of spectacle, are prerequisites for a 'subversive' reading of the picture.

Members of the Rossetti and Swinburne circles could use references to Roman decadence as a shorthand for indicating something exceptionally transgressive. When, in a letter to Swinburne, Edward Burne-Jones wanted to convey the extreme obscenity of some drawings he and Solomon had made, he called them 'pictures . . . such as Tiberius would have given provinces for';[33] Swinburne's passing allusion to Nero, in the article on Solomon, functions similarly. But to cite Tiberius and Nero as personifications, respectively, of the twin motifs of voluptuousness and cruelty was also a commonplace of the most conventional Victorian denunciations of Roman imperial decadence.[34] The women's sadism appears fascinating in Swinburne's account of *Habet!*, and despicable in Royal Academy reviews; but both readings depend on the perfectly respectable characterisation of the decadent Roman woman as the archetypal subversion of normative femininity. When Royal Academy critics unwittingly mimicked the words of Swinburne's fictional critic, that the subject was 'a scene better forgotten', they were placing the picture almost beyond the pale; but they were also validating the picture's 'subversive' credentials in the public press.

In 1887 the anti-feminist journalist Eliza Lynn Linton published a series of articles on the women of history including 'The Roman matron and the Roman lady', devoted to proving that increased personal and political

[33] Undated letter (British Museum, MS Ashley A. 3871), reproduced in LeBourgeois (1973) 93. [34] See for example Lewes (1863).

freedom for women led inexorably to moral decline. The climax of the argument was a scene of Roman women in the amphitheatre, watching gladiators 'among whom are lovers, once held and now discarded, whose death will be all the more exciting for the memories of the past'. The narrative then gathers momentum:

> When the trumpet sounds . . . how those languid, heavy-lidded eyes open wide and blaze with hungry fire! how the mobile nostrils dilate as they scent the coming reek of blood! And when the fatal cast has been made . . . when the conquered lifts his hand and prays the people for his life, while the victor waits for the determining sign – how their eager faces press forward above the bearded throng – their hearts wildly beating, their white bosoms heaving, their nervous hands tightly clenched, with the cruel thumbs turned up, and their shrill voices, sharpened to a scream, crying out, 'Habet! habet! hoc habet!'[35]

The passage reads as if it is a description of Solomon's *Habet!*, which Linton, born in 1822, could have seen at the Royal Academy exhibition of 1865. But the similarity may be misleading. Both Linton and Solomon were drawing on a stock repertoire of Roman decadence motifs used in many other representations, literary and pictorial, such as the historical novels by Bulwer-Lytton and Whyte Melville mentioned above. Even Pater included an amphitheatre scene in his historical novel, *Marius the Epicurean* of 1885. Throughout the novel, Pater tests the familiar conventions of the genre of Roman historical fiction; in the amphitheatre scene he introduces a version of the moralising authorial intervention used in so many previous novels:

> That long chapter of the cruelty of the Roman public shows may perhaps leave with the children of the modern world a feeling of self-complacency. Yet it might seem well to ask ourselves . . . not merely, what germs of feeling we may entertain which, under fitting circumstances, would induce us to the like; but, even more practically, what thoughts, what sort of considerations, may be actually present to our minds, such as might have furnished us, living in another age and in the midst of those legal crimes, with plausible excuses for them: each age in turn, perhaps, having its own peculiar point of blindness, with its consequent peculiar sin – the touchstone of an unfailing conscience in the select few. (ch. 14)

Solomon's *Habet!* might also be seen as testing his contemporaries' 'blindness', making the scene visible in vivid colour and detail, but without the contextualisation that might induce a feeling of comfortable moral superiority. The composition places us in the midst of decadence; we are compelled to imagine the horrifying event that occurs slightly to our left, as the direction of the women's gazes indicates, but certainly in the space we ourselves occupy. Whether or not we decode the full range of clues to sadomasochism and homoeroticism, we cannot evade the sexuality of our passive position before the women's gazes.

[35] Linton (1887) 255.

The works of Solomon, Pater and Swinburne perhaps offered artful challenges to the contemporary moral presuppositions that most fictional and pictorial representations of Rome were content to confirm, yet Roman decadence could serve either project. Indeed, the nineteenth-century authors and artists might be accused of a deficiency of inventiveness, so faithfully do they repeat the standard motifs, down to details such as the heavy-lidded eyes of the female spectators. Invention lies elsewhere, in the way the decadence motifs are deployed to radically different ends, from Linton's campaign against the women's rights movement to Solomon's exploration of recondite areas in sexual politics. The range of amphitheatre scenes alone should be sufficient to abolish the notion, evident in some recent research, that classical reference supported any monolithic cultural ideology.[36]

Another common interpretative strategy is to treat classical reference as a cloaking or distancing device, disguising, neutralising or sanitising potentially transgressive content by invoking the legitimacy of the classical. This approach is prevalent in art history, for instance in the claim that a classical subject such as Venus could make acceptable the depiction of the female nude in the nineteenth century; that has been repeated so often that it seems matter of fact. But Linton's ancient Roman parallel has the reverse effect, and stunningly so; comparison to the stock motif of the women in the amphitheatre intensifies the danger of the women's rights movement to the point of crisis. Solomon, too, raises the stakes to their maximum; in the amphitheatre, sadistic desire is no harmless foible but a matter of life and death. Roman decadence, far from distancing or neutralising issues of present import, can exacerbate them until 'self-complacency', in Pater's phrase, becomes inconceivable.

It might even seem possible to raise the opposite objection: that the historical parallel with Roman decadence is excessive relative to its contemporary import. But works of historical representation are not commodities to be exchanged for their equivalent values in contemporary relevance. Discounting Linton's text for its propagandistic motive fails to neutralise the power of the stock motif of the women in the amphitheatre. Indeed, we might suspect ourselves of attempting to distance the image of Roman decadence when we deflect our attention to ulterior motives. Solomon's Roman pictures deny us this self-complacency. We may scrutinise *Habet!*, *The toilette of a Roman lady* and *Heliogabalus* for their messages about sexuality, but the context of Roman decadence, with its implications of 'pure and unmodified evil', leaves us finally uncertain which way the messages tend.

[36] See for example Kestner (1989).

10 Christians and pagans in Victorian novels

Frank M. Turner

The Victorians and Edwardians wrote about both Greece and Rome, but they wrote about them differently. They turned out numerous multi-volume histories of the politics and culture of Greece: Connop Thirlwall's eight volumes, George Grote's twelve volumes, Evelyn Abbott's three volumes, G. B. Grundy's two volumes, as well as W. E. Gladstone's seven volumes on Homer, Benjamin Jowett's three volumes of Plato, Ernest and Percy Gardner's many volumes on Greek sculpture and Lewis Farnell's numerous volumes on Greek religion to mention only the most prominent. On the subjects of Roman history and culture the Victorians and Edwardians were much more reticent, producing many fewer and much less distinguished histories of Rome.

As W. H. Auden wrote many years ago, 'The historical discontinuity between Greek culture and our own, the disappearance for so many centuries of any direct influence, made it all the easier, when it was rediscovered, for each nation to fashion a classical Greece in its own image.'[1] The situation with Rome was markedly different. Rome was a physical presence. Roman ruins dotted the landscape because Rome had governed much of the island for several centuries. Roman history had to be sure provided a point of reference for the British to think about their own political institutions and imperial role in the world but usually a cautionary one. The Roman republic with which eighteenth-century Britons often compared themselves had fallen into despotism.[2] As the pages of Gibbon had demonstrated, the Roman empire itself had decayed into anarchy, corruption and military defeat. Rome was thus not a comfortable political example.

For the Victorians, the shared presence of the Christian faith constituted the single most important connection between their lives and those of the Romans under the empire. Concern for the faith largely replaced the eighteenth-century concern for Roman politics in the minds of the Victorian generations. The rise of Christianity within the Roman empire for the Victorians and even many Edwardians more than compensated for the

[1] Auden (1948) 2. [2] Turner (1993) 231–61.

disappearance of the empire itself. Indeed for many Victorian writers the empire had simply served as a providential vehicle for the emergence of the faith. Furthermore, and for this essay most significantly, the nineteenth century witnessed the most intense religious controversies that Britain had seen since the seventeenth century. Controversy over the early history of Christianity within the Roman empire became a vehicle for carrying out those debates.

The novel provided the device through which the Victorians and their contemporaries from eastern Europe to America debated among themselves the issues of Christianity under the Roman empire and in their own day. Examining this literary phenomenon in 1923, Randolph Faries listed over two hundred novels written by British and American authors on Roman life between the 1820s and the First World War.[3] The overwhelming majority of these works related to early Christianity. They ranged from enormously popular narratives such as Bulwer-Lytton's *The Last Days of Pompeii* (1834), the American Lew Wallace's *Ben Hur* (1880), and the Polish Henryk Sienkiewicz's *Quo vadis?* (1895) to less popular ones that closely argued and carefully encoded issues of contemporary Victorian religious conflict.

The authors of the Roman novels, following the example of Walter Scott, repeatedly indicated that they were not making up their stories from whole cloth. They followed a general practice of adding footnotes indicating which ancient sources had furnished information. Wishing to substantiate and champion the historic rise of the Christian faith, the novelists filled their narratives with fictitious details of those developments which had been more sparsely related by the ancient historians. Moreover, the Victorians regarded the Romans of late antiquity as living through an age of transition similar to their own. As Richard Jenkyns has recently argued, the authors of these novels assumed 'the doctrine of the unchanging heart' whereby the characters who populated the ancient scenes were very much like modern men and women.[4]

For many Victorians the most famous and enduring novel of Rome was Sir Edward Bulwer-Lytton's *The Last Days of Pompeii* of 1834. Bulwer-Lytton carried his reader through the streets of ancient Pompeii made familiar by the recent excavations. In that regard, the days prior to its dramatic destruction, serving as the backdrop of the story, provided the kind of sublime moment rendered in prose that artists, such as J. M. W. Turner, Joseph Wright of Derby and John Martin had attempted to capture in their paintings of the eruptions of Vesuvius. The plot itself involves the story of

[3] Faries (1923). The publication of Rhodes (1995) came to the author's attention too late to have its analysis incorporated into the present essay.

[4] Jenkyns (1995) 143.

a villainous priest of Isis, a young Christian convert and a beautiful pagan woman who also eventually converts to Christianity. The novel closes not with the destruction of the city but rather with the marriage between the young converts, who survive the disaster.

The religious themes of *The Last Days of Pompeii* were quite straightforwardly Christianity versus paganism, in this case primarily the mysterious cult of Isis which suggested some resonance, but a generally unarticulated one, with the popular Protestant perception of Roman Catholicism. Within the novel there was nothing problematic about the Christian faith itself. Upheld by a congregation of brave faithful souls, Christianity appears as a clear creed 'which, shedding light over this world, gathers its concentrated glory, like a sunset, over the next'.[5]

Yet despite its popularity *The Last Days of Pompeii* represented a path not taken for later Victorian novelists of Rome. What emerged after 1834 was a series of novels in which generally the plot resolves not around pagans versus Christians, but Christians versus other Christians in the first five centuries of the Common Era, or a conflict between pagans and Christians which resolves itself with the victory of a very particular version of Christianity.

What brought about this change in focus was the Tractarian Movement. In 1833 John Henry Newman and others commenced publishing *Tracts for the Times*, to reassert the position of the Church of England against what they regarded as the dangers posed by the English state in the wake of events from Catholic Emancipation of 1829 through the First Reform Bill of 1832. In contrast to earlier evangelical writers, the Tractarians contended that the true doctrines of the Church of England stood rooted in the patristic age and most especially in the history of the first four centuries of the church, the years of the Christian church under the Roman empire. In this respect the Tractarian Movement put into contemporary cultural play the early history of the church.

By 1836 the Tractarian Movement, by then most closely associated with John Henry Newman, E. B. Pusey, John Keble and Isaac Williams, had begun to transform itself so as to champion certain features of Catholic Christianity that most of their Protestant contemporaries found offensive. First, in their doctrines on church authority and the sacraments the Tractarians asserted very considerable authority for both bishops and individual priests. Second, Pusey in particular became associated with the teaching of fairly extreme fasting. Third, Isaac Williams stirred up a fury by arguing that the church should pursue a practice of reserve, whereby many doctrines of the church including the atonement should not be

[5] Bulwer-Lytton (1898) 390.

widely or frequently preached but rather reserved for those whose lives indicated they took the faith seriously. To the vast majority of their contemporaries including evangelicals, broad churchmen, and high churchmen the teachings, writings and behaviour of the later Tractarian Movement displayed Roman Catholic sentiment. Their suspicions were confirmed as in 1845 several of Newman's younger friends and finally Newman himself converted to the Roman Catholic church. The drift towards Roman Catholicism continued a few years later with an even larger number of conversions in the wake of the Gorham Judgement of 1850, the same year in which Cardinal Wiseman re-established the Roman Catholic hierarchy in England.

It had been Newman who brought the world of ancient Christianity into this arena of religious and cultural conflict. Through the publication of *The Arians of the Fourth Century* (1833) and *The Church of the Fathers* (1840), the latter being a collection of previously published anonymous articles, Newman transformed the early history of the Christian church into controverted territory for Victorian Christians. As Newman later acknowledged in 1857, *The Church of the Fathers* had been directed 'originally against Protestant ideas'.[6] Whereas Bulwer-Lytton had portrayed the old battle between pagans and Christians, Newman encoded modern religious controversy among Christians into the world of fourth-century Christianity. He was claiming that territory for a modern Christian vision that emphasised priests, monasticism, asceticism and celibacy. In the early 1840s he had also organised a brief-lived monastic retreat at the village of Littlemore just outside Oxford. Pusey for his part hoped to establish Anglican convents for women.

The earliest and most prominent novelist to engage Newman's vision of the ancient world was Charles Kingsley in his once famous *Hypatia* of 1853. The story of Hypatia itself was well known and had been succinctly related by Edward Gibbon:

> Hypatia, the daughter of Theon the mathematician, was initiated in her father's studies; her learned comments had elucidated the geometry of Appollonius and Diophantus, and she publicly taught, both at Athens and Alexandria, the philosophy of Plato and Aristotle. In the bloom of beauty, and in the maturity of wisdom, the modest maid refused her lovers and instructed her disciples; the persons most illustrious for their rank or merit were impatient to visit the female philosopher; and Cyril beheld, with a jealous eye, the gorgeous train of horses and slaves who crowded the door of her academy. The rumour was spread among the Christians that the daughter of Theon was the only obstacle to the reconciliation of the prefect and the archbishop; and that obstacle was speedily removed. On a fatal day, in the holy season of Lent, Hypatia was torn from her chariot, stripped naked, dragged to

6 Newman (1868) x.

the church, and inhumanly butchered by the hands of Peter the reader, and a troop of savage and merciless fanatics: her flesh was scraped from her bones with sharp oyster-shells, and her quivering limbs were delivered to the flames. The just progress of inquiry and punishment was stopped by seasonable gifts; but the murder of Hypatia has imprinted an indelible stain on the character and religion of Cyril of Alexandria.[7]

For Gibbon the story was a brief one illustrating the danger of fanaticism in the service of superstition.

Charles Kingsley transformed Gibbon's single paragraph into a two-volume novel of 671 pages subtitled 'New foes with an old face'. Kingsley portrayed fifth-century Alexandria as a vast melting-pot of peoples of various ethnic origins and religious outlooks. The two dominant personalities are Cyril himself and the philosopher Hypatia. Her gender is always the foremost issue. What makes her interesting as a philosopher is simply the fact that she is a woman, not the character of her philosophy itself. Kingsley wished to demonstrate that the Christianity characterised by monks, celibacy and strong bishops, which was associated with the Tractarians and Roman Catholics, stood opposed to women and to healthy male–female relationships as well as the true version of the faith.

Kingsley's narrative follows the story of Philammon, who leaves a monastic setting to discover what the world is really like. This journey eventually leads him to Alexandria where he encounters peoples of differing ethnic background, a vast array of different intellectual traditions including various forms of Platonism and a Christianity largely identified with monks. He rather quickly becomes familiar with the beautiful and charismatic Hypatia whose classroom Kingsley describes as 'the last haunt of the Muses'.[8] As well as writing a commentary on Plotinus and indicating some curiosity about Christianity, she is teaching her students and auditors that they possess within themselves a spark of divinity.

By contrast Philammon also encounters in the streets of Alexandria sectarian religiosity fuelled by the fanaticism of monks. These monks dislike the Jews, the Greek philosophers and other Christians. The monks run riot against any of these groups at what seems like a moment's notice. Philammon thus quickly becomes disillusioned with monks and also aware of the sharp divisions among Christians. He finds the one holy Catholic church to be anything but unified. Indeed he finds himself from time to time in sympathy with Jews and heathens rather than with his monastic fellow Christians.

Thus discouraged with Christians, Philammon attempts to understand the teachings of the beautiful Hypatia. Philammon soon desires to become the instrument of Hypatia's conversion. He intends to rebuke her for her

[7] Gibbon (1994) II 945–6. [8] Kingsley (1881) I 97.

sins, but does not know what they might be in such a philosophical woman. Shortly thereafter he becomes enamoured of philosophy and sees himself as a heathen. By the middle of the novel Philammon, now known for his association with Hypatia, is pursued by a crowd of angry monks. Hypatia herself soon becomes part of the plot of the local ruler who hopes to make himself emperor. She imagines herself as ruling with him. Eventually Hypatia condemns her own unphilosophical ambition as their plot fails.

After the failure of the coup, Cyril mobilises his monks against Hypatia. Raphael, a Jew who has converted to Christianity by the force of love rather than the attractions of celibacy, attempts to warn Hypatia of her danger. This is to no avail. She is murdered by the monks. In his retrospect on these events Kingsley commented:

> True, he [Cyril] and his monks had conquered; but Hypatia did not die unavenged. In the hour of that unrighteous victory, the Church of Alexandria received a deadly wound. It had admitted and sanctioned those habits of doing evil that good may come, of pious intrigue, and at last of open persecution, which are certain to creep in wheresoever men attempt to set up a merely religious empire, independent of human relationships and civil laws; – to 'establish', in short, a 'theocracy', and by that very act confess their secret disbelief that God is ruling already. And the Egyptian Church grew, year by year, more lawless and inhuman.[9]

Thereafter that church fell into 'a mere chaos of idolatrous sects, persecuting each other for metaphysical propositions, which, true or false, were equally heretical in their mouths, because they used them only as watchwords of division'.[10] Furthermore, with the death of Hypatia philosophy itself was silenced in Alexandria.

Although Kingsley admitted that the theologians of the eastern church had developed metaphysical ideas essential to Christianity, throughout *Hypatia* he none the less contrasted the history of an effeminate, mystical eastern church with the emergence of an increasingly strong church in the west led by extraordinarily masculine figures and receiving new strength from the infusion of new blood from both northern and western Europe. He contended that the eastern church had been drawn from practice to speculation and that 'the races of Egypt and Syria were effeminate, overcivilised, exhausted by centuries during which no infusion of fresh blood had come to renew the stock'.[11] This situation 'afforded material out of which fanatics might easily be made, but not citizens of the kingdom of God'.[12] Severe social consequences had resulted from this situation in the ancient world:

> The passionate Eastern character, like all weak ones, found total abstinence easier than temperance, religious thought more pleasant than godly action; and a monas-

[9] *Ibid.* II 321. [10] *Ibid.* 322. [11] *Ibid.* I xviii. [12] *Ibid.* xix.

tic world grew up all over the East, of such vastness that in Egypt it was said to rival in numbers the lay population, producing, with an enormous decrease in the actual amount of moral evil, an equally great enervation and decrease of the population.[13]

As a long term result of this repression of libido, the eastern church could not survive the later onslaught of Islam.

The life of the east had severed the church from its two divine roots – 'the very ideas of family and national life'.[14] Kingsley was determined to argue not only that Christianity is compatible with sexuality in marriage but that such sexuality was necessary to the very life and growth of Christianity. Serious difficulties arose when sexuality was thwarted or unnaturally denied as in monastic life. Kingsley's hatred of the ideal of celibacy is well known. His wife, whom he deeply loved and with whom it is known he enjoyed a fulfilling sexual relationship, had herself almost entered a Puseyite convent. This anxiety over a happy marriage almost lost permeated his attack on ancient and modern celibacy and monasticism.

In his preface, Kingsley, like other Victorian novelists of the Roman empire, indicated that the evils of the heathen world were 'utterly indescribable'.[15] Yet Kingsley did most memorably and for some contemporaries, such as Tennyson, too graphically relate the murder of Hypatia, which was *a describable evil* carried out by Christian monks against a brilliant and beautiful woman. Kingsley wrote,

She shook herself free from her tormentors, and springing back, rose for one moment to her full height naked, snow-white against the dusky mass around – shame and indignation in those wide clear eyes, but not a stain of fear. With one hand she clasped her golden locks around her; the other long white arm was stretched upward toward the great still Christ appealing – and who dare say, in vain? – from man to God. Her lips were opened to speak; but the words that should have come from them reached God's ear alone; for in an instant Peter struck her down, the dark mass closed over her again . . . and then wail on wail, long, wild, ear-piercing, rang along the vaulted roofs, and thrilled like the trumpet of avenging angels through Philammon's ears.

Crushed against a pillar, unable to move in the dense mass, he pressed his hands over his ears. He could not shut out those shrieks! When would they end? What in the name of the God of mercy were they doing? Tearing her piecemeal? Yes, and worse than that."[16]

Here Kingsley was describing the brutality and the unleashed sexual fury of the monks against the female philosopher who had been involved in heterosexual love.

It is important to observe that such Roman scenes, from Bulwer-Lytton's portrayals of feasts onward, allowed Victorian writers to indulge their readers in a direct description of sadistic behaviour and implied forbidden

[13] *Ibid.* xix. [14] *Ibid.* xix. [15] *Ibid.* vii. [16] *Ibid.* II 289.

sexual activity that could only with difficulty be included in novels set in the nineteenth century. There is a direct line of descent from these Victorian dramas of Christian life and persecution in Rome to the movies of the twentieth century which have vividly portrayed torture and sexual extravagance. The Roman setting and the Christian protagonists allowed the world of the melodrama, with all of its questionable morality and its image of a moral order that might suddenly collapse, to enter the polite, respectable Victorian home in an acceptable guise. The cultural cover for these portrayals of violence, sadism and sexuality was the presentation of these events in the context of a moral tale that encoded the rise of some form of pure Christianity over the moral and physical challenges of pagans or dissolute Christians. Later in the century, when novels set in the Roman empire and other tales were presented on the stage in London, even nonconformists attended these plays, which were full of excitement, morally questionable scenes and violence, because they seemed to be a portrayal of sacred history.[17]

The tendency towards sadistic melodrama also appeared in the much calmer pages of John Henry Newman's *Callista* (1856), written as a Roman Catholic response to Kingsley. Set in North Africa during the third century, the novel relates the story of a pagan woman, Callista, who eventually converts to Christianity and then shortly thereafter dies a martyr. Throughout, Newman notes the evils of the pagan world but leaves the details to his reader's imagination. For example, at one point, describing a procession of pagans, he comments, 'And then they struck up a blasphemous song, the sentiments of which we are not going even to conceive, much less attempt in words.'[18] On another occasion, he writes, 'Well is it for us, dear reader, that we in this age do not experience – nay, a blessed thing that we cannot even frame to ourselves in imagination – the actual details of evil which hung as an atmosphere over the cities of pagan Rome.'[19] They were 'scenes of unspeakable pollution'.[20] The unspeakable quality of the evil, of course, licensed and even encouraged the sadistic fantasy of the reader.

Newman does, however, make some direct appeals to the religiously prurient imagination. After Callista is martyred on the rack, her body is exposed to the elements and the vultures. Then the Christians, including Agellius, the man who loved her, reclaim the body. Describing the actions of Agellius, Newman writes, 'He has stooped down and scooped up such portions of the sand as are moistened with her blood, and has committed them to a small bag which he has taken out of his bosom.'[21] Callista's remains are then taken to a cave to become a holy relic through which

[17] Mayer (1994)16–17. [18] Newman (1873) 13. [19] *Ibid.* 113–14. [20] *Ibid.* 115.
[21] *Ibid.* 375.

miracles will be wrought. Agellius later brings to the cave his brother Juba, who through witchcraft has been possessed by an evil spirit . The following scene ensues:

He [Juba] held back, and exerted himself with all his might to escape, foaming at the mouth, and from time to time uttering loud shrieks and horrible words, which disturbed, though they could not interrupt the hymn. His bearers persevered: they brought him close to Callista, and made him touch her feet with his hands. Immediately he screamed fearfully, and was sent up into the air with such force that he seemed discharged with some engine of war: then he fell back upon the earth apparently lifeless.

The long prayer was ended; the *Sursum corda* was uttered. Juba raised himself from the ground. When the words of consecration had been said he adored with the faithful. After the mass, his attendants came to him; he was quite changed: he was quiet, harmless, and silent; the evil spirit had gone out; but he was an idiot.

This wonderful deliverance was but the beginning of the miracles which followed the martyrdom of St. Callista. It may be said to have been the resurrection of the Church at Sicca.[22]

This scene might have occurred in a gothic novel. Again, as in *Hypatia*, the victim of the tale is a woman, who is killed in a sadistic manner, here on a rack described as a bed and then handled in death by a possessed idiot. The ancient setting provided a protective colouration for Newman to explore religious practices which his contemporaries regarded as illustrating the worst of continental Roman Catholic practices and as a restatement of his argument in favour of granting veracity to ecclesiastical miracles.

One moves to a very different Roman world in Walter Pater's *Marius the Epicurean: his sensations and ideas*, published over a quarter century later in 1885. Just as the Tractarian Movement had established Kingsley and Newman's Roman landscape, Pater's was established by the late Victorian debate over the position of religion and culture in Victorian intellectual life. What is impressive about this work is Pater's capacity to see both religion and philosophy less as speculative creeds than as modes of social expectation and interaction. There are none of the scenes of gothic excess in this exceedingly cerebral work. *Marius the Epicurean* mimicked other religious novels and spiritual autobiographies of the day that traced the intellectual journey of a protagonist from some form of childhood or family religion through a series of alternative creeds and religious associations. Marius by contrast moves from traditional Roman religious observances through various ancient philosophies, including Epicureanism, Platonism and Stoicism, and finally ends his life among Christians, if not necessarily as a yet consciously faithful Christian.

Marius the Epicurean is set in the world of the Antonines and in the reign

[22] *Ibid.* 380–1.

of Marcus Aurelius. Like Gibbon before him, Pater saw that era as an extraordinarily special moment in the history of the west. Different religions and philosophies were challenging each other, but in a remarkably civil manner. Christianity was for Pater a developing historical construct rather than a providential event. Pater portrayed the Christianity of the era as the epitome of the Arnoldian vision of religion as culture which had replaced an earlier more nearly ascetic and millennialist faith. In point of fact, Pater saw this ancient cultured Christianity as in the process of shedding the elements that Arnold associated with modern Hebraic Protestant Nonconformity. For example, according to Pater, Christians at this time no longer believed the apocalypse might occur at any moment. Pater explained, 'Millenarianism – the expectation of the speedy coming of judgment – with all the consequences it involved in men's tempers was dying out. Every day the contrast between the church and the world was becoming less trenchant.'[23] The church needed no longer to endure 'subterranean worship'.[24]

And as the church had attained new safety under pagan 'saints' such as Antoninus Pius and Marcus Aurelius, it had adopted new attitudes towards the world which rejected an earlier narrow asceticism that Arnold also associated with Protestant Nonconformity. According to Pater,

> In the life of the church, as in all the moral life of mankind, there are two distinct ideals, either of which it is possible to follow – two conceptions, under one or the other of which we may represent to ourselves man's effort after the better life. . . . The ideal of Asceticism represents that moral effort as essentially a sacrifice, the sacrifice of one part of human nature to another, that it may live in what survives the more completely; while the ideal of Culture represents it as a harmonious development of all the parts of human nature, in just proportion to each other. It was to the latter order of ideas that the church, and especially the church of Rome, in this period of the Antonines, was lending herself. In this earlier 'Peace' she had set up for herself the ideal of spiritual *development*.[25]

What this church championed was chastity within the family and an emphasis on the family drawn from the best traditions of Roman life. Furthermore, the church was carrying out notable acts of charity, and the image of the Madonna, according to Pater, 'just then rising upon the world like the dawn', was inspiring a new respect for women.[26]

The instigator of this cultured Christianity, which eschewed rigorism, asceticism, sectarianism and misogyny, was the church of Rome itself. By this deft analysis Pater, who was always drawn to the Anglican high church, associated the ancient Roman church with all the most conventional Victorian values – 'the ideal of woman, of the family, of industry, of man's

[23] Pater (1885) 355. [24] *Ibid.* 357. [25] *Ibid.* 357–8. [26] *Ibid.* 350.

work in life'. He cleansed ancient Christians of all the excesses with which both Kingsley and Newman had associated them. He portrayed an ancient, patristic church that could without the Reformation serve as the source for a modern high church of England. Pater thus sought to deny that the ancient church could provide any precedent for modern evangelical religion, with its emphasis on morality, preaching and concern for the second coming of Christ.

But the battle over the territory of the first five centuries would not end so easily nor so calmly as Pater's aesthetic portrait of an ancient religion of culture. Evangelically minded late Victorian Christians would plant their claim to the ancient Roman territory. Their champion was one of the most prolific and beloved late Victorian Christian authors – F. W. Farrar, Archdeacon and Canon of Westminster, the author of *Eric*, a best-selling book for the young and a similarly successful life of Jesus as well as many other works of history and devotion. In 1891 he published *Darkness and Dawn or, scenes in the days of Nero* and in 1895 *Gathering Clouds: A tale of the days of St Chrysostom*. Both volumes went through several editions.

Farrar may be termed an evangelical, broad churchman. That is to say, he accepted much biblical criticism and was willing to see the Church of England embrace a wide spectrum of theological opinion. Yet at the same time his most fundamental religious and moral instincts were evangelical. The Christian faith was about personal redemption and the coming to a new life in Jesus Christ. What Farrar disliked was the sin of the world, especially the sins of the flesh, and sectarianism in the Christian church. One endangered souls and morality; the other endangered the proper role of the Christian church in modern society.

Each of Farrar's novels – and he hesitated to call them novels since he made extensive use of the narratives of ancient historians – had a distinct evangelical purpose. *Darkness and Dawn* represented an effort not unlike the contemporaneous *Ben Hur* and *Quo vadis?* to draw the poorly documented story of the early church and prominent early Christians on to the stage of well documented Roman history. The question that he posed for this novel was why did Christianity triumph? His answer put most simplisticly is that it triumphed because the providence and will of the Christian God overcame the evils of the Roman world.

Tacitus provided Farrar with most of his historical materials. The reader meets all the major figures of Nero's court, his mother, his wives, Seneca and others. With the exception of Seneca, Farrar portrays each of these people as utterly evil with virtually no redeeming qualities according to both Christian or Roman estimations. Seneca for his part represents the inadequacy of the best available pagan philosophy. There also runs throughout both novels a general condemnation of Roman women of all ages or what Farrar at one point terms the 'base mob of Roman Matrons'.[27] These pagan women possess no morals, no concern for family, no ability to give men or children real love.

Farrar's ancient Christians live in the interstices of Roman society and in the midst of sin and potential persecution. He writes of them,

> But for the poor Christians of Rome, though the days were so evil, life had neither tumult nor terror. They had found that which more than compensated them for the trials of the world. Their life was a spiritual life. To them, to live was Christ. They possessed the strange secret of joy in sorrow, the boast of which upon the lives of the Stoics was an idle vaunt. That secret lay in a spiritual conviction, an indomitable faith, above all, in an In-dwelling Presence which breathed into their souls a peace which the world could neither give nor take away. The life which was to most of their contemporaries a tragedy without dignity, or a comedy without humour, was to them a gift sweet and sacred, a race to be bravely run under that lucent cloud which shone with the faces of angel witnesses, – a mystery indeed, yet a mystery luminous with a ray which streamed to them out of God's Eternity from the Glory of their Risen Lord.[28]

Farrar here draws the reign of Nero into an evangelical vision of history – a vision actually long established – whereby that persecution was one of many providential moments in the sacred history of the faith.

Farrar felt compelled to reveal the extent of Roman evil, which he does through the various murders by Agrippina, Nero and others, yet in some manner also sought to justify both that evil and its portrayal. As he writes at one point, 'There is a marvelous force of illumination in a great crime, but it is the lurid illumination of the lightning-flash, revealing to the lost Alpine wanderer the precipices which yawn on every side.'[29] The evils of which he writes include wives murdering husbands, fratricide, matricide, adultery, political betrayal, the massacre of slaves described in elaborate detail, and imperial banquets and orgies.

Through all of this mayhem the Christians persevere. Finally Farrar introduces the figures of St Peter and St Paul, who are rapidly martyred along with other Christians. Before his martyrdom St Paul confronts Nero. Persecutions of this sort reveal for Farrar the inner being of the early Christian faith:

> On that day the terrible massacres began which were to baptize the infant Church in a river of blood, and to consecrate Rome in the memory of Christendom as the city of slaughtered saints. For there Paganism was to display herself, naked and not ashamed, a harlot holding in her hand the brimming goblet of her wickedness, drunken with the blood of the beloved of God. . . . Herein lay the secret of the victory of Christianity. In the Rome of Nero heathendom showed the worst that she could *be*, and the worst that she could *do*; and Christianity showed, coinstantane-

[27] Farrar (1891) 245. [28] *Ibid.* 293. [29] *Ibid.* 314.

ously, that manhood can preserve its inherent grandeur when it seems to be trampled into the very mire under the hoofs of swine.[30]

Thereafter Farrar gives detailed descriptions of the martyrdoms in the same kind of detail that would be recorded in the epic early Christian movies of the twentieth century.

But Farrar's moral is clear. The faith, virtue and courage of Christians in the providence of God allowed them to overcome the pagan world. From the blood and ashes of martyrs arose a pure faith. Moreover, there was clearly a moment when the faith was pure and the last of the apostolic truths had been delivered to the faithful. It was in this moment in the history of Christianity that evangelicals saw the true evangelical faith forged. This was the moment of Christian triumph. Thereafter would ensue centuries of decline and corruption which necessitated the Protestant Reformation. The latter movement reclaimed the earlier corrupted truth.

Darkness and Dawn provided the first act of the evangelical drama of early Christianity. It chronicled the triumph of the church over the world. In *Gathering Clouds,* published four years later, Farrar introduced the second element of the evangelical drama, the triumph of the world over the visible church. For the evangelical vision of the history of the faith, the original faith had to be planted in its purity in the age of Christ and the apostles, who had established the church and through divine inspiration written the works of the New Testament. But evangelicals then required a second act. The second event was the corruption of the visible church, the rise of medieval Roman Catholicism, and the emergence of other superstitions that would in time be purged by the events of the Reformation and the establishment of a reformed faith.

In *Gathering Clouds* Farrar locates this moment in the history of St Chrysostom and his years in Constantinople. Certain themes of this work return to those of Kingsley. Farrar repeatedly criticises the monasticism of the eastern church as unscriptural.[31] He also repeatedly reverts to his own unique misogynist outlook and portrays Chrysostom confronting one kind of political difficulty after another because of his challenges to women. In particular he points to the saint's loathing of 'superannuated coquettes'.[32] Throughout the novel, however, his chief target is 'sacerdotal wickedness'.[33] Farrar presents a long dialogue on celibacy and fasting urging that each has often been misinterpreted in the service of priestcraft. He also argues through his characters that the eucharist does not involve a sacrifice.

In addition to these familiar themes Farrar introduces the familiar condemnation of nominal versus real Christianity which had been the

30 *Ibid.* 482–3. 31 Farrar (1895) 36, 45. 32 *Ibid.* 298. 33 *Ibid.* 490.

subject of evangelical polemic from the days of Wilberforce onward. According to Farrar, by the close of the fourth century the church had become tolerated in the Roman world. But it was no longer the band of faithful persons prepared to face martyrdom. Priests and laymen had been corrupted by power, by money and especially by sex. Farrar comments,

> It was the evil lives of so many nominal Christians; the fact that genuine, untainted goodness seemed to have become entirely etiolated; the usurping claims and worldly lives of so many priests; the haughty and tyrannous ambition of so many prelates; the furies of mutual antagonism which rent Christians into fierce dissensions respecting incomprehensible minutiae of theological definition; the violence and fury of hordes of intolerant monks; the revolting self-maceration of multitudes of half-idiotic hermits.[34]

Or as one of Farrar's ancient characters states, and as Farrar himself may well have felt in regard to his own time, 'I fear that many things are called 'Catholic' nowadays . . .which are neither Scriptural, nor primitive, nor Christian, nor in any sense true.'[35]

Chrysostom has to fight what he regards as nominal Christianity, hypocrisy, superstition and pharisaism among his clergy. But in addition to these spiritual sins Farrar also sets out much more fleshly ones as he described one corrupt clergyman:

> He was notoriously one of the *auriscalpii*, who abused their priestly position to lead captive silly women laden with lust; one of those who, having frightfully abused even the safeguarded office of a *public* confessor, which Nectarious abolished because of the iniquities to which it led, had used every influence to get the office restored. He was one of those who, sanctioned by the abuse of custom, had lived with a young and beautiful *agapet*, whom he called 'his spiritual sister', and for whose richly dressed loveliness he always secured a prominent place in St Sophia.[36]

He and other priests and laymen take part in shocking debaucheries and orgies. The Church itself had thus become infected with virtually all aspects of the decadence of the late empire.

Chrysostom himself makes the mistake of challenging the position of the empress, as again Farrar's misogynist theme enters the picture. This action brings him down and with him many other Christians. Christian groups within the city begin to battle each other. Farrar describes these battles in very considerable detail as he does the tortures which Christians impose on each other, including tearing off eyebrows, torching wounds, whipping with leaded thongs and dislocating of joints one by one on the rack. All of this is carried out in the name of a hypocritical faith that has become nominal rather than real.

Farrar believed the end of Chrysostom's position and influence in

[34] *Ibid.* 71. [35] *Ibid.* 177. [36] *Ibid.* 228.

Constantinople had far-reaching consequences for the church. The church had less and less influence over the emperors in Constantinople. The dispute between the east and the west widened. As the power of the western emperor eroded, the authority of the Bishop of Rome grew steadily. The tribes from the east overran the empire. The stage was set for the demise of real Christianity in the face of a Christianity which had become part and parcel of the world.

In terms of the impact of the Roman novel, by staking out an evangelical claim to the territory of the Christian church under the Roman empire, Farrar had laid the groundwork for the image of early Christians that George Bernard Shaw would pillory in *Androcles and the Lion* (1913). In a very real sense that play provides the satiric capstone to the entire Victorian attempt to appropriate early Christianity for the purpose of modern religious polemics. To satirise contemporary evangelical Christians, Shaw needed only to reduce to humorous caricatures the image of what evangelical Christians regarded as their early Christian predecessors.

11 Screening ancient Rome in the new Italy*

Maria Wyke

In 1914 Italians flocked to see the newly released historical film *Cabiria*, which was being presented to the public as the work of the great national poet Gabriele d'Annunzio. A booklet was distributed, under the name of the poet, to the Italian press and sold to spectators at the film's regional premières within which the significance of the historical setting of *Cabiria* (and, therefore, its potential attraction for modern audiences) was spelled out:

> The third century BC, the historical epoch some great images of which are here gathered and linked in an adventurous fiction, brings forth perhaps the most tragic spectacle that the struggle of the races has given to the world. Its events and heroes seem to act in accordance with the power of a tireless flame. The blast of war transforms peoples into a kind of inflammable material which Rome strives to mould to its own likeness. Hostile fortunes – as one sees in the invasion of Hannibal 'born in full armour' – do not seem to erase but to deepen this tremendous imprint. Peace – which will be Roman over the whole Mediterranean – is still an entirely empty name . . . [T]he soul of Rome is swollen by an antagonistic and fearless will. No natural energy equals in irresistible rhythm the power and perseverance of the city founded by a savage hero in whom the violent spirit of Italic Mars is married to the mysterious spirit of Oriental Vesta.[1]

The purpose of this chapter is to explore the intimate and insistent relationship between the ancient Roman past and its cinematic display in modern Italy, a relationship highlighted by d'Annunzio's bombastic rhetoric. The present tenses of the poet's historical account of the Punic Wars between Rome and Carthage place the militancy of the Roman republic, its fearless will and violent perseverance against the menace of Africa, in the here and now of early twentieth-century Italy, while Roman warfare is already

* This paper was variously delivered during the period 1995–6 at the University of Washington (Seattle), the National Film Theatre (London), New Mexico State University at Las Cruces and the Institute of Historical Research (London). I am very grateful for all the helpful comments I received on those occasions. Most of the research for this paper was completed with grants generously provided by Somerville College, the British Academy, the British School at Rome and the Wingate Foundation.

[1] The full text is reproduced in facsimile in Pastrone (1977) 21–8. It was also incorporated into an anticipatory interview with the poet d'Annunzio in the *Corriere della sera* of 28 February 1914. Unless otherwise stated, all translations are my own.

troped as a cinematic experience – as a spectacle of racial struggle, as heroic acting and as material as inflammable as the film reel itself (a characteristic highlighted in *Cabiria*). Culminating in an analysis of *Cabiria*, I shall examine the ways in which the Italian film industry's projection of a Roman past on to cinema screens during the period 1912 to 1914 gradually developed as a discursive practice for the construction, dissemination and legitimation of an Italian national identity, an identity that was grounded in pretensions to a new Roman empire on the shores of Africa.[2]

During the course of the nineteenth century, Italy's struggle for independence as a nation-state had been fought on the terrain of *romanità*. *Romanità* was, to use Eric Hobsbawm's term, an 'invented tradition' deployed to justify Italy historically, to cement group cohesion and legitimate action in the name of continuity with ancient Rome.[3] Opposed to unification and political reform, the Catholic church used archaeology as the material trace of a providential connection between classical and Christian Rome and projected publicly both the Colosseum and the cross as signs of the enduring power of the papacy. The nationalists, however, sought a corresponding but counter political authority in the republican past to which the French revolutionaries and America's Founding Fathers had also appealed. Already in 1798 the *risorgimento* revolutionaries had attempted to found a new Roman republic replete with senators, tribunes and consuls instead of popes, priests and martyrs, and continued in their political discourse, in coins, seals, standards, public ceremonial and street festivals, to secularise the monuments and landscape of papal Rome and to replace Christian with civic symbols. The Forum was pitted against the Colosseum, the republican *fasces* against the Christian cross.[4] Iconographically the Italian general Giuseppe Garibaldi acquired the potential to usurp the features of a militant Christ and by 1860 a lithograph could depict him, in the final throes of the struggle for liberty, receiving a sword from the republican hero Cincinnatus and a rifle from George Washington (by now firmly established as the Cincinnatus of the New World). By means of such strategies, the revolutionaries hoped that Italians would recognise that the origins of their civilisation stretched back further than the emergence of the Christian church at Rome and would claim that city as the natural (because historically precedented) capital of a new, unified and secular Italy.[5]

2 For further discussion of the nationalistic agenda of Italian films set in ancient Rome, see also Wyke (1997).

3 Hobsbawm and Ranger (1983). Cf., more generally, Lowenthal (1985) 44 and 53.

4 Springer (1987) 3 and 65–74.

5 On Garibaldi's identification with Christ, see Dalle Vacche (1992) 101. For the republican rhetoric of the revolutionaries, see Bondanella (1987) 158–65 where the lithograph is illustrated; Lovett (1982) 20; Springer (1987) 136–57, 163 and 169.

After unification in 1861, the new nation of Italy continued to exploit *romanità* in its political discourses. Still needing to justify itself historically in the face of continuing opposition from the Vatican, requiring a cohesive national history for its disparate peoples and validation of its claims to authority, territory and international prestige, the new body politic proclaimed itself heir to both the civic virtues and the military victories of its Roman past. Thus celebrations held in 1911 to mark the fiftieth anniversary of Italian independence and unity included a display of Roman remains at the Baths of Diocletian. Opening the *mostra archeologica*, its organiser Rodolfo Lanciani proclaimed that it should form the basis of a future museum dedicated to the Roman empire 'where Italian youth may seek inspiration for all those virtues which rendered Rome, morally as well as materially, mistress of the world'. This evident shift in the discourse of *romanità*, from the language of republicanism to that of imperialism, was propelled by the expansionist ideology of Italy's colonialists whose ambition it was to claim a share, along with other European powers, of the decaying Ottoman empire in Africa. Despite the expression by some Italians of considerable reservations about the merits of empire, by 1911 preparations were underway to seize the North African colonies of Tripolitania and Cyrenaica from Turkey and, in an attempt to arouse a popular *coscienza coloniale* (colonial consciousness), nationalists appealed to the imperial successes of Rome's legionaries in order to shape the city not just as the moral heart of modern Italy but as the political centre of renewed empire in the Mediterranean.[6]

During the subsequent military campaigns of 1911–12 conducted to establish the new Italian colony of Libya, advocates of territorial expansion constantly sought justification in tangible signs of an earlier Roman presence in North Africa. Libya was denied its own indigenous cultural history and identity to become merely the repository of modern Italy's self-discovery as an imperial power. Archaeological knowledge of Rome's ancient empire was everywhere deployed to depict modern colonial ambitions in the more comfortable terms of a destined homecoming.[7] The edition of the magazine *L'illustrazione italiana* for 14 January 1912, for example, displayed a full-page photograph of a Roman mosaic which was said to have been discovered by Captain Ferdinando Lucchesini of the eleventh light-infantry during troop movements at Ain-Zara *(fig. 22)*. According to the captain's own accompanying account, the mosaic awakened astonishment in all the many visitors to the site due to

[6] Calendoli (1967) 108; Segrè (1974) 3–32; Gaeta (1981) 128–41; Hobsbawm and Ranger (1983) 267; Gori (1988) 12; Cubberley (1988) xii; Cagnetta (1979) 15–34; Canfora (1980) 39–40; Bondanella (1987) 165–6; Visser (1992) 7–8; Moatti (1993) 128.

[7] Fuller (1992) 213, 215 and 220.

the precision, delicacy and multiplicity of its designs, and the variety and vivacity of its colours. As if to underscore the political capital to be gained from the discovery, the magazine also reported that during the official celebrations of the new year in Tripoli, the civil and military governor, General Caneva, held a morning reception at which he bestowed courteous words 'full of profound Italian sentiment' on all his well-wishers and, in particular, alluding to the newly discovered mosaic, prompted some attendant students to spread abroad among their companions the opinion that 'our presence in Tripolitania and Cyrenaica has the value not of a new conquest, but of a fitting return to which the grand traditions of our Latin motherland have driven us'.[8] The magazine itself abetted just such an interpretation of the mosaic by juxtaposing the photograph of it with one whose caption read 'a patrol of lancers reenter Ain-Zara after a reconnaissance'.[9] The reproduction of an Italian postcard in the English magazine *The Sphere* towards the end of 1911 testifies to the widespread success of such appeals to the material traces of a Roman presence in Africa. It depicts a combative Italian sailor on the shores of Tripolitania. He is portrayed in the act of grasping the sword of empire from the scabbard of a Roman soldier whose skeleton lies partially buried in the African sands.[10]

The literary guardians of Italy's aspirations to empire in the Mediterranean also drew on the name of ancient Rome to give further impetus to the colonial cause. Italy's potential status as a great imperial power to be built up on the foundations of the Roman remains in Africa became a major theme of the nationalist poets' revolt against the modest political pretensions of the *risorgimento*. War was exalted as a path to predestined greatness.[11] Thus, just after the beginning of the war in Libya, in an oration delivered on 26 November 1911 and dedicated to the dead and wounded of the preceding two months' hostilities, the poet Giovanni Pascoli justified the African adventure as a fulfilment of Italy's historical right to succeed ancient Rome in ownership of Libyan soil and to continue its civilising mission. As he advanced towards Ain-Zara, Pascoli declared: 'We were already there. . . . We left signs that not even the Berbers, the Bedouins and the Turks could erase; signs of our humanity and civilisation, signs . . . that we are not Berbers, Bedouins and Turks. We are returning.'[12] Similarly, Gabriele d'Annunzio himself famously glorified the justice and the heroism of the war against Turkey in a series of bellicose poems which were printed in the Milanese newspaper the *Corriere della sera* throughout the campaign period of October 1911 to January 1912 and published

8 *L'illustrazione italiana* (14 January 1912) 44. 9 See *ibid.* 36 and 37.
10 See Bondanella (1987) 165–6 for an illustration and discussion of the postcard.
11 Segrè (1974) 17–18.
12 Quoted in *ibid.* (1974) 22. Cf. Fuller (1992) 213; Cagnetta (1979) 17.

immediately as the fourth book of his *Laudi del cielo, del mare, della terra e degli eroi* (Praises of sky, sea, land and heroes). In *La canzone d'oltremare* (The song beyond the seas), Victory invites Italy to come to Africa:

> With me, with me towards the burning Desert,
> with me towards the Desert without sphinxes,
> which awaits the imprint, the furrow and sowing;
>
> with me, fertile race who girds yourself
> anew to replant the ancient trace
> on which you yourself and your destiny draw . . .

Both d'Annunzio's exaltation of the Libyan campaign in *La canzone d'oltremare* and his subsequent description of the historical setting of the film *Cabiria* appeared in the pages of the *Corriere della sera*. Regular readers of the Milanese newspaper over the period 1911–14, therefore, would have had little difficulty in understanding that not only were traces of ancient Rome to be found in modern Italian warfare but that modern Italian warfare could be traced through d'Annunzio's cinematic narrative of an ancient struggle between the races. If the present incorporated the past, the past could also incorporate the present.

During the Libyan campaign the Italian film industry was likewise transformed into an instrument of propaganda, into a site for the popularisation of a colonial foreign policy. The Banco di Roma, which had considerable investments in North Africa and had encouraged the pursuit of a Libyan colony, also controlled the Roman production house Cines which accordingly produced a whole series of newsreel reports from the theatre of war, documentaries and a number of fiction films with an African setting.[13] The film historian Gian Piero Brunetta has frequently argued that the Italian feature-length fiction films set in ancient Rome (which began to be produced with some regularity from 1912) were also propagandistic because they were steeped, in his view, in the nationalistic and imperialistic tropes of *romanità* that had provided such sustenance for the Libyan adventure. The practice of cinema-going brought huge audiences out of their homes into a shared, collective space and thus rendered their experience of *romanità* a more public event than the private reading of a poem, a novel or a newspaper. The specific and developing technologies of cinema could also accommodate masses of people on screen before whom, or even for whom, the central characters of the historical fiction acted. Through these crowds of extras, mass audiences were able to visualise on screen their own collectivity and gain a stake in the history of Rome. According to Brunetta, the cinematic narration of Roman history implicitly assimilated ancient virtues and glories to present situations; the parade of imperial eagles,

[13] Dall'Asta (1992) 50 n.8; Sorlin (1996) 45.

fasces, Roman salutes, battles and triumphs which marched across Italian cinema screens during the period 1912–14 could supply vivid historical symbols of Italian nationhood and stir up among spectators a frenzy for more contemporary combat.[14]

Italy's historical films of this period have therefore been generally regarded as highly suitable vehicles to project the still relatively new nation's sense of its own identity and as highly successful attempts to improve morally, civically and patriotically their often illiterate spectators.[15] Yet the first such feature-length film, Enrico Guazzoni's *Quo vadis?* (shot by the Roman production house Cines during 1912 and released in 1913), contains no overt reference to Africa, associates the Roman eagles, the *fasces* and the triumphal processions with the decadence and cruelty of the emperor Nero, and solicits audience identification with the heroism of Nero's Christian victims.[16] The film's deployment of *romanità* appears to hark back to the rhetorical strategies of the Catholic church prior to and after unification, rather than replay those of the *risorgimento* revolutionaries or Italy's strident colonialists. It spectacularly displays not the dannunzian 'struggle of the races' but internal persecution, not glorious Roman warfare but shameful Roman tyranny, and it exalts not the fearless will of Rome's armies abroad but the brave martyrdoms of its Christians at home.

Following the customary conventions that had early been established for the cinematic narration of history, the plot of *Quo vadis?* is borrowed from a nineteenth-century historical novel. The novel was written by the Polish Catholic Henryk Sienkiewicz and concerns two star-crossed lovers, the Roman soldier Marcus Vinicius and his Christian beloved Lygia. Their love is blessed by the leader of Rome's Christian community, St Peter, but endangered by the emperor Nero who burns Rome, persecutes the innocent Christians as scapegoats and has Lygia throw into the arena tied on the back of a bull. She is magnificently rescued from death by the strongman Ursus, her faithful protector, and her lover Vinicius (now a convert to Christianity) appeals to the assembled crowds for mercy and stimulates rebellion against the rule of the bestial emperor. The film closes with a visitation from Christ which encourages the fleeing St Peter to return to Rome and with the suicide of a disheartened Nero in woodlands outside the city. In the nineteenth century such narratives of the triumph of the

14 Brunetta (1986) 57–8, (1990), 123, (1991), 64–5, (1993) 160–77. Cf. Brunetta and Gili (1990) 9–13; dall'Asta (1992) 20–1.

15 Bernardini (1982) 192–3; Bernardini and Gili (1986) 34; Cardillo (1987) 25–37; Hay (1987) 151–2; Brunetta (1991) 13–14; Dalle Vacche (1992) 3–4; Sorlin (1996) 1.

16 For a more detailed discussion of Enrico Guazzoni's *Quo vadis?*, see Wyke (1994) and Wyke (1997) ch. 5. A print of the film, accompanied by Spanish intertitles, can be found in Cineteca Nazionale.

early Church over Nero's persecutions had been inextricably bound up in wider political discourses concerning the battles in Italy over the temporal powers of the papacy. Sienkiewicz's hugely successful novel, originally serialised between 1894 and 1896 in the *Gazeta Polska* and subsequently published in numerous translations world-wide, reads as a Christian apology whereby Peter stands for the Catholic church, Nero for Italy's secular government and Christ's miraculous appearance on the Appian Way as divine sanction for the revitalisation of the Vatican's authority in modern secular Italy. For Sienkiewicz, Rome is self-evidently and for ever to be the city of Christ.[17]

The film *Quo vadis?* appears to offer a similar allegory for the conflict between church and state which had continued in Italy into the twentieth century. Long after unification, the Vatican was still refusing to recognise the secular state's existence and a mass movement had developed to reclaim national life for Catholicism.[18] The film's simple symbolic iconography pits the religiosity of the Christian cross and the fish against the militancy of the Roman standards and eagle, the peaceful hands held open and up in prayer against the aggressive soldiers' salute, the plain living and selfless friendship of the early Christian community against the sumptuously cluttered, orgiastic and cruel imperial court. Through the film's evocation of a papal *romanità*, Italian spectators were invited to interpret the climatic rescue of Lygia as the salvation of Catholic Italy from the tyranny of the secular state.[19] Such a reading of the film would surely have pleased the financial backers of Cines. Funded by Catholic banks, the production house had been organising its film-making activities as a way of extending Catholic influence in Italian society and confronting the controversial issue of Catholic involvement in the government of the nation.[20]

Guazzoni's *Quo vadis?* treated the paraphernalia of Roman rule as contested national symbols. However, on its release, the film itself was presented by the press as a glorious product of the Italian nation. It was widely admired, both at home and abroad, for its innovative feature length, its narrative complexity, its huge sumptuous set designs, elaborate costumes and archaeologically detailed props, its naturalistic acting, its use of long shots and close-ups designed to alternate individual and collective experience of imperial Rome, its skilled development of crowd movement through a newly expanded depth of field and its use of point-of-view shots to engage spectators with its astonishing spectacle of Roman history.[21] The specialist

[17] See d'Amico (1946); Highet (1949) 462–4; Lednicki (1960) 55; Wyke (1997) ch. 5.

[18] Webster (1960) 3–9; Jemolo (1960) 81–3 and 134–5.

[19] Cammarota (1987) 15–16 argues for such a reading of the film. Cf. Wyke (1997) ch. 5.

[20] Forgacs (1990) 50; de Vincenti (1988) 26.

[21] Paolella (1956) 163–6; Cary (1974) 6–7; Bernardini (1982) 149–50; Elley (1984) 124; de Vincenti (1988) 14–15; Wyke (1997) ch. 5.

Turinese magazine *L'illustrazione cinematografica* for 20–5 May 1913, for example, proudly boasted that:

> with regard to cinematographic technology, this can be considered a magnificent victory, given that it is not easy to offer a vision at once so rapid and pressing and so steady, radiant and dark that nonetheless leaves eyes fresh and nerves calm.
>
> Our sincere and unconditional applause may greet therefore the bold, but successful, initiative of this film's producers. In their work we do not see a casual and detached occurrence; but the first stone of a new and stupendous edifice in which are enclosed the fortunes of the cinematography of the future. This is the furthest step yet taken towards conquest.[22]

Thus the Italian press and film industry, eliding the narrative ambivalence of *Quo vadis?* and underscoring only its technical and aesthetic sophistication, everywhere promoted it as a prized national artefact. Whatever the symbolic significance of the film's extravagant narrative of Neronian Rome, its visual brilliance was thought capable of enhancing the prestige of the Italian film industry at a time when Italy was seeking to elevate itself to the ranks of the great industrial powers, and provided sufficient justification for the frequent parade in Italian film reviews of military metaphors such as 'victory' and 'conquest'.[23]

The cult of *romanità* appears to have been homogeneous neither in Italy's cultural formation generally nor in its cinematic productions of Roman history. If *romanità* was an ambiguous concept, an invented tradition capable of assimilating modern Italy both to the glories of the Roman empire and to the Christian values which were regarded as having destroyed the pagan past, it is not surprising that such ambiguity seeped into the cinematic reconstructions of Italy's ancient history which were themselves subject to other, sometimes conflicting, aesthetic, technological and economic determinants. In the case of *Quo vadis?*, and despite the views of Brunetta, it is clear that in early 1913 there was as yet no intimate union between the *romanità* of Italian cinema and that of Italy's colonialists.

The strategies for representing ancient Rome on screen which Italian silent cinema inherited from the nineteenth century were only gradually reshaped after the conquest of Libya better to suit the nationalistic and imperialistic agenda of modern Italy. Following the immense critical and commercial success of *Quo vadis?* in the early months of 1913, two films about the volcanic destruction of the ancient Italian city of Pompeii were released in August from competing studios in Turin.[24] Both films followed

22 This review, among others, is quoted in Martinelli (1993) 175–82. See also Turconi (1963) 48–9.

23 On the prestige thought to accrue to Italian historical films, see generally Brunetta (1986) 56–9; dall'Asta (1992) 19–20; Sorlin (1996) 16–43.

24 For more detailed discussion of these two films, see Martinelli (1993) 296–301 and 314–19; Martinelli (1994); Redi (1994); Wyke (1996) and Wyke (1997) ch. 6.

preceding patterns in their dependency for their plot-line on a nineteenth-century historical romance, this time by the English writer Lord Edward Bulwer-Lytton. Published in 1834 and subsequently circulated in many translations, *The Last Days of Pompeii* brings the ruins of Pompeii to life by recounting a sensational, melodramatic love story against the backdrop of the doomed city. Glaucus, an Athenian gentleman resident in Pompeii, falls in love with another Greek resident of the city, the beautiful Ione. Jealous of their love, the evil Egyptian priest Arbaces who presides over the local worship of Isis, murders Ione's Christian brother and contrives to have Glaucus accused of the crime. When Vesuvius erupts and overwhelms the corrupted city, a blind flower-girl called Nydia, who is hopelessly in love with Glaucus, organises his rescue from the arena where he has been condemned to the lions, and drowns herself only after she has selflessly conducted the lovers to the safety of an escaping ship. The religiously sentimental outcome finds Glaucus and Ione now happily ensconced in Athens, married and converts to Christianity.[25]

Both the film directed by Eleuterio Rodolfi for the Ambrosio production house (*Gli ultimi giorni di Pompei*) and that directed by Giovanni Enrico Vidali for Pasquali (*Ione, o gli ultimi giorni di Pompei*) undertake various repressions and alterations of Bulwer-Lytton's Pompeian fiction in order to mesh more comfortably with the cultural identity being formulated for the Italian nation after its African conquests.[26] Glaucus and Ione are not demarcated as sensitive, democratic Athenians to be set against avaricious, decadent Romans.[27] Nowhere is there a secret Christian community to warn the citizens of Pompeii of a coming punishment for their immorality and impiousness. Nor do the lovers convert to Christianity to mark the films' closure. Instead the city is represented as a racially homogeneous community endangered by a *foreign* evil which the eruption of Vesuvius must expunge. Once the central characters have been introduced in the opening sequences of both films, it is the priest Arbaces and his vile lust for Ione which propel the narrative proper. He is visually demarcated as Other, a non-Roman. His elaborate head-dress and costume, the exotic architecture and religious artefacts of his temple to Isis, his black slaves and

[25] For discussion of Bulwer-Lytton's novel, see Leppmann (1966) 133–6; Eigner (1978) 146–7; Jenkyns (1980) 82–6 and 317–18; Mayer (1984–5) 42 and 47–8; Mayer (1994) 19–20; Wyke (1997) ch. 6; Turner (in this volume); Vance (1997).

[26] A relatively complete print of the Ambrosio film, containing some coloured sequences, exists in the archives at UCLA. Fragmentary prints are viewable at the Library of Congress and Cineteca Nazionale. To my knowledge, however, the Pasquali film survives only in the British National Film Archive and is currently incorrectly listed as an Ambrosio film directed by Mario Caserini.

[27] In the Ambrosio version, Glaucus is described as Athenian at the film's opening and when his release from the arena is demanded, but this Greekness has no narrative function within the film.

Egyptian props, all identify the priest within the iconographic terms of orientalism as belonging to the racially inferior, decadent east.[28]

In the ensuing film narratives, there unfolds a multiple colonialist rescue fantasy in which innocent western women must be saved from the lascivious predations of eastern aggressors. In the Ambrosio film, Arbaces entices Ione into his exotic terrain only to have his attempted violation of her body thwarted by her brother. Temporary safety from assault is provided in the archaeologically detailed and recognisably Pompeian home of Glaucus. After the hero's arrest, Nydia is similarly imprisoned in the vaults of Isis' temple and, on her escape, requires the assistance of a Pompeian aristocrat to denounce the Egyptian priest. The Pasquali film intensifies this colonialist narrative drive by differentiating markedly between the behaviour of a black and a white slave towards the imprisoned girl. It is only the sympathies of a white slave that prevent Nydia from being mercilessly beaten on several occasions by the vicious African servant of Arbaces, and it is the white slave who helps her send a plea for help to Glaucus' friends. As Ella Shohat has observed, such rescue fantasies manufacture a role for the western male as liberator from oriental aggression and thus provide an apparent justification for colonial domination.[29]

Both the Ambrosio and Pasquali films, therefore, simplify and reshape the narrative of Bulwer-Lytton's novel to offer their spectators a cinematic history of Pompeii which takes them on a satisfying voyage of purification and redemption from African contamination. Within this new filmic narrative, the thrillingly depicted eruption of Vesuvius functions to cleanse an Italian community threatened by external African agencies. The climactic death of Arbaces and the spectacular movement of the Pompeian crowds through the collapsing fabric of their city communicates cinematographically the collective racial fears generated by Italy's imperial ambitions, when the supposed barbarism and oriental decadence of the Ottoman empire was a pressing and constant nightmare that could only be countered by the establishment of a new, Roman empire in the Mediterranean.[30] Compared to *Quo vadis?*, the narrative structures and iconography of these two films are far more in keeping with a dannunzian display of 'the struggle of the races' and 'the power of the tireless flame' – a struggle and a flame which must lead inevitably to the destruction of Rome's African enemies.

Better still, by October 1913, another Roman historical film was released which this time set the struggle of the races on the shores of Africa itself.

28 For the discursive structures of orientalism generally, see Said (1978).

29 Shohat (1991) 62–3.

30 For the cultural threat to Italy thought to be posed by the Ottoman empire, see Visser (1992) 7–8. For this interpretation of the two Pompeii films, cf. Calendoli (1967) 78; de Vincenti (1988) 25–6; Brunetta (1991) 67–8 and (1993) 166–7; dall'Asta (1992) 40; Wyke (1997) ch. 6.

Although this new film had the same director and came from the same production house as *Quo vadis?*, it was far more convincingly enmeshed in the contemporary colonialist rhetoric of Italian imperial conquest. The subject matter for Enrico Guazzoni's film *Marcantonio e Cleopatra* (Cines, 1913) was a highly appropriate vehicle through which to express Italian pretensions to an African empire. Even in antiquity, the defeat of the Ptolemaic queen had been treated as a political necessity in order to protect Rome itself and establish peace in the Mediterranean. In the Roman propaganda generated around the time of the battle of Actium, Cleopatra had been marked as doubly Other – both Egyptian and Woman – and, therefore, doubly deserving of defeat by an Octavian who represented the patriotic restoration of the authority of Rome, the west and the Male Principle.[31] The narrative of Octavian's victory over the tyranny of Cleopatra, of Rome's triumph over Egypt, then became a founding myth of western culture and, precisely at the moment in the nineteenth century when the western nations were looking to occupy the fragmenting Ottoman empire, Cleopatra was refigured in the western imagination as an orient inviting penetration.[32] On a bronze medallion struck in 1826 to commemorate publication of a detailed French account of Egypt, for example, France is seen to disclose the secrets of an Ottoman province in the guise of a Roman general unveiling a bare-breasted Egyptian queen. The colonialist project is provided with an ancient and successful precedent, and geographical conquest and exploration of a land is naturalised as sexual possession of a woman's body.[33] It is that colonialist myth of western victory over and possession of a feminised east – better even than d'Annunzio's more equitable marriage of 'the violent spirit of Italic Mars' with the 'mysterious spirit of Oriental Vesta' – that lies at the core of Enrico Guazzoni's film.

Before initiating the historical narrative proper with the disembarkation of Antony's troops on Egyptian shores, *Marcantonio e Cleopatra* opens with actuality shots of Pharaonic monuments borrowed from documentaries such as *Paesaggi egiziani* and *Regno dei faraoni* which had been produced and distributed by Cines during the Libyan campaign.[34] The film literally cannot escape a colonialist intertext and puts on display a fantastic spectacle of politically resonant landscapes, monuments and troop movements. Beautifully crafted parades of Roman soldiers on African soil

[31] Hughes-Hallett (1990) 21–143; Wyke (1992) 100–12; Hamer (1993) xvi–xvii and 1–23.
[32] Hughes-Hallett (1990) 252–80.
[33] Curl (1994) 132. For the feminisation of the orient more generally, see Said (1978) 188 and 206–8; Shohat (1991) 46–62.
[34] de Vincenti (1988), 25. The opening documentary sequence survives in a print at Cineteca Nazionale, but not in that held by the Library of Congress. For more detailed discussion of the film, see Wyke (1997) ch. 4.

appear on numerous occasions and for long sequences of the film. Antony himself begins the film as a commanding Roman soldier in military uniform but ends it, once ensnared by the sinister enchantress, as a subservient 'Egyptian' in Pharaonic head-dress and robe. Cross-cutting neatly juxtaposes Antony's life of leisure and subservience at the savage, feminine Ptolemaic court with Octavian's life of authority at the civilised, masculine senate house at Rome and Octavian's life of activity commanding another set of Roman troops on their way to war and victory. Roman civilisation is about to triumph over Egyptian barbarity and Octavian to save Rome itself from oriental emasculation and depravity.

The closure of *Marcantonio e Cleopatra*, in order to keep the moral high ground for ancient Rome (and thus, by extension, for modern Italy), works to diminish any pathos which might accrue to the suicide of Cleopatra. In the final moments of Shakespeare's canonical play, which the Italian film invokes in its title, Caesar cloaks the body of Cleopatra with some dignity: 'Bravest at the last, | She levelled at our purposes and, being royal, | Took her own way' (*Antony and Cleopatra* V.2). As if in defiance of the Shakespearean tradition, the intertitle in Guazzoni's film which follows on Octavian's discovery of Cleopatra's body declares 'truly an inglorious ending for the last of the Ptolemies, the setting of Egypt's star salutes the dawn of Roman rule'.[35] The final sequence of *Marcantonio e Cleopatra* then exceeds the bounds of the Shakespearian tragedy to display, for the gratification of its Italian spectators, Octavian's triumphant parade on horseback through Rome, accompanied by *fasces* and standards, trophies of shields and spears and a procession of the vanquished. The final shot is of Octavian high up beneath a statue of winged Victory, standing and saluting the cheering crowds. On this concluding image is imposed the Latin motto 'AVE ROMA IMMORTALIS' (Hail Rome the Eternal City).[36] If Rome is indeed eternal, then the cinematic language of justification for Octavian's conquest of Egypt can easily translate into a justification for and celebration of the more recent conquest of Libya. Here, as elsewhere in the contemporary rhetoric of an aggressive Italian nationalism, Italy's imperial project is sustained by an appeal to Roman origins and historical continuity: modern Italy is doing nothing less than carrying on the civilising mission of Augustus Caesar. The colonialist structures of feeling in *Marcantonio e Cleopatra* were not lost on reviewers at the time of its release. While many dwelt enthusiastically on the fine cinematography and careful historical reconstructions of the film, the critic Vachel Lindsay declared

35 This intertitle is missing from the print at the Cineteca Nazionale.

36 The sequence of the triumph at Rome survives in the print at the Library of Congress but is entirely missing from the print at the Cineteca Nazionale – a clearly mutilated version accompanied by scarcely any intertitles.

that *Marcantonio e Cleopatra* 'is equivalent to waving the Italian above the Egyptian flag, quite slowly for two hours'.[37]

Six months after the release of Guazzoni's *Marcantonio e Cleopatra*, spectators were able to witness perhaps the most intimate union of sophisticated cinematography and the exaltation of Italian imperialism when the film *Cabiria* achieved its various premières in April 1914. Its original, if rather complex, plot-line orchestrated a sense of familiarity in cinema audiences by borrowing narrative detail from historical novels about Carthage, such as Gustave Flaubert's *Salammbô* (1862) and Emilio Salgari's *Cartagine in fiamme* (1906), and set-piece sequences from earlier historical films, such as the muscular feats of a protective strongman from *Quo vadis?* and the eruption of a volcano from the various versions of *Gli ultimi giorni di Pompei*.[38] The fictive Cabiria, who gives her name to the title of the film, is abducted by pirates from her Sicilian home after it is destroyed by the eruption of Etna. Still only a small and innocent child, she is taken to a slave-market in Carthage where she is bought by the high priest Kharthalo in order to be sacrificed to the city's idol Moloch. Rescued from the fiery jaws of the god by the Roman patrician Fulvius Axilla and his giant slave Maciste (who are reconnoitring the strength of Rome's arch enemy), Cabiria is recaptured by the Carthaginians but placed under the protection of Hannibal's niece Sofonisba. Meanwhile the power of Rome in the Mediterranean is threatened by Hannibal's ingenious crossing of the Alps and by the destruction of the Roman fleet at Syracuse. Ten years pass and Cabiria, now grown into a lovely young woman, is once again condemned to be sacrificed to Moloch. But after Scipio defeats the Carthaginians and their allies on African soil, Cabiria is once again rescued and sails away to Rome in the embrace of her lover Fulvius.

Cabiria has been described by historians of silent cinema as the most ambitious project of any film industry up to 1914, and as completely altering the entire conception of historical films and the whole process of film-making. The film was in production for nearly two years from June 1912. It cost the equivalent of twenty films of the period to make and lasted well over three hours. Its original theme was realised through specifically cinematic techniques and constituted a substantial advance over the current style of cinematic narration. The film's sweeping narrative drive was propelled over a ten-year period in the wars between Rome and Carthage not through the juxtaposition of a series of static shots, but through the

[37] Quoted in Ball (1968) 168 from *The Art of the Motion Picture* (New York 1915). For other reviews of the film, see Martinelli (1993) 42–5.

[38] Ghigi (1977) 733; Elley (1984) 84; Usai (1985) 51. Prints of *Cabiria* survive in a number of archives including Cineteca Nazionale and the British Film Institute, as well as being available for purchase on video.

sophisticated intercutting of carefully edited and dynamic sequences. It was projected in the grandest theatres of the principal cities of Italy, the rest of Europe and the United States throughout 1914 and long thereafter, and in both domestic and foreign journals met with ample billing and unconditional praise. Milan's *Corriere della sera* dedicated to it the longest film review yet featured in its pages and, like *Quo vadis?* before it, *Cabiria* was hailed internationally as an 'epoch-making photoplay', 'a motion picture milestone' and the 'world's biggest picture to date'.[39]

Extraordinary enthusiasm greeted the monumentality of *Cabiria*'s sumptuous, full-scale three-dimensional set designs – an architectural fantasia on African themes (massive columns, ornate ceilings, imitation marble floors, intricate mosaic patterns and giant elephant motifs) – and the clarity of its panoramic location shooting in Sicily, the Alps and the deserts of Tunisia through whose wide landscapes poured huge crowds of civilians, soldiers, horses, elephants and camels. Reviewers were also astonished (and sometimes perplexed) by the innovative use of a mobile camera which, placed on a dolly, tracked through the sets to follow its moving subjects through a vastly extended cinematic space and thereby engaged spectators in the grandeur of the historical reconstruction. An increased attention to the use of close-ups and a sophisticated deployment of natural and artificial lighting correspondingly underscored facial expressions and gestures to add intimacy to the historical narration. An imposing cultural guarantee was further provided for *Cabiria* by the attribution of its authorship to the leading exponent of Italian nationalism, Gabriele d'Annunzio, whose signature was superimposed over the opening title of the film. Although his precise contribution to the film's production has been much debated, it appears that d'Annunzio merely emended the names of various protagonists and edited the intertitles of a film already constructed by Giovanni Pastrone. Both Pastrone and the Turinese production house Itala-Film none the less presented *Cabiria* to distributors, the press and the public as the work of the poet who was also called upon to attend its Italian premières and lend his name to associated publicity.[40]

For Italian critics the technical innovation of *Cabiria* combined with its attribution to d'Annunzio rendered it unquestionably a new cinematic vision of history that brought to life an epoch of immense significance to

39 Prolo (1951) 8–10; Usai (1985) 80–3; Cardillo (1987) 52–3; Martinelli (1992) 75.

40 For the widely discussed technological sophistication of *Cabiria* and its advance over earlier film-making, see Prolo (1951) 9–10 and 67–71; Robinson (1955) 24–5; Calendoli (1967); Leprohon (1972) 31; Cary (1974) 7–9 and 44–5; Seaman (1976) 96–7; Ghigi (1977) 733–4; Prolo's preface to Pastrone (1977) 5–16; Bernardini (1982) 7–9; Elley (1984) 81–4; Liehm (1984) 10; Usai (1985) 5–7 and 44–95; Cardillo (1987) 48–53; Bondanella (1987) 207–8 and (1988) 3–4; Salt (1991) 49–50; Brunetta (1991) 55–6; Martinelli (1992) 79; dall'Asta (1992) 32; Dalle Vacche (1992) 27–53; Quarantotto (1993) 181–3; Sorlin (1996) 37–8.

the present, and their reviews became steeped in the very tropes of d'Annunzio's own nationalistic rhetoric of *romanità*. For example, the Naples magazine *Film* for 23 April 1914 declared:

The general impression was of amazement together with admiration. Our public, accustomed to the trash with which cinema poisons the history of yesterday and the minds of today, found itself at a stroke transported to a colossal and formidable setting, resounding with true war and relentless battle. The cardboard circuses and the extras' shabby boots had disappeared and two great peoples were tearing each other to pieces in an incurable hatred that was living and throbbing. . . . *Cabiria* is one of those things that will last. It will last because at that instant the vulgar art of cinema ceases and history succeeds, true history, history as lived and seen through the marvellous eyes of a very great poet. D'Annunzio has breathed new life into old burnt-out ashes, he has exhumed from their obscure tombs the names and the races which terrified the world, he has erected on their foundations an unforgettable civilisation which was living still in our memory as legend. And Itala-Film, as far as it is concerned, has completed the enormous marvel of bringing to life bloody ghosts, not only granting them power and life, but discovering still in the ancient veins of our weary and lethargic humanity, a spark to ignite a fire of enthusiasm.

Cabiria undoubtedly hymns the grandeur of ancient Rome. Through its technical and aesthetic craftsmanship, the civilisation and moral force of the Romans is continually contrasted with the crudity, perfidy and deceitful inconstancy of the Carthaginians.[41] The first two episodes, for example, position the innocent child Cabiria in two vividly contrasting settings. The film opens at the child's home in Catana, Sicily. The introductory dannunzian intertitle sets the scene for a bucolic idyll: 'It is evening, already the contest of the goatherds closes inspired by the Doric Muse on uneven flutes "to which wax grants the perfume of honey". And Battus returns from the fields to the city, to his garden at Catana in sight of Etna.' Cabiria's father is then seen to enter his home – a grand Greco-Roman temple of giddying perspectives, splendidly decorated with fine statues, vases and drapery *(fig. 23)*. Accompanied by many servants who carry in the produce of his lands, Battus holds out to his wife for admiration a bunch of grapes and a lamb. Together they pass into the pleasant garden where the child Cabiria is playing innocently with some puppets. The entire scene is marked as a happy rural idyll, an ordered site of fertility and virtuous familial serenity all cruelly disrupted by the subsequent eruption of the volcano.[42] In the next episode, Cabiria is to be seen inside the temple of Moloch at Carthage imprisoned in an exotic atmosphere of bloody ceremonial. The exterior of the gigantic temple reproduces the grim features of a horned, three-eyed monster with flared nostrils and gaping jaw through which pass the tiny figures of Moloch's worshippers. The interior is an architectural catalogue

[41] Calendoli (1967). [42] For discussion of this scene, see Usai (1985) 58–9.

of cinematic art nouveau, dominated by a massive seated statue of Moloch covered with obscure symbols, alchemic, mystical and astral *(fig. 24)*. The especially commissioned *Sinfonia del fuoco* (Symphony of fire) composed by Ildebrando Pizzetti stimulates an atmosphere of tension to accompany the terrifying recitation of the grand priest, who is animated sinisterly by a harsh and intermittent light that falls on him from below: 'King of two regions, I invoke you, I breathe the deep fire born of you, the first born. Accept the hundred innocent children. Swallow! Devour! Be sated! Carthage gives you its flower.'[43] The virtuous Roman republic is thus set against the barbaric kingdom of Carthage, order and culture against human sacrifice and tyranny. Or, as one Italian reviewer put it, on the shores of Africa and Italy stand 'two forces face-to-face, one composed of terror, the other of sweetness, one composed of pillaging, hate and violence, the other of frailty and innocence'.[44]

The closing moments of *Cabiria* disclose that such a historical narrative forms a clear intertext with the strident dannunzian rhetoric of *romanità* elaborated during the height of the Libyan adventure. After the grown-up Cabiria has been rescued from her second condemnation to death an intertitle proudly declares: 'Disarmed by defeat at Zama, Carthage submits to the inevitable yoke. The Latin ships once again cross the sea where the first naval victory proclaimed the name of Rome to the waters from the beak of Duilius' ship.' The consul Gaius Duilius was the commander of a Roman fleet which defeated the Carthaginians in a sea-battle during the first Punic War. He had been heroised in ancient historiography as the celebrant of Rome's very first naval triumph, whose victory was honoured with the erection of a column in the Forum decorated with the bronze beaks of captured Carthaginian ships. Duilius also appears in the fifth stanza of *La canzone d'oltremare*, where d'Annunzio declares to Italy that

> with all your ship-bows I sail south,
> dreaming of the column of Duilius
> which I shall make beaked with a new beak.

In both texts, Duilius marks the originary moment of Roman maritime supremacy in the Mediterranean whose victory over an African enemy requires constant renewal. Between d'Annunzio's ode to maritime victory during the Libyan adventure and the intertitle of *Cabiria* which celebrates Rome's defeat of Carthage, past and present are elided in the perpetual replay of destined conquest in the Mediterranean. The historical narrative of *Cabiria* thus speaks to its Italian spectators as analogy for and prophecy of the present domination of Africa. In this dannunzian key, the cinematic

[43] See *ibid.* 46–8 and 62–7.

[44] From *Il Mattino* for 18 April 1914, quoted in Martinelli (1992) 75–8.

reconstruction of ancient war and conquest operates as a perfect imaginary match of contemporary colonial dominion and as 'a spark to ignite a fire of enthusiasm' for continued Italian empire on African soil.[45]

Both the internal narrative of *Cabiria* and contemporary extra-cinematic discourses about the film draw attention to it as a moment when the meeting of cinema and ancient Rome produced an historical vision of enormous political persuasion. In the body of the film, Archimedes is seen to harness the powers of sunlight, through an ingenious system of mirrors, in order to burn the Roman fleet assaulting Syracuse. In the reading of this sequence offered by Paolo Cherchi Usai, the inventor is depicted sympathetically (and self-referentially) as if faced with a dilemma identical to that of the film's director – namely how to put the light filtered through a camera at the service of a battle for power. The system he invents becomes a metaphor for Italian cinema itself during the period 1912–14, when it became an instrument of destruction and liberation 'in the struggle of the races'.[46]

[45] For the colonialist strategies of *Cabiria*, see Calendoli (1967); Leprohon (1972) 30; Cary (1974) 7–9; Seaman (1976) 98; Prolo's preface to Pastrone (1977) 5–16; Elley (1984) 81–4; Liehm (1984) 10; Bondanella (1987) 208; Cammarota (1987) 18; dall'Asta (1992) 25; Dalle Vacche (1992) 27–52; Sorlin (1996) 37. Contrast Parigi (1994) 69 who regards such a reading of the film as very strained.

[46] Usai (1985) 73.

12 A flexible Rome: Fascism and the cult of *romanità*

Marla Stone

> Rome is our point of departure and our point of reference: it is our symbol, or if you will, our myth.[1] Benito Mussolini, 1922

The Roman Empire, as an idea and as a model, represented a central and diffused component of Italian Fascist ideology and culture. During the twenty years of the Fascist dictatorship, images of and allusions to imperial Rome came to saturate state-sponsored culture. Such references appeared across the cultural landscape of Fascist Italy in locations from the fine arts to mass culture, giving form to expressions as varied as neo-Roman monuments depicting Mussolini as a Roman emperor and popular films which blended Hollywood spectacle with a call to Roman strength and unity. The Italian Fascist regime's interest in establishing its historical rootedness and imperial Rome's identity as the last time that a unified, dominant Italy existed, made *romanità* one of the most determined tropes of Fascist ideology and culture. *Romanità*, the quality of Romanness, for the Fascists, meant a profound spiritual and historical destiny to be made real through Fascism.

This chapter investigates Italian Fascism's mobilisation of imperial Rome as an aesthetic and ideological imperative and the transformation of *romanità* over the course of the dictatorship. Notions of *romanità* had already been exploited in various contexts in earlier decades; this chapter seeks to foreground the specific part played by this idea in Fascist ideology (though this is a phenomenon which in many ways develops out of earlier ideological trends). *Romanità*, in Fascist hands, was an extremely malleable and changing ideological construct. The meanings and uses of *romanità* shifted, as political and cultural conditions varied between 1922 and 1943. In addition, according to the identity and function of the event, ideologues, bureaucrats and artists stressed various characteristics of the Roman empire which suited their own contemporary purposes. 'Rome' gave form to ideological constructs such as economic autarchy, Italian military

[1] Benito Mussolini, as quoted in Cornelio Di Marzio, 'Il pensiero di Mussolini, "La romanità" e la Storia', *Bibliografia Fascista* 14. 3 (March 1939) 197.

prowess, imperial destiny, demographic urgency, the cult of the leader, national culture and Fascism's civilising mission. At the same time, the Italian Fascist 'Rome' was flexible and shifting: during the Fascist ventennium, 'Rome' appeared in Fascist culture to support both nationalism and internationalism, peace and war, stasis and change, patrician and popular.

In the last few decades, scholars have begun to analyse the extensive role of *romanità* in Fascist ideology and culture. The first research on the Fascist appropriation and re-interpretation of Italy's Roman past confronted the subjects of academic and intellectual life. Luciano Canfora and Mariella Cagnetta have assessed the impact of the Mussolini regime and its ideological pressures upon the fields of classics and Roman history. They have also investigated the government and party-supported institutes and journals, such as *Istituto di Studi Romani* (Institute for Roman Studies), through which the regime diffused the cult of *romanità* and gave it the cloak of legitimacy.[2] Romke Visser has written convincingly of the doctrinal primacy of *romanità* in Fascist ideology overall; he postulates *romanità* as a key factor in the consensus of the intellectual classes and nationalist elites for Fascism.[3] Both Emilio Gentile and Romke Visser have examined the ways in which the cult of *romanità* emerged after Italian unification as part of the secular religion of the state, to be expanded and transformed by Fascism.[4]

As a whole, such research has revealed the many ways – from adapted research agendas to conferences hailing politically expedient themes to revisionist historical interpretations – in which Fascist rule reshaped the field of Roman history. The history of official support for classical archaeology in the 1930s has also shed light on the Fascist uses and abuses of the idea of Rome. Government and party interest in isolating the monuments of imperial Rome – the only Rome which counted in official eyes – often meant the destruction of the relics of other, less desirable epochs, such as the medieval and baroque. Fascist-sponsored archaeological projects often also translated into excavations hastily executed with deadlines and propaganda exigencies overriding scholarly concerns.[5] The hurried excavation and reconstruction of the Mausoleum of Augustus and the Ara Pacis to meet the 1938 deadline of the 2000th anniversary of the birth of Augustus is but one dramatic example.[6]

Fascist interest in linking the Rome of the Caesars – Rome at its military height and epoch of greatest unity – and the Rome of Mussolini began in the 1920s, as the newly instated regime searched for legitimacy. From the start, Fascist ideology looked back to the Roman empire as a source of stability and tradition. Fascism came to power presenting itself as the force

[2] See Cagnetta (1976) and (1979); Canfora (1976) and (1977). [3] Visser (1992)
[4] Gentile (1990) and (1993). [5] Manacorda and Tamassia (1985). [6] Kostof (1978).

which would unite Italy and Italians after centuries of disunity and foreign occupation. Early Fascist rhetoric spoke about 'renovation' through a 'return to Roman values'; the Roman values elevated by Fascism in its first decade centred on idealist notions of the *patria* in which the nation/state was a spiritual and universal force through which its citizens achieved identity and fulfilment.[7] With this, the regime collapsed the Roman empire into Fascist conceptions of the state as the transcendent agent through which Italy's historical greatness would be achieved. According to Fascist ideology, this 'ethical state' which drew its roots from the empire founded by Augustus was the antidote to the chaotic materialism of liberalism and Marxism. The Roman empire, according to Fascist ideologues, was an organic and stable society, in striking contrast to the disorder and individualism represented by liberal democracy.[8] This early version of *romanità* celebrated the institutions and laws of Rome, using *romanità* for domestic purposes as way to 'make the *patria* great'.

Fascist symbolism, as it developed in the 1920s, located the Roman legacy at its core and depended heavily upon *romanità* for its coherence. The Fascist imaginary which dominated Italian visual culture between 1922 and 1943 mobilised an endless array of *fasci*, eagles, Romulus and Remus she-wolves, Roman battle standards, soldiers, triumphal arches and columns. Fascism's primary symbol and its namesake, the *fascio*, the double-edged axe bound by rods, was taken from the lictors who carried *fasci* behind the Roman magistrates as symbols of authority. As one contemporary explained, the *fascio* perfectly suited Fascism because 'during all the centuries of Roman power it represented Roman power; it was the sign of collective force in the face of individual force . . . [the *fascio*] symbolises unified, co-ordinated public power, without the suppression of the individual'.[9] Fascism appropriated its gestures, as well as its symbolism, from Rome with the *passo romano* (Roman march) and the Roman salute.

With the Fascist conquest of Ethiopia and the declaration of empire in 1935, *romanità* came to serve the ends of empire, the cult of the *Duce*, militarism and xenophobia.[10] As the Fascist regime radicalised in the wake of the war in Ethiopia, *romanità*, in both content and form, became more militant and exclusive: Fascist propaganda used ancient Rome's domination of the Mediterranean as the rationale and justification for the Fascist empire of Mussolini. Fascist conquests in North Africa and the Aegean, argued Mussolini, were only moves to regain lands properly and historically belonging to Italy.

7 Franco Ciarlantini, 'Il Fascismo e la romanità', *Augustea* (21 April 1938) 2.

8 Pietro Cogliolo, 'La romanità ed il presente rinnovamento italico', *Le professioni e le arti* 6 (June 1933) 5. 9 *Ibid.*

10 A development to some extent foreshadowed in the pre-Fascist period. Cf. Wyke earlier in this volume.

The League of Nation's economic sanctions against Italy in 1936 for its invasion of Ethiopia and the regime's attendant autarchy campaign lent *romanità* a new force and a new character. *Romanità* linked to autarchy gave historical support to the argument for the superiority of Italian models, styles and products.[11] Government and party calls to reject foreign influences and to have culture reflect national and historical traditions touched all aspects of Italian society, from language and industry to fashion design and architecture. The argument for autarchy held that Italy was so rich in tradition and resources – in fact, the source of the most important of all western traditions – the classical – that other influences only corrupted it. Marcello Piacentini, the architect responsible for the urban renewal of Rome, Brescia, Bergamo, Genoa and the University City in Rome was widely perceived as the official architect of the regime and as representing the traditionalist, monumentalising wing of government-supported architecture. In July 1938, he declared: 'one must have the courage to carry out some rejections, and prepare for a stabilisation of values more our own; more our own in terms of epoch and more our own as a people.'[12] The search for cultural expressions 'more our own' together with the charged rhetoric of *italianità* (Italianness) and *romanità* accelerated the official search for an updated Roman aesthetic style.

The cult of the *Duce* – the cult of the charismatic authoritarian leader – was buttressed by *romanità*. By the middle 1930s, as Mussolini solidified his dictatorship and as Achille Starace, the Party Secretary, created the mass structures for the diffusion of the leader cult, the reigns of Julius Caesar and Augustus were reinterpreted to match Mussolini's. Thus, Julius Caesar and Mussolini shared 'the will to fix a unifying and balanced centre and a common will to action'.[13] Mussolini's purposes, like those of Augustus, were to forge 'political, family and social order . . . [to] re-stabilise the Roman peace after decades and decades of civil struggles and bloody wars'.[14] In this reading of *romanità*, Mussolini, just like Augustus, was a lawgiver and peacemaker who created a unified state based on laws applied equally to all citizens.[15]

As the 1930s progressed and Fascist Italy solidified its alliance with Nazi Germany, the regime radicalised *romanità* to provide a eugenic explanation of Italian and Fascist superiority and African and Slav inferiority.[16] In the wake of the war in Ethiopia, *romanità* assimilated a racial component,

[11] For a discussion of the intellectual formulations of 'cultural autarchy', see Marino (1983), part three, 'La disgregazione della cultura autarchica', especially section II, 'La bonifica della cultura'. [12] Marcello Piacentini, *Il Giornale di Italia* (15 July 1938).

[13] Ciarlantini, 'Il Fascismo e la romanità' 2. [14] *Ibid.* [15] Cagnetta (1976) 141–59.

[16] *La menzogna della razza*, exhibition catalogue (Bologna 1994). Though here too one might compare, for instance, the comments of D'Annunzio in 1914, discussed by Wyke earlier in this volume.

often depicting Africans and political opponents (such as the Spanish Loyalists) as barbarian or subhuman. Fascist propaganda increasingly stressed the idea that present-day Italians were racial descendants of the Romans. In this reading, Liberal Democracy and Marxism were the creations of lesser races; statism rooted in the universal idea of Rome was the natural governing system of a race descended from the Caesars. After the passage of the anti-semitic Racial Laws in 1938, Fascist propaganda included Jews among the non-Latin barbarians threatening the reborn Roman empire. The racial reading of *romanità* reached a wide audience with the 1937 film, *Scipione l'Africano* (Scipio, the African), by the director Carmine Gallone. This film, one of the most celebrated propaganda films of the Fascist era, foregrounded the rhetoric of empire as a way of conveying messages about the nation and race. The film re-invented the conflict between Rome and Carthage as the battle of unity and authoritarianism against chaos and democracy, as action against debate and irresolution. Gallone stressed the newly radicalised politics, depicting the Carthaginians as uncivilised, swarthy and 'semitic'.[17] The film won Fascist Italy's highest cinema prize, the "*Duce* Cup for Best Italian Film", at the 1937 Venice Biennale Film Festival.

More than race, however, late Fascist culture elevated bombastic historical and national categories to produce a kitsch 'Roman' style known as the *stile littorio*. With the greatest force and the least grace after the capture of Addis Ababa and declaration of empire in 1936, the regime mobilised a hyperbolic iconography of *romanità* and empire which came to colour all aspects of life in Fascist Italy. An array of posters, children's books, postcards and other consumer items carried images of Romanised Fascist legionnaires and neo-gladiators conquering Italy's colonies of birthright in the Mediterranean and Africa. The *stile littorio* favoured over-sized soldiers and athletes depicted in a monumental neo-Roman style. Late *romanità* in architecture offered 'a neo-imperialist style based on the monuments of ancient Rome'.[18] Without much subtlety, this iconography and architectural idiom asked Italians to identify the Rome of Augustus with the Italy of Mussolini.

The trajectory of *romanità* through the arts paralleled its ideological one. The Fascist Party had assumed power in 1922 with neither a determined

17 Nowell-Smith (1986) 154; *Il Gazzettino* (11 July 1937). According to James Hay it 'met with only lukewarm critical reaction' at the Cinema Show (1987:115) and according to Gian Piero Brunetta, it failed 'because of blocks of dialogue which broke up its internal rhythm, as well as the silliness of its expression and technique' ((1975): 77). Perhaps because of this ancient Rome was not much exploited in other films of the Fascist era. Cf. Wyke (1997) 22.

18 Meyer (1995) 193. Cf. Benton in Ades et al. (1995) 120–8 on the shifting architectural fashions of Fascist Italy.

cultural agenda nor an art of Fascism: Fascism's shallow roots in civil society, owing in large part to the rapid assumption of power, had precluded the development of an 'art of the state'.[19] In the years after 1922, Fascist cultural bureaucrats, themselves coming from a various political and cultural backgrounds from nationalist to futurist, developed a hybrid cultural politics which embraced a range of aesthetic styles including expressionist, neo-classical, abstract and futurist. From the start, Fascist ideology spoke of embracing modernity and tradition and of its ability to reconcile the two. This multi-valenced cultural politics meant that the Fascist approach to *romanità* in the arts began without a prescribed vision.

At first, the cult of *romanità* in the arts was flexible and played a wide range of functions. In art and architecture, a component of *romanità*, classicism, was in some way embraced by the majority of Italian interwar artists. The 'return to order' movement of the 1920s called for a cultural revision which foregrounded issues of order and balance in composition.[20] This revival of interest in the classical tradition, in the classical technique of representation and in classical imagery had a profound impact on the post-World War I cultural landscape even before the Fascist rise to power.[21] In Italy, many modern artists such as Giorgio De Chirico, Carlo Carrà and Mario Sironi foregrounded such classical elements as composition, volume and line after periods of futurist and surrealist experimentation. Achille Funi, for example, who would develop a historically inspired fresco style in the 1930s, executed 'his paintings and murals with . . . classically draped figures and [a] rich Pompeian colour scheme'.[22]

Classicism, like its related ideological construct *romanità*, offered a variety of readings. Modernists and traditionalists in the arts reacted in contrasting ways to official calls to mine the Italian past for aesthetic inspiration. Both artists and bureaucrats who wanted a contemporary-inspired Fascist culture and those who sought a retrograde official culture of Romanised art resurrected the 'classical tradition' as the appropriate source of inspiration for Fascist culture. C. E. Oppo, an advocate of a modern, classically inspired art and Secretary General of the Roman Quadriennale, articulated the call to a 'modern classicism': 'Fascism . . . must have the courage to bear the weighty crown . . . of our great artistic heritage with the ease of an old gentleman wearing a monocle. . . . In Italy there can be no neo-classicism simply because classicism has never grown old. In Italy one is either a classicist or nothing.'[23] For modernist-inspired

19 On Fascist arts policies see Stone (1998).

20 The Tate Gallery exhibition of 1990, *On classic ground*, addressed the issue of the post-World War I 'return to order' movement in the arts. See Cowling and Mundy (1990).

21 Fagiolo dell'Arco (1990).

22 Cowling and Mundy (1990) 107.

23 Cipriano Effisio Oppo, *Critica Fascista* V. 3 (1 February 1927), 44, as reprinted in Schnapp and Spackman, (1990) 264.

artists such as the *Novecento* group, a loosely connected group of artists united in 1922 primarily in an attempt to find an aesthetic at once traditional, modern and quintessentially Italian, *romanità* meant a classicism of style and form, in contrast to one of content.

One of the ways in which artists responded to official calls to make art more useful and more Italian was to turn to classical art forms. In the mid-1930s, some leaders of the *Novecento* evolved a style of public art called *pittura murale* (mural painting). In addition to celebrating the use of murals, *pittura murale* emphasised historical themes, especially classical myths. The *Manifesto della pittura murale* (Manifesto of mural painting) published by Massimo Campigli, Achille Funi, Carlo Carrà and Mario Sironi in December 1933, declared that 'in the Fascist State art must have a social function: an educational function'.[24] These *Novecento* artists proposed the creation of a Fascist, Italian, classical *and* modern style through mural painting.

Most of the celebrities of Fascist culture produced large-scale projects for the buildings and monuments of the party and the government and for government-sponsored exhibitions. Early appearances of the forms included the murals at the 1930 Monza Triennale: Achille Funi and architect Giuseppe Pizzigoni painted a cycle illustrating scenes from the *Aeneid* and a collective of eight painters did murals for the first floor of the exhibition. The 1933 Milan Triennale opened with a grand statement on the new centrality of *romanità* and of the fresco: the walls of the Palace of Art were covered in the murals of Massimo Campigli, Achille Funi, Gino Severini, Arturo Martini and Carlo Carrà. De Chirico contributed a mural called 'La cultura italiana' (Italian culture) to the Fifth Triennale of Milan and Carlo Carrà painted one entitled, 'L'Italia romana' (Roman Italy).[25]

Murals, mosaics and bas-reliefs coincided with Fascist patronage agendas in both form and content: they were all long-standing types of public art which combined Italian traditions dating from antiquity with Fascism's interest in broadening the social participation of cultural production and reception – and exploring their rhetorical possibilities. Patronage of murals, mosaics, medallions and bas-reliefs represented great statements of *romanità*; such forms reinforced the regime's connection to ancient Rome and allowed it to emulate explicitly the great Roman imperial patrons, thereby providing an alternative model to that offered by the bourgeois elites who had ruled Italy since unification. The Roman-inspired frescoes, mosaics and bas-reliefs gave off a classical aura which buttressed the

24 'Manifesto della pittura murale', *La colonna* (December 1933), as reprinted in Simonetta Lux, 'Avanguardia, traduzione, ideologia: itinerario sironiano attraverso un ventennio di dibattito' (unpublished essays, Rome 1985–6) 272.

25 These reproductions are located in illustrations numbers 115 and 116 in Barocchi (1990). On the controversy provoked by these murals see Fraquelli in Ades et al. (1995) 132.

message of the regime's longevity and historical rootedness. Some Fascist bureaucrats believed that such forms strengthened the authority of the state in ways that more contemporary ones could not. Murals and mosaics were also a home-grown response to the increasing hegemony of mass culture.

Figures inside and outside of the Fascist hierarchy seized upon public art as the way to make art more accessible to the masses and to steep artistic production in *romanità*. Fascist populist discourses, a depressed art market and demands for cultural autarchy, led to the production and consumption of vast numbers of frescoes, murals, mosaics and public statuary by the government and the party. Increasingly from 1930 on, such *romanità*-inspired public forms constituted a primary element of state patronage. In fact, in order to guarantee that artists could commit themselves to works of public art, the regime passed the 'Two Percent Law' in 1938. The law legislated that 'in all public works two percent of the total construction costs will go toward decoration'.[26]

Appropriations of Roman forms, such as mosaics, murals, bas-relief and monumental public statuary, escalated with the declaration of empire in 1935. Roman-inspired art forms fitted into Fascism's critique of the foreign, especially French, influences upon healthy Italian artistic traditions. Mosaics, murals and monumental statuary often took Roman themes, as well as forms, especially readings of Roman history and myth which coincided with Fascist priorities. According to many Fascist bureaucrats, officially sponsored competitions for 'Roman' art forms symbolised a regeneration based on national traditions. Frescoed murals, a long-standing element of public art, combined an Italian tradition dating from ancient Rome with commitment to the Fascist cultural priorities. The fresco had a long trajectory through Italian culture and history from the classical period to the Renaissance.

From the mid-1930s on, the major national art exhibitions, the Venice Biennale and Roman Quadriennale, mobilised the Roman cult by offering lucrative prize competitions for frescoes, bas-relief, garden statuary and medallions based on Roman themes such as 'they build the cities', 'legionnaires' or, simply 'the Empire'. The 1936 Venice Biennale, which wove together a number of rising ideological strands, offered two competitions: one for 'seven frescoes' and one for 'eight statues to decorate a central hall chosen for this purpose'.[27] All submitted works had to be 'on themes of Fascist life'. Yet it is important to note that this rising *romanità* in the arts co-existed with powerful support for non-historicist modernism in official

[26] Antonio Maraini, ed., *L'ordinamento sindacale fascista delle belle arti* (Rome 1939) xi.
[27] *Le mostre d'arte in Italia* II. 6 (June 1935) 1.

culture, as represented by groups such as the futurists and Fascist bureaucrats such as Giuseppe Bottai.[28]

In Fascism's second decade, the cult of *romanità* in the fine arts moved beyond form to demand more explicitly rhetorical content.[29] The winning murals at the 1936 Venice Biennale shared a common orientation of both style and substance. Celebrated works stayed close to the assignment of 'themes of life in Fascist Italy' and bore the mark of the Italian 'return to order' movement and an over-arching *romanità* and *italianità*. In one such fresco, Otello Chiti's *La partenza* (The departure), a son bids farewell to his family as he departs to defend Italy. The father remains at home to feed the soldiers and defend the land through cultivation. The themes, the unity of Italy and its empire, and the idea that all citizens must contribute to Italy's regeneration are drawn from the regime's interpretation of *romanità*. Steeped in sentimentality and references to both antique and quattrocento painting, it responds to the call to mine Italian painterly styles. The mood is quiet and static, evoking the healthy, organic life of the countryside. The painting is 'classical' in its attention to balance, harmony and composition *(fig. 25)*. In another example, Cafiero Tuti's *Opera assistenziale* offers a crowded village scene in which party officials donate cakes and grain to villagers. Here Fascism has produced an organic, harmonious and peaceful society not unlike that of the official interpretation of ancient Rome.

As the 1930s became the 1940s, official culture fused the languages of *romanità*, cultural autarchy and Nationalist Socialist cultural ideology. *Romanità* in the fine arts moved from attempts to forge a 'modern classicism' to outright mimicking of Roman styles. At the 1940 Venice Biennale the official portrait competition called for work which would present 'eternal humanity in art' – a formulation which mirrored both the classical ideal and the Nazi precept that art must be seen as a transcendent category, not shaped by political and social contingencies.[30] The competition for

28 In recent years, scholars have addressed the diverse and multiple nature of Fascist cultural politics. For the visual arts, Laura Malvano describes the multiplicity of images supported or accepted by Fascism and Fascism's changing use of those images: Laura Malvano, *Fascismo e la politica dell'immagine* (Turin 1988). The notion of Fascist artistic diversity came into general acceptance with the 1982 Milan exhibition *Anni Trenta: Arte e cultura in Italia* exhibition catalogue (Milan 1983). See also the catalogue from the recent exhibition, *Art and power: Europe under the dictators* (London 1995).

Reassessments of the architectural legacy of Fascist Italy have been particularly fertile. See: Giorgio Ciucci, *Gli architetti e il fascismo* (Turin 1989); Diane Ghirardo, 'Italian architects and Fascist politics: an evaluation of the rationalists' role in regime building', *Journal of the Society of Architectural Historians* 39, 2 (May 1980): 109–27, and *Building New Communities* (Princeton 1989); Silvia Danesi and Luciano Panetta, eds., *Il razionalismo e l'architettura in Italia durante il fascismo* (Venice 1976); Dennis Doordan, *Building modern Italy* (New York 1989).

29 Braun (1990) 345.

30 *XXII esposizione biennale internazionale d'arte*, catalogue exhibition (Venice 1940) 19.

garden statues declared that it recaptured 'an antique and characteristic Italian tradition'.[31] With the belligerent rejection of international influences and the search for 'imperial culture', the 'looking back' to classical Rome became more pronounced and exclusionary. The Venice Biennale exhibition catalogue of 1940 introduced the seventh competition for 'an interpretation of the antique in painting, sculpture, engraving or drawing'.[32] Here artists were being asked to imitate directly the styles of classical antiquity. 'Studying the legacy of the ancients directly', wrote the Secretary General of the Biennale, Antonio Maraini, '. . . would allow artists to remain faithful to the genius of the race.'[33]

Filippo Sgarlata's bas-relief, *It is the plough that draws the sickle, but the sword which defends it,* which was prized at the 1938 Venice Biennale, provides an example of the hyperbolic *romanità* of late Fascist culture *(fig. 26)*. In the bas-relief, the static and monumental figures of a soldier and peasant unite to feed and protect the empire. The classicised rendering represents Sgarlata's attempt to replicate the style of imperial Rome. The frescoes added to the façade of the main pavilion of the Venice Biennale the same year exhibit another variety of *romanità* in the arts. In the case of Francesco Gentilini's *The birth of Rome*, a Roman-inspired fresco was the perfect medium for conveying the message of historic empire. It is a naturalist-archaic pastoral scene of peasants surrounding Rome's founders, Romulus and Remus.[34] Here the attention to composition, the harmony of forms, the Pompeian-inspired colour scheme, the strong sense of line and colour and the obvious Roman theme all show deference to the exigencies of *romanità*.

In mass culture, *romanità* played many roles, providing a malleable and accessible organising principle – and an aesthetic trove – for artists, cultural bureaucrats and cultural consumers during the late 1930s. In addition to a vast array of films, cartoon strips, illustrated magazines and children's books drawing on aspects of *romanità*, official exhibitions and fairs in the 1930s depended heavily on militant *romanità*. The *Mostra augustea della romanità* (Augustan exhibition), the *Triennale delle terre italiane d'oltremare* (Triennale of Italian overseas territories), the *Fiera di Tripoli* (Tripoli fair), the *Fiera del Levante* (Fair of the Levant), together with the exhibitions held in the Circus Maximus represented central mass culture events in Fascist Italy: each one of them embraced *romanità* as its leitmotif.

The most extensive mobilisation of Romanness in Fascist official culture was the 1937 celebration of the bimillenium of the birth of the Emperor

[31] *Ibid.* [32] *Ibid.* [33] *Ibid.*

[34] *XXI esposizione biennale internazionale d'arte, 1938*, exhibition catalogue (Venice 1938) 41. The 1932 façade and the 1938 frescoes still stand on the Biennale grounds, though in a state of disrepair.

Augustus, the *Mostra augustea della romanità* (Augustan exhibition). This exhibition observed the 2000th anniversary of the birth of Augustus as the occasion for a vast archaeologically focussed exhibition celebrating the Roman empire at its apex. With the *Mostra augustea della romanità*, Fascism represented itself as the inexorable culmination of millennia of Italian history.[35] The Augustan exhibition, held in the heart of Rome, was a vast extravaganza which revivified the 'historic' Rome of Augustus through an empiricist discourse of Roman superiority. Archaeologists and classical scholars provided a full and 'scientific' depiction of Rome under the Emperor Augustus, complete with a scale reconstruction of the city, in addition to an enormous array of art and artefacts of the era.[36]

But, as one reviewer explained, '*romanità* is life, not erudition'.[37] The Augustan exhibition's purpose was not historical reconstruction, but recruiting the past for the present. In text and image, historical representation transformed the contemporary Fascist empire under Mussolini into the modern day incarnation of Augustus' empire. A quotation from Mussolini in the entry hall to the exhibition offered its guiding injunction: 'Italians, make certain that the glories of the past are surpassed by those of the future.'[38] Here Caesarism and Mussolinianism cross-fertilised to present a neo-Roman Fascist empire.[39]

The reconstructions of Augustan monuments and art, together with the vast numbers of artefacts collected and restored for the occasion, stressed the connection between the past glories of Augustus – empire-builder, peacemaker and warrior – and present victories of Mussolini. The link, though constant in the exhibition, was most explicit in the paired monumental statues of Augustus and Mussolini which flanked the entrance to the *Mostra augustea della romanità*. The exhibition was organised around sections addressing aspects of life in ancient Rome, such as law, family, culture, military, etc: the main sections of the exhibition were devoted to 'the glorification of Julius Caesar and Augustus Caesar, the formation of the Empire, the struggle against the barbarians . . . and to the rebirth of *romanità* under Fascism'.[40]

In order further to stress the symbiosis of Augustus and Mussolini, the Fascist party reopened another grand exhibition, the *Mostra della rivoluzione fascista* (the exhibition of the Fascist revolution) on the same day as the Augustan exhibition. In dramatic coordination, Mussolini inaugurated the *Mostra augustea* together with the reopened Exhibition of the Fascist

35 *Mostra augustea della romanità*, 4th edn., exhibition catalogue (Rome 1938).
36 See Cagnetta (1976), Silverio (1983).
37 'Verso la mostra della romanità', *Augustea* (30 May 1937). 38 Malvano (1988) 153.
39 'Il Duce inaugura oggi le mostre imperiali', *Corriere della sera* (23 September 1937).
40 'Verso la mostra della romanità'.

revolution, one within an hour of the other.[41] Their simultaneity reinforced Fascism's imperial/militarist and now backward-looking self-image. The dual events stressed the unity of the Roman past and the Fascist present, and the cultural environment occasioned by the creation of empire. As *Corriere della sera* declared: 'The contemporaneous inauguration on the first day of the Year of Augustus of the spectacular *Mostra augustea* and the renovated *Mostra della rivoluzione fascista* is full of significance. *Romanità* and Fascism are manifestations of the same spirit. The two great historical phenomena which led to the creation of the Empire of Augustus and to our Empire represent two moments in the millennial life of a people who have rediscovered their own virtues and reconquered their youth.'[42]

The exhibitions, hailed as 'the *Mostre* of eternal Roman strength' and as 'great documents of Italic glory', were two sides of the same coin. They functioned as complementary, educative elements in the 'Renaissance of Roman virtue, stimulated by Fascism'.[43] The Augustan exhibition presented the Fascist interpretation of the Roman empire and its value as providing eternal inspiration and purpose for the Italian people; the Exhibition of the Fascist revolution illustrated the Fascist resurrection and incarnation of those Roman values. The contemporaneous inaugurations wrapped the Exhibition of the Fascist revolution in a cloak of ancient, historically-predestined empire. 'Italians will re-see', one reviewer wrote, 'when visiting its rooms, a magnificent summary of the glorious and epic deeds that have given the Patria its new Empire.'[44] Their co-existence in two locations in the heart of Rome spread the Fascist cult of empire and its interpretation of Mussolini as the incarnation of Augustus across the capital. The presence of two 'imperial' exhibitions physically inscribed Fascism upon the city.

Imperial Rome's geographic and economic strength and its 'civilising mission' provided contexts for two other successful Fascist events – the Tripoli fair and the Fair of the Levant. In both, architecture and history were the vehicles for the Fascist rebirth as the predestined continuation of ancient triumphs. The Tripoli fair used Roman monuments in North Africa to introduce tourists to Fascist colonial and expansionist policies. The Fair of the Levant stressed the Mediterranean as an historical Italian trading region, as destined to be dominated by Italian cargo ships as it was by Roman galleons. At the end of the decade, the Triennial of Italian overseas

41 The *Mostra augustea della romanità* opened at ten a.m. and the *Mostra della rivoluzione fascista* at eleven a.m.

42 'La fiamma sacra della rivoluzione', *Corriere della sera* (23 September 1937).

43 Cagnetta (1976) 148.

44 'La Mostra della rivoluzione a Valle Giulia', *Corriere della sera* (22 September 1937).

territories held in Naples resurrected Roman history and myth to posit a conception of empire distinguished from the British model. According to this 1940 exhibition, Italian conquests in Ethiopia and Libya were the modern day expression of Rome's civilising mission, bringing enlightenment and a Pax Mussoliniana to Africa. 'Fascism', declared the exhibition catalogue, '[has] moved beyond the traditional conception of European colonies . . . [by] putting its overseas possessions on a national and imperial programme and having them participate directly in Italian life.'[45] Further, Fascist colonisation in Abyssinia and the brave actions of 'the legionnaires of Mussolini' represented not aggression, merely Fascism's civilising mission in the face of 'the barbarism of the Negus'. The exhibition's first section, 'The exhibition of Roman expansion', provided a 'synthesis of the continuity, not just ideal, but real, of the civilising mission achieved by Italy throughout history . . . [especially] the expansion and domination of Urbe [Rome] in Africa, Asia, and *Mare Nostrum* [Our Sea].'[46]

In mass culture, *romanità* was presented as the historical imperative linking all Italians; within this, the contemporary city of Rome became the 'Third Rome' – the Rome to follow and surpass that of the Caesars and that of the popes. The city of Rome was, for many Fascist-organised events, rallies and demonstrations, the stage on which the drama unfolded. Fascist mass culture focussed on Rome as the national, spiritual and historical capital. A series of exhibitions held in the Circus Maximus in the late 1930s attempted to make these connections explicit and to materialise the promises of the Fascist New Rome. Between the Palatine Hill and the Aventine Hill, on the ruins of the Circus Maximus, the Fascist party constructed an exhibition city which connected Fascist advances in autarchy, healthcare and recreation to historical Roman triumphs. Between 1937 and 1939, the Circus Maximus, the 'glorious Roman cradle', housed the regime's largest mass culture events: the Exhibition of the Dopolavoro (after-work activities), Exhibition of national textiles, and the Autarchy Exhibition. Each of these used monumental architecture, sculpture and the surrounding Roman ruins to forge a Romanised cult of military strength and national resurgence.

As part of the 'marketing' of war and empire, the Fascist party built a theme park/ideal Fascist city in the heart of historical Rome. In the case of the exhibitions held in the Circus Maximus, *romanità* was recruited as spectacle and stage set. The Fascist theme park, constructed in an architectural idiom which can be called modern classicism, depicted a clean world of

45 *Prima mostra triennale delle terre italiane d'oltremare*, exhibition catalogue (Naples 1940).
46 *Ibid.*

social peace, harmony and Fascist predominance, devoid of the dirt, conflict and ambiguity of the real city outside. The sleek, monumental promenades, fountains and triumphal passageways of the exhibition city bespoke social order and progress. The pavilions and walkways, using marble and metal, combined modernity and imperial monumentality.

The scale was grand. Forced-perspective architecture directed the visitor's gaze toward the main façades and walkways. For each of the exhibitions, the spectator faced entry boulevards drawing the eye towards a central façade or a series of monumental sculptures. To stress the regime's conception of the new Roman empire and the hierarchies of Fascism at war each exhibition was built around a central axis/ triumphal boulevard. These constructions stood in over-sized contrast to the crowded medieval ghetto neighbourhoods on the other side of the Palatine Hill which the regime was in the process of tearing down, relocating its working-class inhabitants to new suburbs on the outskirts of Rome.

By building an imperial theme park between the Roman Forum and the Aventine Hill, the dictatorship forced spectators to associate the Roman past and Fascist present and future. The Fascist empire, according to the exhibition, could be comfortably nestled in the glorious Roman cradle. The choice of the Circus Maximus, the ruins of the Roman empire's site of sport and leisure, was richly symbolic. It was a reminder of the regime's desire to occupy physically the space left millennia earlier by the Romans. Architects constructed the building of the Circus Maximus in order to further the connection. The use of a red-brick second storey by Adalberto Libera and Mario De Renzi for their *Padiglione dei congressi* (Conference pavilion) at the *Mostra delle colonie estive* (Exhibition of summer camps) mirrored the colours and materials of the imperial Roman residences on the Palatine Hill which looked down upon the exhibition, making clear the historical legacy of ancient Rome. The repeated use of marble, fountains and columns reinforced the symbiosis with the Roman monuments in the Roman Forum, just the other side of the Palatine.

Such a 'framing' of Rome turned the city and its Roman monuments into a spectacle. The architectonic embodiment of imperialist rhetoric transformed the Fascist theme park into an imperial city. Classical proportions, triumphal arches and columns, although stylised, predominated. The urge towards classicism was greatest in the *Mostra autarchica* of 1938. Mario De Renzi, Giovanni Guerrini, Mario Paniconi and Guido Pediconi executed a general plan emphasising a central axis which concluded on the dominant autarchy pavilion. The façade of the main pavilion of the *Mostra autarchica* consisted of 'aluminium and glass [which] sends blinding rays and broadcasts in cubic characters, the word AUTARCHY'. Below the giant metal letters spelling out 'AUTARCHY' hung an enormous metal Roman imperial eagle. Underneath the eagle, along the pediment, ran the words, in capital letters: 'MUSSOLINI HA SEMPRE RAGIONE' (Mussolini is always right). This overbearing combination of text and monumental sculpture left no doubts regarding the dominance of the dictator and the empire. As it reinforced the regime's staging of itself as the new Roman empire, this architecture also deepened the spectators' fantasy of participation in a grand new imperial project. The monumental proportions and imperial Roman motifs simultaneously inspired and overwhelmed the spectator, encouraging a collective engagement with Fascist achievements.

The Roman location of the Circus Maximus played a critical ideological role in reinforcing the idea of a Fascist-enabled national unity – a national unity grounded both in the present and in the historic past. For many of the spectators whom the regime transported to Rome by bus, train or truck, these events represented their first introduction to the Italian nation. The regime used the Roman location 'at the heart of the nation' to stress Fascism's connection to ancient Rome and to elevate Rome as the spiritual, national home of all Italians. The site 'is one of the most beautiful legacies of the past', declared the catalogue of the *Mostra delle colonie estive*: 'on one side are Rome's two 'hills of destiny' . . . which are symbols of the most splendid classicism: the hills which witnessed the glories of more than a millennium'.[47] On many nights, floodlights illuminated 'the archaeological promenades, the baths of Caracalla, the Palatine and the Aventine'.[48] The dramatised Roman ruins towering above the exhibition city provided a theatrical staging of the Fascist historical mission. Against such a backdrop, the predestination of Fascist triumph was clear.

The final and most extensive celebration of *romanità* was to be the *Esposizione universale di Roma* (Universal exhibition of Rome), or *EUR*, which the regime planned as a grandiose Fascist-built 'new' Rome located between the actual Rome and the sea. The Mussolini dictatorship planned for 1942 to commemorate twenty years of Fascist rule and five years of empire with a vast, marble exhibition metropolis. Mussolini had repeatedly promised a third Rome equal that of the Caesars and the popes: EUR was to be the physical incarnation of that promise. As early as 1925, Mussolini's rhetoric envisioned an expansion of the city to its ancient grandeur: 'The third Rome will spread over other hills, along the banks of the sacred river all the way to the beaches of the Tyrrhenian Sea. It [is] a path which must

47 *Mostra nazionale delle colonie estive e dell'assistenza all'infanzia*, exhibition catalogue (Rome 1937) 6.

48 'Foglio d'ordini', n. 190 (13 November 1937), Archivo centrale dello stato, Rome, Presidenza consiglio dei ministri (1936–8) 14.1.1224.

be the longest and widest in the world; [it will] bring the products of *mare nostrum* from a resurgent Ostia all the way to the heart of the city.'[49]

The *Duce*'s imperial urban monument was to be a complementary 'new Rome' in marble and granite which would both rival and extend the existing city all the way to the sea – a physical symbol of Italy's domination of the Mediterranean.[50] The extensively organised and publicised *Esposizione universale di Roma* was to represent the culmination of Fascist urbanism and official culture.[51] It was to consist of a series of permanent monuments and temporary exhibition pavilions. The plan, designed by Marcello Piacentini – the era's great advocate of monumental, Roman-inspired architecture – was based on Roman urban design, focussing upon a grand central axis which linked the isolated monuments. The monuments were elevated and included a church whose dome was second only to St Peter's, and the Palace of Italian Civilisation, a square Colosseum replete with 216 arches. *EUR* is full of bombastic bas-relief, mosaics, inscriptions and triumphal statuary, all depicting Fascism as the new Rome.[52]

The planned celebration of twenty years of Fascism was to include exhibitions on *romanità*, Italian civilisation, popular traditions, science, contemporary art and Fascist politics.[53] This extravaganza, advertised as the 'Olympiad of Civilisations', would have offered a total of seventy-three different exhibitions.[54] The *Mostra della romanità*, a museum of Romanness, was to constitute a central part of the exhibition city. *EUR* never opened, as construction was suspended in late 1941 due to the Second World War. Instead of the imperial city it promised, Fascism left behind an eerie, monumental, marble ghost-town that would eventually be transformed into a suburb of offices by the Republic of Italy.

Fascist culture and ideology depended heavily upon Roman imperial motifs, from Roman military and economic might to the primacy of classical aesthetic forms to the Roman 'civilising mission'. Imperial Rome, especially the age of Augustus, was a usable past which played a number of roles between 1922 and 1943. Through Fascist eyes, *romanità*, the elusive quality of Romanness, was flexible enough to meet Fascism's changing politics. In politics, it could offer a rationale for the authoritarian rule of law or for imperialism. In the arts, *romanità* was translated as both a call to modern classicism and a demand for copies of Roman monuments. Under Italian Fascism, Rome was an idea, an aesthetic and a location with infinite possibilities and identities.

49 Franco Ciarlantini, 'E'42', *Augustea* (15 July 1938) 3.
50 Ciucci (1989) 181.
51 On the *Esposizione universale di Roma* see: Calvesi and Guidoni (1987); G. Pagano, M. Piacentini, L. Piccinato, E. Rossi, L. Vietti, 'Il piano regolatore dell'esposizione universale di Roma, 1941–42', *Casabella*, X. 114 (June 1937).
52 Benton in Ades et al. (1995).
53 Calvesi and Guidoni (1987) I:104–39.
53 *Ibid.* 104. This figure does not include the various attractions, such as 'sound and light' shows and aquatic parks.

13 The Nazi concept of Rome*

Volker Losemann

The 'Nazi concept of Rome' exemplifies the very disparate attitudes of the Nazi party leadership towards antiquity in general.[1] Nevertheless, despite all the conflicts over questions of historical ideology, which characterised the structure of power in the Third Reich, Hitler's main contention – that the 'race question' was the 'key to world history' – was not disputed.[2] The position of Hitler as the supreme leader (Führer) justifies looking first at his concept of antiquity and his view of Rome before going on to discuss the views of other leading Nazi ideologists. Finally, central aspects of the Nazi attitude towards ancient Rome will be illustrated in a wide range of sources, ranging from National Socialist newspapers and periodicals to the academic articles of leading classicists.

The importance of his ideas on antiquity has already received some attention in major historical studies of Hitler and National Socialism. Ernst Nolte in his book *Three Faces of Fascism* mentions as Hitler's most important 'distant models' Rome and Sparta.[3] Hitler's admiration for antiquity, especially for Rome, can indeed be found in the 'legends' about the 'apprentice years of the dictator', as Josef Greiner showed in *The End of the Hitler-Myth* (1947), a book which is severely criticised today.[4]

The approach to the Nazi view of the ancient world originates in Hitler's historical conceptions, which were based on his racial theories. These historical conceptions were already established in *Mein Kampf*, where he had written:

> Especially in history instruction one should not let oneself be deterred from studying antiquity. Roman history, rightly conceived in very broad outlines, is and remains the best teacher not only for today but probably for all times. The Hellenic ideal of culture, too, should be preserved for us in its exemplary beauty. One must not allow the differences of the individual races to tear up the greater racial community. The struggle that rages today involves very great aims: a culture fights for its existence, which combines millenniums and embraces Hellenism and Germanity together.[5]

* I wish to thank M. Bode and Prof. R. M. Errington, PhD (both Marburg) for the translation of the manuscript, which is not easy in its terminology.

1 Cf. Villard (1972), Losemann (1977) 17–26 and Christ (1982) 195–210.

2 Hitler (1939) 470. 3 Nolte (1965) 415. 4 Greiner (1947) 84. 5 Hitler (1939) 631.

Hitler developed some of his dominant ideas beyond the general lines of his racist view of history towards a programme for ruling. The connection between his views of history and his conception of rule seems to be based on his ideas of world empires, which he had expressed in connection with the Roman empire. The Roman model certainly provided him with themes for a 'history of German world power'. In the fact that it was 'fundamentally a peasant state' Hitler saw the reason why Rome was able to become 'the crystallisation point for a world empire'.[6] These speculations were a source for his concept of a peasant utopia, whose characteristics included the 'maintenance of agrarian ways of life', the defence of the land with 'one's own blood' and a 'gigantic growth of power'.[7]

Hitler was also convinced of the importance of ancient precedents, in particular that of major buildings as symbolic expressions of power. His building programme which, as J. Thies argued, was intended to make Berlin 'capital of the world' and to provide the physical framework for a 'German leadership of the World', was based on ancient models.[8]

Naturally, Hitler admired the architecture of classical Greece. According to Albert Speer, Hitler even compared himself to Pericles.[9] But even when he conjured up the common ground of 'Hellenism and Germanity' as in the passage of *Mein Kampf* quoted above, the Athenian example was never so important for his building and ruling programme as was Rome.[10] Sparta was also much more important than Athens: here he saw the prototype of a minority ruling class of high racial quality. Hitler was fascinated with Sparta, which he regarded as the 'purest racial state in history' with 'the greatness of this blood'. Hitler saw in Sparta, just as in the early 'peasant state Rome', the archaic condition of racial unity inherent in an agrarian society. Moreover the Spartan social structure seemed to him proof of the social-Darwinist principle of the 'survival of the fittest' and the 'destruction of the weak'.[11]

It was Hitler himself who extrapolated from Sparta and Rome the future power-structure in eastern Europe. [12] This is also the reason for Hitler's interest in the most important image-building events of German history, the colonisation of eastern Europe in the Middle Ages and the development of the Prussian state.[13] Central premises of Nazi ideology can be found in his visions of Sparta, Rome and the medieval Empire in Eastern Europe. They have in common their character as models for the programme of future German rule: imperialist expansion and archetypal methods of securing internal power, as well as being societies with an agrarian structure in which original racial purity was realised.

[6] Weinberg (1961) 119. [7] Thies (1976) 72–3. [8] *Ibid.*
[9] Fest (1973) 724 n.115. Cf. Näf (1986) 116–19. [10] Kroll (1996) 345.
[11] Losemann (1984) 23–4. [12] Nolte (1965) 415. Cf. Hitler (1980) 279.
[13] Thies (1976) 103–4.

These are the most important examples of Hitler's obsession with the ancient world. His fixation on Rome can be discerned at the very beginning of his career.

On 20 September 1920, Hitler gave a 'long speech about the attempt of the Romans to expand their power throughout the whole world'.[14] Drafts and notes for his early speeches show the important role of Rome in Hitler's historical comparisons. He also mentioned the 'parasitic existence of the Jews', when talking about 'the rise of Rome'.[15] The question of the fall of Rome was also a topic which Hitler talked about at this time. This emerges from the following scene, as described by Alfred Rosenberg, the chief ideologist of the Nazi Party. At their first meeting in the house of the nationalist (völkisch) writer Dietrich Eckart in autumn 1919, he and Hitler both found themselves 'very soon in a talk about history, about the reasons for the collapse of the Roman Empire, and I soon found' – writes Rosenberg – 'the same opinions in another man, that I had myself formed after studies in various subjects'.[16] The image of Hitler, as he presented himself, is that of a man who was already in his early days thinking about the great subjects of history – no doubt part of a calculated attempt to portray himself as a politician and statesman.

Fundamental to Hitler's understanding of Rome was, as Thies and most recently Alex Scobie have shown, the example of monumental Roman state art,[17] by which his programme of rule was inspired:

> For, only when comparing the dimensions of the antique State buildings with the contemporary private houses will one understand the overpowering sweep and force of this stress on the viewpoint to allot the first place to the public works. What today we admire in the wreckage and fields of ruins of the old world as the few still outstanding colossuses are not business palaces of the time but temples and State buildings; that means works the owner of which was the public. Even in the splendor of the later Rome, first place was not taken by the villas and the palaces of individual citizens, but by the temples and the *thermae*, the stadia, circuses, aqueducts, basilicas, etc., of the State; that means of the entire people.[18]

These are 'terms of a history of architecture tinged with Social Darwinism', as Thies pointed out.[19] In this view even the monuments of the Germanic Middle Ages, the 'cathedrals, town halls, and grain markets, as well as watch-towers, are the visible sign of a conception which ultimately corresponded to that of antiquity.'[20] Hitler's architect Albert Speer has stressed the importance of the architectural ideas: He 'recognized the importance of Hitler's "Versammlungsarchitektur" as part of his plan to establish his domination over masses of people who could be molded into a single unified body when enclosed in one all-embracing building'.[21]

[14] Hitler (1980) 226. [15] *Ibid.* 191. [16] Cf. Bollmus (1970) 18.
[17] Scobie (1990) 20–3. [18] Hitler (1939) 362–3. [19] Thies (1978) 421.
[20] Hitler (1939) 363. [21] Scobie (1990) 19.

During his visit to Rome in May 1938, about which he long enthused, the Führer spent several hours in the Colosseum. It is a telling detail that he wanted to be alone with the ancient monuments – another instance of his self-stylisation.[22] His vivid impressions from this visit resulted in changed plans for the 'Kongreßhalle' in Nuremberg and, generally, in his own building plans, he sought to surpass ancient monumentality. The 'Kongreßhalle' actually exceeded the size of the Colosseum.[23] These plans, however, did not merely aim at a special 'ceremonial atmosphere' – as in the internal decorative structure of government buildings – which, as G. L. Mosse says, was meant to produce an intimidating effect on the visitor or spectator.[24] Faithful to ancient models, 'buildings for eternity' were to be constructed. The strongest expression of megalomania in these architectural plans is to be found in drawings which Hitler had made to fix the 'ruin value' of his buildings.[25]

In this 'blueprint for world domination', it was Rome which played the most important part. 'The most natural way for the formation of great States – the way in which most great States have arisen – was to begin', as Hitler declared in a speech on 27 November 1937, 'with a crystallisation point of the political and later the cultural life which then, as the capital city, often gave its name to the State'.[26]

Even the territory was to be developed following the Roman example. Hitler found the speed with which 'Roman legions managed . . . to cross endless stretches of land'[27] remarkable. 'Under the direction of Caesar, and during the first two centuries CE, it was by means of the construction of roads and tracks that the Romans reclaimed the marshlands and blazed trails through the forests of Germania. Following their example, our first task in Russia will be to construct roads', he concluded.[28] Revealing in this context is Scobie's observation 'that it is nearly always the Romans, and not the Spartans to whom Hitler refers when praising military discipline and expertise in the ancient world'.[29] Thus, in this respect, Rome surpassed the 'purest racial state in history'.

Among these ideas and remarks regarding Roman bureaucratic and army organisation belongs, too, the comparison between the Roman and the British empires and its application to the era of the Punic Wars, which occurs as early as 1937 in the famous Hossbach-Protocol, an important document where Hitler explained his long-term war aims. From this the question of the historical roles of Hitler and Neville Chamberlain and Germany and Great Britain respectively was developed. Neither wanted to be forced into the role of Carthage.[30] In the critical time before the outbreak

[22] *Ibid.* 32. [23] Thies (1983) 62. [24] Mosse (1976) 218. [25] Thies (1976) 76.
[26] Baynes (1942) 600. [27] Hitler (1980) 125. [28] Hitler (1953) 537–8.
[29] Scobie (1990) 22. [30] Losemann (1977) 19.

of the Second World War, Hitler disclosed in a very drastic manner what Roman history had taught him: 'One should never be in the predicament of not knowing where a conflict will come from', he says in a remark reported by Speer, and continues: 'In every peace treaty the next war is already built in. That is Rome! That is true statesmanship!'[31] In wartime, too, the model of the Roman empire had lost nothing of its fascination. 'Even today' – he said in November 1941 to Himmler – 'the Roman Empire never had its like. To have succeeded in completely dominating all neighbouring peoples! And no empire has spread so unified a civilisation as Rome did.'[32] What Hitler liked and aimed to imitate, was criticised in 1939/40 by Simone Weil in a comparison of the rule of ancient Rome and Hitler.[33]

A precondition for the success of this exemplary programme for domination was – and this Hitler emphasised in his *Table Talk* – compliance with the race laws: 'A people cannot lay claim to mastery of the world unless it is ready to pay with its blood. The Roman Empire had recourse to freedmen only when its own blood was exhausted.'[34] The perspectives of race history shaped not only his ideas about the rise of Rome, but also in a very obvious way the picture of the decline of this world power.[35] Hitler was convinced that Rome was not 'broken' by Germans or Huns, but by the Christians:[36] 'The day when Christianity abolished the frontier between the classes', was largely responsible for the Roman patriciate having been soaked up by the masses – a ruling class which, once it had obtained wealth, violated a 'basic race law' when it limited the number of births.[37] The vindictive rancour against Christianity characteristic of remarks in 1941 and 1942 may be seen in his repeated identification of Christianity with Bolshevism: 'Christianity was pre-Bolshevism, was the mobilisation of the slave masses by the Jews in order to undermine the state.'[38] This passage, where the two most important enemies of National Socialism are attacked, is an important indication of the inner consistency of Hitler's argumentation. The comparison appears for the first time in 1924 in a pamphlet of one of Hitler's mentors, the nationalist (*völkisch*) writer Dietrich Eckhart. Its title, 'Bolshevism from Moses to Lenin. Dialogue between Adolf Hitler and me', is programmatic for Hitler's anti-Semitism and for his view of history.[39]

Hitler's historical awareness, his aims and conceptions of rule remained constant in these formulations even up to his last hours. In his so-called 'Political Testament' he mentions Sparta and Prussia, but also the 'Germanic expansion eastwards',[40] and the 'political ambition . . . the

31 Speer (1975) 221.
32 Hitler (1953) 111. It is remarkable that Hitler also admired the British empire in principle.
33 Weil (1960) 18–60. 34 Hitler (1953) 253. 35 Cf. Demandt (1984) 190.
36 Hitler (1953) 95. 37 *Ibid.* 261. 38 Hitler (1980) 96. 39 Nolte (1965) 329–37.
40 Hitler (1962) 48,63 and 54.

moral hardiness and material power' of ancient Rome. This latter, however, is marred by his disappointment at the role of the Italians in the Second World War.[41] In his real political last will and testament, dated to 29 April 1945, a few hours before his suicide, he demanded of the nation's leaders and their followers a scrupulous adherence to the race laws and to a ruthless resistance against the 'poisoners of all peoples [*Völkervergifter*] of the world, international Jewry'.[42]

In no other historical theme did Hitler express so active an interest, then, as in Roman history.[43] The above examples suggest the consistency of his ideas – from his early years, through his seizure of power up to the end of the Second World War. The connection between his attention to history and his plans for domination and control of power has also, I hope, emerged clearly. Here as with his architectural plans, the reactionary but at the same time utopian character of his concept of history can be seen. In these statements of Hitler's the difference between past and present is blurred, if not erased. This is not really history at all but rather a collection of short formulae of interpretative fragments, which he fits into a framework of racial ideology.

Hitler's historical ideas, which incorporated central ideological premises, establish a general framework for the Nazi conception of Rome. Especially in the early years after the seizure of power, however, there is no impression that a well-defined and binding concept of history existed, although many calls for a 'fight for a new history' were to be heard. There was undoubtedly a contradiction between Hitler's own positive assessment of Roman antiquity and the extreme admiration for Germanic pre-history by other leading Nazi ideologists, particularly Rosenberg.

As chief ideologist of the party, Rosenberg might have become the leading representative of a Nazi view of history but his position in the Nazi hierarchy was not strong. He can, however, claim special interest as the main proponent of a 'Germanic Weltanschauung'. His barely readable work, *Myth of the Twentieth Century*, was based on H. St. Chamberlain and his *Grundlagen des 19. Jahrhunderts* (Foundations of the nineteenth century).[44] The basic pattern of Rosenberg's interpretation of history is the struggle of a high-quality Nordic race against hostile inferior powers – embodied foremost in the Asiatic opposition race of the Jews. According to Rosenberg, the 'types of ancient Greece and ancient Rome' belonged to 'the first waves of Nordic Indo-Germanic peoples' which perished due to 'racial bastardisation' in the 'national and ethnic chaos [*Völkerchaos* – H. St. Chamberlain's term] of the Hellenistic period and late antiquity'. As the main culprit of this 'mediterranean racial chaos', Rosenberg unmasks

[41] *Ibid.* 118. [42] Nolte (1965) 364. [43] Kroll (1996) 346.
[44] Losemann (1977) 21–3. Cf. now D'Onofrio (1997).

'degenerate Etruscity'. From this stock, according to Rosenberg, the Catholic priesthood of the 'Jewish mercy religion' Christianity developed. Against this abstruse background, Rosenberg places the 'Rome question', for him the keyword for a bitter conflict with the Roman Catholic church.[45] All this has little to do with real history. Even Nordic Man is hardly defined biologically. He is to be found, according to Klaus von See, in a 'supra-historical, mystical idea' – in Rosenberg's much used phrase, in the 'Rassenseele' (race-soul).[46]

Heinrich Himmler was, like Rosenberg, committed to the programme of 'Germanising' German history. Himmler did not leave it at that, but as we know, pushed forward an active 'Germanisation policy', including killing, kidnapping and human breeding programmes.[47]

In view of strong demands for 'Germanising' German history, historians and classicists feared that a total revision of current historical views might emerge, which, for instance, might have called into question the whole *raison d'être* of Roman studies. This background to the programmatic discussion of the relationship between the ancient world and National Socialism was very important. In close connection with that, a 'dispute about the level of German culture' took place between Hitler's Germany and Fascist Italy. In 1934 Mussolini had responded to the theories of those who admired Germany 'with the pity of superiority'. They came, as he said, 'from representatives of a people, which at the time when Rome had Caesar, Virgil and Augustus, did not even have letters with which they could transmit evidence of their life'. In this dispute many anti-Roman voices were raised.[48] It is one of the eccentricities of the Nazi view of history that in this sort of question, particularly in the discussion about the 'high level of German culture', Hitler himself tended to accept Mussolini's position; he compared the relatively low level of German culture with the Athenian Acropolis as symbol of Greek civilisation.[49] He thus took up Mussolini's comment, without altering its tendency, although it had enraged Rosenberg's followers.

Their views in this programmatic discussion were represented by the school teacher Walter Eberhardt in his article 'Die Antike und wir'.[50] This article appeared in the 'National Socialist Monthly', also in the pamphlet series 'National Socialist Science', and was reviewed in the party newspaper *Völkischer Beobachter*. It is safe to say that it reflected the official opinion of the party and was authorised by the party, since the author soon afterwards received a chair of classics.[51]

For the present purpose it is important to note that Eberhardt saw the

[45] Losemann (1977) 21–3. [46] von See (1994) 309. [47] Losemann (1988) 280–1.
[48] *Ibid.* 277. [49] *Ibid.* 278. [50] Eberhardt (1935) 115–27.
[51] Cf. Losemann (1980) 69–70.

'Roman phenomenon' from a racial viewpoint as something mostly alien. In the 'Roman substance' some 'Etruscan blood' was mingled. All in all, he saw the early, peasant Rome, 'the hard times up to the Punic Wars' much more positively.[52] But particularly with regard to the expansion of Roman rule and culture in the age of Augustus he shows, like Rosenberg, a critical distance towards Rome. He criticises the Roman claim to world domination, as expressed in Virgil's *Aeneid* or in the *Res Gestae* of Augustus, from a Germanic point of view:

> We think of the expeditions of Drusus and Tiberius and the punitive expedition of Germanicus and feel the wall which separates us from Roman cultural ideas. We make a bridge to the present and discover that it was always basically the Latin idea of civilisation supported and enlarged by arguments of the French Revolution, under the banner of which 1900 years later the First World War was waged against us, the barbarians on the far bank of the Rhine.[53]

Thus Eberhardt draws a negative picture of the Roman empire, which belongs to the nineteenth-century tradition of 'political Germanism'.[54]

In the early years after the seizure of power, many articles were published of the same type as 'Die Antike und wir'. The authors tried to prove the importance of their field, be it classical languages in school or university, Greek or Roman history or classical archaeology, for the Third Reich. Quite typical was the reaction of Gerhart Rodenwaldt (1886–1945), an archaeologist. In a list which turned up in his estate he had collected Hitler's remarks on antiquity.[55] For classicists Hitler's opinions gave some general starting points from which they could demonstrate the importance of, e.g., Roman history. This kind of argument in defence of Roman history can also be found in the work of distinguished classical historians.

In contrast to Eberhardt's extremely anti-Roman position, Helmut Berve (1896–1979), who had written several programmatic articles in the thirties, showed a more moderate position in his paper 'Antike und nationalsozialistischer Staat'.[56] He several times referred to Hitler's well-known phrases from *Mein Kampf*, regarding Roman history. Even when Berve mentioned the 'difficulties concerning the race question', he nonetheless accepted the effects of 'race instinct', 'race politics' and 'race deterioration'. From Roman history he mentioned the citizenship laws of Augustus and the 'end of the ancient world in general, which was caused by the decomposition of the ruling race'.[57] Here, too, the points of contact with Hitler's conception are obvious.

As well as Berve, the Berlin ancient historian Wilhelm Weber (1882–1948) took part in this programmatic discussion. In the 1930s and

[52] Eberhardt (1935) 119–21. [53] *Ibid.* 122–3. Cf. Scobie (1990) 137.
[54] Losemann (1988) 262. [55] Marchand (1996) 350. [56] Berve (1934). [57] *Ibid.* 163–7.

1940s Weber was one of the 'most important historians of Rome' working in Germany.[58] Furthermore, he belonged to the group of political or politicising professors well known from the Wilhelmine and Weimar periods. Weber's commitment to the monarchy and the Reich, his belief in a 'saviour' and 'leader', his anti-democratic position, his invocation of the 'experience of the front', his anti-Versailles slogans put him, like many of his colleagues, into the political context of the so-called 'conservative revolution'.[59] In his argumentation Weber often made use both of ancient and modern examples. All this seems to indicate a predisposition towards Nazism. Certainly Weber had no difficulties after Hitler's seizure of power in taking up topics like 'leader' and 'empire' in their ancient and modern form. He found a suitable occasion in the 'celebration of the foundation of the Reich and renewal of the Reich by the Führer' on 30 January 1935. As far as the ancient world is concerned, the theme which keeps repeating itself is the '4000–year history of our German-Teutonic people'.[60] With these anti-Roman remarks, Weber joins the discussion about the 'cultural level of the Germanic peoples'.

Weber's monarchistic convictions were expressed most vehemently in his best known, but also most controversial work *Princeps. Studien zur Geschichte des Augustus* (1936).[61] This had already been largely completed in 1930, so must be regarded primarily as a product of the 1920s.[62] What we have of it, in the one volume which was written, is an extremely detailed and highly eccentric commentary on the *Res Gestae.* Above all, however, the idealisation of the *princeps* as a superman (Nietzsche's sense) reached its peak here. In his remarkable picture of the rule of Augustus, Weber looks behind the outer facade of the principate, behind which he sees not only 'the will to achieve power' (*Wille zur Macht*), but also 'belief in the best blood'.[63] It is worth pointing out here that Weber had no good opinion of Augustus' efforts to preserve 'the purity of the blood' (Suetonius *Augustus* 40). He comments on this especially in connection with the conservative attitudes shown by Augustus' citizenship policy, which demonstrated, he suggests, the 'static character' of his rule, just as did his well-known 'refusal to extend the frontiers' (Tacitus *Annals* 1. 11.5). Weber argues here from the point of view of the logical development of the Empire and from that of its subjects.[64] Thus at the time when the *Princeps* was probably drafted, before 1933, the ideology of the 'Reich' had already gained priority over the ideology of race – a reflection of conservative attitudes of the pre-Nazi period.[65]

While Weber idealised Augustus, Fritz Schachermeyr described *Die*

[58] Christ (1982) 210–25. [59] Mohler (1972). [60] Weber (1935) 10. [61] Weber (1936).
[62] Stahlmann (1988) 174. [63] Weber (1936) 240.
[64] Stahlmann (1988) 168. Cf. Weber (1936) 68–75. [65] Cf. Stahlmann (1988) 174.

Nordische Führerpersönlichkeit im Altertum. As early as April 1933 a short sketch was published in the party newspaper *Völkischer Beobachter* – thus aiming at a broad appeal. An extended version was published as an academic article later on.[66] Schachermeyr, whose main interest was in Greek 'leaders', took up 'leadership' not only in the conservative pre-Nazi sense, but also identified himself with far-fetched positions such as those expressed by H. F. K. Günther ('Rasse-Günther') in his 1929 work 'A racial history of the Hellenic and Roman people'.[67]

The work of Joseph Vogt (1895–1986), which has been analysed and criticised recently by D. Königs, shows that Vogt very early adopted 'nationalist [*völkisch*] and racist thoughts',[68] and later on 'took up central elements of the race teaching and Nazi ideology', especially in those works that were aimed not so much at his fellow academics as at a broader readership.[69]

Characteristic topics show how he adopted the Nazi concept of Rome. Vogt treated two current themes in his related articles 'Population Decline [Bevölkerungsrückgang] in the Roman empire' (1935) and 'Race mixing [Rassenmischung] in the Roman empire' (1936), in *Vergangenheit und Gegenwart,* a periodical for history teachers.[70] When examining the 'population change', Vogt concluded that it was the 'racial decline of formerly creative peoples, Greeks and Romans, which had made the infiltration of Orientals and the entrance of the Germans possible'.[71] The choice of words is revealing. In the perspective of race theory, the Roman empire as a whole is seen negatively as an example of a continuing 'blending of peoples and races', which becomes obvious especially in the cities: 'Because the cities are an arbitrary mixture [of the population], the result was an ever decreasing quality of the genetic make-up.'[72] In the end, everything that can be summarised as Romanisation led, from the point of view of race theory, to the decline and fall of the Roman empire. Vogt referred to well-known predecessors: in this category belong not only famous race ideologists like Houston Stewart Chamberlain, J. A. Gobineau and Hans F. K. Günther, but also fellow classicists such as Otto Seeck, Mikhail Rostovtzeff and Tenney Frank.[73] As these authors show, there was a certain interest on the part of classicists – not just in Germany – in these questions. These themes, 'population decline' and 'race mixture in the Roman empire' – standard topics for any racial history – Vogt also made accessible for a broader audience in the newspaper article of 1 November 1936: 'Ein Weltreich stirbt an Rassenmischung. Römische Geschichte im Spiegel der Bevölkerungspolitik'.[74]

[66] Schachermeyr (1933). Cf. Losemann (1980) 55–63. [67] Losemann (1980) 58.
[68] Königs (1995) 105–13. [69] Christ (1990) 95. [70] Vogt (1935) and (1936)
[71] Vogt (1936) 11. Cf. Christ (1990) 84 and Königs (1995) 203. [72] Vogt (1936) 11.
[73] Vogt (1935) 653–4. [74] Cf. Königs (1990) 313.

Such ideas also found their way into the schools. Lessons in ancient history, Latin and Greek were to be held 'with a special regard to eugenics and racial development' (*Rassenkunde*), as the *Amtsblatt* (gazette) of the responsible ministry wrote.[75] One of the messages of Roman history in this sense was that 'the deterioration of the strength of the people and racial health' had started soon after the Punic Wars. Augustan culture was then the 'exemplary attempt to renew the biological and moral foundations of the national character'. In the end, the 'abominable race mixture' which was especially obvious in the big cities ('the metropolis is the grave of a people') inevitably led to the fall of Rome.[76] It remains unclear, however, how far this concept, which shows some overlap with Vogt's and Weber's ideas, was actually taught in the schools.[77]

A preliminary conclusion from all these programmatic statements on Roman history will show on various levels – the remarks of Hitler and his followers, articles by well-known classicists, the teaching offered in schools and in Nazi periodicals – at least outlines of a Nazi concept of empire: following Hitler's programme for domination, a positive view was developed of the creation of a world empire, and of the practice and organisation of rules expressed in the development of a large empire and in monumental state architecture. The Roman example of 'leadership' as exemplified by Augustus is also seen positively. From the point of view of the Germanic ideologists, who were very aggressive especially in the early 1930s, the Roman empire was primarily a negative phenomenon. These people, however, because of the alliance with Fascist Italy, were forced to show restraint. In the context of Nazi race ideology the Roman empire stands for 'ethnic chaos' (*Völkerchaos*), concentrated in the cities. 'Race mixing' causes downfall. Hitler agreed of course with this concept of race theory, but it is perhaps important to note that he was primarily interested in Rome as a model for ruling a world empire.

This was not a clear-cut and systematic concept which would imply a particular interpretation of Roman history. Some room for manoeuvre was thus left for classicists. But the most prominent classicists, in particular, had no problem integrating key elements into their own work, following the slogan 'Die Antike und wir'.

From the programmatic discussions of the relationship between antiquity and National Socialism in the early 1930s a link can be made with several 'Gemeinschaftswerke' (co-operative works) which appeared in 1942 and 1943 from the official organisation 'War Service of the Classics'. They follow a comparable line of argument as, in the first years of the war, the humanities were under pressure to prove their relevance. The different

75 Walsdorff (1935) 27*. 76 *Ibid.* 29*–30*. 77 Cf. Gies (1992) 5; Malitz (1998).

disciplines were called upon to contribute to an 'idea for a new European order'.[78] The first results of the 'War Service of the Classics', organised by Berve, were published in the two-volume book *Das neue Bild der Antike*. How 'new' was this picture? The answer is not straightforward. In most of the articles of the second volume concerning Roman history one can trace the 'continuity of traditional approaches and evaluation'.[79] Only a few modernising approaches were included, such as that of Vogt, who examined the 'concept of space and organisation of space in Roman politics' (*Raumauffassung und Raumordnung*).[80] Very typically, Ernst Kornemann (1868–1946) published a lecture in 1941 on the Roman empire as the 'first European large-area political structure' (Großraumgestaltung) – an illustration of the effect of war on the choice of topics.[81] In these geopolitical concepts, taken over from Karl Haushofer, we are reminded of the developmental and organisational concepts Hitler had articulated when he described his own conquest plans in terms of Roman expansion. Thus too when Vogt, Kornemann and Berve adopted the 'Reichsgedanke' (ideas of empire) as a theme for their work, at the beginning of the Second World War, they linked this explicitly to current German war aims.[82]

To return to the Roman aspect of the *Neue Bild der Antike*, G. Rodenwaldt tried to link Roman state architecture with Hitler's building programme in Berlin (*pro maiestate imperii*).[83] Franz Miltner, who confronted 'Die Antike als Einheit in der Geschichte' with the contemporary, alien world of the east, was probably the contributor most influenced by race ideology. But although the editor Berve had underlined the importance of 'racial self-awareness' for the allegedly new view of ancient history in his introduction to the volume, the book as a whole was in no way based on race theory, something which Fritz Schachermeyr, an adherent of race theory, criticised at the time.[84]

Rome and Carthage, the second 'Gemeinschaftswerk' produced in the 'War Service of the Classics', was focussed on the key question, posed by the editor Vogt in the introduction, of the importance of 'racial conflict' in the wars between these two powers.[85] With this a topic was taken up which had played an important role in Hitler's historical comparisons. Already in the nineteenth century, the conflict between Rome and Carthage had been recast in modern terms and used for propaganda purposes. Identifications changed, but it was England which served for various purposes as 'the modern Carthage'.[86] In the later stereotypes of 'racial history', the 'Nordic Romans' were contrasted with the 'Semitic trading people, the

[78] Cf. Losemann (1977) 108. [79] Christ (1982) 209. [80] Berve (1942) II 100–32.
[81] Cf. Christ (1996) 258–61. [82] *Ibid.* 255–74. [83] Cf. Berve (1942) II 356–73.
[84] Cf. *ibid.* I 6–7 and Schachermeyr (1943) 119. [85] Vogt (1943) 7. [86] Ameling (1993) 2.

Carthaginians', while this anti-Semitic stereotype was transferred by the Nazis to England. In the Nazi concept of Rome, this topic came close to being a model. Racist categories shape the articles of Schachermeyr, Vogt and the archaeologist R. Herbig. Anti-Semitic interpretations can be found particular in Vogt, writing about 'Septimius Severus and his Dynasty'[87] and in R. Herbig on 'The archaeological picture of the Punics' (Puniertum).[88] On the other hand, however, some articles appear which tend to negate the importance of race as a factor in history.[89]

It is therefore no wonder that official Nazi Germany was disappointed with the conclusions reached in 'Rome and Carthage', especially with the section on the 'racial conflict' between Rome and Carthage. For the reviewer in the party newspaper *Völkischer Beobachter*, the conclusion was 'dubious and conspicuously small'.[90]

The fact that differences appeared between the official party position and the efforts of classicists working on a modern view of antiquity surely offers no justification for a reassuring conclusion. On the contrary, the conformity in principle and the obliging ease with which many scholars took over aspects of the Nazi doctrine remains cause for concern. It is of course necessary to recall that research in the classics moved on a level quite different from the programmatic demands of the Nazi ideologists for a racial history of the ancient world and the consequent statements of certain classicists. Weber, who had been close to the Nazis very early on, summarised the efforts of classicists in the cause of a new National Socialist picture of antiquity in February 1944 in this way: 'Everything is as it was long before 1933!'[91]

Weber did not restrict himself to making such harsh criticisms. In his own 'war service with the pen' he showed how he could do better than his colleagues. At the end of 1943 Weber contributed an essay on 'The rise and fall of the Roman empire' to the periodical *Wille und Macht* (Will and Power) – an instructor's manual for the leaders of the 'Hitler-Jugend'. This article comes close to a genuinely Nazi concept of Rome. The contents may be briefly sketched: he starts with the 'foundation of the races', emphasises the 'determining power of the aristocracy' in peasant Rome, describes the 'extension of the state' and 'the rise of monarchy and World Empire', the 'growth and change' of which were affected by 'opposing powers', and he sketches the 'century of crises'. At the end he has a section on 'the Germans'.[92]

This 'life-cycle of Rome' was dictated by the laws of 'blood' – for Weber

87 Vogt (1943) 346–66. 88 *Ibid.* 139–77. 89 Christ (1982) 209.

90 Cf. the article 'Römer und Punier', *Völkischer Beobachter* (14 August 1943) and Losemann (1977) 115. 91 Losemann (1977) 83. 92 Weber (1943) 1–41.

a synonym for 'race'. Weber concentrates on the following points: in contrast to his interpretation in the *Princeps*, a work of the 1920s, Augustus' citizenship and manumission policies are now justified by the danger of the 'dilution of the ruling class of Roman citizens'.[93] Also the grant of citizenship to the extended population of the empire, the *Constitutio Antoniniana*, is interpreted negatively: from now on Rome really became a 'cosmopolis', – the term can be traced back to Oswald Spengler – and drowned in the 'Empire of the "Roman" citizen masses' concentrated in the cities, with which Weber, like Vogt, associates only negative characteristics.[94] The empire as a whole offers the vision of a 'wild mixing of peoples', in which Jews and Christians are seen as 'enemies of the Empire' and 'oppositional elements'.[95] The life-cycle of Rome comes to its end when 'the young peoples of the North advance to the last attack', the aim of which Weber saw, expressed in contemporary terminology, as being 'to recover the living space [*Lebensraum*] of their ancestors'.[96] These are the main points of his racist interpretation of the decline and fall of Rome. In the context of the Nazi European ideology which was mobilised in the last years of the war, Weber makes Rome a kind of timeless advanced post of Europe in the struggle against Asia. Weber follows here the official line of the cultural propagandists. If we ignore the efforts to integrate these war-related aims, we can trace behind the contemporary political propaganda a simple basic structural model of racial history, which fulfills at least some of Hitler's requirements. How close Weber comes to these ideas can be seen in the way the 'model theme' of the Nazi concept of Rome, 'Rome and Carthage', was dealt with during the end phase of the Second World War.

In the party newspaper *Völkischer Beobachter*, on 20 September 1944 in the face of German defeat, the 'Roman example' was conjured up again, in the Nazi context of racial ideology, this time with regard to the crisis in the Second Punic War after the disaster at Cannae. Germany (Rome) was fighting against the 'Semitic trading people of Carthage', and against 'World Jewry'. In the race ideology, Jews and Carthaginians had somehow been merged.

To the very end of his rule Hitler clung to the 'Roman example'. As late as 1 March 1945 he instructed his propaganda minister Goebbels 'to publish extensive treatments of the Punic War in the German press'. 'Beside the Seven Year War', Goebbels wrote in his diaries, 'the Punic War is the great example, which for us can serve as a model. The Punic War brought a decision of world historical importance, which had consequences lasting for several centuries. And like the present struggle concerning Europe the

[93] *Ibid.* 12. [94] *Ibid.* 17–8. Cf. von See (1994) 222. [95] Weber (1943) 14.
[96] *Ibid.* 21.

struggle between Rome and Carthage was not decided in one war.'[97] Following these desparate and defiant remarks it should not be forgotten that parts of Hitler's concepts of rule and race, where Rome had been a 'distant model', were realised with devastating consequences in a war of large-scale destruction.

97 Fröhlich (1995) 394.

14 Ruins of Rome: T. S. Eliot and the presence of the past*

Charles Martindale

Fragments are my theme, fragments, ruins, bits and pieces – even rubbish: for ruins and rubbish may be said to constitute the condition of modernity itself, according at least to my prime exhibit, T. S. Eliot's *The Waste Land,* or at least according to one influential reading of it. The cultural significance of the poem, published along with *Ulysses* in literary modernism's grand climacteric of 1922, makes it a text of central importance for any account of modernity's relation to the classical tradition and of the presence of ancient Rome in our century. What follows will constitute an extended gloss on one line in *The Waste Land*: 'These fragments have I shored against my ruins'.

1 And other withered stumps of time Were told upon the walls

Eliot's views about classicism, tradition and empire (including his espousal of Virgil as the indisputable European classic), which he set out in various prose essays and in the *Criterion*, reflect widespread interwar discussion both in Britain and in continental Europe. Traditional histories suggest that the appeal of antiquity fades during the modern period; at the least we can say that many of the different discourses in which Rome has been entangled split up and reform. But classics, at any rate in Britain, continued to dominate the school curriculum until 1918, and most of the leading modernists, like most of their first readers, received a traditionally classical education. Rome continued to be seen as the model for understanding modern Europe and the likely outcome of events there. Oswald Spengler, from his particular perspective, put it thus: 'Romanism [*das Römertum*] – with its rigorous sense of factuality, lacking in geniality, barbaric, disciplined, practical, Protestant, *Prussian* – will always provide us in our search

* This is a considerably shortened and restyled version of an essay first published in *Arion*, 3rd series 3 (1996) 102–40. It is a pleasure to thank the following for contributing bits and pieces to my argument: Catharine Edwards, Wolfgang Ernst, Duncan Kennedy, Peter McDonald, Michelle Martindale, George Myerson, Liz Prettejohn, Vanda Zajko.

for analogies with the key to the understanding of our own future.'[1] Among the many who agreed with at least the general drift of this was Adolf Hitler: 'Roman history, properly comprehended in its broad outlines, is and remains the best teacher not only for today, but indeed for all times' (*Mein Kampf*).[2] Modernism, which brought with it a reaction against Romantic taste and doctrine and a renewed emphasis on the creative uses of imitation and allusion, helped to make possible a more positive evaluation of Latin literature, overshadowed by Greece for much of the previous century. Theodore Ziolkowski in his *Virgil and the moderns* goes so far as to present the period between the wars as a renewed *aetas Virgiliana*, with Virgil as 'a prophet of modernity,'[3] able to provide succour for the contemporary *mal de siècle*, the widespread sense of disintegration and fracture. In many respects interpretations of Virgil's works may not have differed greatly from each other, but they could serve politically very different ends. The critic and classical scholar J. W. Mackail wrote in *Virgil and his meaning to the world of to-day*, published in the same year as *The Waste Land*: 'We stand now, as Virgil stood, among the wreckage of a world; he can give light and guidance to us in the foundation of a new world upon its ruins.' Part of that light was, in Mackail's view, commitment to a united Italy including 'the larger hope of its concord or coalescence with the spiritual power which still lives in the name of Rome'.[4] Mackail was a socialist, but many from elsewhere in the political spectrum would have concurred with the analysis, while differing on the precise forms this Virgilian guidance should take.

For Gareth Reeves Eliot is a Virgilian poet, not just a poet endebted to Virgil and interested in Virgil's position in history, but one sharing his sensibility at a fundamental level. Certainly Eliot, who while editor at Faber sponsored the publication of Jackson Knight's *Roman Vergil*, came to see the link between Virgil and Dante as central to Western civilisation, a link which thus became, in Frank Kermode's words, 'a sort of key to his historical imagination',[5] with Roman culture as a *figura* of Christian culture. In his two essays on Virgil, 'What is a classic?', originally delivered as his Presidential address to the newly formed Virgil Society in 1944, and 'Virgil and the Christian world', first given as a radio talk in 1951, Eliot sought to lay out a saving myth for modern discontents by his Anglo-Catholic reassertion of Virgil's adequacy as a cultural icon and 'the classic of all Europe'.[6] Eliot's conceptions owe a heavy debt to the Austrian Catholic writer Theodor Haecker, a socialist and staunch anti-fascist, whose bolder reinscribing of Virgil as an embryonic Christian mystic in his popular and influential *Virgil, Father of the West* (1931, English translation 1934) Eliot

[1] Cited Ziolkowski (1993) 12. [2] Cited *ibid.* 14. [3] *Ibid.* 6.
[4] Cited *ibid.* 35; see too p.25. [5] Cited Reeves (1989) 1.
[6] Eliot (1957) 70 ('What is a classic?').

somewhat toned down for his sober and pragmatic British audiences.[7] For Haecker no satisfactory account of Virgil could 'omit the Faith'; to 'judge of Virgil only in the light of his past and immediate present, and not at all in the light of the future, which was implicit in that past and that present' would be 'preposterous and against reason'.[8] The feline Eliot, while to a degree sharing the view of Virgil as an adventist Christian, is circumspect in his formulation of it, bowing gravely to the scholars. Thus of Eclogue 4, long read as a prophecy of the Incarnation, he writes: 'That Virgil himself was consciously concerned only with domestic affairs or with Roman politics I feel sure.' If the poem can be read as a prophecy, that is because 'a prophet need not understand the meaning of his prophetic utterance', and because 'if there is such a thing as inspiration – and we do go on using the word – then it is something which escapes historical research'.[9] One of Eliot's enduring concerns is the relationship between temporality and timelessness, which he sees as coexisting within both empire and classic. Virgil's works can be read under the aspect of time, but also under the aspect of the timeless; neither reading excludes the other, and neither reading is adequate without the other.

For Eliot Virgil is a classic, since his writings display the requisite maturity of mind and manners and style, the requisite comprehensiveness, the necessary absence of that provinciality which 'indicates . . . the decay of a common belief and a common culture'.[10] Where Romantic criticism had favoured the supposed primitive vigour of Homer, Eliot celebrates the 'refined' and 'civilised' character of Virgil's world, a 'world of dignity, reason and order'; Eliot tells us that as a schoolboy, despite his preference for the Greek language, he found himself at ease with Virgil as he was not at ease with Homer.[11] C. S. Lewis in 1942 gave the most succinct statement of this view: 'With Virgil European poetry grows up';[12] in espousing it, as in other ways, Eliot reveals himself as more 'advanced' in sensibility than (say) Ezra Pound, who retained the Romantic hostility to things Roman in general and to Virgil in particular.[13] The Eliotic Virgil is also and above all the supreme poet of empire:

> What Virgil proposed to his contemporaries was the highest ideal even for an unholy Roman Empire, for any merely temporal empire. We are all, so far as we inherit the civilisation of Europe, still citizens of the Roman Empire, and time has not yet proved Virgil wrong when he wrote *nec tempora pono: imperium sine fine dedi.* But, of course, the Roman Empire which Virgil imagined and for which

[7] For Haecker see Reeves (1989) 96–116; Ziolkowski (1993) 48–52. [8] Haecker (1934) 8.
[9] Eliot (1957) 122–3 ('Virgil and the Christan world'). [10] *Ibid.* 61 ('What is a classic?').
[11] *ibid.* 124–5 ('Virgil and the Christian world'). [12] Lewis (1942) 37.
[13] Pound declared that 'since the study of Martial there is nothing I approach with such nausea and disgust as Roman life'; see Stray (1992) 60.

Aeneas worked out his destiny was not exactly the same as the Roman Empire of the legionaries, the pro-consuls and governors, the business men and speculators, the demagogues and generals. It was something greater, but something which exists because Virgil imagined it.[14]

Behind the city of Rome, then, is the city of God. Again Haecker, more explicit and more unbuttoned, can be used to gloss Eliot's judicious restraint: Virgil celebrates that 'Roman Empire, after whose pattern all subsequent, and all future, empires have been and will be made – they are all but partial resuscitations of that one empire which never has been, and never will be, overthrown'.[15] For Eliot Virgil's idea of empire allows a solution, at the political level, of the relationship of macrocosm and microcosm: 'His devotion to Rome was founded on devotion to the land; to the particular region, to the particular village, and to the family in the village. To the reader of history this foundation of the general on the particular may seem chimerical . . . And yet it may be the man who affirms the apparently incompatible who is right.'[16] Such idealised regionalism had long been fashionable among right-wing thinkers, including Charles Maurras, monarchist and anti-Semite, whose ideas had earlier interested Eliot.[17] There is also, as we have seen, an important connection between Virgil's classic status and his imperial vision; as Kermode observes, quoting from the final section of 'Burnt Norton', 'The classic, like the Empire, must be thought of as "timeless . . . except in the aspect of time".'[18] Both classic and empire exist within history, but also transcend history, evincing both permanence and change and enabling us to grasp, or at least to experience in practice, the relationship between them.

Reeves claims that Eliot's two essays present us with a Virgil distinct from the Virgil we encounter in his earlier work; and he considers that the younger Eliot pioneered a different, darker Virgil, a 'poet of apocalyptic doubt'.[19] Here we may feel that a powerful contemporary reading of Virgil is being imposed retrospectively on Eliot. It is true that, as Eliot developed as a poet and as a man, his use of Virgil, like his use of other monuments of high culture, changed: from bricolage, fragments perhaps ironically recalled or desperately shored against his ruins, he achieved a more unitary vision in his later Christian poetry as the committed interpreter of a Western Christian *imperium*. But there is no evidence to suggest any about-turn in his conception of Virgil and good reason to doubt it; his Latin teacher at Harvard who presumably helped shape his view was E. K. Rand,

[14] Eliot (1957) 130 ('Virgil and the Christian world'). [15] Haecker (1934) 64.
[16] Eliot (1957) 126.
[17] For Eliot and Maurras see Margolis (1972) 87–99; Reeves (1989) 91–4; Moody (1994) 63–5.
[18] Kermode (1983) 60; for the relationship between permanence and change, a central concern of both Eliot and Kermode, see eg pp. 42–5. [19] Reeves (1989) 10.

a strong believer in an adventist Christian Virgil. Reeves also exaggerates the importance of Virgil as a presence in the poems; in particular his attempt to impose, through Virgilian resonances, a single dominant pattern on *The Waste Land* fails, as all such attempts are likely to fail (for is that not part of the nature of the waste land of modernity?). Indeed one might argue that if any Latin poet presides over the poem it is not Virgil but the slippery Ovid, whom Charles Tomlinson plausibly names as 'a chief ancestor of literary modernism':[20] we have the repeated use of the myth of Tereus, Procne and Philomela linked to the poem's preoccupation with sound and silence, speech and speechlessness; the role of the Ovidian Tiresias who fluctuates in gender and who, according to Eliot's own note, sees 'the substance of the poem'; and in general a concern with the anthropological substratum of Ovidian story, not least over the reference in the *Fasti*, important for the genesis of Frazer's *Golden Bough*, to the priest at Nemi, a slave who had killed his predecessor in office, destined himself to be killed in his turn (this combination of the sophisticated with an interest in the primitive is typical of modernism). Virgil within Eliot's poetry – and to this extent we may accept Reeves' point – proves more fragmentary and 'fugitive'[21] than the dominating and unified figure presented in the essays might have led one to expect.

The essays on Virgil were written long after the composition of *The Waste Land*, and they come from a very different political environment. But there is a considerable degree of continuity in Eliot's commitments and in the words of power within which they were framed – commitments to authority, order, discipline, hierarchy, classicism, empire, culture and, above all, tradition. Thus the idea of the classic and its relationship to history which in 1944 Eliot set before the Virgil Society, formed in the darkest days of the war in order 'to bring together those men and women everywhere who are united in cherishing the central educational tradition of Western Europe',[22] is consonant enough with the doctrines of 'Tradition and the individual talent', first published in 1919. In Eliot's theory, which

20 Tomlinson (1983) 1; for Eliot and Ovid see, in addition to the chapter in Tomlinson, Stephen Medcalf, 'T. S. Eliot's *Metamorphoses*: Ovid and *The Waste Land*' in Martindale (1988) 233–46.

21 Reeves (1989) 14.

22 From a letter to the *TLS* 18 December 1943, signed by Eliot, Mackail, V. Sackville-West and others; for the full text see Blandford (1993) 79. The Society was designed, according to this letter, to 'play an important part in the intellectual life of the country, in reversing the present descent to vulgarisation of taste and debasement of standards'. A leader in the *TLS*, entitled 'Homage to Virgil', supports the Society's aims, calls Virgil 'one of the most valuable common possessions of a distracted humanity', and asserts that 'it would be difficult to name a more civilizing influence' (Blandford (1993) 78). The Society's constitution of 1952 stated: 'The purpose of the society is to unite all those who cherish the poetry of Virgil as the symbol of the cultural tradition of Western Europe' (Blandford (1993) 89). Subsequent presidents included Mackail (1945) and Lord Wavell (1948).

Kermode well describes as 'Cubist historiography, unlearning the trick of perspective and ordering history as a system of perpetually varying spatial alignments',[23] apparent opposites, tradition and novelty, classicism and modernism, change and stasis, can be reconciled.

In the years following the First World War classicism – which could be a matter quite distinct from the status and reputation of the writers of classical antiquity – was frequently allied to right-wing politics; and Eliot is usually, and in many ways reasonably, thought of as a conservative thinker. But Eliot's 'conservatism' entailed positions which, in current debates, would often be construed as radical. In recent skirmishes over the status of the canon upholders of tradition usually employ the rhetoric at least of objectivism. By contrast, Eliot's intellectual sympathies were, throughout his career, to a large degree culturalist and relativistic, in ways that can be traced back to the philosophical training he received at Harvard. In the last of a series of papers he gave to Josiah Royce's logic seminar at Harvard in 1913–14 he argued against a unitary conception of the self; the self becomes a self only when 'conscious of being several selves'.[24] He agreed with the pragmatist Charles Peirce that there are no originary cognitions, only an infinite chain with neither end nor beginning.[25] It is difficult, or even impossible, to translate one culture satisfactorily into the terms of another, or to enter an alien mental set. Interpretations are historically situated but historical truth is fugitive since, as Eliot put it in 1926, 'the past is in perpetual flux, although only the past can be known'.[26] In all this we may sense, in Eliot, a tension between an extraordinary sensitivity to flux and a countervailing rage for order, a tension which could be related to the despair both of infinity and finitude that critics have detected in *The Waste Land*.[27] And there is also the paradoxical, or self-frustrating, nature of any such reactive traditionalism, since, in the words of Elie Kedourie, 'the essential condition in the holder of a traditional faith is that he should not know he is a traditionalist'.[28]

There are a number of thinkers on the right with whom Eliot can usefully

[23] 'A Babylonish Dialect', in Cox and Hinchcliffe (1968) 229. For Kermode the poem reveals 'behind the temporal disaster of Babylon' the continuing 'timeless pattern of the eternal city'(231); and he concludes his essay thus: 'When the *Quartets* speak of a pattern of timeless moments, of the point of intersection, they speak *about* that pattern and that point; the true image of them is *The Waste Land*. There the dreams cross, the dreams in which begin responsibilities.' Contrast Eagleton (1970) 147: 'Eliot's "Tradition" is a labile, self-transformative organism extended in space and time, constantly reorganised by the present; but this radical historical relativism is then endowed with the status of absolute classical authority.' [24] Jain (1992) 144. [25] *Ibid.* 137.

[26] Quoted *ibid.* 145 (from the Introduction to *Savonarola*, a poem by Charlotte Eliot, the poet's mother).

[27] For the former Jain (1992), preface, x–xi; for the latter Medcalf in Martindale (1988) 242.

[28] Quoted Lowenthal (1985) 371.

be connected, from the disreputable and fanatical Maurras, founder of *L'Action Française* whom Eliot compared to Dante's Virgil leading the French to the temple gate,[29] at one extreme, to the highly reputable scholar E. R. Curtius at the other. From his Harvard professor Irving Babbitt Eliot had early learned the need for an authority outside the individual, which he located first in a literary tradition and then in a wider Christian culture, where tradition, in a more unconscious form, was constituted as much by religion and politics as by literature.[30] The link between classicism and right-wing politics is particularly clear in the writings of T. E. Hulme, commended by Eliot in the *Criterion*. In his essay 'Romanticism and classicism' from *Speculations* (1924) Hulme observes that 'if you asked a man of a certain set whether he preferred the classics or the romantics, you could deduce from that what his politics were'. He dismisses romanticism as 'spilt religion', calls for a poetry that is 'properly classical', 'all dry and hard', and predicts a classical revival which may not necessarily be perceived as such.[31] *The Waste Land* could become, from such a perspective, classical as well as a classic. Eliot had already linked his notion of literary history with what Hulme terms 'the sane classical dogma of original sin';[32] in 1916, in a syllabus for a series of Oxford University extension lectures, he wrote: 'The beginning of the twentieth century has witnessed a return to the ideals of classicism. These may roughly be characterized as *form* and *restraint* in art, *discipline* and *authority* in religion, *centralization* in government. . . . The classicist point of view has been defined as essentially a belief in Original Sin – the necessity for austere discipline.'[33] Eliot made the *Criterion* into a vehicle for a sustained defence of classicism so defined, one supposedly quite consonant with the novelties of modernism. But was the commitment to wholeness and the unity of tradition at one with the fractured nature of his own experimental poetry? In 1926, in a reply to Middleton Murry, he declared that the essential difference between classicism and Romanticism was 'the difference between the complete and the fragmentary, the adult and the immature, the orderly and the chaotic'.[34]

There is a similar emphasis on the *unity* of tradition in the writings of the great German scholar Ernst Robert Curtius, who produced the first translation into German of *The Waste Land* (1927), who was introduced to English readers in the pages of the *Criterion* and whose culminating work, *European Literature and the Latin Middle Ages*, was described by Eliot, on its appearance in 1952, as 'the best book to be published this year and for

[29] Margolis (1972) 95; Jain (1992) 59. Eliot also dedicated his long essay on Dante to Maurras.
[30] See Margolis (1972) 4–9; for Eliot and Babbitt see also Jain (1992) 40–59.
[31] Hulme (1936) 114, 117–18, 125. [32] *Ibid.* 117. [33] Text from Margolis (1972) 11.
[34] *Criterion* October 1923; cited Margolis (1972) 56.

many years'.[35] Curtius, who saw his book as contributing to 'the preservation of Western culture', used it to criticise the fragmentation caused by the specialised study of national literatures:

> To see European literature as a whole is possible only after one has acquired citizenship in every period from Homer to Goethe. . . . One acquires the rights of citizenship in the country of European literature only when one has spent many years in each of its provinces and has frequently moved about from one to another. One is a European when one has become a *civis Romanus*.[36]

That unity, a unity of both time and space, is a Latin-based unity, and at its core once again is the link between Virgil and Dante, 'an arc of flame' which 'historically . . . is the sealing of the bond which the Latin Middle Ages made between the antique and the modern world'.[37] The parts of the whole which constitutes the empire of European letters within Curtius' account are not individual works of literature but the *topics*, *communes loci*, which provide the building blocks, in a manner analogous to letters in an alphabet and which are, in Curtius' archaeological metaphor, 'rooted in the deeper strata of the soul' constituting 'the cellars – and foundations! – of European literature'.[38] Curtius' new synoptic method allows him to see the single entity which is the Western tradition and within which 'the European mind preserves its identity through the millenniums',[39] and, in setting out this method, he once again resorts to an archaeological metaphor: 'A person standing on the ground before a heap of ruins cannot see the whole that the aerial photograph reveals.'[40] Curtius also desired 'a creative renewal of the relations between France and Germany';[41] and Germany's apostasy from civilised values was often connected with a lack of regard for Virgil. Curtius noted that in France the defeat of Germany in 1918 was seen as 'a sign of the reestablishment of traditional Western values'.[42] Haecker has a whole chapter on Virgil and the Germans, in which he explores the reasons for the loss of 'that knowledge which until the eighteenth century the German nation, as a member of the Holy Roman Empire, shared with every good European . . . that Virgil is a fixed star'.[43] For Curtius that loss had removed the key to the understanding of the Latin Middle Ages: 'Only when we are once again able to comprehend Virgil in all his poetic

35 For Curtius see Finley (1975) 193–214; Gelley (1966) 579–94; Uhlig (1990) 193–207; Martindale (1993) 24–5; Eliot's laudatory notice is still quoted on the jacket of editions of *European Literature and the Latin Middle Ages*. 36 Curtius (1979) foreword, viii, and 12.

37 *Ibid.* 358. 38 *Ibid.* 105 and 79.

39 *Ibid.* 395. As Gelley (1966) puts it, for Curtius the canon is 'fundamentally beyond history' (594). 40 Curtius (1979) foreword, ix. 41 So Gelley (1966) 585.

42 So Ziolkowski (1993) 7. Ziolkowski (35–8) shows how even in Walter Wili's *Vergil* (1930) the German hostility to Virgil and Rome which the author generally tries to combat reasserts itself in the concluding paragraph in which Virgil is characterised as 'un-Greek and un-German'. 43 Haecker (1934) 102.

greatness, of which we Germans have lost sight since 1770, shall we wholly appreciate Dante.'[44]

Rome is not so positively presented in Eliot's poetry as in his prose. In particular *Coriolan* (1931) gives us a totalitarian, militaristic Rome, not then the Rome of Virgil's imagining but the Rome of the business men and speculators, the demagogues and generals. *The Waste Land* has been figured as, in part, a response to the crisis of the First World War, which was a crisis of Western and therefore Roman imperialism.[45] Rome is never mentioned in the poem, and is not included in the list of great cities in the apocalyptic picturing of urban collapse in 'What the Thunder said', a passage which is both an image of the Last Judgement and a reflection of post-war political chaos and which itself may well have Virgilian resonances:[46]

What is the city over the mountains
Cracks and reforms and bursts in the violet air
Falling towers
Jerusalem Athens Alexandria
Vienna London
Unreal

But even if absent, Rome is a present absence. In an earlier version of 'The Fire Sermon' Fresca is described as exploring a page of Gibbon (presumably *The Decline and Fall*) – though Gibbon was subsequently crossed out in favour of *The Daily Mirror*.[47] *The Waste Land* is a London poem, but London had long been seen as the heir of Rome, even as maybe more truly Rome than the modern city which bears the name; or such is the burden of a famous opening sentence by another expatriate American, Henry James:

The Prince had always liked his London, when it had come to him; he was one of the Modern Romans who find by the Thames a more convincing image of the truth of the ancient state than any they have left by the Tiber. . . . If it was a question of an *Imperium*, he said to himself, and if one wished, as a Roman, to recover a little the sense of that, the place to do so was on London Bridge . . . (*The Golden Bowl*, ch. 1)[48]

In 1928 Eliot argued that Britain was the 'mediating part' of Europe, 'the connection between Europe and the rest of the world' as being 'the only member of the European community that has established a genuine empire – that is to say, a world-wide empire as was the Roman empire'.[49] Eleanor

44 Curtius (1979) 358.

45 See Cook (1979) 341–55; also Trotter (1986) 143–53, who suggests that the poem owes something to imperial frontier myth, Janowitz (1990) 8–9, 18–9, 177–8, and Vance (1989) I 387: 'Beneath T. S. Eliot's *Wasteland* [*sic*] lie the history and mythology of imperial Rome, fragmented and transposed to our century in the dying British Empire.'

46 So Reeves (1989) 34–5. 47 See Valerie Eliot (1971) 23.

48 On James' appropriations of Rome, see Lyon above.

49 Quoted Reeves (1989) 85 (from 'A Commentary', *Criterion* (7 March 1928), 194).

Cook rightly points out that *The Waste Land* can be plotted on three maps as it were, a map of London, a map of the world, and a map of the European theatre of war from 1914 to 1918, whose centre-point is Rome.[50] As we have seen, Rome is evoked obliquely through allusions to Virgil and Ovid, and there is also a trail of references to the maritime Phoenicians and to Rome's imperial rival Carthage, including the allusion to Dido's lavish *laquearia*. In 'The Burial of the Dead' the speaker hails an old comrade-at-arms from the war from among the crowd flowing over London Bridge with words that evoke Rome's decisive naval victory over Carthage which established her Mediterranean hegemony: 'You who were with me in the ships at Mylae!' This is a moment in the poem which, with particular drama, collapses history, collapses, that is, the present into the past, or brings the past into the present, so that the waste land is seen under the aspect of eternity.

2 What are the roots that clutch, what branches grow
Out of this stony rubbish? Son of man,
You cannot say, or guess, for you know only
A heap of broken images

The conception of poetry as a quasi-archaeological activity is not uncommonly encountered among modern poets. In such writing the poet excavates the past – including the layers buried in the language which survive as traces within current significations – and comes up with something living, or which can have at least a kind of life. The historical substrata behind the present scene are disclosed; the past is found *in the present*. In his 1947 essay on Milton Eliot tells us that, if we are to understand the dissociation of sensibility that afflicted English poetry around the Civil War, 'we must seek the causes in Europe, not in England alone; and for what these causes were, we may dig and dig until we get to a depth at which words and concepts fail us'.[51] Causes are not perhaps the main concern in Eliot's depiction of London as a modern waste land, but there is certainly a process of digging and digging, and that in Europe – and indeed the world – not in England alone; while in 'What the Thunder said' we may reach a depth where words fail us or increasingly end in silence. The first part of the poem in particular, 'The Burial of the Dead', concerns things buried deep, from the dull roots stirred by the spring of the opening to the corpse (whether literal or metaphorical) in Stetson's garden at the close. Whether any painful process of disinterment will bring fresh life or only renewed pain is unclear; Stetson's corpse is described in terms which suggest a root or bulb, and digging it up – as 'the Dog that's friend to men' may do – will only prevent

[50] Cook (1979) 341–2. [51] Eliot (1957) 153 ('Milton II').

it from sprouting. Eliot's theory of poetic language is also in part an 'archaeological one', in terms of recessive layers of meaning; in *The Use of Poetry* (1933) he defines the 'auditory imagination' as 'the feeling for syllable and rhythm, penetrating far below the conscious levels of thought and feeling, invigorating every word; sinking to the most primitive and forgotten, returning to the origin and bringing something back, seeking the beginning and the end'. These layers in the language are brought to simultaneous life as the poet 'fuses the old and obliterated and the trite, the current, and the new and surprising, the most ancient and the most civilized mentality'[52] to create a poetry at once modern and, in Eliot's sense, classical.

We might distinguish two models for our understanding of the past, which may conveniently be termed 'historical' and 'archaeological', the former diachronic, the latter synchronic, palimpsestic. History and archaeology, so conceived, would both offer a form of presence, but presence of a different kind. History represents, *re*presents, the past as a completed story, a story of absent events, of change over time, of causes and effects, befores and afters; archaeology offers a fuller degree of presence, but it is a more obviously fragmentary presence, as tangible fragments of the past are presented to our senses. Now of course this distinction could easily be blurred; one could point out, for example, that an archaeological object, even to be recognised as such, has to be narrativised, historicised, always already. It is a pleasant paradox that archaeology, while seemingly allowing that the object can transcend time and change, has to present it within time (which is why the fragment or ruin is so described in the first place), while history, even as it presents a strictly temporal sequence, implies a position 'outside time', as it were, from which the story can be told. Both discourses, in other words, involve a shuttle between the aspect of time and the aspect of the timeless, but they do so for rather different purposes and with rather different results. Eliot's poetic practice and theory of tradition (both involving a sort of literary cubism which abolishes perspective and linear chronology,[53] and dissolves or refigures time) show the strong attraction to him of archaeology in this special sense. *The Waste Land* with its bricolage of intertexts and competing discourses can thus usefully be related to Freud's famous comparison, in 'Civilisation and its discontents' (1930) of the city of Rome and the human mind as palimpsests: 'Now let us, by a flight of imagination, suppose that Rome is not a human habitation but a psychic entity with a similarly long and copious past – an entity, that is to say, in which nothing that has once come into existence will have passed away and

[52] Eliot (1964) 118–19 ('Matthew Arnold').
[53] Cf. Kermode in Cox and Hinchcliffe (1968) quoted above.

all the earlier phases of development continue to exist alongside the latest one.'[54] Freud, a collector of classical antiquities, had a lifelong interest in archaeology (then in its heroic phase), and frequently employed archaeological metaphors in connection with psychoanalysis, archaeology offering him an 'enticing picture of time made perfectly legible in layered deposits of matter'.[55] The unconscious becomes Freud's way of collapsing the distinction between past and present into a potent simultaneity, rather in the manner of the Eliotic tradition. We seem to be dealing here with something that might be deemed crucial to the formation of modernism.

While a bifocality in respect of the aspects of time and timelessness may be inherent in any version of the past, it is more evidently and more overtly so in the case of Rome, to the extent indeed that it has become an important and explicit part of what 'Rome' traditionally signifies. Any great city – like any potent name – becomes the locus of multiple layered significations, some complementary, some competing, even at war, through the stories or histories told about it, through the people associated with it and who have loved or hated it, through the travellers who have visited and written about it. Rome, like any other city, is not only a physical location but a place of the mind, textually inscribed and as frequently discovered through literature as by more 'direct' encounter. And it is a site of opposed, or seemingly opposed, meanings, weakness and strength, glory and decadence, stability and instability, historicity and transcendence, a sign of tradition but also of flux and rupture. The legacy of Greece and Rome has been for many at once grounds for assurance and testimony of decay. The most potent physical symbols of the ancient city are themselves ruins which proclaim *inter alia* the loss of the past – indeed the adjective 'Roman' invites the noun 'ruin' as a 'natural' complement as readily as it does 'empire'. Rome, in a way that could be called paradigmatic at least for the West, is at once the site of historical change and the *urbs aeterna* (this very formulation with its switch into Latin itself could be said to mirror the movement from the aspect of time to the aspect of eternity); hence its attraction for Eliot. Thomas Greene, in his impressive and influential study *The Light in Troy*, figures the Renaissance's recovery of Roman antiquity in just such terms. In a sense one could argue that the key difference between humanist and earlier responses to Rome lay in a much heightened sense of disjuncture, a conviction that antiquity had died and so needed to be brought back to life again, together with an increased preoccupation with its physical remains. Petrarch, who for Greene inaugurates the new sensibility by recognising 'the possibility of a cultural alternative', uses *ruinae* to describe

[54] See Freud (1930/1985) 257 (this passage is quoted at greater length in Kennedy above); for an excellent discussion see Barkan (1991) 10–19; also Janowitz (1990) 50–3.

[55] Bowie (1987) 23.

both those remains and lost or fragmentary ancient writings.[56] Metaphors of disinterment are frequent; and there must inevitably be fears as well as excitement about digging up corpses. Of that great classic of ruin literature Du Bellay's *Antiquitez du Rome*, Greene writes: 'It is at once a homage, a challenge, a ritual of summoning, a gesture of disinterment, a reconstruction, and a demystifying reflection on all these aspects of itself'; and he adds 'They are all tinged with the suspicion of failure, even the demystification.'[57] There seems a distinctly Eliotic flavour to much of this, and Eliot is indeed duly invoked in Greene's characterisation of the relation of past and present in the *Antiquitez*: 'More directly threatening to the speaker is the thought that 'In my beginning is my end': I recognize from these ruins the futility of poetry, of enterprise, of civilisation. . . . I understand that my port is my shipwreck.'[58]

The Waste Land can be related both to the ruin poem, which in English literature can be traced back to Anglo-Saxon times, and to the poetic fragment which achieved considerable popularity in the nineteenth century, although ruin and fragment now take a modernist form which we can relate to the crisis of the First World War. Any reader of, say, Anne Janowitz' suggestive study *England's Ruins*, which explores 'the network of relations among ruins, fragments, and nation-making',[59] will be aware of the complex and shifting nature of the possible ideological entailments of ruin. A ruin is evidence of decay, of transience, of the power of time to weaken and destroy, but it can also be read as a site of transcendence. This double aspect is powerfully expressed by Hegel in the *Philosophy of History*:

> The sight of the ruins of some ancient sovereignty directly leads us to contemplate the thought of change in its negative aspect. What traveller among the ruins of Carthage, of Palmyra, Persepolis, or Rome, has not been stimulated to reflections on the transiency of kingdoms and men, and to sadness at the thought of a vigorous and rich life now departed. . . . But the next consideration which allies itself with that of change, is that change, while it imports dissolution, involves at the same time the rise of a *new* life – that while death is the issue of life, life is also the issue of death.[60]

Ruins are likewise signs both of origins and of ends or the end. Ruin also to a degree restores art to nature, or blurs the distinction between them. The immemorial antiquity of the ruin may testify that the present social order too is rooted deep in time and the soil and will thus endure. Temporality thus has its benign aspects. Janowitz comments that 'the paradox of

[56] Greene (1982) 90 and 92. I am particularly endebted to two chapters in Greene's book: 'Petrarch and the humanist hermeneutic', 81–103, and 'Du Bellay and the disinterment of Rome', 220–41. [57] *Ibid.* 222. [58] *Ibid.* 227.

[59] Janowitz (1990) 7. In addition to her book, to which I am substantially endebted, see, on ruins, Goldstein (1972); McFarland (1981); Piggott (1976).

[60] Quoted by Greene (1982) 233.

eighteenth-century ruin was that the figure of decay was at the same time the image used to authorize England's autonomy as a world power'.[61] Ruin and empire, seemingly at odds, may at some deeper level cohere – this too is part of the legacy of Rome, and perhaps of the vision of *The Waste Land*. In any recovery poetry has a crucial role to play; great poetry can restore the past, and that in a way better designed to withstand the depredations of time than any building, even if there can be no full presence. So following Du Bellay Edmund Spenser, in his translation of the *Antiquitez* which he called *The Ruins of Rome*, found in those ruins signs of a lost whole: 'Yet these olde fragments are for paternes borne' (sonnet 27). Janowitz also observes that the poetry of fragment or ruin frequently involves a measure of de-historicising, de-contextualising, a movement away from narrative forms, a process of privatisation, of 'spatialization usurping temporality';[62] the relevance of all that to *The Waste Land* hardly requires elaboration.

3 I can connect
Nothing with nothing.
The broken fingernails of dirty hands.

Rome in Eliot as elsewhere can thus be associated with both ruins and empire. How in the light of this is *The Waste Land* to be read, and what is to be made of its parade of splintered intertexts, its mosaic of quotation, imitation, allusion? On Margate Sands the speaker could connect nothing with nothing, but the trouble with many of Eliot's academic critics is that they find it all too seductively easy to connect everything with everything. In one way the search for meaning is inevitable though maybe doomed to failure. Eliot's notes served to encourage that search but offered little real help towards its resolution; indeed, gravely judicious in their style, they may be no more than moves in an arch and solemn game, played at the expense of reader and commentator alike. But their donnish character connects, illuminatingly, with something pedantic about the poem they at least pretend to annotate; Helen Gardner calls it the 'prim pedantry . . . of the New England lecture-room, suggesting . . . the cultured voice and the card-index of the professor',[63] and it was something that worried, or irritated, more than one early reviewer. Today familiarity has bred not contempt but a taking-for-granted of what once seemed strangest and to some most

[61] Janowitz (1990) 2; for ruin and empire see also Goldstein (1972). [62] Janowitz (1990) 7.

[63] Gardner (1949) 85. For the hostile reaction in some reviews to Eliot's 'pedantry' cf. Cox and Hinchcliffe (1968) 29–30 (*Manchester Guardian*) and 33–8 (F. L. Lucas in *New Statesman*). See too James Longenbach, '"Mature poets steal": Eliot's allusive practice', 176–88 in Moody (1994); and for a more hostile account, with some telling instances of 'plagiarism' in Eliot, F. W. Bateson, 'The poetry of learning', 31–44 in Martin (1970).

annoying or disturbing about the poem; and academic critics in particular have seen in the allusiveness a way of resolving any apparent incoherences and a means of generating interpretations to show what the work is really 'about'. The poem is often read 'historically', with its gaps filled by various hermeneutic manoeuvres, usually either as a declaration of cultural decline and personal or social disintegration or as an achieved search for some kind of redemption. In all this we may find, with Maud Ellmann, a critical tendency to 'treat the text as if it were a photographic negative, tracing the shadows of a lost or forbidden body'.[64] All texts may be fragments, yet some are more fragmentary than others, or at any rate foreground their fragmentariness in a more apparent way. In Eliot's case we have, for example, the use of fluctuating pronouns of uncertain reference, the ruptures and incompletenesses in syntax, the absence of punctuation – should interpretation proceed just as if these destabilising features were absent?

The poem consists of contrasted scenes one upon another; usually the breaks are strongly marked, less often one scene blurs into the next. The various sections have a fragmented character, and at the end there is a flurry of quotations in a confusion of languages specifically described as fragments which the speaker has shored against his ruins, whether these be the ruins of a disintegrated or disintegrating psyche or of a civilisation in this condition or indeed of both – already the romantic ruinists had collapsed the distinction between self and world, as when in *Childe Harold* IV stanza 25, lines 217–18 the poet becomes 'a ruin amidst ruins'. This ending can be read negatively as a further slide into dissolution, or more positively as an attempt at least to set the lands in order by shoring up and repairing the structure with such bits and pieces of culture as are to hand. The poem's fractured character, we may feel, necessarily involves some resistance to easy or immediate cohesion, some resistance to closure. Terry Eagleton, displaying the 'radical' critic's usual suspicion of literature, sees this fracturing as merely a ruse to conceal the writer's totalitarian ambition. We should not be fooled by the avant-garde and experimental nature of the poem into supposing that it is, in any real sense, subversive, since any apparent subversion 'turns out to be merely phenomenal': 'for behind the back of this ruptured, radically decentred poem runs an alternative text which is nothing less than the closed, coherent, authoritative discourse of the mythologies which frame it'.[65] We may grant that this reading makes a kind of sense. Of course any fragment has to be a fragment *of*. But Eagleton's interpretation is itself homogenising, totalising; it is not grounded in any close analysis of the poem, which it treats as though it were a single thing

64 '*The Waste Land*: a sphinx without a secret', 377–93 in Clarke (1990) 377.

65 Eagleton (1976) 149–50; cf. 148 on 'the esoteric allusions which attempt to construct an ideal order' across the poem.

with a unified texture. His earlier reference to 'an ideal order' suggests that Eagleton is reading the poem against Eliot's prose criticism, and finding in that criticism the key to its meaning. Moreover no reason is given why we should see the mythologies in the poem as uniquely authoritative or coherent, why they should be held to constitute frame or grounds – they too can be construed as both fragmentary and labile.

There are several attitudes towards fragments. One can argue that reading (and interpretation) always involves fragmentation. We have seen that there is a politics of fragments. For Eagleton the Eliot of *The Waste Land* is simply an authoritarian conservative, but there were early readers of the poem who reacted very differently. For them the poem spoke of liberation, the breaking up, the fragmenting, of old systems (many welcomed war in 1914 for just such reasons). I. A. Richards quoted words of Conrad in his remarks on *The Waste Land*: 'In the destructive element immerse. That is the way'; and Stephen Spender saw in this phrase and this immersion the key to a whole generation.[66] There is also an aesthetics of fragmentation. Ezra Pound wrote his own Sapphic fragment entitled 'Papyrus':

> Spring.......
> Too long......
> Gongula.......

Richard Jenkyns comments: 'Pound wanted to show how eloquent and enticing a few torn remnants of a poem can be; in some cases they may be more suggestive than the poem complete.'[67] One can maintain too that there is an ethical dimension to fragmentation, and find an integrity in the leaving or respecting of gaps, the refusal to narrativise them. A number of poststructuralist or postmodern writers have so argued, in effect equating totality with totalitarianism. One might seek for a kind of autonomy of the fragment, which would mean that a text would be construed as simultaneously part and whole.[68] Roland Barthes, who would normally be thought a more progressive writer than Eliot, is particularly in love with the form of the fragment, as he seeks for pluralities that might free us from tyrannous modes of differentiation. His 'autobiography', if it is rightly so described, narcissistically entitled *Roland Barthes par Roland Barthes*, is structured as a series of short meditations or *pensées*. On the basis that 'incoherence is preferable to a distorting order' Barthes uses this structure of diffraction as an attempt to escape the tyranny of binary oppositions: 'I am not contradictory, I am dispersed' (*la personne divisée*?).[69] It would be possible to

[66] Spender (1935) 12. [67] Jenkyns (1982) 82.
[68] See Rajan (1985), 'Afterword', 295–310, and in particular 309 n.16 on Deleuze and Guattari. I am also endebted to an unpublished paper by Wolfgang Ernst, 'Archaeologically correct? Representations of ancient Rome in the novel'.
[69] Barthes (1977) 93 and 143; cf. 94.

argue, along Eagletonian lines, that Barthes' fetishisation of the fragment involves an occlusion of a totalising scheme. The organising principle is presented as arbitrary (in *Fragment of a Lover's Discourse* it is the alphabet), but none the less shapes the whole, and closure is effected by gathering the bits into the totality. Still these fragmentary forms obviously resist some forms of connection. In *Writing Degree Zero* Barthes argues that the key to what he calls 'classical language' is a 'relational' economy, 'which means that in it words are abstracted as much as possible in the interests of relationships', so that they become 'the means of conveying a connection'.[70] By contrast in 'modern' writing the word becomes an 'unexpected object':

> Fixed connections being abolished, the word is left only with a vertical project, it is like a monolith, or a pillar which plunges into a totality of meanings, reflexes and recollections. . . . Thus under each Word . . . there lies a sort of existential geology. . . .The Word, here, is encyclopaedic, it contains simultaneously all the acceptations from which a relational discourse might have required it to choose. It therefore achieves a state which is possible only in the dictionary . . . and is reduced to a sort of zero degree, pregnant with all past and future specifications.[71]

We are moving now from an ethics to a metaphysics of fragmentation. Here again the issues can be variously conceptualised. One could argue that the universe is not a whole thing, so we can only have 'bits' of reality; in the notes to *The Waste Land*, a poem strongly informed by solipsistic impulses, Eliot cites a passage from the philosopher F. H. Bradley which implies that, if there is a whole world, it would be different for each perceiver ('In brief, regarded as an existence which appears in a soul, the whole world for each is peculiar and private to that soul'). Or one could say that there is a whole 'out there', but we have only fragments of perception of it (hence the need for healing). The fragment then becomes the paradigm of the ideal whole, or the path to it. In *Childe Harold* (IV stanzas 153–9) the massive St Peter's has to be broken into parts, so that a start can be made along the route of contemplating the grandeur of the whole, a whole later to be figured by the ocean: 'Thou seest not all; but piecemeal thou must break, | To separate contemplation, the great whole' (stanza 157, lines 1405–6). And, of course, we can always read all these discourses of the fragment under the sign of rhetoric. In a brilliant about-turn Barthes acknowledges the overarching rhetoricity from which all his claims to dispersal and difference cannot escape (*le fragment comme illusion*).[72]

For Eagleton, as we have seen, Eliot's poetry is chaotic on the surface but only because 'reality is coded to its roots'[73] as an ideal order is stealthfully constructed in the interests of a conservative ruling elite, and that is the nature and function of the Eliotic tradition. One can argue, however, that

[70] Barthes (1967) 50. [71] *Ibid.* 53–4. [72] Barthes (1977) 95. [73] Eagleton (1990) 317.

in this respect the poetry knows more than the prose essays, or at least knows differently. In the prose there can be a narrowing sense of tradition as Eliot argues for the unity of a specifically *European* culture rooted in antiquity. But it seems a rather different and more generous sort of tradition, and a different sense of the past, that we encounter in *The Waste Land*. Of course many of the great names of western literature are there; but non-European traditions are also invoked, when wisdom is found in the voice of the Thunder, and it is not only elite culture which provides the poem with its constitutive bric-à-brac, but a whole range of popular discourses, by no means all necessarily cited as signs of decay. There seems humility in the poem's possible admission that if salvation is to come from fragments of culture – and we cannot be sure that it will – it may do so as well from a snatch of nursery-rhyme as from the graver monuments of some 'great tradition'. Important too is the poem's acknowledgement of a sense of rupture (often seen as a defining feature of modernism and the avant-garde); the past we have lost – if lost it we have – is not readily or glibly to be recovered. So read, *The Waste Land* comes closer, in its uses of fragmentation, to the writings of the Marxist Walter Benjamin. Benjamin was an inveterate collector of books (he has a famous essay on the subject) and later of quotations, a fetishiser of the collected object, with an ambition to create a work entirely composed of citations from other texts. In her introduction to *Illuminations* Hannah Arendt argues that there is an intimate connection between a sense of a rupture in the tradition and 'the seemingly whimsical figure of the collector who gathers his fragments and scraps from the debris of the past'.[74] In her view Benjamin became a master 'when he discovered that the transmissibility of the past had been replaced by its citability and that in place of its authority there had arisen a strange power to settle down, piecemeal, in the present and to deprive it of 'peace of mind', the mindless peace of complacency'; and she cites his fine saying: 'Quotations in my work are like robbers by the roadside who make an armed attack and relieve an idler of his convictions.'[75] All this sounds a long way from Eliot's theory of tradition, as set out in the seamless carpentry of his prose, but not necessarily from the practice of *The Waste Land*. Arendt writes this whole section of her introduction under the sign of Ariel's song from *The Tempest*, an intertext also in *The Waste Land*, and she concludes, eloquently:

What guides this thinking is the conviction that although the living is subject to the ruin of time, the process of decay is at the same time a process of crystallization, that in the depth of the sea, into which sinks and is dissolved what once was alive, some things 'suffer a sea-change' and survive in new crystallized forms and shapes that remain immune to the elements, as though they waited only for the pearl diver who

[74] Benjamin (1973) introduction 43. [75] *Ibid.*

one day will come down to them and bring them up into the world of the living – as 'thought fragments', as something 'rich and strange', and perhaps as everlasting *Urphänomene.*[76]

So once again, beyond a flawed historicity, the hope of transcendence; the aspect of time can only be understood alongside the aspect of the timeless. A historical reading of *The Waste Land* is always available, but the poem's structure and imagery also encourages an archaeological reading which allows the various elements of this modern 'classic' to be held together in a timeless moment: like Freud's Rome-psyche Eliot's London is a *bricolage* which nonetheless persists and is ever open to the possibility, though not the certainty, of being redeemed.

A form of waste is rubbish, and rubbish certainly features in the world of *The Waste Land*, for example the detritus floating in the Thames, the empty bottles, sandwich papers and other testimony of summer nights. Rome too has been seen as a rubbish heap; in the nineteenth century one of the commonest signs in the city read, precisely, *immondezzaio*. William Vance comments that 'the metaphor of the Forum as an eloquent page that could rightly be read only by scholars and romantics began to compete with the perception of it as a rubbish heap', that is as 'an accumulation of arbitrarily surviving signs without rational relationship or present function'.[77] *The Waste Land* has been established as a modern classic, but for the reader a perception of its contents as in some sense a rubbish heap may yet persist. Janowitz suggests that 'Eliot the ruinist cannot be sure whether or not his collated fragments will be taken simply as junk.'[78] That insecurity, that sense of struggle over its own status which is never certainly or finally resolved, is another feature which separates the poem's use of tradition from the apparent certainties of the prose essays.

sphragis

Discourse, or dialogue, in general could be figured as a continual process of fragmentation and (re)construction of 'new' wholes. This essay, for instance, collects and recontextualises bits and pieces culled from many places, though its rhetoric on the whole, as we say, favours cohesion more than fracture. Like most scholars in the competitive arena of the academy I am also negotiating anxieties about burdensome totalities and equally burdensome fragmentations,[79] fearful alike of infinity and of finitude: how

[76] *Ibid* 54–5. [77] Vance (1989) I 30. [78] Janowitz (1990) 178.

[79] For such oppressions in relation to Eliot and their possible political entailments see 'T. S. Eliot: Conservatism', 74–127 in North (1991), especially 75, 79 ('Prufrock . . . suffers as much from a sense of oppressive totality as he does from fragmentation'), 89, 96, 100, 105, 118. This is now the best account of the politics of modernism.

could I ever read *all* the relevant material?; hasn't *everything* always already been said?; can I articulate anything which is *wholly*, or *partly*, true? Well now that's done: and I'm glad it's over; in the postmodern scholarly waste land, waiting with as much patience as I can muster for refreshment, these fragments I have shored against my ruins.

Bibliography

Ades, Dawn, Tim Benton, David Elliott, Iain Boyd White (1995) *Art and power: Europe under the dictators 1930–1945*. London

Allen, Graham (1994) *Harold Bloom: a poetics of conflict.* Hemel Hempstead

Ameling, W. (1993) *Karthago*. Munich

Andreotti, Libero (1992) 'The aesthetics of war: the Exhibition of the Fascist Revolution', *Journal of Architectural Education* 45 (February): 76–86

Ankersmit, Frank (1995) 'Statements, texts and pictures', in Frank Ankersmit and Hans Kellner, *A new philosophy of history*, 212–40. London

Arnold, Matthew (1860) 'On translating Homer', in R. H. Super, ed. *The complete proseworks of Matthew Arnold* vol. I (1960). Ann Arbor

(1869) 'Culture and anarchy', in Super, ed. *The complete proseworks of Matthew Arnold*, vol. V (1965). Ann Arbor.

Auden, W. H. (1955) 'Introduction', in W. H. Auden, ed. *The portable Greek reader* (first published 1948). New York

Baker, Joseph Ellis (1932) *The novel and the Oxford Movement.* Princeton

Baldick, C. (1983) *The social mission of English criticism 1848–1932*. Oxford

Ball, R. H. (1968) *Shakespeare on silent film: a strange eventful history*. London

Ballhatchet, K. (1980) *Race, sex and class under the Raj: imperial attitudes and policies and their critics 1793–1905*. London

Bann, Stephen (1984) *The clothing of Clio: a study of the representation of history in nineteenth-century Britain and France.* Cambridge

(1988) 'Romanticism in France', in Roy Porter and Mikulas Teich, eds. *Romanticism in national context*, 240–59. Cambridge

(1990) *The inventions of history*. Manchester

(1994) *Under the sign: John Bargrave as collector, traveler and witness*. Ann Arbor

(1995) *Romanticism and the rise of history*. New York

Barkan, Leonard (1991) *Transuming passion: Ganymede and the erotics of humanism*. Stanford

Barocchi, Paola (1990) *Storia moderna dell' arte in Italia.* Turin

Barrell, John (1991) *The infection of Thomas De Quincey. A psychopathology of Imperialism.* London and New Haven.

Barthes, Roland (1967) *Writing degree zero*, trs. Annette Lavers and Colin Smith. London

(1997) *Roland Barthes by Roland Barthes*, trs. Richard Howard. New York

Barton, Tamsyn (1995) 'Augustus and Capricorn: astrological polyvalency and imperial rhetoric', *Journal of Roman Studies* 85: 33–51

Bate, Percy H. (1899) *The English Pre-Raphaelite painters: their associates and successors*. London

Baudelaire, Charles (1993) *The Flowers of Evil*, trs. James McGowan. Oxford
Baynes N. H., ed. (1942) *The speeches of Adolf Hitler 1922–1939*, 2 vols. Oxford
Beard, Mary (1992) 'Frazer, Leach, and Virgil: the popularity (and unpopularity) of *The Golden Bough*', *Comparative Study of Society and History* 34: 203–24
(1996) 'Le mythe (grec) à Rome: Hercule aux bains', 81–104 in *Le mythe au figuré*, 81–104. Paris
Bearce, G. D. (1961) *British attitudes towards India 1784–1858*. Oxford
Becker, Edwin, Edward Morris, Elizabeth Prettejohn and Julian Treuherz, eds. (1996) *Sir Lawrence Alma-Tadema 1836–1912*, exhibition catalogue. Amsterdam and Liverpool
Beckford, William (1824) 'Andrew Guelph and Og of Basan, disciples of Aldrovandus Magnus', *Biographical memoirs of extraordinary painters*, 25–88. London
Bell, Millicent (1991) *Meaning in Henry James*. Cambridge, Mass.
Benjamin, Walter (1973) *Illuminations*, ed. with intro. by Hannah Arendt, trs. Harry Zohn. London
Bergé, F. (1969) 'Napoléon architecte ou le goût de l'histoire', *Les Monuments Historiques de la France* 15.4 (Oct/Dec.):25–57
Bernardini, Aldo (1982) *Cinema muto italiano*, vol. III *Arte, divismo e mercato 1910–1914*. Rome
Bernardini, Aldo and Jean A. Gili, eds. (1986) *Le cinéma italien de La Prise de Rome (1905) à Rome ville ouverte (1945)*. Paris
Berve, H. (1934) 'Antike und nationalsozialistischer Staat', *Vergangenheit und Gegenwart* 24: 257–72
Berve, H., ed. (1942) *Das neue Bild der Antike*, 2 vols. Leipzig
Betts, R. F. (1971) 'The allusion to Rome in British imperialist thought of the late nineteenth and early twentieth centuries', *Victorian Studies* 15: 149–59
Bisztray, George (1991) 'The role of Rome in Hawthorne's *The Marble Faun* and Henry James' *Daisy Miller*', *Rivista di Studi Italiani* 9: 43–52
Biver, M. L. (1963) *Le Paris de Napoléon*. Paris
Blair, Robert (1848) *The life of Robert Blair, Minister of St Andrews, containing his autobiography from 1593 to 1636*, ed. Thomas M'Crie. Edinburgh
Blandford, D. W. (1993) *Pentekontaetia: the Virgil Society 1943–1993*. London
Block, Elizabeth (1984) 'The Rome of Henry James', in Patterson, ed., *Roman images*
Bloom, Harold (1976) *Poetry and repression: revisionism from Blake to Stevens*. New Haven
Boatwright, M. T. (1987) *Hadrian and the city of Rome*. Princeton
Boase, T. S. R. (1954) 'The decoration of the new Palace of Westminster, 1841–1863', *Journal of the Warburg and Courtauld Institutes* 17:319–58
Boime, Albert (1981) *Thomas Couture and the eclectic vision*. New Haven and London
(1990) *Art in an age of Bonapartism 1800–1815*. (Chicago and London)
Bollmus, R. (1970) *Das Amt Rosenberg und seine Gegner*. Stuttgart
Bondanella, Peter (1987) *The eternal city: Roman images in the modern world*. Chapel Hill, N.C. and London
(1988) *Italian cinema: from neorealism to the present*. New York
Bosanquet, Theodora (1924) *Henry James at work*. London
Bowen, Elizabeth (1987) *The Hotel*. London

Bowie, Malcolm (1987) *Freud, Proust and Lacan: theory as fiction.* Cambridge

Boyer, Ferdinand (1937a) 'Autour de Canova et de Napoléon', *Revue des Études Italiennes, organe de l'union intellectuelle franco-italienne* (July/Sept): 202–32

(1937b) 'L'achat des antiques Borghese par Napoléon', *Comptes rendus, Conférence de l'Académie des belles lettres,* 405–17. Paris

(1969a) *Le Monde des arts en Italie et la France de la révolution et de l'empire.* Turin

(1969b) 'Napoléon et la restitution par les musées du Louvre et de Versailles', *Archives de l'art français, vol. XXIV Nouvelle période*, 65–83. Paris

Braun, Emily (1990) 'Political rhetoric and poetic irony: the uses of classicism in the art of fascist Italy', in Cowling and Mundy, eds. *On classic ground.*

Brendel, O. (1953) 'Prolegomena to a book on Roman art', *MAAR* 21:9–73 (reprinted 1979)

Brunetta, G. P. (1975) *Cinema italiano tra le due guerre.* Milan

(1986) 'L'évocation du passé. Les années d'or du film historique', in Bernardini and Gili, eds. *Le cinéma italien* 55–60

(1990) 'No place like Rome: the early years of Italian cinema', *Art forum* (Summer): 122–5

(1991) *Cent'anni di cinema italiano.* Rome.

(1993) *Storia del cinema italiano: il cinema muto 1895–1929*, vol. I. Rome

Brunetta, G. P. and Jean A. Gili (1990) *L'ora d'Africa del cinema italiano 1911–1989.* Trent

Bryce, James (1914) *The ancient Roman empire and the British empire in India. The diffusion of Roman and English law throughout the world. Two historical studies.* Oxford

Buckley, J. H. and G. B. Woods, eds. (1965) *Poetry of the Victorian Period*, 3rd edn. Glenview, Ill.

Bulwer-Lytton, Edward (1898) *The Last Days of Pompeii* (first published 1834). New York

Burrow, J. W. (1981) *A liberal descent: Victorian historians and the English past.* Cambridge

Butler, E. M. (1935) *The tyranny of Greece over Germany.* Cambridge

Buzard, James (1993) *The beaten track: European tourism, literature, and the ways of 'culture' 1800–1918.* Oxford

Byron [G. G. N., Baron] (1980–92) *The complete poetical works* (7 vols.) ed. Jerome J. McGann. Oxford

Cagnetta, Mariella (1976) 'Il mito di Augusto e la rivoluzione fascista', *Quaderni di Storia* 2:139–81

(1979) *Antichisti e impero fascista.* Bari

Calendoli, Giovanni (1967) *Materiali per una storia del cinema italiano.* Parma

Calvesi, Maurizio and Enrico Guidoni, eds. (1987) *E42, Utopia e scenario del regime vol. I, Ideologia e programma per l'Olimpiade delle civiltà* and *vol. II, Urbanistica, archittetura, arte e decorazione.* Venice

Cammarota, M. D. (1987) *Il cinema peplum.* Rome

Camille, Michael (1989) *The Gothic idol: ideology and image-making in medieval art.* Cambridge

Canfora, Luciano (1976) 'Classicismo e fascismo', *Quaderni di Storia* 2:15–48

(1977) 'Classicismo e fascismo' , *Matrici culturali del fascismo.* Bari

(1980) *Ideologie del classicismo.* Turin

Cardillo, Massimo (1987) *Tra le quinte del cinematografo: cinema, cultura e società in Italia 1900–1937*. Bari
Carnochan, W. B. (1987) *Gibbon's solitude: the inward world of the historian*. Stanford
Cary, John (1974) *Spectacular! The story of epic films*. London
Chard, Chloe (forthcoming, 1999) *Pleasure and guilt on the Grand Tour*. Manchester
Chard, Chloe and Helen Langdon, eds. (1996) *Transports: travel, pleasure and imaginative geography. 1600–1830*. New Haven and London
Chaudonneret, Marie-Claude (1989) *Les Muses de Messidor*. Lyons
Chitty, Susan, (1975) *The beast and the monk: a life of Charles Kingsley*. New York
Christ, Karl (1982) *Römische Geschichte und deutsche Geschichtswissenschaft*. Munich
(1990) *Neue Profile der Alten Geschichte*. Darmstadt
(1996) 'Reichsgedanke und Imperium Romanum in der nationalsozialistischen Ära', *Von Caesar zu Konstantin. Beiträge zur römischen Geschichte und ihrer Rezeption*, 255–74. Munich
Christ, Karl and Arnaldo Momigliano, eds. (1989) *L'Antichità nell'ottocento in Italia e Germania*. Berlin and Bologna
Ciucci, Giorgio (1989) *Gli architetti e il fascismo*. Turin
Civil Service Commissioners' reports – see footnotes to Majeed
Clark, Peter (1967) 'A Macaulay letter', *Notes and Queries* 212: 369
Clarke, Graham, ed. (1990) *T. S. Eliot: critical assessments*, vol. II (Early poems and *The Waste Land*). London
Clarke, G. W., ed. (1989) *Rediscovering Hellenism: the Hellenic inheritance and the English imagination*. Cambridge
Clive, John (1973) *Macaulay: the shaping of the historian*. Cambridge Mass.
Colley, Linda (1992) *Britons: forging the nation 1707–1837*. New Haven and London
La Colonna Traianna e gli artisti francesi da Luigi XIV a Napoleone I, catalogue of exhibition held at the Villa Medici, Rome 12 April – 12 June 1988
Conrad, Joseph (1924) 'Henry James: an appreciation 1905', *Notes on life and letters*, 11–19. London
Cook, Eleanor (1979) 'T. S. Eliot and the Carthaginian peace', *ELH* 46: 341–55
Cooper, Emmanuel (1985–6) 'A vision of love: homosexual and androgynous themes in Simeon Solomon's work after 1873', *Solomon: a family of painters*, exhibition catalogue, Geffrye Museum, London and Birmingham Museum and Art Gallery. 31–5
Cork and Orrery, Earl of [J. Boyle] (1773) *Letters from Italy, in the years 1754 and 1755* ed. John Duncombe. London
Coutagne, Denis (1992) 'Le paysage de Rome', in Néto-Daguerre and Coutagne, eds. *Granet peintre de Rome*
Cowling, Elizabeth and Jennifer Mundy, eds. (1990) *On classic ground: Picasso, Leger, de Chirico and the new classicism 1910–1930*, exhibition catalogue, Tate Gallery. London
Cox, C. B. and Arnold P. Hinchliffe, eds. (1968) *T. S. Eliot:* The Waste Land; *a casebook*. Houndmills and London
Cruise, Colin (1995) '"Lovely Devils": Simeon Solomon and Pre-Raphaelite mas-

culinity', in Ellen Harding, ed. *Re-framing the Pre-Raphaelites: historical and theoretical essays*, 195–210. Aldershot, Hants.
Cubberley, A. L., ed. (1988) *Rodolfo Lanciani: notes from Rome*. Rome
Culler, Jonathan (1988) *Framing the sign: criticism and its institutions*. Oxford
Curl, J. S. (1994) *Egyptomania. The Egyptian revival: a recurring theme in the history of taste*. Manchester
Curtius, Ernst Robert (1979) *European literature and the Latin Middle Ages*, trs. Willard R. Trask (first published 1952). London and Henley
Cutts, E. H. (1952–3) 'The background of Macaulay's Minute', *American Historical Review* 58:824–53
dall'Asta, Monica (1992) *Un Cinéma musclé: le surhomme dans le cinéma muet italien (1913–1926)*, trs. from Italian by F. Arnò and C. Tatum. Belgium
Dalle Vacche, Angela (1992) *The body in the mirror: shapes of history in Italian cinema*. Princeton
d'Amico, M. (1946) 'Il "Quo Vadis?"', *Nel centenario di Enrico Sienkiewicz (1846–1946)*, 117–27. Rome
Damisch, Hubert (1987) *L'Origine de la perspective*. Paris
Davies, P. (1985) *Splendours of the Raj. British architecture in India 1660–1947*. London
Dellamora, Richard (1990) *Masculine desire: the sexual politics of Victorian Aestheticism*. Chapel Hill, N.C. and London
Demandt, Alexander (1984) *Der Fall Roms*. Munich
Derrida, Jacques (1995a) *Mal d'archive: une impression freudienne*. Paris
(1995b) 'Archive fever: a Freudian impression', trs. Eric Prenowitz, *Diacritics* 25:2, 9–63
Deslys, C. (1887) *L'Héritage de Charlemagne*. Paris
de Staël, A. L. G. [de Staël-Holstein] (1979) *Corinne; ou, l'Italie*, ed. Claudine Herrmann. 2 vols. Paris
(1987) *Corinne, or Italy*, trs. A. H. Goldberger. New Brunswick and London
de Vincenti, Giorgio (1988) 'Il kolossal storico-romano nell'immaginario del primo Novecento', *Bianco e Nero* 49.1: 7–26
Dewey, Clive (1973) 'The education of a ruling caste: the Indian Civil Service in the era of competitive examination', *The English Historical Review* 88: 265–85
(1993) *Anglo-Indian attitudes. The mind of the Indian Civil Service*. London
Donadio, Stephen (1978) *Nietzsche, Henry James and the artistic will*. New York
D'Onofrio, Andrea (1997) *Ruralismo e storia nel terzo Reich. Il casa 'Odal'*. Naples
Dowd, D. L. (1959) *Napoleon: was he the heir of the revolution? Source problems in world civilisation*. New York
Dowling, Linda (1985) 'Roman decadence and Victorian historiography', *Victorian Studies* 28.4: 579–607
(1986) *Language and decadence in the Victorian fin de siècle*. Princeton
(1995) *Hellenism and homosexuality in Victorian Oxford*. Ithaca and London
Downes, David Anthony (1972) *The temper of Victorian belief: studies in the religious novels of Pater, Kingsley, and Newman*. New York
Duckett, Eleanor (1925) *Catullus in English poetry* (Smith College Classical Studies 6). Northampton, Mass.
Duff, Alexander (1853) 'The English education act of Lord William Bentinck, with illustrative remarks by Dr Duff', *Second report from the select committee of the*

House of Lords, appointed to inquire into the operation of the act 3 & 4 will. 4. c.85 for the better government of Her Majesty's Indian territories, and to report thereon to the house: together with the minutes of evidence, and an appendix and index thereto (Session 1852–3), House of Lords papers 1853: 397–415
[Dupaty, C. M. J. B. M] (1788) *Lettres sur l'Italie, en 1785*, 2 vols. Rome
Dundy, Elaine (1988) *The Dud Avocado* (first published 1958). London.
Dunn, Hugh Percy (1894) 'Is our race degenerating?' *Nineteenth Century* 36: 300–14
Eagleton, Terry (1970) *Exiles and emigrés: studies in modern literature*. London
(1976) *Criticism and ideology*. London
(1990) *The ideology of the aesthetic*. Oxford
Eaton, Charlotte (1820) *Rome in the nineteenth century*, 3 vols. London
Eberhardt, W. (1935) 'Die Antike und Wir', *Nationalsozialistische Monatshefte* 6: 115–27
Edel, Leon (1977) *The life of Henry James* (first published in five volumes 1953, 1962, 1963, 1969, 1972), 2 vols. Harmondsworth
(1990) 'The Italian journeys of Henry James', in Tuttleton and Lombardo, eds., '*The sweetest impression of life*'
Edwards, Catharine (1994) 'Humanity vs. utility? Classics in nineteenth-century English public schools'. Unpublished paper
(1996a) *Writing Rome: textual approaches to the city*. Cambridge
(1996b) 'The roads to Rome', in Liversidge and Edwards, eds. *Imagining Rome*, 8–19
Edwards, Owen Dudley (1988) *Macaulay*. London
Ehrard, A. and J. (1989) 'Brutus et les lecteurs', *Revue européene des sciences sociales* (essays in honour of B. Bacszo) xvii no. 85:103–14
Eigner, E. M. (1978) *The metaphysical novel in England and America: Dickens, Bulwer, Melville, and Hawthorne*. Berkeley
Eliot, T. S. (1957) *On poetry and poets*. London
(1964) *The use of poetry and the use of criticism*. London
Eliot, Valerie, ed. (1971) *T. S. Eliot: The Waste Land: a facsimile and transcript of the original drafts including the annotations of Exra Pound.* London
Elley, Derek (1984) *The epic film: myth and history*. London
Ellison, J. (1990) *Delicate subjects: romanticism, gender, and the ethics of understanding.* Ithaca and London
Ellmann, Richard (1983) 'Henry James among the aesthetes', *Proceedings of the British Academy* 69: 209–28
Fagiolo dell'Arco, Maurizio (1990) '"Classicismo pittorico": valori plastici, magic realism and novecento', in Cowling and Mundy, eds. *On classical ground*
Fansa, Mamoun ed. (1994) *Varusschlacht und Germanenmythos. Archäologische Mitteilungen aus Nordwestdeutschland* (Beiheft 9). Oldenburg
Faries, II, Randolph (1923) *Ancient Rome in the English novel: a study in English historical fiction*. Philadelphia
Farrar, Frederick W. (1889) *The Early Days of Christianity* (first published 1882). London
(1891) *Darkness and Dawn or, Scenes in the Days of Nero: an historic tale*. New York
(1895) *Gathering Clouds: a tale of the days of St. Chrysostom*. New York
Ferguson, Margaret (1984) '"The afflatus of ruin": meditations on Rome by Du Bellay, Spencer, and Stevens', in Patterson, ed., *Roman images*, 23–50

Fest, J. C. (1973) *Hitler*. Frankfurt.
Findlay, L. M. (1973) 'The introduction of the phrase "art for art's sake" into English', *Notes and Queries* n.s. 20: 246–8
Finley, M. I. (1975) *The use and abuse of history*. London
Fioravanti, Giovanna (1990) *Archivio centrale dello stato: Partito Nazionale Fascista – Mostra della Rivoluzione Fascista*. Rome
Fogel, Daniel Mark (1990) 'Henry James' American girls in darkest Rome: the abuse and disabuse of innocence', in Tuttleton and Lombardo, eds., '*The sweetest impression of life*'
Forgacs, David (1990) *Italian culture in the industrial era 1880–1980: cultural industries, politics and the public*. Manchester
Foucault, Michel (1966) *Les Mots et les choses*. Paris
Freud, Sigmund (1899/1962) 'Screen memories (1899)', in *Standard Edition* vol. III, trs. James Strachey. London
(1900/1976) *The Penguin Freud library*, vol. IV *The Interpretation of Dreams*, ed. Angela Richards, trs. James Strachey. Harmondsworth
(1907/1985) 'Delusions and dreams in Jensen's "Gradiva"', 27–118 in *The Penguin Freud library,* vol. XIV *Art and literature*, ed. Albert Dickson, trs. under the general editorship of James Strachey. Harmondsworth (1910/1985) 'Leonardo da Vinci and a memory of his childhood', 151–231 in
The Penguin Freud library, vol. XIV
(1930/1985) 'Civilisation and its discontents', 251– 340 in *The Penguin Freud Library*, vol. XII *Civilisation, society and religion* (1985), ed. Albert Dickson, trs. under the general editorship of James Strachey. Harmondsworth
Fried, Michael (1980) *Absorption and theatricality: painting and the beholder in the age of Diderot*. Berkeley
(1996) *Manet's modernism*. Chicago
Fröhlich, E. (1995) *Die Tagebücher von Joseph Goebbels,* vol. II. Munich
Fuller, Mia (1992) 'Building power: Italian architecture and urbanism in Libya and Ethiopia', in N. Al Sayyad, ed. *Forms of dominance: on the architecture and urbanism of the colonial enterprise*, 211–39. Aldershot
Gabba, Emilo and Karl Christ, eds. (1989 and 1991) *Römische Geschichte und Zeitgeschichte in der deutschen und italienischen Altertumswissenschaft während des 19. und 20. Jahrhunderts*. 2 vols. Como
Gaeta, F. (1981) *Il nazionalismo italiano*. Bari
Galtung, J. (1990) 'Theory formation in social research: a plea for pluralism', in Else Oyen, ed. *Comparative methodology. Theory and practice in international social research*, 96–112. London
Gardner, Helen (1949) *The art of T. S. Eliot*. London
Gautier, Théophile (1915) *Charles Baudelaire: his life*, trs. Guy Thorne. London
(1954) *Emaux et camées*, ed. Adolphe Boschot. Paris
Gay, Peter (1967) *The enlightenment: an interpretation* vol. I *The rise of modern paganism*. London
Geffcken, J. ed. (1902) *Die Oracula Sibyllina*. Leipzig
Gelley, Alexander (1966) 'Ernst Robert Curtius: topology and critical method', *Modern Language Notes* 81: 579–94
Gentile, Emilio (1990) 'Fascism as a political religion', *Journal of Contemporary History* 25, nos. 2/3:229–51
(1993) *Il culto del littorio*. Bari

Ghigi, Giuseppe (1977) 'Come si spiegano le fortune del "pepla" su cui sembra che torni a puntare', *Cineforum* 17.2: 733–46
Gibbon, Edward (1956) *The letters of Edward Gibbon*, ed. J. E. Norton, 3 vols. London
(1966) *Memoirs of my Life*, ed. Georges A. Bonnard. London
(1994) *The History of the Decline and Fall of the Roman Empire* (first published 1776–87), ed. David Womersley, 3 vols. London
Gies, H. (1992) *Geschichtsunterricht unter der Diktatur Hitlers*. Cologne
Gilchrist, F. (1800) *The anti-jargonist or a short introduction to the Hindostanee language*. Calcutta
Goethe, J.-W. von (1970) *Italian Journey*, trs. W. H. Auden and Elizabeth Mayer. Harmondsworth
Goldstein, Laurence (1972) *Ruins and empire: the evolution of a theme in Augustan and romantic literature*. Pittsburgh
Gori, G. M. (1988) *Patria diva: la storia d'Italia nei film del ventennio*. Florence
Gossman, Lionel (1981) *The empire unpossess'd: an essay on Gibbon's* Decline and Fall. Cambridge
Greene, Thomas M. (1982) *The light in Troy: imitation and discovery in Renaissance poetry*. New York and London
Greiner, J. (1947) *Das Ende des Hitler-Mythos*. Vienna
Grosskurth, Phyllis, ed. (1984) *The memoirs of John Addington Symonds*. New York
Habinek, Thomas N. (1992) 'Grecian wonder and Roman woe: the romantic rejection of Rome and its consequences for the study of Latin literature', in Karl Galinsky, ed. *The interpretation of Roman poetry: empiricism or hermeneutics?*, 227–42. Frankfurt-am-Main
Haecker, Theodor (1934) *Virgil, father of the West*, trs. A. W. Wheen. New York
Ḥālī A. H. (1871/1997) *The flow and ebb of Islam. Hālī's Musaddas,* ed. and trs. C. Shackle and J. Majeed. Delhi
Hamer, Mary (1993) *Signs of Cleopatra: histories, politics, representation*. London
Hare, Augustus (1871) *Walks in Rome*. London
Haskell, Francis (1993) *History and its images: art and the interpretation of the past*. New Haven and London
Haskell, Francis and Nicholas Penny (1981) *Taste and the antique*. New Haven and London
Hautecoeur, L. (1953) *Histoire de l'architecture classique en France*, vol. V. Paris
Haverfield, F. (1911) 'An inaugural address delivered before the first annual general meeting of the Society, May 11, 1911', *Journal of Roman Studies* 1: xi–xx
Hawthorne, Nathaniel (1990) *The Marble Faun* (first published 1860), ed. Richard H. Brodhead. Harmondsworth
Hay, James (1987) *Popular film culture in fascist Italy: the passing of the Rex*. Bloomington, Ind.
Heim, J. F. (1989) *Le Salon de peinture sous la révolution*. Paris
Heim, J. F. and Valérie Huet (forthcoming) *Les Salons de peinture sous Napoléon*. Paris
Hemmings, F. W. J. (1971) *Culture and society in France 1848–1898*. London
Highet, Gilbert (1949) *The classical tradition: Greek and Roman influences on western literature*. Oxford
Hitler, Adolf (1939) *Mein Kampf*. New York.
(1953) *Table talk*, trs. N. Cameron and R. H. Stevens. London

(1962) *The testament of Adolf Hitler. The Hitler-Bormann documents February-April 1945*. London
(1980) *Sämtliche Aufzeichnungen 1905–1924*, ed. by E. Jaeckel. Stuttgart.
(1980) *Monologe im Führerhauptquartier 1941–1944*, ed. W. Jochmann. Hamburg
Hobsbawm, Eric and Terence Ranger (1983) *The invention of tradition*. Cambridge
Hogben, W. M. (1981) 'An imperial dilemma: the reluctant Indianization of the Indian political service', *Modern Asian Studies* 15: 751–69
Huet, Valérie (1996) 'Stories one might tell of Roman art: reading Trajan's column and the Tiberius cup', in Jaś Elsner, ed. *Art and text in Roman culture*. Cambridge
Huet, Valérie and John Scheid, eds. (forthcoming) *Autour de la colonne de Marc Aurèle*. Paris
Hubert, G. (1969) 'Napoléon et les arts en Europe', *Les monuments historiques de la France* 15.4 (Oct./Dec.): 3–24
Hughes-Hallett, Lucy (1990) *Cleopatra: histories, dreams and distortions*. London.
Hugo, Victor (1967–70) *Oeuvres complètes*, ed. Jean Massin. Paris
Hulme, T. E. (1936) *Speculations: essays on humanism and the philosophy of art* (first published 1924). London and New York
Isbell, J. C. (1994) *The birth of European romanticism: truth and propaganda in Staël's 'de l'Allemagne' 1810–1813*. Cambridge
Jacques, F. and John Scheid (1992) *Rome et l'intégration de l'Empire, 44 av. JC – 260 ap. JC*, vol. I. Paris
Jaeckel, E. (1981) *Hitlers Weltanschauung*, 2nd edn. Stuttgart
Jain, Manju (1992) *T. S. Eliot and American philosophy: the Harvard years*. Cambridge
James, Henry (1903) *William Wetmore Story and his Friends*, 2 vols. London
(1962) *The Art of the Novel: critical preface*, with introduction by Richard P. Blackmur (first published 1934). New York
(1974) *Letters* vol. I 1843–1875, ed. Leon Edel. London
(1978) *The Tales* vol. II 1870–1874, ed. Maqbool Aziz. Oxford
(1980) *Letters* vol. III 1883–1895, ed. Leon Edel. London
(1984a) *Letters* vol. IV 1895–1916, ed. Leon Edel. Cambridge, Mass.
(1984b) *Literary criticism: essays on literature; American writers; English writers*, ed. Leon Edel. New York.
(1984c) *The Portrait of a Lady* (first published 1881), eds. Geoffrey Moore and Patricia Crick. Harmondsworth
(1984d) *The tales* vol. III 1875–1879, ed. Maqbool Aziz. Oxford
(1985) *The Golden Bowl* (first published 1904), eds. Gore Vidal and Patricia Crick. Harmondsworth.
(1986a) *Roderick Hudson* (first published 1875), eds. Geoffrey Moore and Patricia Crick. Harmondsworth
(1986b) *The Wings of the Dove* (first published 1902), eds. John Bayley and Patricia Crick. Harmondsworth
(1995) *Italian Hours* (first published 1909), ed. J. Auchard. Harmondsworth
Janowitz, Anne (1990) *England's ruins: poetic purpose and the national landscape*. Oxford
Jebb, R. C. (1900) *Macaulay*. Cambridge
Jemolo, A. C. (1960) *Church and state in Italy 1850–1950*, trs. D. Moore. Oxford

Jenkyns, Richard (1980) *The Victorians and ancient Greece*. Oxford
(1982) *Three classical poets: Sappho, Catullus and Juvenal*. London
(1991) *Dignity and decadence: Victorian art and the classical heritage*. London
(1995) 'Late antiquity in English novels of the nineteenth century', *Arion* (3rd series) 3.2 & 3:141–66
Jenkyns, Richard, ed. (1992) *The legacy of Rome: a new appraisal*. Oxford
Johnson, Samuel (1993) 'A journey to the Western Islands of Scotland', in *Johnson and Boswell in Scotland: a journey to the Hebrides*, ed. Pat Rogers. New Haven and London
Jolly, Roslyn (1993) *Henry James: history, narrative, fiction*. Oxford
Jones, S. (1993) *The language of the genes. Biology, history, and the evolutionary future*. London
Jones, Sir Willliam (1786) 'To Sir John Macpherson', 6 May 1786, letter 453 in Garland Cannon, ed. (1970) *The letters of Sir William Jones*, vol. II, 699. Oxford
(1788) 'On the Hindu's [*sic*]', *Asiatick Researches* 1: 422–3. Calcutta
Jordan, Thomas E. (1993) *The degeneracy crisis and Victorian youth*. Albany, NY
Kaplan, Fred, ed. (1994) *Travelling in Italy with Henry James*. London
Keating, Peter (1989) *The haunted study. A social history of the English novel 1875–1914*. London
Kemp, Martin (1984) 'Construction and cunning: the perspective of the Edinburgh Saenredam', in *Dutch church painters*, 30–7. Edinburgh
Kennedy, D. F. (1997) 'Modern receptions and their interpretative implications', in Charles Martindale, ed., *The Cambridge companion to Virgil*. Cambridge
Kermode, Frank (1962) *Puzzles and epiphanies: essays and reviews 1958–1961*. London
(1983) *The classic: literary images of permanence and change*. London and Cambridge, Mass.
Kestner, Joseph A. (1989) *Mythology and misogyny: the social discourse of nineteenth-century British classical-subject painting*. Madison, Wis.
King, C. R. (1994) *One language, two scripts. The Hindi movement in nineteenth century north India*. Delhi
Kingsley, Charles (1881) *Hypatia or New Foes with an Old Face* (first published 1853). 2 vols, London
Kipling, Rudyard (1924) 'A centurion of the thirtieth', *Puck of Pook's Hill*. London
Kleiner, D. E. E. (1992) *Roman sculpture*. New Haven and London
Königs, D. (1995) *Joseph Vogt: Ein Althistoriker in der Weimarer Republik und im Dritten Reich*. Basel
Kopf, David (1969) *British orientalism and the Bengal Renaissance: the dynamics of Indian modernisation 1773–1835*. Berkeley
Kostof, Spiro (1978) 'The emperor and the duce: the planning of the Piazzale Augusto Imperatore in Rome', in Henry A. Millon and Linda Nochlin, eds. *Art and architecture in the service of politics*. Cambridge, Mass. and London
Kroll, F.-L. (1996) 'Geschichte und Politik im Weltbild Hitlers', *Vierteljahrshefte für Zeitgeschichte* 44: 327–53.
Laird, M. A. (1972) *Missionaries and education in Bengal 1793–1837*. Oxford
Lecky, W. E. H. (1897) *History of European morals from Augustus to Charlemagne* (first published 1869), 12th edn., 2 vols. London

LeBourgeois, John Y. (1973) 'Swinburne and Simeon Solomon', *Notes and Queries* 218: 91–5

Leconte de Lisle, Charles (1858) *Poésies complètes*. Paris

Lednicki, Waclaw (1960) *Henryk Sienkiewicz: a retrospective synthesis*. The Hague

Leppmann, Wolfgang (1966) *Pompeii in fact and fiction*. London

Leprohon, Pierre (1972) *The Italian cinema*, trs. R. Greaves and O. Stallybrass. London

Lewes, G. H. (1863) 'Was Nero a monster?', *Cornhill Magazine* 8: 113–28

Lewis, C. S. (1942) *A preface to* Paradise Lost. London

Liehm, Mira (1984) *Passion and defiance: film in Italy from 1942 to the present*. Berkeley

Linton, E. Lynn (1887) 'The Roman matron and the Roman lady', *Fortnightly Review* n.s. 42: 237–58

Liversidge, Michael and Catharine Edwards, eds. (1996) *Imagining Rome: British artists and Rome in the nineteenth century*, exhibition catalogue, Bristol City Museum and Art Gallery

Lombardo, Agostino (1990) 'Italy and the artist in Henry James', in Tuttleton and Lombardo, eds., '*The sweetest impression of life*', 228–39.

Losemann, Volker (1977) *Nationalsozialismus und Antike. Studien zur Entwicklung des Faches Alte Geschichte*. Hamburg

(1980) 'Programme deutscher Althistoriker in der "Machtergreifungsphase"', *Quaderni di Storia* 11: 35–105

(1984) 'Nationalsozialistische Weltanschauung und Herrschaftspraxis 1933–1935', in K. Malettke, ed., *Der Nationalsozialismus an der Macht*, 9–52. Göttingen

(1988) 'Aspekte der nationalsozialistischen Germanenideologie', in P. Kneissl, ed., *Alte Geschichte und Wissenschaftsgeschichte*, 256–84. Darmstadt

Lovett, C. M. (1982) *The democratic movement in Italy 1830–1876*. Cambridge, Mass.

Lowenthal, David (1985) *The past is a foreign country*. Cambridge

Lucas, C. P. (1912) *Greater Rome and Greater Britain*. Oxford

MacCannell, Dean (1976) *The tourist: a new theory of the leisure class*. London

Macaulay, T. B. (1826) 'Thoughts on the advancement of academical education in England' *Edinburgh Review* 43:315–41

(1862) *Macaulay's minutes on education in India*, ed. H. Woodrow. Calcutta

(1880)*The life and letters of Lord Macaulay*, ed. G. O. Trevelyan. London

(1898) *Complete works*, 12 vols. London

(1899) *The Lays of Ancient Rome*, ed. J. H. Flather. Cambridge

(1907) *The marginal notes of Lord Macaulay*, ed. G. O. Trevelyan. London

(1974–81) *Letters*, 6 vols., ed. Thomas Pinney. Cambridge

McClellan, Andrew (1994) *Inventing the Louvre: art, politics and the origins of the modern museum in eighteenth-century Paris*. Cambridge

MacDonald, Bonney (1990a) *Henry James'* Italian Hours: *revelatory and resistant impressions*. Ann Arbor

(1990b) 'The force of revelation: receptive vision in Henry James' early Italian travel essays', in Tuttleton and Lombardo, eds., '*The sweetest impression of life*', 128–48

McFarland, Thomas (1981) *Romanticism and the forms of ruin: Wordsworth, Coleridge, and the modalities of fragmentation.* Princeton
McGann, J. J. (1984) 'Rome and its romantic significance', in Patterson, ed., *Roman images*, 83–104
Macleod, C. W. (1979) 'Horace and the Sibyl' (*Epode* 16.2)', *CQ* 29:220–1
MacPherson, James (1773) *An introduction to the history of Great Britain and Ireland*, 3rd ed. London
Maine, H. S. (1861; 1986) *Ancient law. Its connection with the early history of society, and its relation to modern ideas*, ed. Lawrence Rosen. Tucson
Majeed, Javed (1992) *Ungoverned imaginings. James Mill's 'The History of British India' and orientalism.* Oxford
Malitz, J. (1998) 'Römertum im "Dritten Reich": Hans Oppermann', in P. Kneissel and Volker Losemann, eds., *Imperium Romanum: Studien zu Geschichte und Rezeption*, 518–43. Stuttgart
Malvano, Laura (1988) *Fascismo e la politica dell'immagine*. Turin
Manacorda, Daniele and Renato Tamassia (1985) *Il piccone del regime*. Rome
Marchand, Suzanne L. (1996) *Down from Olympus. Archaeology and philhellenism in Germany 1750–1970*. Princeton
Margolis, John D. (1972) *T. S. Eliot's intellectual development 1922–39*. Chicago and London
Marino, Giuseppe Carlo (1983) *L'autarchia della cultura*. Rome
Marshall, P. J. (1988) 'The Whites of British India: a failed colonial society?' paper delivered at the Institute of Commonwealth Studies, University of London
Martin, Graham, ed. (1970) *Eliot in perspective: a symposium*. London
Martindale, Charles (1993) *Redeeming the text: Latin poetry and the hermeneutics of reception*. Cambridge
Martindale, Charles, ed. (1984) *Virgil and his influence*. Bristol
(1988) *Ovid renewed: Ovidian influences on literature and art from the Middle Ages to the twentieth century*. Cambridge
Martindale, Charles and David Hopkins, eds. (1993) *Horace made new: Horatian influences on British writing from the Renaissance to the twentieth century.* Cambridge
Martinelli, Vittorio (1992) 'Il cinema muto italiano: 1914', *Bianco e Nero*, 1–2
(1993) 'Il cinema muto italiano: 1913', *Bianco e Nero*, 1–4
(1994) 'Sotto il vulcano', in Redi, ed., *Gli ultimi giorni di Pompei*, 35–62
Marx, Karl (1967) *Eighteenth Brumaire of Louis Bonaparte* (first German edn. 1852). Moscow
Matthiessen, F. O. (1980) *The James family: a group biography* (first published 1947). New York.
Maves, Carl (1973) *Sensuous pessimism: Italy in the work of Henry James*. Bloomington, Ind.
Mayer, David (1984–5) 'Romans in Britain 1886–1910: Pain's "The last days of Pompeii"', *Theatrephile* 2.5: 41–50
(1994a) *Playing out the empire: 'Ben-Hur' and other toga plays and films, 1883–1908. A critical anthology*. Oxford
(1994b) *La menzogna della razza*, exhibition catalogue, Bologna
Meyer, Eduard (1910) *Kleine Schriften*, 2 vols. Halle

Meyer, Esther Da Costa (1995) *The work of Antonio Sant' Elia*. New Haven
Metcalf, Thomas (1989) *An imperial vision. Indian architecture and Britain's Raj*. London
(1994) *Ideologies of the Raj*. Cambridge
Mill, J. S. (1858) 'Memorandum of the improvements in the administration of India during the last thirty years', in John M. Robson, Martin Moir, and Zawahir Moir, eds., *Writings on India by John Stuart Mill* (1990) 91–160. Toronto
(1861) 'Considerations on representative government', in Richard Wollheim, ed., *John Stuart Mill. Three essays* (1975) 142–453. Oxford
Mitchell-Boyask, Robin (1994) 'Freud's reading of classical literature and classical philology', in eds. S. L. Gilman, Jutta Birmele, Jay Geller, V. D. Greenberg, eds., *Reading Freud's reading*, 23–46. New York
Moatti, Claude (1993) *The search for ancient Rome* (first published 1989), trs. A. Zielonka. London
Mohler, A. (1972) *Die konservative Revolution*, 2nd edn. Darmstad
Mommsen, Theodor (1996) *A history of Rome under the emperors*, eds. A. and B. Demandt, trs. Clare Krojzl, ed. with introduction by Thomas Wiedemann. London
Moody, A. D., ed. (1974) The Waste Land *in different voices*. London
ed. (1994) *The Cambridge companion to T. S. Eliot*. Cambridge
Moore, George (1972) *Confessions of a Young Man* (first published 1889), ed. Susan Dick. Montreal and Kingston, Ontario
Morgan, Thaïs E. (1993) 'Reimagining masculinity in Victorian criticism: Swinburne and Pater', *Victorian Studies* 36: 315–32
Mort, Frank and Nead, Linda (1996) 'Sexuality, modernity and the Victorians', *Journal of Victorian Culture* 1: 118–30
Moses, H. (1824–8) *The works of Antonio Canova*. London
Mosse, G. L. (1976) *Die Nationalisierung der Massen*. Frankfurt
Näf, B. (1986) *Von Perikles zu Hitler? Die athenische Demokratie und die deutsche Althistorie bis 1945*. Frankfurt
Napoléon (1969) catalogue of exhibition held at Grand Palais, Paris
Napoléon Ier, 1802, la paix d'Amiens, le Concordat, le Consulat à vie (1952), catalogue of the exhibition held at Malmaison
Nehru, Jawaharlal (1946/1989) *The discovery of India*. Delhi
Néto-Daguerre, Isabelle (1991) 'Correspondance de François-Marius Granet', PhD thesis, Université de Paris IV Sorbonne. Paris
Néto-Daguerre, Isabelle and Denis Coutagne (1992) *Granet peintre de Rome*. Aix-en-Provence
Newman, John Henry (1868) 'Advertisement to the third edition, 1857', *The church of the Fathers*, 4th ed. London
(1873) *Callista: a sketch of the third century* (first published 1856). London
(1890) 'The Patristical idea of Antichrist', *Discussions and arguments on various subjects*, 7th ed. London
Nietzsche, Friedrich (1978) *The use and abuse of history*, trs. Adrian Collins. Indianapolis
Nisard, J. M. N. D. (1834) *Etudes de moeurs et de critique: les poètes latins de la décadence,* 3 vols. Brussels

Nisbet, R. (1980) *History of the idea of progress*. New York
Nolte, E. (1965) *Three faces of Fascism*. London.
Nordau, Max (1896) *Degeneration*, Eng. trans., 9th edn. London
Normanby, C. H. Phipps, Marquis of (1825) *The English in Italy*, 5 vols. London
North, Michael (1991) *The political aesthetic of Yeats, Eliot and Pound*. Cambridge
Nowell-Smith, Geoffrey (1986) 'The Italian cinema under fascism', in David Forgacs, ed., *Rethinking Italian Fascism*. London
O'Malley, L. S. S. (1965) *The Indian Civil Service*. London
Pater, Walter (1867) 'Winckelmann', *Westminster Review* n.s. 31: 80–110
(1885) *Marius the Epicurean*, 2nd edn. London
(1973) *Essays on literature and art*, ed. Jennifer Uglow. London
Patterson, Annabel, ed. (1984) *Roman images*. Baltimore and London
Paolella, Roberto (1956) *Storia del cinema muto*. Naples
Parigi, Stefania (1994) 'La rievocazione dell'antico', in Redi, *Gli ultimi giorni di Pompei*, 67–84
Parliamentary papers – see footnotes to Majeed.
Pastrone, G. (1977) *Cabiria*, ed. M. A. Prolo. Turin
Pemble, John (1988) *The mediterranean passion: Victorians and Edwardians in the south*. Oxford
Pérouse de Montclos, J. M. (1969) 'Les traditions classique et révolutionaire dans l'urbanisme napoléonien', *Les Monuments Historiques de la France* 15.4 (Oct./Dec.): 67–79
Piggott, Stuart (1976) *Ruins in a landscape: essays in antiquarianism*. Edinburgh
Port, M. H. (1995) *Imperial London: civil government building in London 1851–1915*. New Haven and London
Prendergast, Christopher (1997) *Napoleon and history painting: Antoine-Jean Gros's La bataille d'Eylau*. Oxford
Prettejohn, Elizabeth (1996) 'Recreating Rome in Victorian painting: from history to genre', in Liversidge and Edwards, eds., *Imagining Rome*, 54–69
Prolo, M. A. (1951) *Storia del cinema muto italiano*. Milan
Quarantotto, C. (1993) 'Cinema di d'Annunzio e cinema dannunziano 1908–1938', in F. Perfetti, ed. *D'Annunzio e il suo tempo*, 169–97. Genoa
Quennell, Peter (1971) *The Colosseum*. London and New York
Raby, F. J. E. , ed. (1959) *The Oxford book of Medieval Latin verse*. Oxford
Rajan, Balachandra (1985) *The form of the unfinished: English poetics from Spenser to Pound*. Princeton
Ratcliff, C. (1988) *Komar and Melamid*. New York
Rawson, Claude (1995) 'Musing on the Capitol', *Times Literary Supplement* 4815 (14 July): 3
Read, Donald (1979) *England 1868–1914: the age of urban democracy*. London
Redi, R., ed. (1994) *Gli ultimi giorni di Pompei*. Naples
Reeves, Gareth (1989) *T. S. Eliot: a Virgilian poet*. Houndmills, Hampshire and London
Rhodes, Royal W. (1995) *The lion and the cross: early Christianity in Victorian novels*. Columbus
Richard, C. J. (1994) *The founders and the classics: Greece, Rome and the American enlightenment*. Cambridge, Mass.
Richardson, Joanna (1971) *Verlaine*. London

Ridley, Ronald T. (1992) *The eagle and the spade: the archaeology of Rome during the Napoleonic era 1809–1814*. Cambridge

Robinson, David (1955) 'Spectacle', *Sight and Sound* 25: 22–7 and 55–6

Rowe, John Carlos (1984) *The theoretical dimensions of Henry James*. Madison, Wis.

Said, E. W. (1978) *Orientalism*. London

Salt, Barry (1991) 'Il cinema italiano dalla nascita alla Grande Guerra: un'analisi stilistica', in R. Renzi, ed. *Sperduto nel buio: il cinema muto italiano e il suo tempo (1905–1930)*, 49–58. Bologna

Schachermeyr, F. (1933) 'Die nordische Führerpersönlichkeit im Altertum', in *Humanistische Bildung im nationalsozialistischen Staat*, 36–43. Leipzig

(1943) 'Fachbericht Alte Geschichte', *Rasse* 10: 118–20

Schnapp, Jeffrey and Barbara Spackman, eds. (1990) 'Selections from the great debate on fascism and culture: *Critica Fascista* 1926–27', *Stanford Italian Review* 8.1–2: 264

(1992) 'Epic demonstrations: Fascist modernity and the history of the 1932 exhibition of the Fascist revolution', in Richard Golsan, ed. *Fascism, aesthetics and culture*. Hannover and London

Schefer, Jean-Louis (1995) *La lumière et la table*. Paris

Schorske, Carl E. (1991) 'Freud: the psychoarchaeology of civilisations', in J. Neu, ed. *The Cambridge companion to Freud*, 8–24. Cambridge

Schueller, Herbert M. and Robert L. Peters, eds. (1968) *The Letters of John Addington Symonds*, vol. II *1869–1884*. Detroit

Schwab, Raymond (1984) *The oriental renaissance: Europe's rediscovery of India and the east*. New York

Scobie, Alex (1990) *Hitler's state architecture. The impact of classical antiquity*. London

Seaman, A. R. (1976) 'Cabiria', *CinemaTexas Program Notes* 11.4: 95–101

Sedgwick, Eve Kosofsky (1995) 'Shame and performativity: Henry James's New York prefaces', in David McWhirter, ed. *Henry James's New York edition: The construction of authorship*, 206–39. Stanford

Segrè, C. G. (1974) *Fourth shore: the Italian colonization of Libya*. Chicago

Sellers, M. N. S. (1994) *American republicanism. Roman ideology in the United States constitution*. London

Settis, S. (1985) 'La colonne Trajane: invention, composition, disposition', *Annales ESC* (Sept./Oct.) no. 5: 1151–94

(1988) 'La colonna', in S. Settis, A. La Regina, G. Agosti, V. Farinella *La colonna Traiana*, 45–255. Turin

Seymour, Gayle Marie (1986) 'The life and work of Simeon Solomon (1840–1905)', PhD thesis, University of California, Santa Barbara

Shackle, C. and R. Snell (1990) *Hindi and Urdu since 1800. A common reader*. London

Shaffer, E. S. (1975) *'Kubla Khan' and the fall of Jerusalem. The mythological school in biblical criticism and secular literature 1770–1880*. Cambridge

Sheikh, F. (1989) *Community and consensus in Islam. Muslim representation in colonial India 1860–1947*. Cambridge

Sheriff, M. D. (1996) *The exceptional woman: Elisabeth Vigée-Lebrun and the cultural politics of art*. Chicago and London

Shohat, Ella (1991) 'Gender and culture of empire: toward a feminist ethnography of the cinema', *Quarterly Review of Film and Video* 13.1–3: 45–84
Siegert, B. (1994) 'The fall of the Roman empire', in Hans Ulrich Gumbert and K. Ludwig Pfeiffer, eds. *Materialities of communication*. Stanford
Silverio, A. M. L. (1983) 'La Mostra Augustea della Romanità', *Dalla mostra al museo: dalla Mostra archeologica del 1911 al Museo della civiltà romana*, 77–90. Venice
Sinfield, Alan (1994) *The Wilde century: effeminacy, Oscar Wilde and the queer movement*. London
Sirkin, G. and N. R. (1972–3) 'John Stuart Mill and disutilitarianism in Indian education', *Journal of General Education* 25: 231–6
Smiles, Sam (1993) *The image of antiquity: ancient Britain and the romantic imagination*. New Haven and London
Sorlin, Pierre (1996) *Italian national cinema 1896–1996*. London
Speer, Albert (1975) *Spandauer Tagebücher*. Berlin
Spender, Stephen (1935) *The destructive element*. London
Springer, Carolyn (1987) *The marble wilderness: ruins and representation in Italian romanticism 1775–1850*. Cambridge
Stahlmann, I. (1988) *Imperator Caesar Augustus. Studien zur Geschichte des Principatsverständnisses in der deutschen Altertumswissenschaft*. Darmstadt.
Stephen, Leslie (1899) *Hours in a Library*, vol. II. London
Stewart, S. (1993) *On longing: narratives of the miniature, the gigantic, the souvenir, the collection*. Durham and London
Stirling, A. M. W. (1926) *The Richmond papers*. London
Stone, Marla (1993) 'Staging Fascism: the exhibition of the Fascist revolution', *Journal of Contemporary History* 28:215–43
(1998) *The patron state: art and politics in Fascist Italy*. Princeton
[Strachan-Davison, J. L.] (1879) 'Froude's Caesar', *Quarterly Review* 148: 453–89
Stray, Christopher (1992) *The living word: W. H. D. Rouse and the crisis of classics in Edwardian England*. London
(1998) *Classics transformed: schools, universities and society in England 1830–1960*. Oxford
Suleri, Sara (1992) *The rhetoric of English India*. Chicago and London
Surtees, Virginia (1971) *The paintings and drawings of Dante Gabriel Rossetti (1828–1882): a catalogue raisonné*, 2 vols. Oxford
Swart, Koenraad W. (1964) *The sense of decadence in nineteenth-century France*. The Hague
Swinburne, A. C. (1924) *Collected poetical works*, 2 vols. London
(1871) 'Simeon Solomon: notes on his 'Vision of Love' and other studies', *Dark Blue* 1: 568–77
(1974) *A year's letters*, ed. Francis Jacques Sypher. New York
Symons, Arthur (1906) *Studies in seven arts*. New York
Symonds, Richard (1986) *Oxford and empire: the last lost cause?*. London
Tacitus (1989) *Annals*, trs. Michael Grant. London
Tanner, Tony (1992) *Venice desired*. Oxford.
(1995) *Henry James and the art of nonfiction*. Athens, Georgia
Teuffel, W. S. (1873) *History of Roman literature*, trs. Wilhelm Wagner, 2 vols. London

Thies, J. (1976) *Architekt der Weltherrschaft. Die Endziele Hitlers.* Düsseldorf
(1978) 'Hitler's European building programme', *Journal of Contemporary History* 13: 413–31
(1983) 'Nazi architecture – a blueprint for world domination: the last aims of Adolf Hitler', in D. Welch, ed., *Nazi propaganda: the power and the limitation*, 45–64. London
Thomas, Stephen (1991) *Newman and heresy: the Anglican years.* Cambridge
The three Graces, Antonio Canova (1995) exhibition catalogue, National Gallery of Scotland, Edinburgh
Tintner, Adeline R. (1986) *The museum world of Henry James.* Ann Arbor
Tomlinson, Charles (1983) *Poetry and metamorphosis.* Cambridge
Trevelyan, Charles (1838) *On the education of the people of India.* London
Trotter, David (1986) 'Modernism and empire: reading *The Waste Land*', *Critical Quarterly* 28: 143–53
Tulard, J. (1989) *Dictionnaire Napoléon.* Paris
Turconi, Davide (1963) 'I film storici italiani e la critica americana dal 1910 alla fine del muto', *Bianco e Nero* 1–2: 40–54
Turner, Frank M. (1981) *The Greek heritage in Victorian Britain.* New Haven
(1989) 'Why the Greeks and not the Romans in Victorian Britain?', in Clarke, ed., *Rediscovering Hellenism*, 61–81
(1993) *Contesting cultural authority: essays in Victorian intellectual life.* Cambridge
Tuttleton, James W. (1990) 'Preface', in Tuttleton and Lombardo, eds., *'The sweetest impression of life'*, 1–7
Tuttleton, James W. and Agostino Lombardo, eds. (1990) *'The sweetest impression of life': the James family and Italy.* New York and Rome
Uhlig, Claus (1990) 'Tradition in Curtius and Eliot', *Comparative Literature* 42: 193–207
Usai, P. C. (1985) *Giovanni Pastrone. Il castoro cinema 119.* Florence
Vance, Norman (1985) *The sinews of the spirit.* Cambridge
(1997) *The Victorians and ancient Rome.* Oxford
Vance, William L. (1989) *America's Rome,* 2 vols. New Haven and London.
Van Den Abbeele, G. (1988) *Travel as metaphor.* Minneapolis and Oxford
Vauthier, G. (1911) 'Denon et le gouvernement des arts sous le Consulat', *Revue des Annales* 4:336–65
Verlaine, Paul (1969) *Oeuvres poétiques,* ed. J. Robichez. Paris
Veyne, Paul (1991) 'Propagande expression roi, image, idole, oracle', *La société romaine*, 320–42. Paris (a version of this paper was published in English as 'Conduct without belief and works of art without viewers', *Diogenes* 143 (1988) 1–22).
Vidal-Naquet, Pierre (1995) *Politics ancient and modern*, trs. Janet Lloyd. Oxford
Villard, P. (1972) 'Antiquité et Weltanschauung Hitlérienne', *Revue d'histoire de la deuxième guerre mondiale* 22: 1–18
Visser, Romke (1992) 'Fascist doctrine and the cult of the *Romanità*', *Journal of Contemporary History* 27: 5–22
Viswanathan, Gauri (1990) *Masks of conquest: literary study and British rule in India.* London

Vogt, Joseph (1935) 'Bevölkerungsrückgang im römischen Reich', *Vergangenheit und Gegenwart* 25: 652–65
(1936) 'Rassenmischung im römischen Reich', *Vergangenheit und Gegenwart* 26: 1–11
Vogt, Joseph, ed. (1943) *Rom und Karthago*. Leipzig
von See, K. (1994) *Barbar, Germane, Arier: Die Suche nach der Identität der Deutschen*. Heidelberg
Walsdorff, F. (1935) 'Der Unterricht in der alten Geschichte und den alten Sprachen unter dem Gesichtspunkt der Erbpflege und Rassenkunde', *Deutsche Wissenschaft, Erziehung und Volksbildung*, 27*-34*. Berlin
Walsh, T. J. (1981) *Second Empire opera*. London
Washbrook, D. (1982) 'Ethnicity and racism in colonial Indian society', in Robert Ross, ed. *Racism and colonialism*. The Hague
(1991) '"To each a language of his own": language, culture, and society in colonial India', in P. J. Corfield, ed. *Language, history, and class*. Oxford
Waugh, Evelyn (1962) *Brideshead Revisited* (first published 1945). Harmondsworth
Webb, Timothy (1996) '"City of the soul": travellers in Rome', in Liversidge and Edwards, eds., *Imagining Rome*, 20–37
Weber, Wilhelm (1935) *Vom neuen Reich der Deutschen*. Berlin.
(1936) *Princeps. Studien zur Geschichte des Augustus*. Stuttgart.
(1943) 'Das Alte Rom. Ursachen für Aufstieg und Niedergang des Römischen Reiches', *Wille und Macht* 11: 1–41.
Webster, R. A. (1960) *The cross and the fasces: Christian Democracy and Fascism in Italy*. Stanford
Weeks, Jeffrey (1981) *Sex, politics and society: the regulation of sexuality since 1800*. London and New York
Weil, Simone (1960) *Ecrits historiques et politiques*. Paris.
Weinberg, G. L., ed. (1961) *Hitlers Zweites Buch*. Stuttgart.
Weinbrot, H. D. (1993a) *Britannia's issue: the rise of British literature from Dryden to Ossian*. Cambridge
(1993b) 'Politics, taste and national identity: some uses of Tacitism in eighteenth-century Britain', in T. J. Luce and A. J. Woodman, eds. *Tacitus and the Tacitean tradition*, 168–84. Princeton
Wharton, Edith (1993) *Roman Fever*. London
White, Hayden (1973) *Metahistory: the historical imagination in nineteenth-century Europe*. Baltimore
Wilde, Oscar (1962) *The letters of Oscar Wilde*, ed. Rupert Hart-Davis. London
(1966) *Complete works of Oscar Wilde*, intro. Vyvyan Holland. London and Glasgow
(1979) *Selected letters*, ed. Rupert Hart-Davis. Oxford
(1989) *Oscar Wilde's Oxford notebooks: a portrait of a mind in the making*, ed. P. E. Smith II and M. S. Helfand. New York and Oxford
Williams, Wynne (1993) 'Reading Greek like a man of the world: Macaulay and the classical languages', *Greece and Rome* 40.2:201–16
Wilson, H. H. (1836) 'Education of the natives of India', *The Asiatic journal and monthly register of British and foreign India, China, and Australasia* 19: 1–16
Winckelmann: la naissance de l'histoire de l'art à l'époque des Lumières (1991), Actes

du cycle des conférences prononcées à l'Auditorium du Louvre du 11 déc. au 12 fév. 1990. Paris

Wiseman, T. P. (1992) 'Of grammar and grandeur', *TLS* (May 29):11–12

Womersley, David (1988) *The transformation of the Decline and Fall of the Roman Empire*. Cambridge

Wyke, Maria (1992) 'Augustan Cleopatras: female power and poetic authority', in A. Powell, ed. *Roman poetry and propaganda in the age of Augustus*, 98–140. London

(1994) 'Make like Nero! The appeal of a cinematic emperor', in J. Elsner and J. Masters, eds. *Reflections of Nero: culture, history and representation*, 11–28. London

(1996) 'Cinema and the City of the Dead: reel histories of Pompeii', in C. MacCabe and D. Petrie, eds. *New scholarship from BFI Research*, 140–56. London

(1997) *Projecting the past: ancient Rome, cinema and history*. New York

Ziolkowski, Theodore (1993) *Virgil and the moderns*. Princeton

Index

Note that individual ancient Romans are listed under the name by which they are most familiar in English.

Lightning Source UK Ltd.
Milton Keynes UK
UKHW010639031220
374534UK00001B/7

9 780521 036177